HABITS OF THE
CREATIVE MIND

RICHARD E. MILLER
Rutgers University

ANN JURECIC
Rutgers University

BEDFORD/ST. MARTIN'S
Boston | New York

For Bedford/St. Martin's

Vice President, Editorial, Macmillan Higher Education Humanities: Edwin Hill
Editorial Director for English and Music: Karen S. Henry
*Publisher for Composition, Business and Technical Writing
and Developmental Writing:* Leasa Burton
Executive Editor: Molly Parke
Developmental Editor: Christina Gerogiannis
Production Editor: Kendra LeFleur
Production Assistant: Erica Zhang
Production Supervisor: Victoria Anzalone
Marketing Manager: Emily Rowin
Copy Editor: Arthur Johnson
Indexer: Jake Kawatski
Director of Rights and Permissions: Hilary Newman
Senior Art Director: Anna Palchik
Text Design: Laura Shaw Design, Inc.
Cover Design: Billy Boardman
Cover Art: Courtesy Anannya Dasgupta
Composition: Cenveo Publisher Services
Printing and Binding: R. R. Donnelley

Manufactured in the United States of America.

0   9   8   7   6   5
f   e   d   c   b   a

For information, write: Bedford/St. Martin's, 75 Arlington Street, Boston, MA 02116
(617-399-4000)

ISBN 978-1-4576-8181-3

Acknowledgments

Coates, Ta-Nehisi. "Fear of a Black President." From the *Atlantic.* August 22, 2012. Reprinted by permission.

Text acknowledgments and copyrights appear at the back of the book on page 352 which constitute an extension of the copyright page. Art acknowledgments and copyrights appear on the same page as the art selections they cover. It is a violation of the law to reproduce these selections by any means whatsoever without the written permission of the copyright holder.

ABOUT THE AUTHORS

Habits of the Creative Mind is co-written by two nationally recognized figures in the field of composition. Richard E. Miller has written and lectured extensively on how digital technology is transforming higher education. He is an award-winning teacher, an avid blogger, an amateur graphic novelist, and a poet. Ann Jurecic is the author of *Illness as Narrative*, which examines how writers, both literary and amateur, have used writing to make meaning of illness, loss, and impermanence. Her academic work explores the intersection of writing studies, literary studies, and the medical humanities. Jurecic is also an award-winning teacher and she writes a column for the medical journal *The Lancet*. Richard E. Miller and Ann Jurecic teach at Rutgers University.

PREFACE

Habits of the Creative Mind is a collection of essays about writing, each one written to spur reflection on what's involved in training the mind to make the world a more interesting place to live, and each one followed by prompts to generate more writing in return.

It is also a textbook, but a special kind of textbook—one that sees writing as a technology for confronting the unknown. As such, it promotes questioning over arguing; curiosity over conviction; and mindful practice over mindless repetition.

In other words, *Habits of the Creative Mind* is a textbook designed to break with the convention of the textbook: it is writing about writing that is meant to be read, rather than skimmed or glossed or painted over with a highlighter; it is writing about writing that is also meant to reward rereading.

We wrote *Habits of the Creative Mind* for teachers and students who want to learn how to use writing to break free from conventional thinking. We were motivated by our conviction that education, properly understood, is the process of cultivating creative and curious minds. The students entering college now have labored under a different definition of education: they have spent twelve or more years in standardized and metrics-driven education systems, where they have learned that the most important question to ask is, "Will this be on the test?" In their experience, writing for school entails following a formula to produce whatever it is the testers are testing for that year. They don't know how accomplished writers think about writing and they don't practice the habits of mind that make writing a meaningful activity. Very few of them have had the experience of pursuing self-directed research about a question, problem, or puzzle that is motivated by their own intellectual curiosity. Our goal in writing *Habits of the Creative Mind* has been to provide students with a new experience of writing. We want them to see writing as a technology to think thoughts that are new to them. We want them to ask questions, explore, read, discuss, lose track of time, take risks, make wrong turns, and try again. We want them to experience the essence of what it means to have a creative mind.

Habits of the Creative Mind is built on a set of core principles.

Writing is a Technology for Thinking Thoughts that are New to the Writer
The central tenet of *Habits of the Creative Mind* is that writers come to know what they think through acts of writing. To gain access to writing's unique power to educate, though, one must learn how to ask genuine questions, as opposed to questions that are statements in disguise. To this end, we provide prompts throughout *Habits* that have students begin with a question they can't answer or write their way to a question they can't answer. For writing to generate thoughts that are new to the writer, the writer must learn how to ask questions that are generative: writing and questioning are inseparable.

The Habits of Mind that Support Good Writing are Teachable and Learnable
Experienced writers, performers, and artists, all of whom are in the business of creating new ideas and new insights, have developed habits that contribute to their success. They are curious, attentive, engaged, open to new ideas, persistent, flexible, and reflective, and creative. Students become stronger writers by practicing these habits of mind as they read, research, write, revise, and reflect. Our approach to teaching habits of mind aligns with the *Framework for Success in Postsecondary Writing*, a document jointly produced by the Council of Writing Program Administrators, the National Council of Teachers of English, and the National Writing Project, that identifies eight habits of mind that are "essential for success in college writing."

Creativity Takes Practice, Lots and Lots of Practice
Creativity can be taught and it can be learned, not once and for all (like riding a bicycle), but through regular, sustained practice (like

playing a musical instrument or doing high order mathematics). This is why our book is entitled *Habits of the Creative Mind:* creativity is best understood as a set of habits acquired through practice—practice asking unanswerable questions, practice confronting the limits of one's understanding, practice encountering ambiguity, practice making connections. The "Practice Sessions" that follow each of the essays in *Habits* focus the student's attention on the mental operations that drive the work of the intellectually curious and creative mind—connecting, reading, reflecting, and researching, as well as writing and revising.

The Essay is the Ideal Form for Practicing the Habits of the Creative Mind

We seek to reclaim Montaigne's use of "essay" as a form that accommodates meditative, speculative, deliberative thinking and writing. *Habits* itself provides a sustained introduction to this use of the essay: we have composed each of the lessons as an essay that explores one of the many complex issues that are raised when writing is understood as a way of *making* meaning. By emphasizing this use of the essay, we aim to demonstrate how writing can be used to show a mind at work on a problem. With practice writing this kind of essay, students are in a position to transfer the habits of mind they have acquired to new contexts and to produce writing in any genre that requires writers to demonstrate insight, reflectiveness, and a capacity for dealing with complexity.

Writing is a Way of Paying Attention

To produce writing worth sharing one has to have thoughts worth thinking—and that requires a commitment to paying attention. The essays in *Habits* model what it means to pay attention to what one reads, writes, and thinks as a daily practice. After each essay, the students are prompted to practice paying attention, over and over again, in a range of contexts using a variety of sources. The habit of paying attention to what one sees, reads, and thinks opens the door to using writing as a technology for thinking new thoughts. At the same time, the habit of writing enhances one's capacity for paying attention. The activities are mutually reinforcing and mutually beneficial.

Habits of the Creative Mind **is a textbook for the twenty-first century, with readings included and readings a click away.**

The creative mind thrives on making connections. We want our students to be able to make connections with texts they share in common, and we also want them to have the opportunity to follow their curiosity wherever it might lead. To support both focused and open-ended acts of connection over the course of a semester, we provide the following resources:

- Thirty-four original essays, authored by us, that both explain and model habits of the creative mind. Each essay is followed by an "Explore" section that points to other exemplary essays (many available online) and to relevant Web sites.

- Eleven profiles of writers, artists, and performers who demonstrate the many different ways the creative mind can express itself when it is "at work." Each profile of how a writer moves from an initial question or puzzle to a finished work serves as an invitation to further research.

- More than seventy-five "Practice Sessions," some focused on exploring ideas discussed in the essays we've authored, others directed at the included readings, and still others that encourage students to pursue open-ended online research.

- Three readings that serve as a shared resource for assignments. These essays, by Ta-Nehisi Coates, Jill Lepore, and Susan Sontag, provide examples of curious and creative minds at work: they are driven by questions and address problems of broad public concern.

- Eight images, including works of art and a visual puzzle, support the practices of paying attention, re-seeing, and arguing differently. Many of the essays in *Habits* were written in response to questions raised by the limits of representations; all three of the included readings are centrally concerned with the problems posed by images and representations.

We also wrote *Habits of the Creative Mind* for teachers who see teaching itself as a creative art.

We've organized the essays into twelve sections, each related to a practice that is central to essay writing. We don't, however, see *Habits* as a "course in a box." Creative teachers recognize even the best syllabi need to be modified to match the evolving abilities of each unique class of students. *Habits of the Creative Mind* has been designed with the expectation that teachers will select the sequence of essays and practice sessions that are most productive for their courses and their students. Although *Habits of the Creative Mind* opens with clusters of essays about "Unlearning," "Paying Attention," "Connecting," and "Asking Questions," and later addresses more complex habits of mind, such as "Reflecting," "Arguing," and "Diverging," there's no ideal or recommended itinerary for moving from one habit to the next. Our hope is that *Habits of the Creative Mind* will be a catalyst for invention and innovation for teachers as well as students.

Acknowledgments

This book is the result of decades of teaching, thousands of hours of contact with students in all sorts of classrooms, hundreds of presentations at conferences, and extended conversations with the teachers and colleagues who have most shaped how we think about how to cultivate the habits of the creative mind. Our suggested readings and our bibliography can be read as a partial catalogue of the many voices that have contributed to our effort to realize this project.

We want to thank our friend Anannya Dasgupta for her permission to use her stunning photograph, "Splash of Orange," for the cover of our book. We also thank the students who gave us permission to use examples of their writing: Chris Osifchin, Erik Rose, Donald Shimazu, and Annie Stiver. For their invaluable feedback as our manuscript took shape, we thank Jeffrey Andelora, Mesa Community College; Victoria Boynton, SUNY Cortland; Heather Brown, Monmouth University; Bettina Calouri, Mercer County Community College;

Anthony Edgington, University of Toledo; Tim Jensen, Oregon State University; Erica Kaufman, Bard College Institute for Writing and Thinking; Nancee Kesinger, Mesa College; Denise Knight, SUNY Cortland; Thomas LaPointe, Bergen Community College; Tami LeHouillier, Western Nevada College; Noralyn Masselink, SUNY Cortland; Jennifer Militello, River Valley Community College; Michael Murphy, Oswego State University of New York; Alice Myatt, University of Mississippi; Emmanuel Nelson, SUNY Cortland; Adam Penna, Suffolk County Community College; Alex Reid, University of Buffalo; Howard Tinberg, Bristol Community College; Megan Titus, Rider University; and Amanda Irwin Wilkins, Princeton University. We want to acknowledge everyone at Bedford who worked with us to bring *Habits of the Creative Mind* to light. Joan Feinberg, who provided career-long support and guidance; Leasa Burton, publisher nonpareil, and the Bedford/St.Martin's team: Edwin Hill, Karen Henry, Molly Parke, Christina Gerogiannis, Kendra LeFleur, Cara Kaufman, Emily Rowin, Billy Boardman, Kalina Ingham, Martha Friedman, and Arthur Johnson. Locally, we want to thank Stephanie Hunt for her editing assistance getting the original manuscript in shape for submission.

—Richard E. Miller

—Ann Jurecic

Get the Most Out of Your Course with *Habits of the Creative Mind*

Bedford/St. Martin's offers resources and format choices that help you and your students get even more out of your book and course. To learn more about or to order any of the following products, contact your Bedford/St. Martin's sales representative, e-mail sales support (**sales_support@bfwpub.com**), or visit the Web site at **macmillan-highered.com /habits/catalog**.

Choose from Alternative Formats of *Habits of the Creative Mind*

Bedford/St. Martin's offers a range of affordable formats, allowing students to choose the one that works best for them. For details, visit **macmillanhighered.com/habits/catalog**.

- *Paperback:* To order the paperback edition, use **ISBN 978-1-4576-8181-1.**

- *Popular e-book formats:* For details, visit **macmillanhighered .com/ebooks.**

Select Value Packages

Add value to your text by packaging one of the following resources with *Habits of the Creative Mind.* To learn more about package options for any of the following products, contact your Bedford/St. Martin's sales representative or visit **macmillanhighered.com/habits/catalog.**

Writer's Help 2.0 is a powerful online writing resource that helps students find answers whether they are searching for writing advice on their own or as part of an assignment.

- **Smart search** Built on research with more than 1,600 student writers, the smart search in *Writer's Help* provides reliable results even when students use novice terms, such as *flow* and *unstuck.*

- **Trusted content from our best-selling handbooks** Choose *Writer's Help 2.0 for Hacker Handbooks* or *Writer's Help 2.0 for Lunsford Handbooks* and ensure that students have clear advice and examples for all of their writing questions.

- **Adaptive exercises that engage students** *Writer's Help* includes *LearningCurve,* game-like online quizzing that adapts to what students already know and helps them focus on what they need to learn.

Student access is packaged with *Habits of the Creative Mind* at a significant discount. Order ISBN 978-1-319-05650-6 for *Writer's Help 2.0 for Hacker Handbooks* or ISBN 978-1-319-05649-0 for *Writer's Help 2.0 for Lunsford Handbooks* to ensure your students have easy access to online writing support. Students who rent a book or buy a used book can purchase access to *Writer's Help 2.0* at **macmillanhighered.com/writershelp2.**

Instructors may request free access by registering as an instructor at **macmillanhighered.com/writershelp2.**

For technical support, visit **macmillanhighered.com/getsupport.**

***Portfolio Keeping*, Third Edition, by Nedra Reynolds and Elizabeth Davis** provides all the information students need to use the portfolio method successfully in a writing course. *Portfolio Teaching*, a companion guide for instructors, provides the practical information instructors and writing program administrators need to use the portfolio method successfully in a writing course. To order *Portfolio Keeping* packaged with the print book, contact your sale representative for a package ISBN.

Instructor Resources

You have a lot to do in your course. Bedford/St. Martin's wants to make it easy for you to find the support you need—and to get it quickly.

A chapter for instructors titled "Teaching Creativity and Curiosity" is available at **macmillanhighered.com/habits/catalog**. In "On Teaching Writing with *Habits of the Creative Mind*," the first of three essays in the chapter, Miller and Jurecic discuss how to teach students that writing is a technology for thinking new thoughts. In "On Evaluating Student Writing," they share their thoughts on practices for soliciting, reading, and responding to the writing students produce as they seek to acquire the habits of the creative mind. And in "Creative Teaching at Work: Mike Rose," the authors showcase one example of what it means to link creativity and teaching.

A WPA correlation grid that aligns *Habits of the Creative Mind* with the revised Council of Writing Program Administrators' Outcomes Statement for first-year composition (as of July 17, 2014) is available as a PDF that can be downloaded from the Bedford/St. Martin's online catalog at **macmillanhighered.com/habits/catalog**.

Teaching Central offers the entire list of Bedford/St. Martin's print and online professional resources in one place. You'll find landmark reference works, sourcebooks on pedagogical issues, award-winning collections, and practical advice for the classroom—all free for instructors. Visit **macmillanhighered.com/teachingcentral**.

Bedford Bits collects creative ideas for teaching a range of composition topics in a frequently updated blog. A community of teachers—leading scholars, authors, and editors such as Andrea Lunsford, Elizabeth Losh, Jack Solomon, and Elizabeth Wardle—discuss assignments, activities, revision, research, grammar and style, multimodal composition, technology, peer review, and much more. Take, use, adapt, and pass the ideas around. Then, come back to the site to comment or share your own suggestion. Visit **bedfordbits.com**.

CONTENTS

ORIENTING

....

Y ou are about to enter unfamiliar territory: *Habits of the Creative Mind* is not organized like a typical writing handbook. We don't make the claim that there's only one way to write, or that writing is fun and easy if you just know the right tricks. And we don't focus on the arts of persuasion or the arts of argumentation. Our work on this book began with the premise that the best writing develops from the exercise of habits of mind that include curiosity, creativity, attentiveness, openness to new ideas, persistence, flexibility, and reflectiveness. Starting with this premise compelled us to rethink what a textbook is and what it asks of both students and teachers.

We begin with two letters, the first addressed to students and the second to teachers. Both letters challenge the prevalent practice of teaching writing through formulas. And both make the case that writing is best understood as a technology for thinking new thoughts and for exploring the unfamiliar and the unknown.

On Habits of Mind: A Letter to Students and Other Readers

"Curiouser and curiouser!" cried Alice (she was so much surprised, that for the moment she quite forgot how to speak good English); "now I'm opening out like the largest telescope that ever was! Good-bye, feet!" (for when she looked down at her feet, they seemed to be almost out of sight, they were getting so far off).

Alice's Adventures in Wonderland begins with our heroine having nothing to do. It's not that Alice is alone: she's with her sister and could choose to do what her sister is doing—reading silently. But the book her sister is reading doesn't interest Alice because it has no pictures or dialogue. Alice has a problem—she's bored.

The resources we now have for relieving boredom were not available to Lewis Carroll's Alice one hundred and fifty years ago: she can't text a friend or stream her favorite videos out there on the grass. Uninterested in reading, she lies in the sun, trying to get up the energy to pick some daisies, when a rabbit wearing a waistcoat runs by. In an instant, Alice is transformed: "burning with curiosity," she races after the rabbit, commencing her "adventures in Wonderland" that continue to attract readers to this day.

How does this happen—the jump from idling in listless boredom to embarking on a curiosity-driven adventure?

Both as writing teachers and as parents, we have heard a lot about boredom. The assigned readings are boring. The writing assignments are boring. School is boring. No one willingly seeks out boredom, yet there is this general sense that one is constantly at risk of being bored. And once one is bored, then everything is boring.

Look at Alice. The rabbit runs by her and at first she thinks nothing of it. Indeed, she doesn't even "think it so *very* much out of the way to hear the Rabbit say to itself 'Oh dear! Oh dear! I shall be too late!'"

A talking rabbit? Whatever.

It's not until the rabbit stops and looks at his pocket watch that Alice snaps out of her torpor, jumps to her feet, and, in an act that has since entered the language as a synonym for plunging into another world, goes "down the rabbit hole."

There is, of course, no such thing as a talking, waistcoat-wearing, pocket watch-checking rabbit. The sisters sitting on the bank, the book without pictures, the rabbit, the rabbit hole: all of these ordinary, easily recognizable possibilities were brought together in an imaginative act by Lewis Carroll. How did he do it? How does any writer make the jump from being bored (and boring) to being creative? From plodding mechanically to being engaged and engaging?

Habits of the Creative Mind is based on a simple premise: no one wants either to be bored or to be boring. Entire industries are founded on this premise: show business, gaming, gambling, theme parks, wine and spirits. We understand that entertainment and distraction are popular antidotes to the fear of being bored, but we also believe that the central role of education is to guide students in the cultivation of creative and curious habits of mind.

Nothing is inherently interesting—not the weeping willow in the park, or the lecture on global warming, or the Monet water lily painting hanging in the gallery, or the rabbit scampering into the bushes. Everything in the material world of objects and in the immaterial world of ideas can be tuned out, mocked, or trivialized. Everything we experience through our senses or gain access to with our minds can be dismissed by someone else as *boring*.

So nothing is inherently interesting; but everything—from the ways single-celled bacteria communicate, to the running back-channel chatter in the brain, to the evanescent patterns made when smoke rises from a candle's flame—has the *potential* to be made interesting. The mind can be trained to transform what would otherwise seem mundane and unremarkable into an opportunity for thoughtful reflection. We can make the world interesting to ourselves and to others through sustained acts of attention, and we can gain access to curiosity and creativity through practice.

We've written this book to provide ways for you to learn how to make the world a more interesting place and how to make your interests of interest to others. For this to happen, you will need to cultivate a sense that what is unknown is exciting, and you will need to transform your way of thinking about the world into an open-ended adventure. Of course, taking pleasure in confronting the limits of one's own understanding does not come naturally to anyone: we all avoid situations where our ignorance might be exposed, our faulty reasoning brought to light. And this tendency is precisely why practicing being attentive, curious, and creative is essential; it's a way of confronting, engaging with, and responding to the unknown. A commitment to working at the edge of one's own understanding is, we believe, what lies at the heart of the educational enterprise.

In this book, we focus on writing as one way to practice the encounter with the unknown, but as you'll see, we understand writing to encompass more than just putting words on-screen. In fact, we often use the word *composing* to emphasize our sense that writing is an ongoing act of making sense of the world—an act that necessarily involves working with sounds and images, perceptions and intuitions, and everything else in the realm of experience that shapes both what and how we think.

That said, we do maintain that there's an important distinction between informal personal writing and writing-to-learn. Most of us don't need help posting the events of the day to Facebook or spinning memories into anecdotes. Writing-to-learn is a different beast altogether, one that involves the dual practice of private introspection and public research, driven forward by cultivating the mind's connective powers. Writing-to-learn is therefore both an activity and the experiences that arise when one is engaged in that activity. It is a way of approaching writing as a set of tools (or, as we'll say often in this book, a "technology") for thinking new thoughts, and it is a way of gaining access to the limitless possibilities suggested by the image of a cursor flashing on a blank screen. The daily practice of writing-to-learn establishes and brings to light an ever-evolving relationship between the writer and the word and between the writer and the world.

Getting started requires three things: a desire to better understand yourself and your place in the world; access to writing materials and the Internet; and a commitment to making time for the work of cultivating curiosity, creativity, and learning. *Habits of the Creative Mind* provides you with a structure and a host of activities, prompts, and exercises to assist you in your practice of writing-to-learn, but you have to meet the project halfway by being open to the possibility that using writing to explore your mind's connective powers can help you both to think new thoughts and to think in new ways.

We know that skepticism is an inevitable part of the process of thinking about ideas that are strange or unfamiliar, so we expect you to be skeptical along the way. But it is up to you to keep that skepticism in check so that you don't become dismissive as soon as you find yourself being asked to think in unfamiliar ways about what thinking is and about what it means to be a thoughtful person. We're not asking for a lot. If you've ever found yourself wishing that you understood the world a little better or that you had a clearer sense of how to make the world a better place, then you're as open as you need to be to give our approach to writing a try.

We've designed *Habits of the Creative Mind* to be read cover to cover or to be dipped into and out of at will. And we've structured the book to reflect the philosophy of consciousness that underlies our approach to writing. There is no single, linear path through the process of learning to write well; indeed, what makes learning to write well so difficult is that it can't be learned by moving in orderly steps from the easiest concepts to the most complex. Every aspect of the writing process is complex. Every act of writing has the potential to lead the writer down one rabbit hole or another. Writing always takes time. Confronting the unknown is always challenging. Responding to this challenge is always a messy process. Any book that presents writing in a different light is not a book whose goal is to get you to learn how to use writing to think thoughts that are new to you.

Accordingly, in our book you won't find a series of chapters that walk you through the nuts and bolts of creating an outline or developing a thesis. Instead, we've written a collection of essays to guide you in learning how to use writing as a technology for thinking new thoughts. Some of the essays are just a few pages long, while others are much longer; all of them reflect the assumption that learning to think new thoughts is a complicated process and that the only way to get started is to plunge in.

If you choose (or if your teacher chooses) to move through the sections in order, you'll find that themes introduced near the beginning of the book return later for modification and reconsideration. And whatever path you take to develop the habits of the creative mind, at some point you're sure to find yourself thinking, "Why didn't I learn about X first?" This frustration is an inevitable part of the process of learning; as you do the hard work of mastering the encounter with your own ignorance, you are sure to think, "There has to be an easier way!" There isn't. So instead of wishing that this book simplified writing into a series of steps that move you from brainstorming to polished draft, we invite you to think of the essays that follow as pieces in a mosaic designed to provide you with assistance in learning the art of reflection; the design will come together only when you can step back and contemplate the whole.

We've also imagined that, as you practice using *Habits of the Creative Mind*, your own curiosity will lead you to explore the resources that the Web puts at your disposal: a vast array of long-form essays and works of creative nonfiction; informational sites that cover the rules and mechanics of grammar; and free video tutorials for resolving whatever technological problems you may run into along the way. We see *Habits of the Creative Mind*, in other words, as a book that is implicitly connected to all the creative archives that can be accessed on the Web and to reference materials that cover everything from punctuation to usage to the conventions governing the citation of online resources. Once you begin to make some of these implicit connections explicit, you'll be on your way to realizing the overarching goal of this book: to make creativity a daily habit of mind.

On the Origins of *Habits of the Creative Mind*: A Letter to Teachers

....

"The first step toward a more creative life is the cultivation of curiosity and interest, that is, the allocation of attention to things for their own sake."
— MIHALY CSIKSZENTMIHALYI

Habits of the Creative Mind is designed to help students learn to use writing as a technology for practicing thoughtful engagement with the world. In choosing to approach writing as a "habit of mind," we mean to shift the instructional emphasis away from rhetorical modes and argumentation to practices that actively encourage learning through writing—chief among them creativity and curiosity, but also attentiveness, openness, engagement, flexibility, persistence, and reflectiveness.

Between us, we have more than forty years' experience teaching writing. We've taught in high school, community college, and public and elite research universities. We've taught basic skills classes, expository writing classes, creative nonfiction classes, research writing classes, and classes for students finishing their dissertations. We've worked in writing centers, trained writing tutors, taught graduate students to teach writing, and served as administrators in writing programs big and small.

Wherever we've worked, we've had to confront this paradox: despite decades of educational reform, writing isn't better than it was when we first stepped into the classroom, it's simply different. Twenty-five years ago, the writing that students composed during the first week of class was disorganized, poorly thought out, and incurious. Today the writing that our students produce during their first week is organized, formulaic, and incurious.

Why does writing remain an exercise in trussing up banalities for almost all who produce it in school? The short answer to this question is that students today are trained to follow a recipe-based approach to writing and have been rewarded (or punished) by the standardized testing system for their ability (or inability) to produce writing that is clear and concise. The directions for producing this kind of writing are no secret.

The recipe-driven essay has three parts: introduction, body, conclusion. The introductory paragraph lays out the author's thesis, which often takes the form of "X is the case because of A, B, and C." The body contains a series of paragraphs, each of which provides details about one of the three reasons for accepting the thesis. The conclusion restates the thesis and summarizes the body paragraphs. In its barest form, the essay so defined begins with an assertion of an irrefutable statement, offers evidence that the irrefutable statement is, in fact, irrefutable, and then reasserts the original claim.

We've written this book out of the belief that the best writing is curiosity driven and is carried forward by creative acts of connective thinking. We have found that producing curiosity-driven writing—and, indeed, gaining access to the experience of writing as an act of thinking rather than an act of reporting—only becomes possible once students and teachers alike let go of the recipe-based approach to writing. This book is for teachers who want to help their students learn how to use writing as a means for thinking thoughts that are new to the writer.

What do we offer students to replace the discarded formulas? We help them to cultivate the habits of mind of more experienced writers, because knowing how to be curious, attentive, engaged, open to new ideas, persistent, flexible, reflective, and creative contributes to successful writing. For those who are committed to traditional ways of teaching composition, our call for a shift in writing instruction away from formulas and toward habits of mind may appear idiosyncratic or deliberately countercultural. It is neither. When Ken Bain did research for his book *What the Best College Teachers Do,* he studied the practices of professors at two dozen institutions, ranging from colleges with open admissions to elite research universities, and he found that, regardless of the setting, highly effective teachers create classroom environments in which students "learn by confronting intriguing, beautiful, or important problems, authentic tasks that will challenge them to grapple with ideas, rethink their assumptions, and examine their mental models of reality." These teachers know that students need to replace the mental models they brought with them from high school with more complex models for understanding the world. They also know that such transformations take time, so they routinely "conduct class and craft assignments in a way that allows students to try their own thinking, come up short, receive feedback, and try again." In such challenging and supportive environments, students come to see mistakes and misunderstandings as fundamental to the learning process.

Our approach is also affirmed by the *Framework for Success in Postsecondary Writing*, a document jointly produced by the Council of Writing Program Administrators, the National Council of Teachers of English, and the National Writing Project. The *Framework* maintains that "standardized writing curricula or assessment instruments that emphasize formulaic writing for nonauthentic audiences will not reinforce the habits of mind and the experiences necessary for success as students encounter the writing demands of postsecondary education." The *Framework* also provides a list of the specific habits of mind that are fundamental to success in college, which we've reproduced below:

- Curiosity—the desire to know more about the world.
- Openness—the willingness to consider new ways of being and thinking in the world.
- Engagement—a sense of investment and involvement in learning.
- Creativity—the ability to use novel approaches for generating, investigating, and representing ideas.
- Persistence—the ability to sustain interest in and attention to short- and long-term projects.
- Responsibility—the ability to take ownership of one's actions and understand the consequences of those actions for oneself and others.
- Flexibility—the ability to adapt to situations, expectations, or demands.
- Metacognition—the ability to reflect on one's own thinking as well as on the individual and cultural processes used to structure knowledge.

One way that we have chosen to answer the call of the *Framework for Success in Postsecondary Writing* is to present our thoughts on writing in *Habits of the Creative Mind* in a series of essays rather than in the deathly prose of the textbook. (The word *essay*, recall, has etymological roots that link it to the French verb *essayer*, meaning both "to try" and "to wander.") We have sought to share our thoughts via curiosity-driven writing that simultaneously discusses and demonstrates ways to practice writerly habits of mind, writing that aims to model for any writer—in high school, in college, or out of school—how to practice curiosity, creativity, and engagement with the world beyond the self.

Throughout the book, you will see that we encourage our readers to seek out curiosity-driven writing in nonfiction essays and articles—the kind of writing one is likely to see featured in the *New Yorker, Harper's,* and the *Atlantic Monthly,* or in online sources such as Longform.org or the magazine *n+1.* Why do we turn to nonfiction prose for our models? Because journalism and literary or creative nonfiction, when they are done well, are typically driven by questions that are accessible to a general reader. Take, for example, the book *Outliers,* in which Malcolm Gladwell considers a question that has bedeviled and befuddled psychologists and educators for generations: Is there such a thing as innate talent? If we read Gladwell's work *as writers*—looking carefully at how he thinks about, studies, and structures his response to this question—we can see that he uses his writing as a technology for thinking new thoughts. What we see, in other words, is not an extended version of a five-paragraph essay, but rather a teachable style of thinking that seeks out the unexpected, the confounding, the mysterious.

Are writers born or made? Conventional wisdom would have us believe that talent is innate: either you've got it or you don't. This conventional wisdom is Gladwell's starting point in *Outliers.* He grants that not every painter can achieve what Picasso did, nor can every college football player succeed in the NFL or every scientist win a Nobel Prize. But—and with Gladwell, there is always a *but* that stands conventional wisdom on its head—when psychologists study the careers of gifted people, they find that a good deal of what distinguishes the world-class expert from the rest of the field is not simply innate talent or genius, but something that is available to every single one of us: practice. In fact, psychologist K. Anders Ericsson settled on a measurement of how much practice is needed to succeed: according to Ericsson, it takes ten thousand hours of practice for anyone—whether a musician, an athlete, a lawyer, an artist, a chess player, or a writer—to excel in his or her chosen field.

If Gladwell's work ended here, he wouldn't have taken us much beyond that old vaudeville joke: "Excuse me, sir, can you tell me how to get to Carnegie Hall?" "Practice, my boy, practice." But Gladwell moves on from this discovery, which seems obvious in hindsight, to consider *how* experts practice. Not just any kind of practice will do. No one can become a great or even a good writer by grinding out practice essays for the SAT. (Imagine the violinist who is never asked to play anything beyond major scales.) Gladwell identifies his own transformation from literate person to writer as beginning when the *Washington Post* hired him in 1987. He spent ten years there covering business, science, and the New York region. Those years gave him enough practice to become an expert journalist. Gladwell points out, however, that his work at the *Post* was more than mere practice. It was *deliberate* practice; it required focus and feedback. He worked with editors who would read his work and then tell him what didn't work and why. They regularly evaluated his drafts and sent him back to his desk with instructions on how to revise. That job, he recognizes, was "a supportive learning environment." And that's the "magic" formula for what it takes to become a good writer: the *right* kind of practice in the *right* kind of environment over an extended period of time.

The writers we want our students to emulate are, like Gladwell, writers who practice working in the face of uncertainty. These writers ask genuine questions—difficult questions that can't be answered simply by looking up facts—and they work to produce writing that is informed by deep learning and serious thought. They make connections between their particular interests and something bigger, something outside the sphere of their individual concerns. And they also write in ways that reward rereading; they produce work that has been crafted with attention to linguistic and aesthetic nuance.

In the case of *Outliers*, Gladwell uses his writing to examine the complex relationship between practice, opportunity, and achieved success, and to wonder who gets the chance to practice so many hours early in a career, and who does not. He also ponders what the obstacles to sustained practice are, other than lack of persistence or grit. And from these questions more difficult ones emerge: Is this a society that is willing to create the conditions that allow the greatest number of people to develop their potential? How could that be made to happen?

Other writers we admire—Katherine Boo, Anne Fadiman, Philip Gourevitch, and Daniel Alarcón, for example—move from curiosity to creative expression in other ways. But what all these accomplished— i.e., well-practiced—writers do is what we'd be thrilled to find our students doing with their own writing: they use their writing to take intellectual risks as they venture into the unknown.

When we assign a long-term project, we ask our students to emulate these writers by engaging deeply, over an extended period of time, in the activities of reading and research. As students dig into research, we encourage them to exercise curiosity—to pose questions and to think actively about what they are learning. Or, to put this another way, we ask them to practice working at the edges of their own understanding; to practice wandering off the well-furrowed tracks of their own familiar responses; to practice resisting the allure of knowingness.

Then, before they begin drafting a formal essay, we ask them to narrow their focus to a question, puzzle, or problem that they'd like to write about. We tell them that their essays should respond in thoughtful and interesting ways to their questions. They might explore the complexity of a problem, weighing different perspectives, or they might propose a solution or course of action. The direction each essay takes depends on the writer's own questions, interests, and insights. To help our students avoid the temptation of falling back on the formulas they learned in the past, we tell them to think of the essay as the map of a mind at work on a problem.

And then we ask them to go through the whole process again. And again. And again. Because learning how to ask a question that is compelling, promising, or haunting comes only with practice. Because what is potentially interesting isn't out there at the front of the project waiting to be found, but becomes visible only when the writer practices shifting perspectives and working outside his or her comfort zone. Because learning to accept complexity and to thrive in the shadow of uncertainty takes time, because figuring out how to connect ideas from different disciplines takes practice, and because divergent, creative thinking can't be taught by rote. Each one of these lessons can be learned only through experimentation, failure, and trying again.

To write and think in these ways is not a niche luxury for the idle, the bookish, and the elite. While education increasingly focuses on preprofessional, vocational, and technical skills, students should have chances to develop the habits of mind that will allow them to thrive in the face of complexity and to enjoy getting lost in the process of deep learning. In *College: What It Was, Is, and Should Be,* Andrew Delbanco argues that college should serve as "an aid to reflection, a place and process whereby young people take stock of their talents and passions and begin to sort out their lives in a way that is true to themselves and responsible to others." We don't see this as an idealistic goal; rather, we believe that such an education is an absolute necessity now that we live in a world where each one of us has more information at our immediate disposal than entire previous generations had access to—now that we live, in other words, in a world of information that can never be definitively mastered, perfectly graphed, or thoroughly understood. The fact of overabundant information applies in every discipline, from art history to genomics, from economics to political science; and so, regardless of the field, the work of the writer is no longer to appear to know everything, but rather to raise a question that helps to organize some part of the information and allows the writer to move on to questions of meaning and significance.

A single writing class will never enable a student to rack up the thousands of hours of practice it takes to become an expert writer. (Even if all college courses were devoted to promoting mastery of creative thinking, students might only get a third of the way to accruing those ten thousand crucial practice hours by graduation.) And a single book will never be able to make writing simple or easy or fun (although this is what all the recipe-based self-help guides promise). What a single class can do—and what we aim to do with this book—is to provide a time, a place, and an environment in which the focus is on nurturing curiosity, creativity, and the other allied habits of mind that define a richer, fuller engagement with the world, its challenges, and its beauty. To that end, we offer a wide range of exercises and prompts to help students practice paying attention—exercises that guide them to focus on seeing and reseeing the places, people, things, ideas, and processes that define their many worlds. Other exercises offer guidelines for practicing reading and researching as a writer, asking probing questions, and becoming better attuned to the kinds of questions asked by others. Still other exercises provide ways to practice divergent, connective, and reflective thinking. And, online, to assist you in teaching *Habits of the Creative Mind*, we have posted two essays we've written that discuss a pedagogy for the cultivation of creative minds. The first describes your essential role in modeling the practice of creativity and curiosity both in your teaching and in your own reading and writing. The second provides you with guidelines and advice for commenting on and assessing the work students produce once they've stopped using templates for arguing and have started to ask real questions.

It is our hope that this book will inspire you to see yourself as a creative pedagogue, one who sees the merits of providing your students with an opportunity to learn how to develop an ever-higher tolerance for dwelling in uncertainty—to recognize what they do not know and to have the curiosity and persistence to learn more. We know from experience that writers figure out what they know and what they still don't know *in the act of writing.* When this happens, writing ceases to be a tool for communicating what is already known and becomes a technology for exploring the unknown. While the five-paragraph essay template is designed to generate instant clarity, the writing activities we offer here are designed to teach the virtues of contending with difficulty. Writing without a template—writing that is driven by curiosity and intellectual creativity—can be difficult and frustrating, and writers will have to face failure before they succeed. But only through such persistent and deliberate practice can writers discover how their own minds work and what the evolving shape of their own thoughts might come to be.

BEGINNING

....

The blank screen and the blinking cursor: for most of us, the hardest moment in the writing process is getting started. To get that cursor moving, you need to have something to say, something of interest to others. But how do you just start off being interesting? Where do interesting thoughts come from? It's a mystery—or so it seems.

The three essays in this section discuss how to begin using *Habits of the Creative Mind* to unpack this mystery. The first essay introduces learning's central paradox: when we begin to learn something new, we simultaneously have to unlearn something familiar. A beginning is also an ending. In unlearning formulaic approaches to writing pseudo-arguments, you will be on your way to learning how to think seriously about open-ended questions.

The second and third essays discuss how to use your writing to confront what is unknown to you. In some cases, this process will involve choosing to read and write about topics that are unfamiliar. In other cases, it will involve finding ways to join an ongoing conversation among experts. In every case, you will have to contend with moments of confusion and uncertainty. The more you practice confronting what is unknown to you, the more comfortable you'll become with questions that confront all kinds of complexity and with answers that never settle things once and for all.

On Unlearning

When students enter our writing classes, they often bring with them a set of rules from high school that they use to define good writing. They know that every paragraph should start with a topic sentence that states the main point of the paragraph. And they know that all good essays have five sections or paragraphs: an introduction that states the essay's thesis; three descriptive body paragraphs, each of which discusses a different example that supports the essay's thesis; and a conclusion that restates what has been said in the previous sections. And finally, they are certain that no good essay ever uses the word *I*.

I—or rather we—suspect you know these rules well, since they've been repeated in writing classrooms for decades, with good grades going to those who follow them. But do they *really* produce good writing? Think about it: When was the last time you ran across a five-paragraph essay outside of school? Try looking for one in a news source, a magazine, a book, or even a collection of essays. You might find a modified version of one in an op-ed piece, but most of the writing you find will be organized quite differently. The five-paragraph essay, it turns out, is a very limited form, one best suited to the work of making simple claims and reporting or describing supporting evidence. (It's also easy to skim and easy to grade.)

In college classes, professors often expect students' writing to do a kind of work that is simply beyond the reach of the five-paragraph essay: contending with complexity. You may have had a professor who asked you to develop an argument by working with a handful of original sources, each with a competing point of view; or to support a new interpretation of a text not discussed in class; or to synthesize a semester's worth of lectures into a thoughtful reflection on a complex problem. When professors compose assignments like these, they assume you know how to use your writing to grapple with a genuine problem, puzzle, or question related to a course; they assume you've got something else in your quiver besides the formula for the five-paragraph theme.

So why don't we just give you a new set of rules, one that is capacious enough to provide directions for handling the range of writing tasks college students confront—the response paper in introductory history, the seminar project in advanced economics, the seven-to-eight-page argument for a 300-level psychology or politics or anthropology class? As appealing as that solution is, it's not available to us, because there's not one set of rules for generating good writing that works within any single discipline, let alone across multiple disciplines. The reason for this is not that any judgment of writing quality is inevitably arbitrary, as is often supposed, but rather that writing quality is always a function of context. Thus, what makes for a good paper in a literature class doesn't always make for a good paper in a history class or an econ class, or perhaps even in another literature class taught by a different professor.

How, then, does anyone in any discipline learn how to write about complex challenges? The first step involves unlearning the rules that are at the core of the five-paragraph essay. Taking that first step may seem impossible. We can't unlearn how to walk or how to talk. These habits are so deeply ingrained that a catastrophe of some kind (either psychological or physical) is required to unseat them. And we can't unlearn how to ride a bike or how to swim; we may forget how to over time, but when we return to these activities after a long hiatus, our challenge is not to learn how to do them as if for the first time, but to remember what's involved in keeping the bicycle upright or our body afloat and moving through the water.

Writing is unlike these other activities because each act of writing is not a straightforward repetition of what you've done before. Writing something new requires that you make choices about why you're writing, whom you're writing for, what you think, and what you want your writing to accomplish. So when we say you should unlearn what you learned about writing in school, we mean that we want you to actively resist the idea that writing is governed by a set of universal rules that, if followed, will clearly communicate the writer's ideas to the reader. We can't tell you to forget what you've learned (that would have the same paradoxical effect as telling you not to think about an elephant); and we can't say you shouldn't have been taught the rules governing the five-paragraph essay because, within an educational system dominated by the industry of standardized testing, you must be able to demonstrate that you can produce writing that follows those rules. Rather, we are asking you to question the two assumptions behind the formula for the five-paragraph essay: first, that the primary purpose of writing is to produce irrefutable arguments; and second, that the best writing is immediately understandable by all.

What do we propose in place of these assumptions? That you practice the habits of mind experienced writers exercise when they compose. Experienced writers tend to be curious and attentive. They choose to engage deeply with sources, ideas, people, and the world they live in. They are mentally flexible, self-reflective, and open to new ways of thinking, attributes that allow them to adapt to unfamiliar circumstances and problems. And they are persistent, resisting distraction and disappointment, accepting the fact that writing what hasn't been written before is hard work. When you commit yourself to practicing these habits—curiosity, attentiveness, openness, flexibility, reflectiveness, and persistence—you will also be committing yourself to making a habit of creativity, the practice of inventing novel and useful connections, compelling ideas, and thoughtful prose. As you delve into *Habits of the Creative Mind*, you'll see that we've designed the book to give you practice developing these habits. As you work your way through the book, you won't be working toward mastery of a formula for good writing; you'll be working on developing the habits of mind that increase your sensitivity to context and that allow you to use your writing to explore the unknown. You'll be practicing using your writing to show to others and yourself how your mind—not *any* mind, not *every* mind—works on a problem.

Practice Session One

Reflecting

When we tell students to unlearn the writing rules they learned in high school, they often ask for something—anything—to put in the place of those rules. We start our students on a path toward developing curious and creative habits of mind by telling them that their writing should show their minds at work on a problem. But what does that look like on the page?

Before you can answer that question for yourself, you need to know what kind of thinker you are. How does *your* mind work? What are your mental habits? How do you know? To answer these questions, pay attention over the course of a week to how you write and how you read.

Take notes every day on *everything* you read and write (not just in school or for school). Pay attention to all the times you process words: reading a page, a sign, a cereal box, the screen of a phone or a computer; writing a note, a Facebook post, a text message, a school assignment, a journal entry. For each instance, take note of where and when you read or wrote. Was it quiet? Were you moving? Were you alone?

At the end of the week, consider the following questions and spend at least 30 minutes composing a reflective response about what you've observed. Is the way you read and write better described as a set of rules or as a set of habits? Whichever option you choose, explain why. If you were to teach someone to read and write *the way you do*, how would you do it? What standards would apply?

Practice Session Two

Reading

Select one of the readings included in this book and read it with an eye toward seeing the habits of the writer's mind at work on the page. Read the text through once and then review it, identifying evidence of the writer's habits of mind. Where do you see signs of curiosity, attentiveness, openness, flexibility, reflectiveness, persistence, and creativity?

Next, spend at least 30 minutes jotting down notes about the habits of mind on display in the reading you selected. What do the examples you've found tell you about how the writer thinks?

Writing

The reading you chose to work with is obviously not a five-paragraph theme, and not just because it has far more than five paragraphs! Review the reading again and think about other ways the writer breaks what you thought were rules of writing. Then write an essay that considers why the writer made some surprising choices, writing in ways you thought were discouraged, or at least risky. What do these choices tell you about the writer's habits of mind?

EXPLORE

Can curiosity and creativity be learned? Unlearned? Relearned? Francine Prose recalls learning to write—outside school—by becoming a close and careful reader. In two TED videos, Ken Robinson laments the value placed on standardization and conformity in schools in the United States and United

Kingdom and asks us to reimagine schools as environments that cultivate curiosity and creativity.

Prose, Francine. "Close Reading: Learning to Write by Learning to Read." *Atlantic.* 1 Aug. 2006. Web.

Robinson, Ken. "How Schools Kill Creativity." TED. Feb. 2006. Web.

———. "How to Escape Education's Death Valley." TED. April 2013. Web.

On Confronting the Unknown

In his book *Deep Survival: Who Lives, Who Dies, and Why*, Laurence Gonzales recounts the story of seventeen-year-old Juliane Koepcke who was seated next to her mother on a flight with ninety other passengers when the plane was struck by lightning, causing it to go into a nosedive. The next thing Koepcke recalled was being outside the plane, still strapped into her seat, hurtling earthward towards the canopy of the Peruvian jungle.

What would you think if you were in her place at that moment? What strikes Gonzales is Koepcke's recollection of her thoughts as she fell. Her mind was not filled with shrieking terror, or a hastily pulled together prayer, or feelings of regret. No, Koepcke remembered "thinking that the jungle trees below looked just like cauliflowers." She was moving into her new reality. She passed out while still falling, and when she regained consciousness sometime later, she was on the ground, still strapped into her chair. Her collarbone was broken. There was no sign of anyone else. She decided that the planes and helicopters she could hear flying above would never be able to see her because of the thickness of the tree canopy so she began to walk out of the jungle.

Central to Gonzales's thesis about resiliency is that those who survive a life-threatening crisis see the future as unmapped. Thus Koepcke, falling two miles upside down through a storm, didn't think the obvious thought—that her future was already clearly mapped out. Instead, she was struck by the appearance of the Peruvian forest from above. And when she came to later, having crashed through the canopy, she didn't think—or didn't only think—the obvious thought about what lay ahead for a seventeen-year-old girl without her glasses, walking alone in a jungle, barefoot, slapping the ground with her one remaining shoe to frighten off the snakes that she couldn't see well enough to avoid. She walked for eleven days while she was, as Gonzales described it, "being literally eaten alive by leeches and strange tropical insects." On the eleventh day, Koepcke found a hut and collapsed inside. The next day, as chance would have it, three hunters came by, discovered her, and got her to a doctor.

Gonzales is interested in this question: Why did Koepcke survive this crash, while "the other survivors took the same eleven days to sit down and die"? Gonzales identifies a number of reasons, besides blind luck, for Koepcke's survival. First, rather than follow rules, she improvised. Second, although she was afraid, as the other survivors surely were, she used that fear as a resource for action. And third, while many better-equipped travelers have succumbed to much lesser challenges, Koepcke had "an inner resource, a state of mind" that allowed her to make do with what the moment offered.

As Gonzales pursues his research further, he finds other traits that resilient people share in common: they use fear to focus their thoughts; they find humor in their predicaments; they remain positive. The list goes on, but the item that most interests us is Gonzales's admonition that to survive a crisis, one must "see the beauty" in the new situation:

> Survivors are attuned to the wonder of the world. The appreciation of beauty, the feeling of awe, opens the senses. When you see something beautiful, your pupils actually dilate. This appreciation not only relieves stress and creates strong motivation, but it allows you to take in new information more effectively.

After we read this, it was hard not to ask: If it's possible for someone to be attuned to the wonder of the world when confronted by a situation that is *life threatening*, could writers in far less dire circumstances cultivate this attunement as a habit of mind?

Here's why this connection suggested itself to us: from our years teaching writing, we know how terrifying and humbling the confrontation with the blank screen and the flashing cursor can be—for beginning writers and experienced writers alike. This confrontation is not life threatening, of course, but it can nevertheless trigger fears: Do I have anything worth saying? Can I make myself understood? Will the struggle with the blank screen be worth it in the end? These questions arise because the act of writing, when used as a technology for thinking new thoughts, takes us to the edge of our own well-marked path and points to the uncharted realms beyond.

Ultimately, each time a writer sits down to write, he or she chooses just how far to venture into that unknown territory. To our way of thinking, the writing prompt, properly conceived, is an invitation to embark into unmapped worlds, to improvise, to find unexpected beauty in the challenges that arise. We know from experience, though, that learning to approach writing this way takes practice, and that without such practice, the writing produced in response to a prompt tends to reject whatever is unfamiliar and huddle around whatever is obvious and easiest to defend.

We have designed the prompts in this book to help you use your writing to bring you to the edge of your understanding, to a place where you encounter what is unknown to you. The more you practice using your writing in this way, the further you will be able to take your explorations; you'll find yourself moving from writing about what is unknown to you to what is more generally unknown, and then to what is unknowable. Making this journey again and again is the essence of the examined life; the writing you do along the way tracks your ongoing encounter with the complexity of human experience. The more you do it, the more you know; and the more you know, the more connections you can make as you work through your next encounter with what is unknown to you. You'll never make it to absolute knowledge, but the more you practice, the more comfortable you'll be with saying, "I don't know, but I'm sure I can figure it out."

Or so we say.

We can pose our position as a challenge: Can you make your writing trigger an inner journey that is akin to falling from a plane over the Amazon, with everything that seemed solid and certain just moments ago suddenly giving way, question leading to question, until you land on the fundamental question, "What do I know with certainty?"

We all can count on being faced with challenges of comparable magnitude over the course of our lives—the death of a loved one; the experience of aging, disease, separation, and suffering; a crisis in faith; a betrayal of trust. Writing, properly practiced, is one way to cultivate the habits of mind found in those who are resilient in moments of crisis: openness, optimism, calm, humor, and delight in beauty.

Practice Session One

Writing

One could say that seeing the future as unmapped is something children do, and that part of growing up is learning to have reasonable expectations about what the future holds. What interests Gonzales is how a person responds, regardless of his or her age, when disaster strikes. When the plane you're on splits in half miles above the Earth, it's reasonable to assume that your future is mapped: you are going to die. Gonzales's contention is that those who respond to disaster by suspending that sense that the future is known have, perhaps paradoxically, a better chance of surviving.

The thing is, you don't know how you're going to respond to hugely significant and unexpected events until they happen. What is the most unexpected event that has taken place in your life so far? What made it unexpected? How did you respond to this confrontation with the unknown? In the event, did you settle into the moment, or did your sense of what the future held remain constant and unshaken?

Spend at least an hour writing a profile of how you responded to the unexpected. Feel free to discuss what you would do differently if given another chance, knowing now what you didn't know then.

Practice Session Two

Reflecting

The kinds of crises that interest Gonzales have a cinematic quality to them: planes split apart in midair; a hiker is trapped, miles from anyone else, with his arm pinned by a boulder; a mountain climber dangles over the edge of a cliff, his partner unable to pull him to safety. (Indeed, the last two cases have been made into major motion pictures.) But writers rarely find themselves in predicaments of this kind; their crises tend to be internal and to center on getting to the heart of a matter, finding a way to express a fugitive truth, struggling to put a new thought into words.

What has been the most striking event in your *mental* life? A crisis of faith? An existential crisis? A realization that your way of thinking about love or friendship, truth or beauty, justice or politics, or any other of the concepts that are central to human experience was grounded in a false assumption? How did you respond to this confrontation with the unknown? What happened to your experience of time while this event unfolded? Did you find yourself living from moment to moment, or did your sense of what the future held remain clear?

Spend at least an hour writing a profile of how you responded to the most striking event in your mental life. Feel free to discuss what you would do differently if given another chance, knowing now what you didn't know then.

Practice Session Three

Researching

The writers whose work we've included in *Habits of the Creative Mind* can be said to use the form of the essay to confront something that is unknown to them. Choose one of these readings and write an essay that describes the writer's strategies for confronting the unknown. In tales of survival and resiliency, it is common to stress the hardships confronted and overcome, as well as acts of courage and ingenuity. If these terms strike you as out of place in a discussion of a writer grappling with a question, then provide terms of your own that you find more appropriate.

EXPLORE

What constitutes "the unknown" can take many forms. Jo Ann Beard writes about a radical change in her personal circumstances. Charles Mann imagines a world where people live to be 150 years old. Neil deGrasse Tyson discusses the edge of scientific understanding. And Amy Wallace looks at the deadly consequences of responding to life's uncertainties with inaction. Whatever form "the unknown" takes, writing about an encounter with it involves a confrontation with fear and an effort to get that fear under control.

Beard, Jo Ann. "The Fourth State of Matter." *New Yorker.* 24 June 1996. Web.

Mann, Charles C. "The Coming Death Shortage." *Atlantic.* May 2005. Web.

Tyson, Neil deGrasse. "The Perimeter of Ignorance." *Natural History.* Nov. 2005. Web.

Amy, Wallace. "An Epidemic of Fear: How Panicked Parents Skipping Shots Endangers Us All." *Wired Magazine.* 19 Oct. 2009. Web.

On Joining the Conversation

The literary critic Kenneth Burke described the exchange of academic ideas as a never-ending parlor conversation. "Imagine," he wrote,

> that you enter a parlor. You come late. When you arrive, others have long preceded you, and they are engaged in a heated discussion, a discussion too heated for them to pause and tell you exactly what it is about. In fact, the discussion had already begun long before any of them got there, so that no one present is qualified to retrace for you all the steps that had gone before. You listen for a while, until you decide that you have caught the tenor of the argument; then you put in your oar. Someone answers; you answer him; another comes to your defense; another aligns himself against you, to either the embarrassment or gratification of your opponent, depending upon the quality of your ally's assistance. However, the discussion is interminable. The hour grows late, you must depart. And you do depart, with the discussion still vigorously in progress.

With this extended metaphor, Burke offers us a way to think about how to write academic arguments. Preparing to write a paper about a topic that is new to you is like entering a parlor where a "heated discussion" is already taking place. For a while, all you can do is read what others have written and try to follow the debate. Then, after a bit, you begin to figure out what's being discussed and what the different positions, conflicts, and alliances are. Eventually, after you catch the "tenor" or drift of the conversation, a moment arrives when you feel you have something to contribute to the conversation, and you "put in your oar." And so you begin writing, even as you know that you won't have the last word—that no one will ever have the last word.

Doubtless, there is much about Burke's vision of academic writing that won't surprise you: to write, you need to understand what others have written about the problem or question that intrigues you, and you must be able to represent, analyze, and synthesize those views. You also have to be interested enough in joining the conversation to develop a position of your own that responds to those sources in compelling ways. What *is* surprising about Burke's scenario is that the conversation never ends: it is "interminable." There are no decisive arguments in Burke's parlor, or even any strongly persuasive ones; there is only the ceaseless exchange of positions.

Why, it's reasonable to ask, would anyone choose to engage in a conversation without end? To answer this question, we'd like to walk you through an example of a writer working with multiple sources to explore an open-ended question.

Magazine journalist Michael Pollan writes about places where nature meets culture: "on our plates, in our farms and gardens, and in the built environment." In his article "An Animal's Place," Pollan grapples with the ideas of Peter Singer, a philosopher and the author of an influential book, *Animal Liberation*, which argues that eating meat is unethical and that vegetarianism is a moral imperative. Pollan makes his own view on meat eating clear from the very first sentence of "An Animal's Place": "The first time I opened Peter Singer's *Animal Liberation*, I was dining alone at the Palm, trying to enjoy a rib-eye steak cooked medium-rare." He's being purposely outrageous, dramatizing his resistance to what he knows of Singer's ideas. But he hasn't yet read *Animal Liberation* and he knows that engaging with Singer's text is going to be a challenge, because it's "one of those rare books that demands that you either defend the way you live or change it."

When Pollan opens *Animal Liberation* at his table at the Palm, he transforms the steakhouse into his own Burkean parlor. Having entered the conversation late, he tries to catch "the tenor of the argument." He discovers that Singer not only opposes eating meat but also objects to wearing fur, using animals in experiments, or killing animals for sport. While these practices may seem normal today, Singer argues that they will someday be seen as expressions of "speciesism," a belief system that values humans over all other beings, and that will be looked back upon, in Pollan's phrasing, as "a form of discrimination as indefensible as racism or anti-Semitism." At the core of Singer's book is this challenging question: "If possessing a higher degree of intelligence does not entitle one human to use another for his or her own ends, how can it entitle humans to exploit nonhumans for the same purpose?"

Pollan discovers that, although Singer's ideas were far from mainstream when *Animal Liberation* was first published in 1975, Singer's campaign for animal rights has since gained many intellectual, legal, and political allies. At the time that Pollan's article was published in November 2002, German lawmakers had recently granted animals the constitutional right to be treated with respect and dignity by the state, while laws in Switzerland were being amended to change the status of animals from "things" to "beings." England had banned the farming of animals for fur, and several European nations had banned the confinement of pigs and laying hens in small crates or cages. In the United States in 2002, such reforms had not yet been addressed by legislation, but today animal rights are no longer a fringe issue.

Pollan also discovers that a crowd of scholars and writers is clustered near Singer in Burke's parlor. Among them is Matthew Scully, a political conservative and former speechwriter for President George W. Bush who wrote *Dominion: The Power of Man, the Suffering of Animals, and the Call to Mercy*, a best seller about the routine cruelty toward animals in the United States. Also present is eighteenth-century philosopher Jeremy Bentham, who argued that even though animals cannot reason or speak, they are owed moral consideration because they can suffer. Beside Bentham are legal scholar Steven M. Wise and the contemporary philosophers Tom Regan and James Rachels, and off to the side is novelist J. M. Coetzee, who declares that eating meat and purchasing goods made of leather and other animal products is "a crime of stupefying proportions," akin to Germans continuing with their normal lives in the midst of the Holocaust.

Pollan wants to resist Singer's insistence on the moral superiority of vegetarianism, but before he can build his argument, he needs to find his own allies in the ongoing conversation. He is intrigued by John Berger's essay "Why Look at Animals?" which argues that humans have become deeply confused about our relationship to other animals because we no longer make eye contact with most species. This helps Pollan to explain the paradox that, even as more and more people in the United States are eager to extend rights to animals, in our factory farms "we are inflicting more suffering on more animals than at any time in history." From sources as varied as Matthew Scully's *Dominion* and farm trade magazines, Pollan learns that these farms, also known as Confined Animal Feeding Operations, or CAFOs, reduce animals to "production units" and subject them to a life of misery.

But these sources don't particularly help Pollan to stand up against Singer's insistence that everyone who considers eating meat must choose between "a lifetime of suffering for a nonhuman animal and the gastronomic preference of a human being." Unhappy with either option before him—to refuse to pay attention to the suffering of animals in factory farms or to stop eating animals—Pollan brings a completely new voice into the parlor: not a philosopher or a writer, but a farmer. Joel Salatin, owner of Polyface Farm in Virginia, raises cattle, pigs, chickens, rabbits, turkeys, and sheep on a small farm where each species, including the farmer himself, performs a unique role in the ecosystem. The cows graze in the pasture; afterward, the chickens come in and eat insect larvae and short grass; then the sheep take their turn and eat what the cows and chickens leave behind. Meanwhile, the pigs compost the cow manure in the barn. In this system, the mutual interest of humans and domestic animals is recognized, even when the animals are slaughtered for meat. In life, each animal lives according to its natural inclinations; and when it is slaughtered, its death takes place in the open. Nothing is hidden from sight. Pollan concludes that slaughtering animals, where the process can be watched is "a morally powerful idea." Salatin convinces him that animals can have respectful deaths when they are not, as they are in factory farms, "treated as a pile of protoplasm."

Pollan's visit to Polyface Farm is transformational. He decides that "what's wrong with animal agriculture—with eating animals—is the practice, not the principle." The ethical challenge, in other words, is not a philosophical issue but a practical one: Do the animals raised for meat live lives that allow them to express their natures? Do they live good lives? Pollan decides that, if he limits his consumption of meat to animals that are raised humanely, then he can eat them without ethical qualms. Pollan is so pleased with his creative solution to the problem Singer posed that he even writes to the philosopher to ask him what he thinks about the morality of eating meat that comes from farms where animals live according to their nature and appear not to suffer. Singer holds to his position that killing an animal that "has a sense of its own existence" and "preferences for its own future" (that is, a pig, but not a chicken) is wrong, but he also admits that he would not "condemn someone who purchased meat from one of these farms."

Does this mean that Pollan has won the argument? Not really. The discussion in Burke's parlor has not ended. New voices have entered to engage with both Pollan and Singer, and new ideas have emerged about sustainability, agriculture, economics, and ethics. Curious, reflective, and open-ended thinkers continue to enter, mingle, and depart, "the discussion still vigorously in progress."

Practice Session

Reflecting

For this exercise, we'd like you to read Michael Pollan's "An Animal's Place" and think more about how he uses sources and what it means to be "in conversation" with words on a page or screen. Read the piece with care, taking notes about where and how Pollan uses his sources to develop his own thoughts. After reading, take at least 30 minutes to write answers to these questions about entering into a conversation with sources: Where did Pollan engage with sources in ways that surprised you? Where did he use sources in ways that you'd like to emulate? What different kinds of conversations did Pollan engage in with his sources? Why did he choose to be in conversation with some sources more than others? What have you learned from these exercises about writing "in conversation" with sources?

Reading

Next, we'd like you to read Harriet McBryde Johnson's "Unspeakable Conversations." Johnson's article is also in conversation with Peter Singer, but unlike Pollan, Johnson is primarily interested in Singer's controversial views on euthanasia. Read the article with care, observing the many different ways Johnson joins in conversation with her sources. To start, you might notice sources that serve as the focus of analysis; supply background or information; provide key ideas or concepts; provide positions or arguments to grapple with; or shift the direction of the conversation.

After you've read, spend at least 30 minutes making a list of the many ways Johnson uses her source material. Notice that she may name or quote some sources explicitly, while not identifying every source of information. This is one way in which journalistic writing differs significantly from academic writing, where, of course, all sources must be cited.

Writing

Now that you've read both "An Animal's Place" and "Unspeakable Conversations," we'd like you to compose an essay in which you enter a conversation with Pollan and Johnson and answer the question: To what extent is it possible to define what makes a "good life" (or a "good death") for humans and other animals? Use Pollan's and Johnson's essays both as sources and as models of how to join a conversation in writing.

EXPLORE

Essays about ethical quandaries invite readers to join the fray. Michael Pollan challenges philosopher Peter Singer on the ethics of eating meat. Harriet McBryde Johnson also argues with Singer, but she objects to his stance on the ethics of killing severely disabled newborns. We invite you to join those conversations, and also to see how biologist Sandra Steingraber connects the words of early environmentalist Rachel Carson, author of *Silent Spring*, to current debates about the dangers of fracking.

Johnson, Harriet McBryde. "Unspeakable Conversations." *New York Times Magazine*. 16 Feb. 2003. Web.

Pollan, Michael. "An Animal's Place." *New York Times Magazine*. 10 Nov. 2002. Web.

Steingraber, Sandra. "The Fracking of Rachel Carson." *Orion Magazine*. Sept./Oct. 2012. Web.

Curiosity at Work: Rebecca Skloot's Extra-Credit Assignment

Rebecca Skloot's best-selling book, *The Immortal Life of Henrietta Lacks,* tells the story of a poor African American woman in Baltimore who was hospitalized with cancer in 1951. Before Lacks died, a surgeon removed some of her cancer cells for research without her knowledge, and they were used to grow human cells in a lab for the first time. Lacks's cells, now known as HeLa cells, are still alive today and have been essential to medical research for more than sixty years. Every person who has received a polio vaccine or who lives in a country where polio has been eradicated, for example, is a direct beneficiary of research that used HeLa cells. And yet, before Skloot's book, few people knew of Henrietta Lacks and her immortal cells.

The path that led Skloot to write Lacks's story was long and circuitous. At age sixteen, Skloot registered for a community college biology course to make up the credit she lost when she failed the subject during her freshman year of high school. When the class was studying cell division, Skloot's teacher, Mr. Defler, told his students about HeLa cells and then wrote HENRIETTA LACKS in big letters on the blackboard. He told them that Lacks had died of cervical cancer, that a surgeon had taken a tissue sample from her tumor, and that "HeLa cells were one of the most important things that happened to medicine in the last hundred years." Before erasing the name from the board and dismissing the class for the day, Mr. Defler added one more fact: "She was a black woman."

Skloot followed her teacher back to his office, asking questions: "Where was she from? Did she know how important her cells were? Did she have any children?" Lacks's life is a mystery, Mr. Defler told her, and then he made the kind of comment teachers make: "If you're curious, go do some research, write up a little paper about what you find and I'll give you some extra credit."

That night, Skloot couldn't find any information on Lacks beyond a parenthetical reference in her biology textbook, but she didn't forget about this mysterious woman whose cells had helped protect millions from contracting polio. Some ten years later, when Skloot was working on her undergraduate degree in biology, she took her first writing course, and the teacher began by asking the students to "write for 15 minutes about something someone forgot." Skloot immediately scrawled "Henrietta Lacks" on her page and wrote about how Lacks had been forgotten by the world. Over time, Skloot resolved to write "a biography of both the cells and the woman they came from." As her commitment to her project deepened, her research became "a decade long adventure through scientific laboratories, hospitals, and mental institutions, with a cast of characters that would include Nobel laureates, grocery store clerks, convicted felons, and a professional con artist." She met Lacks's five adult children and their families, which raised new questions for her about race, ethics, and medical research, among them: If Henrietta Lacks's cells were so important to medical science and had given rise to a multibillion-dollar industry, why couldn't Lacks's children and grandchildren afford health insurance?

More than two decades after Rebecca Skloot first heard the name Henrietta Lacks, she finished her book. Putting her research skills to use once more, she tracked down the biology teacher who first told her about HeLa cells and sent him a note: "Dear Mr. Defler, here's my extra credit project. It's 22 years late, but I have a good excuse: No one knew anything about her."

Note: The quotations in this essay are from Rebecca Skloot's blog post, "What's the Most Important Lesson You Learned from a Teacher?" *Rebeccaskloot.com* 8 May 2012.

PAYING ATTENTION

I s it possible to write without paying attention? At first the question seems absurd: How could words move from your brain to your keyboard if you weren't paying attention? Writing doesn't just happen. And yet people text while walking and even while driving, which shows that writing happens all the time without one's full attention. And of course, students can now write papers while also surfing the Net and snapchatting their friends.

Funnily enough, a common response to the mistakes that happen as a result of being distracted is the command to "pay attention." You step off the curb into oncoming traffic and are pulled back to safety by a friend just before you would have been hit. "Pay attention!" You're sitting in class daydreaming when your teacher calls on you. "Pay attention!" You're in a crowd and walk directly into a stranger. "Pay attention!" In each case, the command arrives too late: it's less helpful guidance than it is a rebuke.

We want you to think of writing not as a way of proving you *were* paying attention but as a way *of* paying attention. To this end, we've populated this section with essays that explore how writing can be used to train the mind to focus and the eye to see. We also explore using your writing to reflect on how you think and on how you imagine the thoughts of others. When you use writing in these ways, you are practicing being engaged with and interested in the world.

On Learning to See

When Betty Edwards started teaching high school art classes in the late 1960s, she was baffled as she watched her students having trouble drawing simple, familiar objects. If they could see that the orange was *in front of* the green bottle, why did they draw the two objects *next to* each other? Why was it that the ability of her students to express themselves verbally and to reason mathematically had improved from kindergarten to high school, but their ability to draw hadn't changed much since the third grade? And when her students eventually figured out how to produce drawings that were more accurate, why did the improvement seem to take place all at once rather than gradually?

Around the time that Edwards was pondering why students who learned easily in academic classes had so much difficulty in art class, neuroscientists Roger W. Sperry and Michael Gazzaniga began publishing reports that suggested that the two sides of the brain did different kinds of mental work. The left hemisphere, where language was typically housed, was more systematic and linear. The right hemisphere was more visual, spatial, and synthetic. Once Sperry and Gazzaniga's research got picked up by the popular press, it was reduced to a simple binary opposition: the right brain is creative and the left brain is analytical.

Edwards used this research to make sense of the difficulty her students had seeing what was right in front of them as well as the breakthroughs they experienced when they suddenly began to see differently. In Edwards's view, students were rewarded in their academic classes for being verbal and analytical thinkers; they were required, one could say, to be left-brained. But to draw well, they needed access to visual, perceptual, and synthetic thought; they needed to find a way to see with the right brain. To trigger this apparent hemispheric shift for her students, Edwards developed exercises that quieted the verbal, analytical, and systematizing thinking rewarded elsewhere in the curriculum, so that visual, creative, and associative thinking could come to the fore. As she developed these exercises, Edwards was beginning to understand that, in order to learn how to draw, her students had to stop naming what they were trying to draw and start seeing what was in front of them in a new way—as related lines and connected spaces without names. If they stopped saying "hand," for example, they could learn to stop drawing the symbol for a hand (five stick fingers at the end of a stick arm) and could instead begin to see the intricate pattern that is made by a particular hand resting on the edge of a particular keyboard.

Edwards's explanation of the brain's two dominant operational modes makes a kind of immediate, intuitive sense; indeed, it makes it sound like all you really have to do to draw is to learn how to toggle the switch between your left brain and right brain. The truth, though, is that both the brain and learning how to draw are more complicated than the model of a sharp division between left-brain and right-brain function suggests. We now know from neuroscience that it is more accurate to say that activity in the right hemisphere is *correlated* with creative and divergent thinking and that activity in the left hemisphere is *correlated* with analytic and convergent thinking. While the right part of your brain contributes a good deal to creative potential, your whole brain has to work in concert for you to engage in creative work.

In *A Whole New Mind*, Daniel Pink describes attending a drawing class based on the methods developed by Edwards and learning just how difficult it is to get the whole brain to play along with this new way of seeing. His first attempt at drawing a self-portrait while looking at his face in a mirror was simply terrible. The eyes, nose, and lips were clumsy cartoon versions of these basic components of the human face. Pink's placement of these features in his drawing was equally cartoonish and bore little relation to where the eyes, nose, and mouth are found on a real human face. Pink couldn't draw what was right in front of him, the most familiar, recognizable part of himself, because his preconceptions about faces—which his teacher called "remembered symbols from childhood"—blinded him to the actual contours of the face looking back at him in the mirror. To draw better, Pink needed to stop naming, analyzing, and judging what he saw and practice seeing and sketching lines, patterns, relationships, and relationships between relationships. He had to practice finding increments of simplicity in complex patterns of lines and spaces.

We believe that the kind of seeing Edwards aims to trigger through her teaching practice is a specific instance of the kind of seeing that lies at the core of creative thinking. Indeed, Edwards herself says that "this —

ability to see things differently has many uses in life aside from drawing— ✳
not the least of which is creative problem solving." So, although it surely
seems contradictory, we adapted a couple of Edwards's exercises meant to
restrain the dominance of language to serve our own interest in having you
think differently about the role of language in the creative process.

Practice Session One

Writing

Draw a self-portrait. Start by finding a spot with a mirror and plenty of light
where you can work comfortably for at least 30 minutes. Using a pencil and a
blank sheet of paper, draw your face. Do your best, and don't give up before
you've got all your facial features looking back at you. The drawing may look
awful, and that's okay.

Next, look carefully at the shape of the features and the relationships between
features and think about how and why your portrait turned out as it did. What
went right? Where did you successfully transform perception into image? What
went wrong? What did you *not see* as you were drawing? How did you feel while
you were completing this exercise? How did you feel when you were done? Why?

As a final step, take at least 15 minutes to write an assessment of the act of
seeing that generated your self-portrait.

Seeing

For this exercise, you will use a trick of Betty Edwards's that helps you see without naming—drawing an upside-down image. We'd like you to give Edwards's
exercise a try, following these instructions.

1. Gather your materials: you'll need the Egon Schiele drawing reproduced
   on page 38, a pencil, an eraser, and a sheet of unlined paper. Then find a
   quiet place where you won't be interrupted for at least 30 minutes.

2. When you're ready to begin drawing, turn your cell phone off, close your
   laptop, and take off your headphones. You should do everything you can
   to give this exercise your undivided attention.

3. While you are making your copy of the upside-down Schiele line drawing,
   try not to figure out what you are looking at (and don't turn the drawing right-side up until after you're finished). You'll do a better job if you

Robert Muller by Egon Schiele

aren't trying to name what you are drawing. Focus instead on the lines in the drawing, the relationships between those lines, and the relationships between the lines and the paper's edge. Edwards tells her students: "When you come to parts that seem to force their names on you—the H-A-N-D-S and the F-A-C-E—try to focus on these parts just as shapes. You might even cover up with one hand or finger all but the specific line you are drawing and then uncover each adjacent line."

Writing

When you are done making your copy, we'd like you to reflect upon the *experience* of drawing an upside-down image. Begin by considering the following questions: Was it difficult to stop naming and to start seeing relationships? Are there parts of your copy that are more successful than others? What happened to your sense of time while you were working on your copy?

Then, spend at least 30 minutes writing about what happened *in your mind* while you worked on your line drawing. There's no right answer here. Think of your writing as a sketch of your mind at work. Learning to see begins with learning how *you* see.

Practice Session Two

Reflecting

In the 1940s, a psychologist named Karl Duncker developed a test of problem solving that's popularly known as "the candle problem." The challenge posed to participants is to figure out how to attach a lit candle to a wall without it dripping on the floor below. To complete the challenge, participants can use only the objects pictured here:

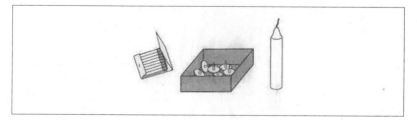

Karl Dunker Candle Problem. On Problem Solving, Psychological Monographs, 58, American Psychological Association. Panel A, na

Take as much time as you need to figure out how you would solve the candle problem, and then write down your solution.

Next, watch Daniel Pink's TED talk, "The Puzzle of Motivation." Pink begins talking about the candle problem and its solution at around the two-minute mark, but we want you to listen to the talk in its entirety. Take notes while you're watching, writing down anything Pink says that surprises you.

After you've listened to Pink's TED talk, we'd like you to spend 45 minutes writing a reflective piece that considers the role seeing played in your response to the candle problem. Did solving the candle problem require a new way of seeing, a new way of thinking, or both? What do you think the implications of the candle problem are for learning?

EXPLORE

Writing about seeing is often precipitated by the experience of learning to draw. John Berger has been drawing his entire life. Adam Gopnik earned a BA and MA in art history but didn't learn to draw until middle age. A classical pianist before changing careers, Peter Mendelsund is a self-taught artist who designs book covers for a living. Each of these writers explores the relationship between how we see the world and how we put the world of our experience into words.

Berger, John. *Bento's Sketchbook: How Does the Impulse to Draw Something Begin?* New York: Pantheon, 2011. Print.

Gopnick, Adam. "Life Studies: What I Learned When I Learned to Draw." *New Yorker.* 27 June 2011. Web.

Mendelsund, Peter. *What We See When We Read.* New York: Vintage, 2014. Print.

On Looking and Looking Again

"Pay attention!"

Walk the hallways of any elementary school, and it won't be long before you hear this exasperated command. Over time, all students learn that what their teachers mean when they say "pay attention" is "sit still and be quiet." The teachers know, of course, that there's more to paying attention than being quiet, but what that "more" turns out to be is something that can't be ordered into existence by the voice of another. So students learn early on how to get their bodies to behave in class, but getting their minds to behave is another matter.

The paradox at the beginning of the process of paying attention seems irresolvable: How does mental focus emerge out of chaos, the attentive mind out of distraction? How does anyone ever learn the inner work of paying attention?

Our answer is: by practice.

But what kind of practice? How does one practice a state of mind?

The poet William Blake offers some guidance on how to think about this paradox in the opening stanza of his poem "Auguries of Innocence":

> To see a World in a Grain of Sand
> And a Heaven in a Wild Flower
> Hold Infinity in the palm of your hand
> And Eternity in an hour

On a first reading, Blake's stanza seems to offer a straightforward proposition about how to trigger a state of deep attentiveness: if you want X (to see the world in a grain of sand), then do Y (hold infinity in the palm of your hand). But if this is what it takes to pay attention, attentiveness of the kind Blake describes seems an impossibility, for how is one supposed to go about grabbing hold of infinity or experiencing "eternity in an hour"?

Perhaps we've misread the stanza. Perhaps Blake is making a statement both about what paying attention involves and what it makes

possible: "To see a world in a grain of sand and heaven in a wild flower [is to] hold infinity in the palm of your hand and eternity in an hour." Read this way, Blake's verse is saying that, if you can learn to "see a world in a grain of sand" or "a heaven in a wild flower," you can gain access to realms beyond what you know and even beyond the limits of thought—you can reach the infinite and the eternal.

From Blake's poem we could conclude that the practice of writing poetry has trained Blake's mind to focus on the particular (a grain of sand, a wildflower) until it leads to something much bigger (a world, a heaven) and onward to realms beyond measure (infinity, eternity). More generally, we can say that Blake shows us that the attentive mind generates insights, connections, and beautiful objects and moves by inference, analogy, and metaphor.

Does this mean that, instead of commanding a distracted student to "pay attention" teachers should try saying, "sit still and be a poet"?

That command wouldn't work any better than the command to pay attention, of course: first, even the best poet can't be a poet on command; and second, poetry is only one possible result of paying attention.

Better by far, we think, to say, "Practice looking and looking again."

A teacher we greatly admire, Ann Berthoff, developed an exercise that we've adapted here to help you experience the kind of seeing Blake describes. To get her students to resee the natural world, Berthoff would bring to class all manner of organic objects—a starfish, the husk of a cactus, dried reeds, a pressed flower—and then have each student take one of the objects home to study for a week.

For our version of this exercise, you'll need to select your own organic object—anything from the natural world will do. You should choose something that you can hold in your hand and that you can put somewhere out of harm's way for a week.

We ask that, for seven straight days, you spend at least 10 minutes recording your *observations* of the object you've selected.

Here's an example of what a day's entry might look like, written by Erik on day five:

> Clearly the plant is dehydrated and dying, and yet, besides
> my dismembering it of its limbs, it still has the same form

and design as it did when I first took it home. The colors of the leaves have noticeably changed, but nothing else has visibly changed as far as I can tell. Of course, the way I'm seeing this object has changed since the first day I laid my eyes upon it.

There are definitely patterns that are quite unmistakable in and on this plant. For instance, the mini-stems that connect the buds to the stem that connects back to the entire organism: there are seven of these mini-stems, and they are all about of equal length. That is interesting. If it is sunlight the buds seek, I would think that maybe one of the mini-branches would push itself considerably farther out so as to receive more energy for its own survival. But, naturally, these buds are probably not competing for energy but rather are working together for the survival and health of the entire plant.

I cannot help but draw a connection to a human body here. You can find multi facets and numerous parts and functions of parts within a single limb of a body. In fact, you can find it in one single human cell. . . . I'm reminded of a quote from Aldous Huxley [who was quoting from William Blake]: "If the doors of perception were cleansed, every thing would appear to man as it truly is, infinite." A person is not just a person with a name, a height and a weight, and a social status; each person is also composed of electricity, of a billion cells that perform who knows how many functions.

My plant here, at first glance, is just a little piece of a shrub. But if you really look at it, there is a lot going on here that makes this plant what it is. Can the physical world ever be described as infinite? Do we really actually know, in an empirical sense, of anything that is infinite? Why do we have a "word" describing something that we have never experienced? Is that evidence or a suggestion from our subconscious mind, our inner spirit, our unseen self, that there is such a thing as infinity? Is there infinity present in my little piece of shrub? I don't know, but I'm willing to bet that as

more powerful microscopes are developed, there will surely be more we will be able to "see" in the physical universe around us, and this will further lend credence to the idea that, yes, with a necessary perspective, it may be possible to hold infinity in the palm of your hand. You won't know it unless you have eyes to see it, or take the time to meditate on it, and even then . . . infinity is a tough thing to swallow and ascribe to what we can perceive with our five senses. But it's not impossible.

Focusing on the plant stem, Erik makes connections to the human body, to a quote he's read in Aldous Huxley, and then back to the Blake poem we used in our writing prompt. Looking closely allows Erik to see beyond the plant back into his own mind. Thinking about how the plant is organized becomes, in this instance, a way to think about how all minds organize perceptions.

Practice Session

Writing
Choose an organic object from the natural world, something that you can hold in your hand and that you can keep out of harm's way for a week. Then, over seven consecutive days, write for at least 10 minutes each day about what you see.

> Describe how your object is put together.
>
> What questions does your object pose?
>
> What does it point to?
>
> Where did it come from?
>
> What is it a part of?

You are free to move your object, to alter it, or to interact with it in any way that furthers your effort to understand how it is put together. You can also read and do research if questions come to mind. Your goal is to see how your object is organized within itself and how it is implicitly connected with other natural objects.

Write every day.

Ponder what your observations and explorations tell you about the object.

Write even if you're stuck.

If you try to sketch your object, does that help you see aspects you would otherwise miss? What if you photograph it?

Write even if you think you've said all there is to say about your object.

There's only one rule: don't anthropomorphize your object. Don't give it a human name. Don't invent a dialogue between yourself and your object. We've found that this approach only serves to obliterate the object—it displaces the act of looking and looking again.

Reflecting

After you've completed your seven days of writing, reread what you've written with the following questions in mind: At the end of all your looking, how would you describe the organization of your organic object? Based on what you've written, how would you describe your own way of looking? What did you see right away? What did it take you a while to see? What kinds of questions did you ask automatically? What kinds of questions emerged late in the process?

Write an essay that reflects on what this exercise of looking and looking again has helped you to recognize about seeing in general and about paying attention in particular.

EXPLORE

Looking, learning, and rethinking can turn the ordinary into something extraordinary. Rachel Carson, Annie Dillard, and Michael Pollan each look at familiar objects or places until they become strange and surprising. Carson lingers by a sea cave that appears only at the year's lowest tide. Dillard looks for hidden treasures in the natural world: monarch pupae, flying squirrels, the streak of green light that bursts from the sun at the moment of sunset. And Pollan explores an orchard with 2,500 varieties of apple trees, including an ancient species from Kazakhstan that may be the origin of all apples.

Carson, Rachel. "The Marginal World." *The Edge of the Sea*. Boston: Houghton Mifflin, 1998. 1–7. Print.
(Available on Google Books via preview.)

Dillard, Annie. "Total Eclipse." *Teaching a Stone to Talk: Expeditions and Encounters*. New York: HarperCollins, 1982. 9–28. Print.
(Available on Google Books via preview.)

Pollan, Michael. "Breaking Ground: The Call of the Wild Apple." *New York Times*. 5 Nov. 1998. Web.

On Encountering Difficulty

In his essay "The Mind's Eye," the neurologist Oliver Sacks confronts the conundrum of free will: "To what extent are we—our experiences, our reactions—shaped, predetermined, by our brains, and to what extent do we shape our own brains?" He is led to this conundrum by consideration of a series of cases of individuals who were born with sight but then became blind. The point that Sacks wants to make in "The Mind's Eye" is deceptively simple: how one responds to becoming blind is idiosyncratic—that is, it is unique to the individual. Sacks did not always think this was the case. Initially, he assumed that responses to going blind were determined by the structure of the human brain and thus were essentially uniform.

Sacks begins his essay by describing an extreme example of what is thought to be the typical response to going blind, where the other senses gain heightened powers as the ability to see recedes. After John Hull, blind in one eye due to cataracts at seventeen, went completely blind at forty-eight, he steadily lost access not only to his visual memories but to what Sacks terms "the very idea of seeing." In this profound state of "deep blindness," Hull claimed that spatial references such as "here" and "there" lost meaning for him. At the same time, he became what he calls a "whole-body seer," someone whose other senses have roared to life to compensate for the loss of vision and who now experiences wholly new ways of engaging with the world.

After first writing about Hull in 1991, Sacks began to hear from others whose own experiences of becoming blind conflicted with this compensatory model of how senses covered for each other. For example, Zoltan Torey's response to going blind was the exact opposite of Hull's: instead of embracing "deep blindness" when he lost his sight in an accident at the age of twenty-one, Torey cultivated the powers of his "inner eye," self-consciously laboring to hold on to his ability to think with and manipulate visual images. What Torey has done since going blind is almost unthinkable: he learned to multiply four-figure numbers by visualizing the operations as if the calculation were written on a blackboard; he taught himself to move and manipulate three-dimensional images in his mind, breaking them apart and recombining the pieces; he even single-handedly replaced the roof on his gabled home. What motivates Torey? A deep need to retain a sense of the visual.

Then there's Sabriye Tenberken, blind since twelve, who has traveled extensively in Tibet, often alone, advocating for the blind. She has cultivated a rich synesthetic inner world, one full of color and feeling, which allows her to use words to paint elaborate and fanciful descriptions of the outside world. While Torey visualizes highly detailed maps and diagrams of the real world, Tenberken delights in holding on to an inner vision that is poetic and playful.

Sacks started out looking for a neurological explanation of these varied responses to becoming blind—i.e., that whereas Hull's visual cortex had atrophied completely, Torey was able to "stave off an otherwise inevitable loss of neuronal function in the visual cortex" as a result of his mental gymnastics. But when Sacks turns his attention to people who can see, he quickly finds a similar range in the visual imagination of sighted individuals: some seeing people can hold images in their minds and manipulate them as Torey does; some, akin to Hull, cannot generate visual images or call them to mind; others can achieve the ability to visualize in great detail only through chemical enhancement.

Where does this leave us? For Sacks, the fact that both the blind and the seeing share a spectrum of possible ways to visualize the outer world illustrates the difference between brain and mind. The power to see has a physical, neurological basis located in the brain. What happens to those impulses once the brain processes them is determined not by the brain alone but by "the higher and more personal powers of the imagination, where there is a continual struggle for concepts and form and meaning, a calling upon all the powers of the self," which we would call *the mind*. Sacks continues:

> Imagination dissolves and transforms, unifies and creates, while drawing upon the "lower" powers of memory and association. It is by such imagination, such "vision," that we create or construct our individual worlds.

Thus, at the level of the individual, there will always be a measure of mystery in the adaptations that occur in response to radical change. We see this mystery as much in Hull's embrace of deep blindness as in Torey's tending the flames of inner vision—in the interplay between the hardwiring of neurology and the software of the self. Such a mystery cannot be unraveled by science alone because the self simultaneously resides in and is created by the work of the imagination as it connects and transforms the memories and associations recorded by and stored in the brain.

To put this another way, we could say that our inner lives are both created and sustained by the imagination; and further, that in times of radical change the very survival of the self depends on imagining what was previously unimaginable—that life without sight is sensually rich, for example, or that one's blindness should be fully embraced. This observation doesn't resolve the mystery, of course, but only further sharpens it: How does one cultivate an imagination capable of such adaptation? How does one learn to live with and within new forms of embodied experience?

Practice Session One

Researching

If you are blind or visually impaired, skip this exercise and go to Reflecting (for blind or visually–impaired students) on the next page. If you are sighted, visit the online *Time* magazine photo gallery *Photos by Blind Photographers*. The opening blurb says that the exhibit "raises extraordinary questions about the nature of sight." What do you see when you look at these photographs taken by photographers who are legally blind? How do the words that accompany each image influence what you see? Can you unsee the words and consider the images simply as photographs? Search the Web for other works by these photographers and for the work of other blind photographers. Follow your curiosity.

Reflecting (for sighted students)

How do blind photographers teach the sighted to see? Using examples of images you have collected through your research, write a reflective essay about what you've learned about blindness and the imagination.

Reflecting (for blind or visually-impaired students)
Consider what the sighted could learn about perception through a representation of your experience. John Hull offers such a representation when he describes the intensity of experiencing rain as a "whole-body seer":

> Rain has a way of bringing out the contours of everything; it throws a colored blanket over previously invisible things; instead of an intermittent and thus fragmented world, the steadily falling rain creates continuity of acoustic experience. . . . The sound on the path is quite different from the sound of the rain drumming into the lawn on the right, and this is different again from the blanketed, heavy, sodden feel of the large bush on the left. Further out, the sounds are less detailed. I can hear the rain falling on the road, and the swish of the cars that pass up and down.

Write a reflective essay that represents your experience of your environment. Does your experience strike you as idiosyncratic? That is, did your individual character, temperament, or will play a role in your perception of your environment?

....

Practice Session Two

....

Writing
John Hull, Zoltan Torey, and Sabriye Tenberken help Sacks to see the power of the individual imagination in shaping how one responds to trauma. But what about ordinary, everyday problems? Does the imagination come into play when confronting a problem that is not life altering?

Choose a mundane problem that arises in the course of your day: a disagreement with a family member; difficulty finding parking; misplacing your keys. Does this sort of problem, in its solution, yield evidence of the uniqueness of each individual's imagination? Or do mundane problems call for mundane solutions? Write an essay that explores multiple ways of solving an everyday problem, and consider whether your example demonstrates the powers of the human imagination.

Practice Session Three

Researching

Each of the readings we've included in this volume serves as an example of a writer encountering difficulty. Choose one of these essays and, while reading it, mark the moments when the author encounters difficulty. When you're done, review the passages you've marked. Are all the difficulties of the same kind? Of the same importance? Of the same intensity?

How does the writer respond to these difficulties? Write an essay in which you examine the writer's approach to difficulty. Although you might be tempted to say that the writer's approach is simply "idiosyncratic," explore in greater detail how the writer responds to difficulty that's encountered in the world of ideas and words.

EXPLORE

Our essay on encountering difficulty works with four examples of how people have responded to losing the ability to see. The material we suggest here further complicates our discussion. Michael Finkel profiles a blind man who sees like a bat. Filmmakers Peter Middleton and John Spinney interpret John Hull's audio-diary of his journey into blindness. A photo gallery showcases images created by people who are legally blind.

Finkel, Michael. "The Blind Man Who Taught Himself to See." *Men's Journal.* March 2011. Web.

Hull, John. "Memory," "Panic," and "Rainfall." Supplements to Peter Middleton and John Spinney's "Notes on Blindness." Audio. *New York Times.* Web.

Middleton, Peter, and John Spinney, directors. "Notes on Blindness." *New York Times.* 16 Jan. 2014. Web.

Photos by Blind Photographers. Time n.d. Web.

Curiosity at Work: David Simon Pays Attention to the Disenfranchised

David Simon has excelled as a writer in many different roles: police reporter in Baltimore; author of two award-winning books, *Homicide: A Year on the Killing Streets* and *The Corner: A Year in the Life of an Inner-City Neighborhood;* screenwriter for *Homicide,* a television series based on his book of the same title; head writer for the HBO series *The Wire;* and cocreator and coproducer of the HBO series *Treme.* In 2010, he was awarded a no-strings-attached $625,000 MacArthur "Genius" Fellowship, which the MacArthur Foundation says "is not a reward for past accomplishment, but rather an investment in a person's originality, insight, and potential." Not bad for a guy who graduated from the University of Maryland with a C average.

What made it possible for Simon to move from cub reporter to chronicler of the collapse of American cities? The decades Simon spent on the beat in Baltimore made him comfortable with not knowing in advance what he was going to see or hear or report: "To be a decent city reporter, I had to listen to people who were different from me. I had to not be uncomfortable asking stupid questions or being on the outside. I found I had a knack for walking into situations where I didn't know anything, and just waiting." Simon learned to listen closely to the people of Baltimore and to pay attention to their multiple points of view. Because of the way he listened, he fell in love with the crime-ridden, impoverished city.

Why has Baltimore gone from being a major US port to a city with one of the highest murder rates in the country? This is a problem that can't be answered in a sound bite. It takes Simon five seasons of storytelling in *The Wire* to bring to light the multiple variables that work together in postindustrial capitalism to create the toxic conditions in which humans are worth less and less with every passing moment, while glistening new buildings rise on Baltimore's Inner Harbor. These rapacious economic and social forces can't be understood in isolation; they have to be seen in action, degrading the value of the lives of gang members as well as those who work in the police force, the failing

shipping industry, the city government, the public school system, and the local newspapers. Like a contemporary Charles Dickens, Simon employs a large canvas, multiple intersecting plotlines, and memorable hard-luck characters to voice his critique of the widening gap between the haves and the have-nots.

In the four seasons of *Treme*, Simon continues exploring the fate of American cities, this time focusing on New Orleans after Hurricane Katrina. Looking beyond the image of New Orleans as the Big Easy, a place where the good times always roll, Simon tells stories about the city's recovery from the hurricane through the eyes of local musicians, a neighborhood bar owner, a "Big Chief" in the Mardi Gras parades, a civil rights attorney, and a jazz musician who has made good in New York. Why does he use storytelling and not journalism or the documentary form to do this work? Simon explains: "By referencing what is real, or historical, a fictional narrative can speak in a powerful, full-throated way to the problems and issues of our time. And a wholly imagined tale, set amid the intricate and accurate details of a real place and time, can resonate with readers in profound ways. In short, drama is its own argument."

Note: The first Simon quote is from Margaret Talbot's *New Yorker* article, "Stealing Life"; the second quote is from "HBO's 'Treme' Creator David Simon Explains It All for You," published in the *New Orleans Times-Picayune*.

ASKING QUESTIONS

"There are no bad questions": this is an incantation repeated year in and year out in classrooms across the country. It represents a well-intentioned effort to establish a comfortable learning environment, but it's a hard sell, since teachers and students alike know that not only are there bad questions, but there are whole categories of questions that are unwelcome in the classroom. There are questions most teachers dread—the intrusively personal question, the cynical question, and the do-you-mind-repeating-what-you-just-said question, to name a few—and there are questions most students dread, such as the teacher's guess-what-I'm-thinking question, the teacher's fill-in-the-blank question, and the question that exposes the student who asked it to ridicule.

Rather than make the demonstrably false assertion that there are no bad questions, we prefer to ask: What is a good question? In this section, we introduce you to two of our favorite question posers, the hosts of *Radiolab*. We also propose an alternative to the thesis-driven writing project: writing your way to a question. And we look at how to prepare for an interview-based project. Questions you hear, questions produced by your own speculative writing, questions you put to others: we give you three different contexts for considering the roles that context, expertise, research, and curiosity play in the production of good questions.

On Asking Questions

We're devoted fans of *Radiolab*, a radio show and podcast on which the hosts, Jad Abumrad and Robert Krulwich, invite listeners to join them "on a curiosity bender." Abumrad is a composer by training and won a MacArthur Fellowship in 2011 for his work on the show, while Krulwich is a science correspondent with over three decades of broadcast experience. Working together, they make the exercise of being curious about the world *sound* like an exciting adventure.

In each show, Abumrad and Krulwich assume the air of happy amateurs who delight in having simple questions open up complex realities. They typically begin with a big question—about science, the arts, medicine, philosophy, or some other aspect of human experience—and then spend an hour exploring a range of responses to the question they've posed. The questions they ask often express an open-minded wonder about the world: Why do we sleep? What is color? What is race? How do we assign blame? To help them with their explorations, they always turn to experts, but they never take what the experts have to say as the final word on the matter. They question, provoke, and at times openly disagree with their guests and with each other.

There's a common pattern in most *Radiolab* shows: Abumrad and Krulwich move back and forth between questions, big ideas, interviews, and stories, inevitably leading their listeners to new problems and new questions, and revealing in the process that the issue they started with is more complicated than it first seemed. We admire how they move from simple wonder to complex possibilities, and we like that multiple answers, insights, and solutions are entertained along the way. We also like that *Radiolab* sounds beautiful. It's important to recognize that the creative soundscapes Abumrad and Krulwich produce are more than mere entertainment. In every episode, they demonstrate how curiosity can generate beauty as well as answers and ideas.

What we admire most about *Radiolab* is that the hosts manage to express in sound and language the whole spectrum of habits of the creative mind. You can hear Abumrad's creativity as a composer in the ways he uses sound to represent ideas that might otherwise remain too

abstract for listeners to grasp. You can hear how open both men are to ambiguity, the unknown, and discovery as Abumrad and Krulwich talk their way through the implications of what they're learning. You can also hear their attention to and engagement with ideas, information, and expertise in the questions they ask. And you can hear their reflectiveness as thoughts digress, reverse, and surprise. Most of all, you can hear their boundless curiosity at work in the shape and progress of each episode.

We'd like you to listen to two episodes of *Radiolab*—one scripted, one open ended—so that you can hear what curiosity as a habit of mind sounds like.

Practice Session One

Listening

In "An Equation for Good," a chapter in *Radiolab*'s "The Good Show" podcast, Abumrad and Krulwich consider an open-ended question that has puzzled evolutionary biologists since Charles Darwin first advanced his theory that species evolve through struggle and competition. If the "fittest" survive through tooth-and-claw rivalry, how can we explain kindness, generosity, and altruism?

Find a quiet place where you can listen to "An Equation for Good" without interruption; the podcast is about 22 minutes long. Use headphones or earbuds so you don't miss a thing.

Next, listen to the podcast again, this time pausing it when necessary to write down the questions Abumrad and Krulwich ask; this is likely to take more than 30 minutes. Keep track of where each question leads. What people and sources do Abumrad and Krulwich turn to for answers? What stories do they tell? Is there a logic to the overall shape of the show? An aesthetic?

Writing

Spend at least 30 minutes creating a visual map that illustrates the development of the hosts' thinking as "An Equation for Good" unfolds. When do their ideas move in a straight line? When do their questions cause a change in direction? Do they ever take wrong turns? If so, are any of the resulting digressions useful? By the end of "An Equation for Good," how far have Abumrad and Krulwich traveled? What do they conclude about the status of the definition of *evolution* as "the survival of the fittest"? (Note: You might want to

experiment with making your map "move"; feel free to use presentation and/or animation software to bring your map to life.)

After you've created your map, pause to reflect on what you've learned. What does your map reveal about Abumrad and Krulwich's methods? Could someone else look at your map and understand what you've learned about how the show is structured? If not, how is what you've produced a map?

Practice Session Two

Listening

Next, we'd like you to listen to the *Radiolab* podcast "Secrets of Success," a conversation between Robert Krulwich and Malcolm Gladwell, author of *The Tipping Point*, *Blink*, and *Outliers*. This podcast shows how questions unfold when a curious person talks at length to a single expert, trying to understand the development and reach of the expert's ideas while also puzzling through whether to accept the expert's conclusions.

Find a quiet place where you can listen without interruption; the interview is about 25 minutes long. Don't forget your earbuds.

When you're done, set aside more than 30 minutes to listen to the podcast again, this time pausing to write down the questions and other prompts Krulwich uses to get Gladwell to explain his ideas about talent, practice, passion, and success.

Writing

Set aside at least 30 minutes to create another map that illustrates the unfolding conversation between Gladwell and Krulwich. When does Krulwich move the discussion in a straight line? When does he seem to change direction? Do any apparent digressions end up looping back to serve the main argument? Are there other digressions that take the conversation off track? Are you convinced by Gladwell's responses to Krulwich's questions?

Practice Session Three

Reflecting

After you've created maps for both "An Equation for Good" and "Secrets of Success," look at them side by side. Spend at least 30 minutes considering what they show you about how curiosity works and how understanding and arguments develop. What do you see that helps you to think about how you might compose a curiosity-driven essay or podcast about a big question like "How can we explain why humans sometimes go out of their way to help strangers?" or "Is there a secret to success?" What are some open-ended questions you'd like to read, listen, or write about?

EXPLORE

We're drawn to works of nonfiction that are question-driven. The podcast *Radiolab* asks questions about anything and everything, including time, tumors, blame, mosquitos, quicksand, and the power of music. While *Radiolab* jumps from topic to topic, the captivating podcast *Serial* devotes twelve episodes to one subject—an investigation into whether a man was wrongfully imprisoned for the 1999 murder of a Maryland teen. Law professor Ruthann Robson asks questions about a different kind of case, one that emerges after she is misdiagnosed with cancer, suffers through chemotherapy and medical mistreatment, and then considers both what her life is worth, and what matters more to her than money.

Radiolab. Podcast.

Robson, Ruthann. "Notes from a Difficult Case." *In Fact: The Best of Creative Nonfiction*. Ed. Lee Gutkind. New York: Norton, 2005. 226–44. Print.

Serial. Season One. Podcast.

On Writing to a Question

What's writing for? In school, the most common answer given to that question is, "To make a point." And so in school one practices having a point that can be succinctly stated in a thesis statement. "Writing is for making points" is itself an example of a succinct thesis statement.

We think the requirement to *start* an essay by committing to a thesis is a good way to kill curiosity. It turns writing into a mindless fill-in-the-blank exercise: Thesis? Check. Three examples? Check. Conclusion that summarizes the previous three paragraphs? Check. This approach to writing is a machine for arguing the obvious; it does not use writing as a tool for thinking new thoughts or for developing ideas that are new to the writer.

For your writing to become a mode of learning for you, you must begin in a state of not-knowing rather than committing yourself to a claim you came up with before you've done any curiosity-driven research. In the "Curiosity at Work" profiles in this book, we showcase a wide range of nonfiction writers who use writing as a mode of learning. Consider the divergent cases of Donovan Hohn and Rebecca Skloot.

Donovan Hohn, a high school English teacher, was reading a student's paper when he first learned about the plastic bath toys—yellow ducks, green frogs, blue turtles, and red beavers—that began washing ashore in Alaska and Australia in the early 1990s. Curious, he began to do some research online. Caught up in the mysteries, he left his job and traveled the earth to follow the path of the toys. He recorded his journey of discovery in his book *Moby-Duck*.

Rebecca Skloot was sixteen years old and taking a biology class when she learned that the first human cells ever grown in a lab were from an African American woman named Henrietta Lacks. Skloot wanted to know more about Lacks, but her teacher had no additional information, and at the time Skloot couldn't find anything more in the library. Many years later, when Skloot decided to become a writer, she tracked down Lacks's family and pieced together Henrietta Lacks's history and the history of her cell line. Then Skloot wrote the best-selling book *The Immortal Life of Henrietta Lacks*.

Neither of these writers began with a thesis that they then set out to prove. Rather, each started with a question and pushed past simplistic discussions of pollution or racism to develop a deeper, richer understanding of the situation's complexity. But where did the questions that Donovan and Skloot began with come from? Were the questions the result of inspiration or just dumb luck?

While there's always an element of chance in any research project, we think you learn how to ask the kinds of questions that stick with you for years by cultivating the habit of generating questions. How does this process work? Once you've developed the habit of generating questions about things that are taken for granted and about things unknown, you will find that you have many questions to choose from and many possible paths to explore. Some questions will seem more important than others, some will nag at you, and some will seem urgent; the very best questions will have all of these attributes.

To help our students develop the intertwined habits of curiosity and questioning, we've adopted a drafting strategy that throws out the familiar essay form. We ask our students instead to write frequent short papers in response to readings, and we tell them that these papers should not contain thesis statements.

At first they're baffled. How can you even begin an essay without a thesis? We tell them to just go ahead and give it a try. We instruct them to look in the assigned readings for moments when an author

- says something surprising or confusing;
- makes an unexpected connection;
- presents a provocative example;
- uses a familiar term in a new or peculiar way;
- or poses an idea or argument that is difficult to accept.

Freed from having to begin with a thesis statement, our students use their responses to readings to puzzle through surprising, confusing, or provocative passages. Consequently, when they write, they aren't reporting what the author said and then agreeing or disagreeing with it; they are focusing on interesting moments in which they sense a tension between their own thoughts, knowledge, or expectations and what an author has written.

Once they've written their way through a passage or a series of passages, we ask them to conclude their response papers with a reflection on what they've figured out over the course of developing their responses. Ideally, their exploration of moments of tension leads them to a compelling question or questions, which they pose in the final sentences of their responses. These should be questions that they can't presently answer and that require more thought, reading, and research—questions they are truly curious about and *want* to answer.

Right now you might be wondering, what's the point of writing to a question you can't answer? Isn't exposing your own ignorance the exact opposite of what you should be doing in school? Good questions!

We think there are many good reasons to use informal writing and drafting to arrive at a compelling question. When you write about passages or ideas in a text or set of texts that confuse or interest you, you are learning to use writing as a tool for thinking. And you'll see that writers discover what they think not *before* they write but *in the act* of writing. You'll also learn how to take more risks with your thinking. Ending with a question you don't know the answer to may feel uncomfortable at first—as if you're revealing a weakness. But openly confronting what you don't know is an essential part of learning to write well. Paradoxically, by writing to a question in a draft, you'll learn how to generate a truly interesting thesis. Once you've drafted a question that you're genuinely curious about, you're ready for the next step: figuring out how to respond to that question. Your response will be a thesis that's worth writing and reading about. Writing to a question also gives you practice with the essential habits of the creative mind: curiosity, openness to new ways of thinking, engagement with learning, and intellectual adventurousness.

Practice Session One

Reflecting

Are you a curious person? Do you express your curiosity most often in school, among your friends, at work, or elsewhere? You may not know the answers to these questions, so we'd like you to pay attention to your own curiosity for a week. Take notes every day, keeping an account of when, where, and how you pose questions, whether out loud to others or silently to yourself.

At the end of the week, spend at least 30 minutes reviewing your notes and learning about your own curiosity. When and where were you most curious? How often did you ask questions in classes? Did you pose more questions in one class or another? Did you ask questions as you read, jotting questions in the margins or in your notes? What was your most vivid experience of curiosity-driven learning in the past week? Was it in school or elsewhere?

Practice Session Two

Reading

In the list of suggested readings in this essay's "Explore" section, on page 63, each writer presents his or her central question in the article's subtitle: "What Should Medicine Do When It Can't Save Your Life?"; "Did American Conservationists in Africa Go Too Far?"; "Why Are We So Fat?"; "Is It a Crime?" Read one of the suggested readings, paying attention to how the writer answers the question posed in the subtitle. Trace how the writer's answer to the main question develops as the piece progresses.

Spend 30 minutes taking notes on how the answer to the question unfolds. Does the writer reverse or qualify your expectations? Are additional questions posed, explicitly or implicitly, that shift the direction of the writer's inquiry or reshape your understanding of the issue?

Reflecting

In our essay, we describe how we ask our students to write to a question. Now we want you to give it a try.

Return to the reading you selected and review it, looking for moments in the argument that catch your attention—passages that are surprising or confusing, make an unexpected connection, present a provocative example, use a term in a new or peculiar way, or pose an idea or argument that is difficult to accept. Then write a draft in which you explore three or more parts of the reading that you find interesting or baffling—places where you feel friction between the text and your own thoughts, knowledge, or expectations.

In the final paragraph of your draft, reflect on what you've learned about the ideas or argument in the reading you selected, and pose a question that has emerged from your work with the passages you've chosen. The standard for assessing the quality of the question you've generated is this: Do you genuinely want to answer it?

Writing

Having arrived at an interesting question, you can now write an essay that allows you to develop your thoughts and figure out your answer. Bring a version of your question into your essay's title or subtitle, as the writers of the suggested readings do. Then go about answering it, working with the reading you selected and the passages you wrote about, as well as any other passages that now seem relevant.

EXPLORE

At the beginning of Practice Session Two, we draw your attention to the subtitles of the essays listed below: each one poses a difficult question and each question leads readers into realms of ambiguity, uncertainty, and ethical confusion. It's unlikely these writers began with their questions already formed; they began instead with challenging cases: a pregnant mother who learns she is going to die; a conservation effort that leads to killings; a graph that shows an explosion in American obesity in the 1980s; a man who forgot to drop his toddler off at daycare and the terrible consequences that followed. Only after much reading, researching, drafting, and revising did the big issues crystalize: How should medicine treat the dying? What is the human cost of protecting endangered species? What has caused an "epidemic" of obesity? And can a terrible mistake also be a crime?

Gawande, Atul. "Letting Go: What Should Medicine Do When It Can't Save Your Life?" *New Yorker*. 2 Aug. 2010. Web.

Goldberg, Jeffrey. "The Hunted: Did American Conservationists in Africa Go Too Far?" *New Yorker*. 5 April 2010. Web.

Kolbert, Elizabeth. "XXXL: Why Are We So Fat?" *New Yorker*. 20 July 2009. Web.

Weingarten, Gene. "Fatal Distraction: Forgetting a Child in the Backseat of a Car Is a Horrifying Mistake. Is It a Crime?" *Washington Post*. 8 March 2009. Web.

On Interviewing

Creative nonfiction, defined by Lee Gutkind as "true stories, well told," is often focused on a personal profile: a portrait of a hero or villain, a talented athlete, or an attractive star. Some of the work in this genre features individuals who are distinctive because of their unusual interests or their exceptional abilities, but there is also work that focuses on those who have earned attention because of circumstance or an accident of history. We are particularly drawn to profiles of individuals contending with contingency, such as Anne Fadiman's account of a Hmong family struggling to take care of a gravely ill child in *The Spirit Catches You and You Fall Down* and Jon Krakauer's portrait of a young, idealistic college grad who dies while camping in Alaska in *Into the Wild*. We also admire writing that unveils mysterious, socially marginal figures, such as Susan Orlean's description of an eccentric Florida orchid hunter in *The Orchid Thief*, and Truman Capote's voyage into the minds of two murderers in the *locus classicus* of the creative nonfiction genre, *In Cold Blood*.

Capote, who is credited with inventing creative nonfiction, once said that the genre requires a writer "to empathize with personalities outside his usual imaginative range, mentalities unlike his own, kinds of people he would never have written about had he not been forced to by encountering them inside the journalistic situation." For Capote, the writer of creative nonfiction must go beyond the journalist's commitment to neutrally reporting verifiable information and must instead, via empathy, strive to reconstruct the assumptions, beliefs, and feelings of another person. For Capote, describing the murders was a relatively simple matter: two drifters break into a farmhouse, kill the owners and their two teenage children, and escape with nothing, having been misinformed about the presence on the property of a safe stuffed with cash. But finding a way into the murderers' inner worlds was a much steeper challenge. How could Capote understand the thinking of the men behind these unthinkable acts? And why would he even want to try?

Once the murderers were captured, Capote interviewed them repeatedly over a three-year period—during and after their trial, throughout their efforts to appeal their convictions, and up to the time of their executions. He also interviewed townspeople, family members of the deceased, family members of the murderers, police officers, jailers, and other inmates. To make sense of the minds behind this senseless act of violence, Capote had to work long and hard. What they had done was clear, but why they had done it could be understood only through painstaking research and leaps of the imagination.

Getting inside the heads of cold-blooded killers—that's the outer limit of the impetus driving creative nonfiction. The more general desire motivating work in this genre is a deep curiosity about how others make sense of the world—and those others can be just about anyone: a family caring for a child in a persistent coma; a young man dissatisfied with the emptiness of contemporary life; a guy who searches swamps for orchids and sells them in an international black market. The realm of creative nonfiction enables us to grapple with the most profound difference there is: what life is like in the mind of another.

．．．．．

The journalist's most important tool for understanding others is the interview. How does one learn to interview? The first rule is easy: be curious.

The art and craft of interviewing, like writing, takes practice. Your first few efforts might feel clumsy, but as you gain experience, conducting interviews gets easier. As you begin, these general guidelines will make the process easier and the results more useful.

BEFORE THE INTERVIEW

- Choose a time and a place for the interview that will put the interviewee at ease. You need to be able to hear each other, so select a location that doesn't distract from the conversation or invite interruptions from others.

- Draft your questions ahead of time, but before you draft them, spend time on background research. Then generate questions that your background research *can't* answer.

- Bring everything you need for note taking to the interview. You'll need paper and pencil or a laptop, of course. If the interview subject agrees to be recorded, you can also bring equipment for making an audio or a video recording. (We find that an audio recording is preferable, because the presence of a video camera often causes the interviewee to speak as if on television.) Be sure to get your subject's permission in advance to record the interview.

DURING THE INTERVIEW ITSELF

- After you ask a question, pause and wait for an answer. Give your interview subject time to think. If she or he is truly stumped, ask whether you should rephrase the question.

- If your interview subject says something you don't understand or refers to something unfamiliar to you, don't be embarrassed to ask more questions.

- Listen carefully to what your interview subject says and how he or she says it.

- Give yourself permission to improvise. Your interview should feel like a conversation, not an interrogation. For this to happen, you need to be willing to stray from what you've written down and follow the interview subject down any unexpected paths the conversation has revealed.

A CAUTIONARY TALE

A while back, we were teaching a course in which students were researching a number of nearby development projects. In one case, the developer had taken down an entire block of local businesses and was in the process of putting up a high-rise of condos and apartments. The developer agreed to meet and discuss his vision of New Brunswick with the team of students working on the case. The students did their research, and at the appointed time, they sat down with the developer in his office, the model of his redevelopment plans laid out in front of his panoramic view of the city.

The lead interviewer asked the developer about the number of apartments he anticipated renting out to students in the new high-rise.

"None," the developer told them. The high-rise wasn't being built for students.

The interview effectively ended at that point, though other questions followed. The students had done research, but their research did not help prepare them for this particular interview with this particular person. They had their one shot with a very busy local entrepreneur, and they used it to ask a question about a matter of concern to them. Unfortunately, the way their question was phrased revealed that they had not imagined a world in which students might not be the central concern. They were, in essence, asking the entrepreneur why he didn't see the world the way they did, instead of using the interview to better understand how *the entrepreneur* viewed the development project and why he viewed it that way.

To the students' credit, they realized that the interview had failed because they had not posed questions that would solicit useful material. So they started over: they drafted a whole new set of questions and requested another chance. In this instance, they were lucky enough to be granted a second interview, but interviewers can't count on their subjects giving them multiple shots, especially if, in their first shot, they seem unprepared, have chosen a poor location, or fail to show that they value the interviewee's time.

Moral?

You may only get one shot. Make it count.

Practice Session One

Reading

Read Gene Weingarten's "Pearls before Breakfast," which is available online at washingtonpost.com, and watch the videos embedded in the article. As you read, keep notes on the many people Weingarten interviews for his article and on how he goes about discovering what and how they think.

After you've read and thought about Weingarten's article, spend at least 30 minutes reviewing your notes and reflecting in writing on Weingarten as an interviewer. When do you think he's most successful at gathering compelling or surprising points of view? Identify instances in which Weingarten elicits a particularly important idea or revealing insight from someone he interviews. How does Weingarten use what he learns from interviews to develop his own thoughts? What does he do as an interviewer that you would like to emulate?

Practice Session Two

Researching

As preparation for writing a nonfiction profile, spend a week researching a little-known subculture or group at your school or in your community. The deeper the mystery, the better. (Over the years, we've had students write about underground music scenes, fire throwing—look it up!—urban gardening, religious practices, body modification, and a dance-influenced Brazilian martial art called *capoeira*.) Your research will require both observing and interviewing.

Begin by doing background research about the activity or subculture. If it's possible to attend a group activity—a performance, a practice session, a ceremony—do so. Observe, listen, and take notes. Describing the activity or subculture will be part of the challenge when you begin to write; you will need to bring the unknown and unfamiliar to light.

The other part of the challenge is getting inside the minds of the participants. You will need to interview at least one participant in depth. Conduct an interview that's at least 30 minutes long, keeping careful notes and, if your subject agrees, recording the conversation. Do your best to ask questions that invite your subject to tell stories. Try to figure out why she or he finds participation in the activity or group *meaningful*.

After you've conducted your interview, you're ready to write a profile. Compose a curiosity-driven essay that explores the subculture or group your interviewee belongs to and its meaning or value.

Reflecting

Take at least 30 minutes to reflect on your experience as an interviewer. Review your notes and the recording you made (if there is one). Then look over the essay you wrote. Where did your use of the interview work best? What would you do differently in your next interview? What do you need to practice to get better results?

EXPLORE

There's an art to the interview. Anne Fadiman, Jon Krakauer, Janet Malcolm, and Susan Orlean each composed book-length nonfiction narratives that grew out of months, even years, of listening, learning, and asking questions. Their prose portraits display both intimate insights and evidence of the mysteries that remain after their interviews ended. We also invite you to read the transcripts of writers interviewing other writers in *The Paris Review* and *The Believer*.

The Believer. Interviews with writers from 2003 to the present. Web.

Fadiman, Anne. *The Spirit Catches You and You Fall Down*. New York: Farrar, Straus and Giroux, 1997. Print.

Krakauer, Jon. *Into the Wild*. New York: Villard, 1996. Print.

Malcolm, Janet. *The Journalist and the Murderer*. New York: Knopf/Random House, 1990. Print.

Orlean, Susan. *The Orchid Thief*. New York: Random House, 1998. Print.

The Paris Review. Interviews with writers, from 1953 to the present. Web.

Curiosity at Work: Michael Pollan Contemplates the Ethics of Eating Meat

What would history look like if it were told from the vantage point of the plant world? This provocative question drives Michael Pollan's *The Botany of Desire*, in which he considers how plants that satisfy the human desire for sweetness (apples), beauty (tulips), pleasure (marijuana), and sustenance (potatoes) have transformed the global landscape. By shifting to "a plant's-eye view," Pollan is able to see anew how the fate of the plant kingdom is inextricably linked to human desire.

In "An Animal's Place," published shortly after *The Botany of Desire*, Pollan moves from the plant world to the animal world to consider the personal, political, and moral puzzles involved in something many people take for granted: eating meat. Pollan begins his essay as a committed meat eater, one who is frustrated by the argument Peter Singer makes in *Animal Liberation* that eating, wearing, or experimenting on animals violates animals' right to live free of suffering caused by humans.

Pollan responds to his frustration with Singer by posing questions and noticing contradictions. Why is it that 51 percent of Americans believe that primates should be extended the same rights as human children, while at the same time "in our factory farms and laboratories we are inflicting more suffering on more animals than at any time in history"? Why are we so confused about our relationship to animals?

From there, Pollan's questions emerge in a steady stream. "When's the last time you saw a pig?" he asks. Is the fact that animals lack certain human characteristics a just basis for raising them for slaughter on factory farms? Pollan is especially intrigued by a question posed by eighteenth-century philosopher Jeremy Bentham, who wrote that we ought to make moral decisions about animals not by asking whether animals can reason or talk—questions that render them less than human—but rather by asking, "Can they suffer?"

And the questions keep coming. "Why treat animals more ethically than they treat one another?" "Wouldn't life in the wild be worse for these farm animals?" "Doesn't the fact that we could choose to forgo meat for moral reasons point to a crucial moral difference between animals and humans?" "What's wrong with reserving moral consideration for those able to reciprocate it?" Do "we owe animals that can feel pain any moral consideration, . . . and if we do . . . how can we justify eating them?" And finally, "were the walls of our meat industry to become transparent, literally or even figuratively, . . . who could stand the sight?"

Pollan's train of thought leads him to a question posed in the title of critic John Berger's essay "Why Look at Animals?" Berger was concerned, says Pollan, that "the loss of everyday contact between ourselves and animals—and specifically the loss of eye contact—has left us deeply confused about the terms of our relationship to other species." Pollan agrees and concludes that if we looked animals in the eyes, and if we created the conditions in which we were also able to look without disgust or shame at how we raise and slaughter them, then we could eat animals "with the consciousness, ceremony, and respect they deserve." In two subsequent books, *The Omnivore's Dilemma* and *In Defense of Food*, Pollan has sought to better understand how to live in accordance with this insight.

Note: For additional discussion of Michael Pollan's "An Animal's Place," see "On Joining the Conversation" on page 27.

EXPLORING

....

Our first history lessons in school are often about "the explorers." Christopher Columbus discovered America; Vasco da Gama discovered the overseas route from Europe to India; Marco Polo opened trade routes in Asia. These captivating stories involve adventure, courage, bravery, and derring-do. There are skirmishes, riches beyond imagining, kings and queens—all sorts of things to fire the imaginations of the young.

Later on, we learn that these stories have been simplified and that exploration itself is rarely the process of moving peacefully through unoccupied, unclaimed territories. Some find the revision of these earlier stories to be upsetting and somehow wrong. But we believe that those who practice being curious with their writing are learning how to explore both the worlds beyond and the worlds within the self. This isn't exploration as represented in fairytales and childhood stories of questing heroes. It's the messier, more disorienting, more complicated work that making sense of human experience and human history demands.

The first essay in this section likens exploration in the Internet age to Alice's trip "down the rabbit hole" and invites you to use your search engines to practice chasing ideas, thoughts, and questions wherever they may lead. In the second essay, we suggest that there is an activity called "creative reading" that parallels creative writing, and in the third essay, we show you how the process of understanding others (as opposed to conquering them) requires acts of imagination, informed by research. Why would anyone want to engage in explorations of these kinds? We close this section with a meditation on the mystery of motivation.

On Going down the Rabbit Hole

"Down the rabbit hole": it's a strange phrase, isn't it? If you've heard it before, it's possible that the first thing it calls to mind is the scene in *The Matrix* where Morpheus offers Neo two pills: "You take the blue pill—the story ends, you wake up in your bed and believe whatever you want to believe. You take the red pill—you stay in Wonderland, and I show you how deep the rabbit hole goes." In the inside-out world of *The Matrix*, reality is an illusion and what seems illusory—that time can be slowed down, that bullets can be dodged, that gravity only applies intermittently—is actually possible in a deeper reality.

Morpheus (the name Ovid gives the god of dreams in his long poem *Metamorphoses*) refers to "Wonderland" and "the rabbit hole" on the assumption that Neo—and those watching the film—will make the connection to Lewis Carroll's *Alice's Adventures in Wonderland*. In that story, a young girl named Alice is sitting on a riverbank, bored with how the day is going, when a rabbit carrying a pocket watch rushes past her. Alice follows the rabbit, who disappears down a rabbit hole. She sticks her head in and begins to fall down the hole, and what follows is a series of adventures that has captivated generations of readers for nearly 150 years.

Think of all that happens to Alice in the few pages that make up the first chapter of her *Adventures*: when she finally hits bottom (when she sees how deep the rabbit hole goes), the rabbit is just turning a corner in another long tunnel, so she gives chase. When she turns the same corner, Alice finds herself in a long hallway with doors on each side, all of them locked. Then she discovers a key that opens a very small door, which leads to a beautiful garden on the other side. Because she is too big to fit through the door, Alice keeps exploring the hallway. She finds a bottle with a note that says DRINK ME. Alice complies, and suddenly she's "shutting up like a telescope" until she's only ten inches tall. She wants to go into the garden but can no longer reach the key to open the small door, and so she begins to cry. She looks down, discovers another small door, opens it, and finds a small cake with the words EAT ME written on top in currants. Which Alice does, of course, leading to this statement at the beginning of the second chapter:

"Curiouser and curiouser!" cried Alice (she was so much surprised, that for the moment she quite forgot how to speak good English); "now I'm opening out like the largest telescope that ever was! Good-bye, feet!" (for when she looked down at her feet they seemed to be almost out of sight, they were getting so far off).

Why is this idea, which is at the heart of both *The Matrix* and *Alice's Adventures in Wonderland*, so appealing? Why do we take such pleasure in imagining that there's the world we experience every day and that, just beyond this everyday world (or just beneath it, assuming rabbit holes go down), there's another world where the laws of the everyday world no longer apply? One explanation for this fantasy's appeal is that the other extraordinary world is action packed: once the rules that govern the ordinary are suspended, anything can happen—rabbits can talk; bodies can bend out of the way of approaching bullets; a boy with a scar on his forehead can fight off the forces of evil. But this isn't really an explanation so much as it is a description masquerading as an explanation. Why are we drawn to the extraordinary?

Ellen Dissanayake has spent nearly five decades exploring the allure of the extraordinary. Working in evolutionary aesthetics, a field she helped to invent, Dissanayake has concluded that humans are hardwired to seek out the extraordinary; it is, she says, in our nature to do so. In making her argument, Dissanayake sets out to establish that the desire to "make special" or to "artify" (she uses both terms interchangeably) serves a number of evolutionary purposes central to the survival of the species—the most significant being that acting on this desire provides concrete responses to anxiety and uncertainty. Over time, certain ways of making special become ritualized: the wedding ceremony or the walk across the graduation stage, for example, or the gift of flowers to someone who is sick. What we find appealing about Dissanayake's thesis is the implication that art is not the set of static images you find on a wall at a museum. Rather, it is a way of doing or making; it's the practice of making special, which can manifest at anytime—at the feast for a visiting dignitary or over coffee between friends.

Is there an art to doing research? We think so. Most handbooks will send you out to do your research with a plan, an outline, or a map of some kind. The idea behind all this preplanning is to protect you from getting lost while mucking about in the endless thicket of information that's out there. That seems sensible if you think of research only as the process of predicting and then confirming results. That is, when this approach to research is followed, it's no accident that the end results are unsurprising; the whole point of this approach to doing research is that there will be no surprises!

We invite you to envision the research process not as a voyage out onto already mapped territory but as a trip down the rabbit hole. We want you to set for yourself the goal of generating research that is extraordinary—research that proceeds by "making special," by "artifying." We want your research to lead you to write something that rewards repeated acts of attention, which, after all, is just another way of defining *extraordinary*.

What does artful, special, or extraordinary research look like? Obviously, there's no formula. But we'd like to offer an example of what it can look like with an excerpt from an e-mail we received from Chris Osifchin a former student who wrote to us a year after graduating.

I've been really getting into Richard Linklater lately, after watching *Dazed and Confused* (my favorite movie of all time) for about the thirtieth time. I watched his movie *Slacker* and also part of *Waking Life*, and what was interesting to me was the portrayal of nothing as everything and how it is displayed in a much more explicit manner than *Dazed*.

I then saw a tweet from an awesome Website, Open Culture, directing Tweeters to the films and works of Susan Sontag. Never heard of her. Isn't it funny how connections come about? As I read more about her, and more of her pieces, I began to make a connection between Linklater's work and Sontag. The first piece of Sontag's work that I read was "Against Interpretation." I found it fascinating, and also true to a point. The best art does not try to mean anything, it just [lies] there in the glory and awe of its creation. . . .

Next, I read a NYT review of Sontag's first novel, *The Benefactor*, and was struck by how similar it seemed to *Waking Life*. The review even says "Hippolyte also dreams numerous repetitious dreams, ponders them endlessly, and keeps encountering Frau Anders, like a guilty conscience. The intent is to present waking life as if it were a dream. And, to present dreams as concrete as daily living." This is precisely what *Waking Life* is portraying. I think the depiction of dreams as reality and reality as dreams or any combination of those is not "without motive or feeling" as the reviewer says, but rather allows you to view things from a less interpretive point of view, as Sontag might [argue for].

Now, after reading this review, I decided to see if Linklater was influenced by Sontag. I literally searched on Google "Richard Linklater influenced by Susan Sontag." Interestingly enough, and why I decided to send this email to you, Sontag mentions Linklater's *Dazed and Confused* in an article on the Abu Ghraib torture incident, "Regarding the Torture of Others." In it, Sontag mentions the increasing brutality of American culture and the increasing acceptance of violence. Not only did this make me think of [*The Ballad of Abu Ghraib*] and reading it in your class, but it also made me think of a specific moment in *Waking Life* [here he provides the link to the YouTube clip of the moment he references]. "Man wants chaos. In fact, he's gotta have it. Depression, strife, riots murder. All this dread. We're irresistibly drawn to that almost orgiastic state created out of death and destruction. It's in all of us. We revel in it!" It seems to me that this connects very well to Abu Ghraib as a whole, not just the immediate actions of the guards. Sontag's observation that "Secrets of private life that, formerly, you would have given nearly anything to conceal, you now clamor to be invited on a television show to reveal," collides at the intersection of American fantasies played out on TV screens all the time and the real world. It's an interesting comment on American society as a whole—who would have thought that reality TV would come back to bite America in a *war*? And with the extension of reality TV that is now, what I can't think to call anything but the "reality Web" (i.e., social media/networks), it is becoming more prevalent than ever. Sontag puts it better than I have—"What is illustrated by these photographs is as much the culture of shamelessness as the reigning admiration for unapologetic brutality."

For our former student, the world of ideas, like the rabbit hole in *Alice in Wonderland*, is endlessly surprising and extraordinary. He begins by writing about rewatching Richard Linklater's movie *Dazed and Confused*, and then before he knows it, he's off on an entirely self-motivated search through film, philosophy, war, and media in search of artists and thinkers who can help him better understand our "culture of shamelessness" and "unapologetic brutality." With genuine curiosity and some practice doing research, you can transform the world of ideas, as Chris did, into an astounding place in which nearly every turn inspires a new connection and thinking itself becomes both art and play.

Practice Session

Researching

Type the words *Ellen Dissanayake* into the Google search engine. Press return.

Everyone who does this at the same time will get the same results. We can call this "ordinary research." If you click on the Wikipedia entry for Dissanayake, you'll find yourself on a page that provides a thumbnail sketch of the author and her work. Again, in gaining this foothold on Dissanayake's work, you'll be doing what any ordinary researcher starting out would do.

It's what you do next that matters. Choose one of Dissanayake's works that you find online and read it.

Your next task is to make your research into this researcher of the extraordinary extraordinary. (We composed that last sentence with *Alice's Adventures in Wonderland* in mind.) Set aside at least an hour for exploratory research. Begin by choosing a phrase, a quotation, a reference, or a footnote from the

Dissanayake work you read and doing another Google search. Read two or more of the recommended links. Then choose a phrase, a quotation, a reference, or a footnote from the second set of works and do another Google search. Repeat. Repeat. And repeat again, until you've burrowed down to an insight or a question that you yourself find extraordinary.

Reflecting

We call the process outlined above, where you move from one linked source to the next, "drilling down." Spend at least 30 minutes reflecting on this process. As you drilled down in your research, beginning with your first search about Dissanayake and ending with an extraordinary insight or question, how did you distinguish between ordinary and extraordinary moments of discovery? What choices yielded genuine surprises? Begin a list of useful strategies to include in your repertoire as a curious researcher, a list you can add to as you continue to practice drilling down.

Researching

Write an essay about your research into the extraordinary that presents a special or artful idea, insight, or question. Don't write a schoolish "report" about your research. Instead, make something special with your words; write something that rewards repeated acts of attention.

Writing

We challenged you to write about your research into the extraordinary in a way that rewards repeated acts of attention—just as Lewis Carroll did in *Alice's Adventures in Wonderland*, and as the writers and directors Lana and Andy Wachowski did in *The Matrix*. Now spend at least 30 minutes writing and thinking about what makes *The Matrix* or *Alice's Adventures* or another work of literature, film, or art worth returning to again and again. What did you do in your own essay to reward repeated acts of attention?

EXPLORE

A rabbit hole can open up anywhere. Tim Cahill's efforts to make sense of conflicting accounts of the Jonestown Massacre lead him into the mind of a madman. Sarah Stillman's research into the war on drugs reveals the deadly consequences of police reliance on young drug informants. David Foster Wallace, dispatched to cover a lobster festival, finds himself on an existential journey to make sense of the joys of eating creatures who have been boiled alive.

Cahill, Tim. "In the Valley of the Shadow of Death: Guyana after the Jonestown Massacre." *Rolling Stone.* 25 Jan. 1979. Web.

Stillman, Sarah. "The Throwaways." *New Yorker.* 3 Sept. 2012. Web.

Wallace, David Foster. "Consider the Lobster." *Gourmet.* August 2004. Web.

On Creative Reading

Once you've learned to read, it's easy to lose sight of just what a complicated business reading actually is. You see the letters *c-a-t*, and without effort you know that together they refer to the furry, whiskered, four-legged purring thing curled before the fire. To accomplish this seemingly simple act of translation, you have had to learn a sign system (the alphabet), a host of rules governing the combination of the signs in the given system (for example, there are vowels and consonants, and they can be put together only in certain ways), and the connection between the signifier (the word that results from the orderly combination of sounds) and the signified (the object, idea, or sensation out there in the world).

Even at this most rudimentary stage, there's an inescapable arbitrariness at the heart of the reading process: Why does *c-a-t* and not some other series of letters signify that furry thing? Why *that* sound for *that* creature? And beyond the arbitrariness of the sign system, there's an even deeper mystery: How does the child watching the parent's finger point to the letters on the page ever make the leap to that moment when the sound, the letters, and the image in the picture book suddenly connect, and meaning gets made?

Solving the mystery of how and why humans developed this ability to work with sign systems is a job for evolutionary neuroscientists, and their answer, when it comes, will apply to humans in general. We're interested in a more personal issue: Once the process of reading has been routinized and internalized, why is it that different people reading the same material reach different conclusions? Or to put this another way, why is there ambiguity? Why is there misunderstanding? What happens in the movement from decoding the characters on the page or screen to creating an interpretation of what those characters, considered in context, might mean that causes one reader's mind to go in one direction and another reader's mind to go in a different direction?

The mystery of the individual response is made clear as soon as class discussion begins. Where'd *that* idea come from? How'd the teacher get *that* out of *those* words? And because students can't see inside the teacher's mind, they often conclude that the connections the teacher is making are arbitrary and, beyond that, that anything other than the reporting of facts is "just a matter of opinion." For many students, the mystery of how teachers—and experts, in general—read is never solved. For these students, the experience of higher-order literacy, where reading and writing become ways to create new ideas, remains out of reach.

Social bookmarking, a gift from the Internet, gives us a way to make visible for others some of the previously invisible workings of the creative reader's mind. Below we walk you through an example of how using social media worked in one of our classes, and then we give you some exercises to get you on your way. Although there are any number of bookmarking tools out there for you to try, we use Diigo because it allows our students to annotate the Web pages they share with the class. They can highlight passages they want to draw attention to or pose inline questions. And just like that, two previously invisible aspects of the reading process—what people read and how they respond to what they've read—become visible and available for others to consider.

So what does *creative* reading look like in practice?

Our example comes from a creative nonfiction course we taught in which the students read *On Photography*, a collection of essays by Susan Sontag that was originally published in 1977 and that remains a touchstone in discussions of how the free circulation of images changes societal norms. We were halfway through the second essay in the collection, "America, Seen through Photographs, Darkly," and had reached the point where Sontag considers the work of Diane Arbus, who presented her subjects, whether they were at the margins of society or at its center, in ways that were strange and disturbing.

Sontag's criticism of Arbus is damning: Sontag argues that Arbus used her camera to depict all of her subjects as "inhabitants of a single village . . . the idiot village [of] America." Here the class encountered a problem that runs throughout Sontag's *On Photography*: there are no photographs. For readers who already know the history of American photography, this isn't a problem; they can just call to mind some of Arbus's most famous images and judge for themselves whether or not Sontag's assessment is fair. But for readers who don't know Arbus's work, the only option is to treat Sontag's assessment as a fact.

Sontag's readers in the 1970s who wanted to know more about Arbus's work would not have had an easy time of it, but today any reader with access to the Internet can check out Arbus's images and assess the validity of Sontag's judgment. Without exerting any more effort than it takes to type "Diane Arbus" into a search engine, our students found the images Sontag refers to in her piece and more: Arbus's shots of circus freaks; the off-balance, bedecked socialites; the nudists; the giant man towering over his miniature parents; and of course, the twin girls.

Once she'd seen the pictures, our student Alice asked: "Well, how did people at the time react? We know Sontag didn't like Arbus's work, but did they?"

As so often happens in our classes, we didn't know the answer to the question our student had posed. (And in this instance, even if we had known, we wouldn't have said so.) Alice asked a good question—both because finding out the answer would end up requiring some creativity on her part and because wondering about how others see what you're seeing always serves to highlight the fact that meaning is both a public and a private matter. So we said, "That's a Diigo moment," which is shorthand in our classes for, "See what you can find out and post the results to our class's social bookmarking group."

Back in her room, Alice set off to answer her own question. She entered some search terms, cast about a bit, and then settled on a path that took her to *Athanor*, a journal published by Florida State University's Department of Art History, and an article by Laureen Trainer entitled "The Missing Photographs: An Examination of Diane Arbus's Images of Transvestites and Homosexuals from 1957 to 1965." Alice posted a link to the piece on Diigo and then highlighted a passage that struck her:

> However, the reaction to her images was intense anger, an emotional response prompted by the cultural war against sexual "deviants." Yuben Yee, the photo librarian at the MoMA, recalls having to come early every morning to wipe the spit off of Arbus's portraits. He recalls that, "People were uncomfortable—threatened—looking at Diane's stuff." Even within the art world, Arbus was thought to be pho-tographing subject matter that was ahead of her time. As Andy Warhol, who had seen some of Arbus's portraits, commented, "drag queens weren't even accepted in freak circles until 1967." Arbus's images were not only disturbing

to her audience on an aesthetic level, but her unabashed and unapologetic views of transvestites touched a deeper nerve in the people who viewed them.

Beneath this quote, Alice wrote about the difference between a time when people spat on images of transvestites in the Museum of Modern Art and her own experience looking at the images a half century later.

How did people respond to Arbus's work at the time? Alice made her way of answering this question visible to the rest of the class. She also found something that was new to her teachers, new to the class, and new to her; in so doing, she gave us a glimpse of what was going on in her mind while she was reading. Yes, it is true that she had just uncovered a piece of information. Yes, it is true that she had not yet done anything with this information. But meaningful engagement with information can happen only *after* one has had the experience of posing an open, exploratory question.

Alice kept looking—it's a requirement in our courses. The next source she posted to Diigo would likely raise the hackles of many teachers: Wikipedia! It's an outrage!

Well, actually, it isn't. If we grant that students are going to use Wikipedia (and SparkNotes and YouTube and, and, and), we can focus on how to use these sources productively rather than insist on unenforceable prohibitions.

So, Wikipedia: Is there a beneficial way to use an encyclopedia? How could the answer to that question be anything other than *yes*?

Alice posted the link to Wikipedia's Arbus entry as well as excerpts from the section of that entry that specifically concern the reception of Arbus's work. She deleted material that was not of interest to her; separated past reactions from more contemporary responses; added an inline comment that directly connected the Wikipedia entry to Sontag's argument; reordered the information so as to place the introductory material in this section of the Wikipedia entry at the end of her own citation; and eliminated entirely a passage where it is observed that "Sontag's essay itself has been criticized as 'an exercise in aesthetic insensibility' and 'exemplary *for its shallowness*'" (italics added).

All of this editorial activity gives us a much richer sense of what Alice did while she was reading. Alice amassed many examples of how the subjects of Arbus's images responded to being photographed; how anonymous viewers at MoMA responded when the photographs were first displayed; and how critics—those who were Arbus's contemporaries and those who came after her—responded to the photographs. Then she concluded her entry with the news that Arbus had photographed Sontag and her son.

Who was this last bit of information news to? Alice. The other students in the course. Her teachers. And given that Sontag herself does not reveal this fact anywhere in *On Photography*, it's safe to say that it would also be news to most, if not all, of Sontag's readers, past and present.

Alice posted this fact to Diigo without comment. She thought she was done.

But the practice of creative reading is never done. In this case there was a question hanging in the air, waiting to be asked. And because the social bookmarking tool made what Alice was reading and how she was reading it visible to the members of the group and to her teachers, it became possible for us to pose the question that could keep the reading process going for Alice: What does the picture Arbus took of Sontag look like?

This question was posed in public for all the other students to see on the Diigo site, just below Alice's entry. And soon enough, Alice posted a link to the image. True, it was only a small, low-resolution image, but it was a start. Or rather, it was a continuation, an extension of a process that started with Alice asking, "How did others see Arbus?" and eventually led to her discovering an image of Sontag and her son looking back at the photographer Sontag describes as "not a poet delving into her entrails to relate her own pain but a photographer venturing out into the world to *collect* images that are painful."

This is one version of what happens when the purpose of reading shifts from the acquisition of information to the exploration of an open-ended question: reading begets more reading, one passage leads to another, and the original text is read and reread in a series of changing contexts, its meaning expanding and contracting depending on the use to which the reader puts it. This is the essence of higher-order reading. Some explorations will be more fruitful than others, and some more valuable for the individual than for a larger community of readers, but the movement from answers to questions, from information to ideas, remains the same.

Practice Session One

Reflecting

The example of creative reading we've described leads from a question about an essay to an image not included in or referenced in the original essay. We first want you to find a reproduction online of Diane Arbus's photograph of Susan Sontag. What light do you think Arbus's photograph of Sontag and her son sheds on Sontag's assessment of Arbus's work in "America, Seen through Photographs, Darkly"? Spend at least 20 minutes figuring out a thoughtful, compelling answer to this question. For the purposes of this exercise, work only with what we've provided. *Don't* seek out the rest of Sontag's essay or more information about Arbus. What does the photograph alone tell you?

Researching

As we've said, the work of creative reading is never done. What information can you find online about the image of Sontag and her son? About *their* relationship? About Sontag's fuller argument in "America, Seen through Photographs, Darkly"? About her argument in *On Photography*? Spend at least an hour researching and reading, keeping careful notes on your discoveries.

Writing

Now you're ready to work on an extended essay about how to read Arbus's images creatively. Continue the research Alice began about how viewers have responded to Arbus's photographs in the forty years since Sontag's judgment, gathering information about one or more lines of response to the photographs. Then make an argument for how you think an Arbus photograph ought to be read. (Note: This series of exercises can be profitably executed using any visual artist.)

Practice Session Two

Researching

Open your own Diigo account. Once a day for a week, we'd like you to bookmark and annotate a page you've visited on the Web. The Diigo tool allows for highlighting, but in our experience most highlighting is done in place of actual reading. We want you to mark those places in your reading where a question of *any kind* is raised for you. An unfamiliar word, data that seems not to compute, an interpretation that doesn't make sense, an odd sentence structure—wherever your reading is stopped, take note of it. At the end of a week, you'll have a profile of your own reading practice.

Reflecting

Now that you have made a version of your own reading practice visible for you to consider, what do you see? Set aside at least 30 minutes to write down answers to these questions: What does your profile reveal about what kind of a reader you are? What habits do you practice currently? Are there instances when your experience of reading was more pleasurable than it was at other times? More productive? More useful? Was your practice of reading markedly different during any of these phases, or was the outcome entirely dependent on what you were reading at the time?

Writing

Using your research and reflections on your reading practices, compose a portrait of yourself as a reader. Where are you now as a reader? Where would you like to be? What specific steps do you need to take to become a lifelong creative reader? Write an essay that analyzes the most important events in your experience as a reader up to the present moment.

EXPLORE

Two of our suggested readings invite you to continue the creative reading of work by Susan Sontag and Diane Arbus: journalist Franklin Foer considers Sontag's critical success alongside her changing relationship to photography, while art critic Peter Schjeldahl's brief remembrance of Arbus seeks to provide a reparative reading of her work. In our third suggested reading, Nathan Chandler uses creative reading to learn about and describe the inner workings of Anonymous—a group of highly skilled hackers who are committed to remaining unknown and unfindable.

Chandler, Nathan. "How Anonymous Works." Howstuffworks.com. Web.

Foer, Franklin. "Susan Superstar: How Susan Sontag Became Seduced by Her Own Persona." Nymag.com. 14 January 2005. Web.

Schjeldahl, Peter. "Looking Back: Diane Arbus at the Met." Newyorker.com. 21 March 2005. Web.

On Imagining Others

We've all heard the proverb "Before you judge someone, walk a mile in that person's shoes." This saying is so well known because it captures the experience we've all had of making a snap judgment that then turns out to be wrong. Understanding another person's motives requires more than just trusting your intuition, and it involves more than just reviewing the evidence about that person reported to you by your own eyes and ears. It also requires an act of imagination that gives you a glimpse of what it is like to experience life as that person does.

But is the imagination really powerful enough or trustworthy enough to approximate the experience of walking a mile in another person's shoes? In our view (that is, as seen through our eyes, when walking in our shoes), the more you practice using your imagination to gain a sense of how others see the world, the better your approximations will become. We're aware that this sense, which is by definition an *approximate* understanding, is not the same thing as *complete* knowledge. Indeed, the very act of trying to produce writing that fully renders the experience of another person can lead to a deeper appreciation for how much of anyone else's experience remains out of reach of your imagination.

One of the most ambitious efforts to imagine the lives of others is the photographer Yann Arthus-Bertrand's 7 billion Others project, which seeks to promote understanding of "what separates and what unites" the world's more than seven billion people. Prior to launching the 7 billion Others project (which began as the 6 billion Others project), Arthus-Bertrand was most famous for the aerial photographs he took for his book *Earth from Above*. From up in the sky, he says, "the Earth looks like an immense area to be shared." But back on the ground, all the local impediments to sharing the earth come back into focus—problems produced by geography, culture, language, religion, wealth, health, and opportunity. To counter this immediate sense of an unshareable world, Arthus-Betrand offers spectacular image after spectacular image in *Earth from Above* of the world's rich natural resources and of the vibrant productivity of its peoples.

Confronted with the problem of how we might better understand each other, in 2003 Arthus-Bertrand and his coworkers began filming thousands of interviews in eighty-four different countries and posting these videos on their Web site. Every interview subject responded to the same list of questions (forty-five in all) about experiences, beliefs, and hopes, a list that included these conversational prompts:

⚹ What did you learn from your parents?

What would you like to hand on to your children?

What was the most difficult ordeal you have had to face in your life?

What do you think is the meaning of life?

Have you ever wanted to leave your country? Why?

Have you seen nature change since your childhood?

What does love mean to you?

What is your greatest fear?

What do you think happens after death?

What did you dream about when you were a child?

Comparing the subjects' answers to these questions to our own answers reveals both what we have in common with others and what remains puzzling and mysterious about the thoughts and lives of others.

The 7 billion Others project provides us with raw material for imagining the lives of others around the globe and across the country. But one can also find the compelling mystery of otherness across the street or across the kitchen table. Imagine, for instance, how different it might be to see the world from the perspective of a parent, sibling, grandparent, or friend, or how you would perceive the world from a wheelchair, or if you couldn't see at all. (You can even find the mystery of otherness within yourself, but that's a paradox we'll consider at another time.)

In the preface to his book *What the Dog Saw*, Malcolm Gladwell captures the sense of otherness within one's own home in a vignette from his childhood. As a young boy, Gladwell would slip into his father's study and marvel at the graph paper covered with rows of penciled numbers strewn across his father's desk. Gladwell knew his father was a mathematician, but what did that mean, really? He writes,

> I would sit on the edge of his chair and look at each page with puzzlement and wonder. It seemed miraculous, first of all, that he got paid for what seemed, at the time, like gibberish. But more important, I couldn't get over the fact that someone whom I loved so dearly did something every day, inside his own head, that I could not begin to understand.

If Gladwell could "not begin to understand" what was going on in his father's mind, why did he persist in wondering about the symbols scrawled on graph paper? He persisted, he explains, because "curiosity about the interior life of other people's day-to-day work is one of the most fundamental of human impulses." Early in life, Gladwell discovered the rewards of confronting the unknown in everyday life, and he held onto his curiosity long after childhood, convinced "that everyone and everything has a story to tell." His curiosity about others' thoughts became the foundation of his career as a writer.

Practice Session One

Reflecting

Go to the 7 billion Others Web site and explore all that it makes available. Set aside at least 30 minutes to watch a few of the testimonials. Listen to how people from all over the world respond to questions about love, fear, family, and more. Then select one film on a specific topic ("After death," "Family," "Meaning of life," and so on), and watch it in its entirety.

After viewing the film, spend at least 30 minutes reflecting on what you saw and heard. Begin by reflecting on the responses of the people interviewed in the video. Then consider your own response to the topic you chose. At which points did you feel the strongest affinity with the people being interviewed? Which responses struck you as being most surprising? Does the 7 billion Others project show that there are seven billion perspectives?

Practice Session Two

Researching

Imagining the lives of others begins with curiosity, openness, and a commitment to listening attentively. One way to practice those habits of mind is to conduct an interview in which you listen closely and carefully to what the person being interviewed has to say. (When you conduct an interview, you should either take notes or get the interviewee's permission to record the interview.)

Option 1: Find a friend or an acquaintance—someone around your age who has a different perspective on the world than you do—and invite that person to talk with you for 30 minutes or more about one or two of the topics that most interest you from the 7 billion Others project, such as "What did you learn from your parents?" or "What do you think is the meaning of life?" Invite stories. Listen for places where your interviewee's beliefs or thoughts are different from your own, and ask questions to expand your understanding of those differences.

Option 2: Find a friend or an acquaintance who is at least twenty years older than you are, and invite that person to talk for 30 minutes or more about childhood and growing up. What was everyday life like when he or she was your age? What are the most dramatic changes that this person has observed in his or her lifetime? What does she or he miss about the past? What changes have been most welcome? Listen for places where your subject's experiences are radically different from your own, and ask questions to expand your understanding of those differences.

Writing

After your interview, review your notes or your recording and write an essay about what it would take for you to see the world as your interview subject does. What else would you need to know about this person that you don't know from your conversation and your previous interactions? How would you know whether you had succeeded in approximating their worldview? At what point do you have to shift from what you know to what you imagine to be the case?

EXPLORE

When we imagine the experience of another person, we might focus on what it would be like to have that person's thoughts, talents, or background. With our suggested readings, we invite you to consider what it would be like either to inhabit another person's body or to be intimate friends with someone who is both enormously talented and self-destructive. Nora Ephron describes life without a plunging cleavage. Lucy Grealy describes life after half of her lower jaw was removed, at age nine, due to cancer. And Ann Patchett describes the challenges involved in being Grealy's close friend.

Ephron, Nora. "A Few Words about Breasts." *Esquire.* May 1972. Web.

Grealy, Lucy. "Mirrorings." *Harper's Magazine.* Feb. 1993. Web.   ·

Patchett, Ann. "The Face of Pain." *New York Magazine.* 1 July 2003. Web.

On Motivation

Why write?

When posting on social media, the writer's motivation is clear: to connect with friends, or to say something others will "like." As in other kinds of "unsponsored writing," such as keeping a diary or maintaining a personal blog, the central activity is giving voice to the self. This can be pleasurable; it can teach you about yourself; it can relieve stress. While there are plenty of people who never feel the desire to engage in unsponsored writing, there's not much mystery as to why some do.

What *is* mysterious is why anyone, outside of a school assignment, voluntarily writes about anything other than the self, its interests, its desires, its travails, and so on. Why write a searching analysis of a social problem, for instance, or a book-length study of voting behaviors, or a biography of someone long dead and wholly unrelated to the writer? Why do something that requires so much time and mental energy, and for which the odds of getting published or having your work read are so low?

When cast in these terms, the motivation to write voluntarily about something other than the self does seem mysterious. But perhaps these are not the best terms for understanding how the motivation to write emerges. So let's move from the hypothetical to the particular and consider the story of how the historian Jill Lepore set out to write a book about Benjamin Franklin and ended up writing one about Jane Franklin, his virtually unknown sister. It's obvious why a historian might want to write about Ben Franklin. He's a major figure in American history; he was an inventor, an ambassador, an educator, and a philosopher; he was one of the most famous people of his time, and he interacted with others in all walks of life. If you're a scholar of American history, writing about him sounds fun.

In "The Prodigal Daughter," Lepore describes settling into reading Franklin's papers and finding herself drawn instead to the sixty-three-year-long correspondence Ben Franklin had with his younger sister Jane. Lepore discovered that Ben Franklin wrote more letters to Jane than to anyone else. "No two people in their family were more alike," Lepore came to realize, even though "their lives could hardly have been more different." Jane Franklin was nearly illiterate, and the few writing lessons her brother gave her ended after he left home when she was only eleven. Aside from letters to family and friends, the only writing she did was to record the dates of major events in a small, handmade book she called her "Book of Ages," which Lepore describes as "four sheets of foolscap between two covers to make a little book of sixteen pages." Turn the pages of this homemade book and you'll move through a list of dates and events: Jane's birth; her marriage at age fifteen; the birth of her first child, and that child's death less than a year later; the births of eleven more children and the deaths, during her lifetime, of all but one of those children.

In contrast to her brother's life, Jane Franklin's life seemed too spare and uneventful to warrant general attention. And yet when Lepore told her mother what she had learned about Ben Franklin's forgotten sister, her mother said, "Write a book about her!" Lepore thought her mother was joking. How could she write a book about a phantom? Who would want to read about her? It seemed like an impossible task, but when her mother's health began to fail, Lepore returned her attention to Jane Franklin's letters "to write the only book [her] mother ever wanted [her] to write."

Although her personal motivation for writing a book about Jane Franklin couldn't have been stronger, Lepore floundered. She tried to write a double biography that placed Jane Franklin's life story next to her brother's, but she abandoned this approach after drafting 250 pages, having found that the juxtaposition only magnified the sadness and sameness of Jane's life. Without a more compelling reason to write than pleasing her mother, Lepore put the project aside. We would say that, at this stage, Lepore had a private motive but not a public one. Her private motive was powerful enough to get her writing, but it didn't provide her with a way to present Jane Franklin's monotonous life as a puzzle, problem, or question that others might find meaningful.

Perhaps the problem was that the questions raised by Jane Franklin's life didn't merit a book-length study. Maybe what was interesting about her life could be stated much more briefly. In "Poor Jane's Almanac," a short opinion piece Lepore published in the *New York Times*, she described Jane Franklin's "Book of Ages" and the political arguments Jane had with her brother after her child-rearing days were done. By highlighting Jane's two modes of writing—the catalog of her losses and her letters to her brother—Lepore found a way to show her readers why they should be interested in her life. Jane Franklin's biography in itself isn't compelling; what is so interesting is what her life's story reveals about the connections between gender, poverty, education, and access to contraception. "Especially for women," Lepore writes, "escaping poverty has always depended on the opportunity for an education and the ability to control the size of their families," neither of which Jane had.

Lepore was stunned by the flood of letters she received in response to the *New York Times* piece. In an interview ("Out Loud: Jane Franklin's Untold American Story"), she described letters from readers about how their mothers, like Jane Franklin, swam against the "undertow of motherhood" to steal the time required to read and learn and engage with the wider world. Taken together, the mass of personal letters helped Lepore see why trying to fit Jane Franklin's life into the form of a biography hadn't worked. Lepore's readers hadn't written to her because they were moved by Jane Franklin's singular, unique life; rather, they wrote because they saw in Jane Franklin a version of their own mothers. At last, Lepore had a public motive for writing at length about Jane Franklin's life: she would use her story to show how poverty, motherhood, and limited education diminished the lives of women in the eighteenth century and rendered achievement outside the home impossible. And that's exactly what she did in *Book of Ages: The Life and Opinions of Jane Franklin*, which was nominated for a National Book Award in 2013.

We began with the question "Why write?" and have ended with a discussion of audience. How did we get here? By following the story of Jill Lepore's struggle to find a satisfying way to write about Jane Franklin's life, we've seen that the movement from a private to a public motive to write involves a shift in the imagined audience for one's writing. For personal reasons, Lepore set out to write a book about Jane Franklin with her own mother as the imagined audience; when Lepore imagined a larger audience of sympathetic readers, she realized she had to reconceive the project. It would still be about Jane Franklin, but Franklin's life story would become a case study of the challenges women in general faced in eighteenth-century America.

Given that virtually all of the writing students do in school is in response to an assignment of one kind or another, and further, that those assignments come with an external motivator (the grading system) and an intended audience (the teacher), it's highly unlikely that you have had an experience like Lepore's while writing in school. Even so, with the assignments in *Habits of the Creative Mind*, we want you to practice imagining that the audience for your work is composed neither exclusively of your friends nor solely of those who are paid to read your work, but rather of sympathetic readers interested in seeing how your mind works on a problem. As you practice imagining a different audience for your work, you will find yourself confronting the writer's central challenge: How do I make what interests me of interest to others?

Practice Session One

Reading
For this exercise read Jill Lepore's "The Last Amazon: Wonder Woman Returns," which is included in this volume, or any of her other writing that is available on the Web. After you've finished reading the piece, spend at least 30 minutes considering Lepore's public motive for writing it. What is the compelling problem, question, puzzle, contradiction, or ambiguity she is exploring? At what point in the reading does she make her central project clear? What does she do to make her project compelling to her audience?

Writing
Public and intellectual motives are often expressed as questions, or as statements that use a complicating or qualifying word such as *but, however,* or *or.* For example, Lepore's motive in *Book of Ages* can be expressed by this statement: Jane Franklin's life appears to be unexceptional, *but* her life provides a valuable example of how poverty, lack of education, and motherhood severely limited what women in the eighteenth-century United States could achieve.

We'd like you to spend at least 20 minutes reviewing the Lepore article you selected and defining the public motive of the article as clearly as you can in just one sentence. Experiment with restating the motive in a sentence that uses *but, or, however,* or some other complicating word. How does the statement you composed help to clarify Lepore's project for you?

Practice Session Two

Researching

We invite you to practice the motivating move that Lepore employs regularly. Specifically, we want you to use details about particular people or historical events to open up larger questions about cultural or social issues, such as motherhood, fatherhood, national identity, education, poverty, or economic opportunity.

To begin, write up a familiar anecdote from your family history. Then follow Lepore's example and consider how you could use the story to shed light on an interesting cultural or social problem, puzzle, or mystery that is bigger than your particular family. In other words, define a public motive for writing by using your family anecdote to rethink a larger issue or idea. Before you try to make a compelling connection, spend at least one hour doing research about the cultural or social issue that interests you.

After you've done sufficient research and feel ready to connect personal experience and public ideas, compose an essay that links your family history to the larger issue you've researched.

EXPLORE

Jill Lepore, whose work is the foundation for our discussion of how the motive to write evolves over time, explains in a recorded interview why she chose to write about Jane Franklin. George Orwell's discussion of motive differs from ours because it focuses instead on how writers are driven by ego, beauty, a desire for knowledge, and political purpose. Oliver Sacks further complicates explanations for motive because of what is now known about how malleable memory is; when memories change over time, motives for past actions can't be recalled with certainty.

Lepore, Jill. Interview by Sasha Weiss and Judith Thurman. "Out Loud: Jane Franklin's Untold American Story." Podcast audio. *New Yorker.* 30 June 2013. Web.

Orwell, George. "Why I Write." *Gangrel* 4 (Summer 1946). Web.

Sacks, Oliver. "Speak, Memory." *New York Review of Books.* 21 Feb. 2013. Web.

Curiosity at Work: Donovan Hohn Follows the Toys

Donovan Hohn was teaching high school English in New York when a student's paper inspired him to pursue his own open-ended research assignment. Hohn had asked his students to practice the "archaeology of the ordinary" by picking an artifact, researching its history, and writing up what they found. One student, who chose to write about his lucky rubber duck, came across a report from 1992 about twenty-eight thousand bath toys that fell off a container ship in the Pacific Ocean. A few years later, the report continued, beachcombers in Alaska began to notice the toys floating ashore—a plastic duck here, another there, arriving year after year. Hohn couldn't get this story out of his head. He started asking questions: Why had some of the toys ended up in Alaska? Where were the rest of the toys? Why didn't they all end up in the same place? He decided to look for answers.

"At the outset," Hohn writes in his book *Moby-Duck*, "I figured I'd interview a few oceanographers, talk to a few beachcombers, read up on ocean currents and Arctic geography, and then write an account of the incredible journey of the bath toys lost at sea." He thought he'd be able to do this work without leaving his desk. But Hohn didn't manage to stay seated for long. He discovered that questions

> can be like ocean currents. Wade in a little too far and they can carry you away. Follow one line of inquiry and it will lead you to another, and another. Spot a yellow duck dropped atop the seaweed at the tide line, ask yourself where it came from, and the next thing you know you're way out at sea, no land in sight, dog-paddling around in mysteries four miles deep. You're wondering when and why yellow ducks became icons of childhood. You want to know what it's like inside the toy factories of Guangdong. You're marveling at the scale of humanity's impact on this terraqueous globe and at the oceanic magnitude of your own ignorance.

In pursuit of answers to his growing list of questions, Hohn crossed the Northwest Passage in an icebreaker. He sailed on a catamaran to the Great Pacific Garbage Patch, a huge expanse of plastic soup—broken-down bits of bottles, toys, and packaging of all kinds—drawn together by ocean currents. He rode out a terrifying winter storm on the outer decks of a cargo ship in the middle of the Pacific, with "shipping containers stacked six-high overhead, . . . strain[ing] against their lashings, creaking and groaning and cataracting with every roll." He sped on a ferry up China's Pearl River Delta to a factory where he saw bath toys being made. He learned how to say "thank you" in Inuktitut and Cantonese.

In the end, Hohn wrote a book about many things: consumer demand for inexpensive goods, the toxins in the Chinese factories where the ducks are made and in the ocean where the toys degrade, and prospects for change. His curiosity took him all the way from an absurd image of a flotilla of plastic ducks to questions about the most pressing environmental concerns the world faces today.

CONNECTING

"Connect the dots": this phrase used to appear atop the pages of activity books designed to help young children practice counting while they worked on improving their fine motor skills. A child, crayon in hand, would draw a line from numbered dot to numbered dot, and at the end of the process, if the child had followed the dots in order, then voilà, there was a picture. If not, there was a mess.

No one would argue that connecting the dots is creative. The child has simply followed the directions to uncover a design. But once we move from children connecting dots to students using their own writing to connect ideas discussed in what they've been reading, we enter a realm where creativity becomes possible. Any two ideas can be connected; any claim can be made; any argument can be put forward. Under such chaotic conditions, how does one make connections that matter?

The essays in this section will help you to resist writing formulas that pre-organize your encounters with the infinite range of connections to be made. To encourage you to practice using your writing to develop new habits for engaging with and exploring what is unknown to you, we want you to think of writing itself as the act of making connections. Writers make connections with the language they use, with the questions they choose to ask, and with the sources they choose to interview. As you experiment with making connections in each of these areas, you will be engaging directly in the creative act of making meaning: the dots you connect will be your own, and the image that results will be of your own design.

On the Three Most Important Words in the English Language

How do you know you're thinking?

This is the kind of question that stops you in your tracks. First, you think, who would ask about something so obvious? And then—well, then you're left with the challenge of putting into words a central facet of your mental life.

When we begin discussing this question in class, we are soon deep in the murk. There's involuntary mental activity, which takes place in any brain-equipped creature—for example, the turtle sunning on a log is passively monitoring the surroundings, scanning for threats. There's instinct, the lightning-quick response to inbound data—the cat pounces on whatever is rustling in the bush, killing, as the common phrase puts it, without thinking. There's dreaming, and there's daydreaming, too. There's all this involuntary mental activity going on up there that we don't control. And then there's thought, which is, in contrast, mental activity over which we have some control. So while we can't unsee what our eyes behold or unhear the sounds that enter our ears, and we can't unsmell, untouch, or unfeel, we can change how we think about what our senses are reporting. And though we can't exactly *unthink* a thought we've had, we can change that thought by *rethinking* it.

We're interested in that stretch of mental activity that you can influence. For the moment, we ask that you grant us the following proposition:

Thinking is the intentional act of making connections.

This act of connecting can take place in language, sound, and images; chefs would doubtless say it takes place in taste, and perfumers in smell. We're open to the medium; what we want to focus on is the array of connections available to the thinker.

We are pretty sure that you'll have reservations about this proposition, but we need you to suspend those reservations for the time being. Don't worry; we'll qualify and complicate it by and by—we promise.

Beginning writers, like beginning thinkers, tend to rely on one connector: the coordinating conjunction *and*. For the beginning writer, writing is the act of connecting like to like, with thoughts or observations linked together via the explicit or implicit use of *and*:

> The house I grew up in had a garden. It also had a garage. It had two floors. *And* an attic.

In this additive mode of composing, the beginning writer can expand the composition as much as the assignment requires. All that the writer needs to supply is more of the same:

> It had two chimneys. It had three bedrooms. *And* one bathroom.

In the hands of an experienced storyteller, this additive mode of composing can serve as the foundation for an episodic epic poem:

> After the end of the Trojan War, Odysseus heads home. On the way back, he and his men sack the city of Ismarus. And then they sail to the land of the Lotus-Eaters. After they escape, they encounter the Cyclops, Polyphemus. And then, and then, and then . . .

Similarly, in the hands of an experienced visual artist, the assumption that *and* links like to like can be exploited to create jarring juxtapositions that bring into being something entirely unexpected. Take the cover image for this book, for instance. The artist, Anannya Dasgupta, uses digital postprocessing tools that allow her to combine and transform two or more images to create a unique image that exists nowhere else in the physical world. In this case, she brought together a photograph she took of a plaster wall, a photograph of a diaphanous curtain, and some fractal images she created using a program on her computer. When these images are combined, the effect is of a three-dimensional surface that is textured with mesh and bumps. She calls the final image *Splash of Orange*. As you can see, when *and* is intentionally used to link like to unlike, surprising things can happen.

Beginning writers are more likely to make connections via addition (A and B and C) than via qualification (A and B but not C). The machinery of the five-paragraph theme makes no room for thinking of this kind; there's just the thesis, the three supporting examples (A and B and C), and the conclusion. Qualification muddies the waters.

It's not that beginning writers have no access to the word *but*. Indeed, when we confer with beginning writers, we often find that their minds are abuzz with qualifications, exceptions, contradictions, and confusions. However, little of this mental activity makes it onto the page because our students have been told repeatedly that the goal of writing in school is clarity. Equating *clarity* with *simplicity*, beginning writers avoid presenting anything that might complicate their efforts to produce an argument that is straightforward and to the point. When this strategy of avoiding complications is rewarded, writing's primary function is reduced to the activity of simplification, and the goal of writing in school becomes nothing more than producing "arguments" that are clear, direct, and easy to follow.

Obviously, writing has a communicative function (moving idea X from point A to point B), but this isn't writing's sole function. Writing can also serve as a technology for thinking new thoughts—thoughts, that is, that are new to the writer. We believe that this use of writing, as a heuristic for venturing into the unknown, is as important as its communicative use. Indeed, it is through learning how to use writing for discovery, comprehension, and problem solving that we come to have ideas that are worth communicating.

Beginning writers start with a thesis and then find evidence to support their position; for them, writing is the process of reporting what fits the thesis and ignoring the rest. The problem with such writing is not that it is unclear but rather that it is, from the outset, *too* clear: it says what it's *going* to say (thesis), then it says it (three supporting examples), and then it says what it said (conclusion). Reading writing of this kind is like being plunged into the great echo chamber of nothingness.

This problem is easily solved: we just insist that our students bring the coordinating conjunction *but* into their writing. Things get messy right away, and clarity, misunderstood as simplicity, gives way to qualification and complexity. At the start, some of the qualifications are silly, and others are improbable. But the qualifications become more meaningful over time, and the prose begins to engage more productively with the complexities of lived experience. The writing begins to capture the shape of a mind at work on a problem.

But is the passkey for entry into critical thinking.

If you want to test out this assertion, we invite you to consider how different Abraham Lincoln's Gettysburg Address would be if it ended after the second paragraph:

> Four score and seven years ago our fathers brought forth on this continent, a new nation, conceived in Liberty, and dedicated to the proposition that all men are created equal.
>
> Now we are engaged in a great civil war, testing whether that nation, or any nation so conceived and so dedicated, can long endure. We are met on a great battle-field of that war. We have come to dedicate a portion of that field, as a final resting place for those who here gave their lives that that nation might live. It is altogether fitting and proper that we should do this.

Lincoln speaks at the dedication of the cemetery at Gettysburg, Pennsylvania, for the Union casualties of the Battle of Gettysburg. He invokes the nation as if it were one thing, but the nation is at war with itself. Those who have gathered for the dedication of the cemetery do so to recognize the sacrifice of those who died so that the "nation might live."

If the speech ended here, it would end with the statement that recognizing the fallen is "altogether fitting and proper." Lincoln's intent is clear: it's appropriate to recognize those who have died defending the liberties of those who are still living. He's saying aloud what everyone present already knows; the point he is making is obvious to all.

But the speech *doesn't* end here. Lincoln continues:

> But, in a larger sense, we can not dedicate—we can not consecrate—we can not hallow—this ground. The brave men, living and dead, who struggled here, have consecrated it, far above our poor power to add or detract. The world will little note, nor long remember what we say here, but it can never forget what they did here.

Everything hinges on the qualification that Lincoln introduces in the third and final paragraph of his speech. What those who are assembled are doing is "altogether fitting and proper," *but* the living do not, in fact, have the power to do what those who have died have done.

With this qualification, Lincoln is able to shift the audience's attention from an understanding of dedication as a commemorative event bounded in time to its redefinition as an open-ended activity carried out by the living in the service of a vulnerable ideal:

> It is for us the living, rather, to be dedicated here to the unfinished work which they who fought here have thus far so nobly advanced. It is rather for us to be here dedicated to the great task remaining before us—that from these honored dead we take increased devotion to that cause for which they gave the last full measure of devotion—that we here highly resolve that these dead shall not have died in vain—that this nation, under God, shall have a new birth of freedom—and that government of the people, by the people, for the people, shall not perish from the earth.

Lincoln's use of *but* at the beginning of the third paragraph of his address allows him to connect dedication as a ceremonial event to the ongoing activity of being dedicated to some higher ideal. The connection is not like to like: coming to the dedication is not the same thing as dedicating oneself to the preservation of the nation. Without the *but*, we have a speech that thanks people for coming to a battlefield; with that qualification, we have a speech that links the deaths that took place on the battlefield to a larger set of ideas, values, hopes, and aspirations.

How do you get from critical thinking to creative thinking? Here's a rubric that oversimplifies to the point of distortion:

and	Foundation for thought	Basis for black-and-white, yes/no, binary thinking
but	Foundation for critical thought	Enables qualifications, exceptions, conditions, ambiguity, uncertainty
or	Foundation for creative thought	Enables alternatives, possibilities; is future oriented

We know this table can't withstand rigorous critical examination. Indeed, we'd say the table predicts its own dismantling, since it assumes both a critical thinker who will respond to the clear-cut grid by qualifying the table's assertions and a creative thinker who will imagine other grids or other ways of modeling the relationship between coordinating conjunctions and modes of thought.

So, just like the overly simplified left brain/right brain distinction discussed in "On Learning to See" (pages 35-40), our table doesn't fully depict how thought happens. It's just a heuristic device, a helpful strategy for identifying different mental operations; it's a way to get you to think about thinking as the process of making connections.

With those qualifications, we stand by this assertion:

> Consciously introducing *but* and *or* to your mental activity
> is a surefire way to generate new thinking.

It really is that simple.

Practice Session One

Reflecting

Find three images that are important to you. They can be pictures of you or pictures you took yourself; pictures from the Internet; pictures of historical events or pictures of historical importance; pictures of art objects; even advertisements. They need not all be important in the same way.

Place the images before you. What are the implicit connections between them—A and B and C? A or B or C? A and B but not C? A or B and C? The possibilities are not infinite, but they are multiple. Spend at least 5 minutes jotting down notes about the implicit connections—connections that are not openly expressed but that are capable of being understood—between the images as they are laid out before you.

When you've completed your reflections, change the order of the images. What happens to the implicit connections? Repeat the exercise above with the newly ordered images.

When you've completed these two reflections about connections, take at least 20 minutes to write a reflective account of what happened to the connections when you reordered the images. Why does their order make a difference?

Practice Session Two

Reading

We'd like you to look at Ta-Nehisi Coates's essay "Fear of a Black President" (p. 274). Read it through once; then return to it and mark where Coates makes connections.

Make a list of explicit (expressed) or implicit (unexpressed) *and* connections that set information or ideas next to each other.

Then list connections that explicitly or implicitly use the word *but* to establish qualifications, exceptions, conditions, ambiguity, or uncertainty.

Next, list connections that explicitly or implicitly use the word *or* to point out alternatives or possibilities.

Finally, spend at least 30 minutes writing a reflective piece about the connections you listed in the *but* and *or* categories. Which connection is the most important? Which is the most surprising?

Practice Session Three

Researching

After our students compose the first draft of an essay, we often find ourselves saying something along the lines of, "Yes, you've chosen a promising topic (or made a valid observation), but the issue is more complicated than it first appears." Then we invite them to make their thinking more complex by connecting to new ideas or information using *but* or *or* instead of *and*. These objections, qualifications, and additions can't be pulled out of thin air, however. They have to be discovered through reading, research, and thought.

Ta-Nehisi Coates's article "Fear of a Black President" (p. 274) offers a sharp critique of the first term of Barack Obama's presidency. While it's easy to take a polarized position on Coates's argument by simply agreeing or disagreeing with him, it's more interesting to use his work as a starting place for thinking more deeply about the points he raises.

Select three or four passages that confuse, surprise, disturb, or otherwise interest you, and then spend at least 2 hours doing research into the events or history Coates presents. As you dig down into your research, pay attention to places where you learn things that deepen or complicate your understanding of Coates's argument and your own thinking. In other words, look for places where you can make new connections.

Writing

Write an essay that discusses how your research has informed and altered your thinking about Coates's argument. As you write, use the "three most important words" (and variations) to present research that adds to, qualifies, contradicts, or suggests alternatives both to Coates's ideas *and* to your own previously held opinions.

EXPLORE

We've suggested that critical thinking begins with the word *but*. Roxane Gay feels she meets one definition of what it means to be a feminist, but not another. In Etgar Keret's short story, the narrator tells us about a crushed car he has in his living room, but something about the story—and the narrator— seems a little off. Physician Siddhartha Mukherjee knows the arguments for and against antidepressants, but he thinks both arguments distort what is currently known about the treatment of depression. Joyce Carol Oates knows there's a long tradition of writers gaining inspiration from the natural world, but she thinks differently about the ants crawling across her table.

Gay, Roxane. "Bad Feminist." *VQR* Fall 2012. Web.

Keret, Etgar. "Car Concentrate." Trans. Nathan Englander. *Granta.* 2 Jan. 2014. Web.

Mukherjee, Siddhartha. "Post-Prozac Nation: The Science and History of Treating Depression." *New York Times.* 19 April 2012. Web.

Oates, Joyce Carol. "Against Nature." *Antaeus* 57 (Autumn 1986): 236–43. Print.

On Writing by Formula

In math and science, a formula is a hard-and-fast rule or fact. The chemical formula for water, for example, is H_2O, and the algebraic formula that defines the equivalence of energy and mass is $E = mc^2$. The beauty of such formulas is that they remain true, regardless of when or where they are used. Formulas in cooking, which we usually call recipes, are sometimes more flexible. If you're making a cake and you use a little less flour than the recipe calls for, you'll still end up with a cake at the end of the process. But if you substitute an equal amount of baking soda for the baking powder listed in the recipe, you'll push kitchen chemistry past its point of flexibility; what comes out of the oven will look more like a plate than a cake.

If we shift our attention to human communication, we can see how cultural formulas differ from scientific formulas. When applied to culture, the primary meaning for *formula* is "a set form of words for use in a ceremony or ritual." Most events involving human communication—purchasing something in a store, sending a child to school, even quitting a job—aren't ceremonies or rituals and, thus, aren't governed by strict formulas. And, even when the focus is narrowed to a specific ceremony or ritual, the cultural formula for what to say isn't universal, like a scientific formula, but, rather, is context-specific and subject to change over time. Take the marriage vow: the formula for what to say depends on the country in which the ceremony is to occur, whether the vow is to be made in a secular or a religious setting, and, if the setting is religious, the denominations of the participants. In the Episcopal Church, for example, the formula for what the bride and groom vow has changed over time: prior to 1922, the bride vowed "to love, cherish, and obey" the groom; since 1922, brides and grooms have vowed "to love and to cherish" one another. As of 2012, Episcopal churches have the option of consecrating the wedding vows of same sex couples.

As this example suggests, cultural formulas loosely define the conventions that govern a given ritual or ceremony. How loosely? Enter a church of a different denomination or a mosque or a synagogue or an ashram and the formula for creating a marriage bond changes. And if you head over to City Hall to get married by a justice of the peace, where the ceremony is pared down to its essentials, you'll find that a formula still applies: the presiding authority oversees an exchange of vows; there's still an opportunity to seal the vows with a kiss; and there are still papers to be signed afterwards. Even in those ceremonies where the participants write their own vows, there's no escaping the convention of being heartfelt, sincere, and personal. Popular entertainment, for example, is often formulaic. Many of you are likely to be familiar with the formula for the horror film ("Don't go in there!"), and you may even recognize the formula for parodying horror films. ("I know only dumb people in horror movies go into places like this alone, but here I go." Screams follow.) Formulas like these, which build on audience expectations, can be picked up either by watching a bunch of popular horror films or by having someone who knows the formula tell it to you.

If the formulas that govern everything from wedding vows to movie plots are flexible, what about the formulas that govern the thoughtful essay? Are they similarly flexible? We'd be surprised if you thought so, since the tendency of writing teachers from elementary school onward is to represent the recipes or templates or rules of thumb for generating the kind of writing valued in school as hard and fast. We, on the other hand, would say that following these formulas does not produce writing that is thoughtful or compelling or reflective; it just produces writing that can be graded according to the degree to which it has followed the assigned formula. When the work at hand is delivering expected information back to the teacher, such as in an essay exam, formulaic writing is an entirely appropriate mode of response. But when the goal is independent thinking, original insights, or the production of writing that others will read voluntarily, writing that follows a formula is incapable of delivering the goods.

A formula for originality is a contradiction in terms. If your writing is going to help you to think new thoughts, it will be because you are using your writing to practice curiosity, creativity, attentiveness, and engagement. The only way to produce thoughtful prose is to actually be thoughtful; the only way to produce writing that is compelling is to feel compelled by ideas, events, and issues; the only way to produce writing that is reflective is to regularly engage in acts of reflection. In all of these realms, writing is not filling in blank spaces on a form; it is the act of exploring the possible.

. . . . .

At this point in our essay, we intended to demonstrate how we distinguish between writing that's formulaic and writing that's driven by curiosity. But we've discovered that a funny thing happens when you write about writing by formula: every path we've gone down to illustrate what's wrong with formulaic writing has ended up being formulaic itself. If we were teaching a class, we'd ask our students to brainstorm with us about the paths we might take after we've discussed how the meaning of "formula" changes with the context. Since we can't do that with you, our readers, we're going to ask you to join us in a thought experiment about the options available to us. We'll go through them in turn.

Show why the writing in our classes is better than the writing produced under other approaches. "Piece of cake!" we say. This was, in fact, the first path we tried. Given that we are arguing for using writing as a technology for producing thoughts that are new to the writer, it seemed only logical that we would then go on to provide our readers with an example from one of our classes that shows what "non-formulaic" writing looks like. Going in this direction felt natural, necessary, and appropriate.

It also felt familiar. And this is why, eventually, we had to admit that it didn't work. It's not that we lack examples of writing from our classes that we feel amply demonstrate the advantages of developing the habits of the creative mind. Indeed, we have showcased our students' work in a number of other essays in this book. But when we tried to frame our argument about curiosity-driven writing, we found ourselves trapped in the solipsistic activity of arguing for the superiority of writing that we ourselves have assessed as superior.

There's another problem with moving the discussion of curiosity-driven writing to examples from our own classrooms; when it comes to making our case, we hold all the cards. We don't have to show you the writing that didn't succeed; we don't have to take you through the portfolios of students who didn't make progress over the course of the semester. We just have to find examples that prove our point. And then you, the reader, have only two options: you can either agree that we've proven what we've set out to prove or you can argue that our example isn't actually writing that explores new ideas and possibilities; it's just writing to a new formula.

So much for using examples from our classes in this context. Next! **Show why the writing produced in classes that emphasize formulaic writing is bad.** "Easy as pie!" we say. To head off in this direction, all we needed was an exemplary five-paragraph essay. After much research, though, we had to conclude that there was no archive of "the universally agreed upon greatest five-paragraph essays in history" for us to draw on. A sample five-paragraph theme posted on a college Web site seemed promising at first, but the sample turned out to have been copied without attribution from an online paper mill. Even the paper mill sites themselves proved to be a poor source for exemplary five-paragraph essays: it turns out these sites don't claim that the writing they are selling is actually good; they just say it's what your professors are looking for.

Our inability to find a compelling example of the five-paragraph essay led us to see that we were arguing against a phantom. We can search for "prize-winning five-paragraph essays," but no prize winners come up. We can point to a testing industry that provides models for students to emulate with clear thesis statements, clear supporting evidence and analysis, and clear structures, but we can't find compelling examples of school systems or university administrations that insist that formulaic writing of any kind is ideal for conveying important thoughts. In fact, as we continued to drill down on this problem, we were surprised to discover that the critique of formulaic writing has a long history. Michelle Tremmel, writing in 2011, found more than 120 articles published over the past fifty years in professional journals for writing teachers that were "clearly against the five-paragraph theme."

Our failed search for the exemplary five-paragraph essay showed us that we had set ourselves the wrong task. We didn't need to develop an argument against writing by formula because that argument has already been made many times over—to, as far as we can determine, very little effect. Instead, we needed to ask a different question: why is it that students are taught to excel at a form of writing that the preponderance of writing teachers agree isn't actually "good writing"? Our answer to this question, when it finally came, surprised us: teaching students to produce formulaic essays and arguments has never actually been about teaching students to write like good writers. It has instead been about teaching them to be clear and rule-abiding language users.

So, in the end, we concluded that there's actually no point in delineating the limits of the five-paragraph essay or any other writing formula because learning to be a clear and conventional language user has little to do with learning to be a writer. If familiar formulas are really just recipes for clarity, without regard for the writer's thoughts and ideas, we don't need to include them in our discussion of writing at all.

Now what?

Make a joke? We believe in the power of humor to create opportunities that reason alone can't make available. And, the truth is, we are in a funny situation: two writing teachers have given themselves the worst writing prompt ever: "make an unconventional argument against convention." Our predicament is funny in the way only contradictions, paradoxes, and koans can be: there's a fugitive meaning captured by the situation we've put ourselves in that can only be understood through the experience of being caught in the trap.

So, let's admit it's funny that, in our meditation on writing by formula, we've written ourselves into two dead ends: we can't provide unconventional evidence that our approach is better and we can't find anyone who argues convincingly that good writing requires conforming to conventions. We're Don Quixote and Sancho Panza, tilting at windmills.

If we really want to shift the conversation about writing from following a formula to practicing habits of mind, we need to take a different approach. We can't look to a single piece of student writing to bear the burden of illustrating either the habits of a creative mind or the robotic prose of a student trained to produce writing that can be assessed by machines. Instead, we need to ask some new questions: What habits of mind are being encouraged by questions that ask for the faithful reproduction of the main points in a lecture? By questions that ask the writer to agree or disagree with a simple explanation for a complex event? By an assessment system that stresses clarity over shades of meaning?

We'd like you to take some time to think about these questions and to reflect on your own experiences producing writing in school. We think your reflections are likely to support our contention that the emphasis in your education has been on order, clarity, and concision more than exploration, questioning, and the joys of digression.

Change direction. Having produced three different discussions of formulaic writing, we finally wrote ourselves to an understanding of why this particular transition has been so difficult. To comprehend how writing is based in habits of mind, one must look at the work of writers who are in the habit of writing. We want our students to ask difficult questions and get lost in the rabbit holes of research; we want them to know what it's like to get trapped in dead ends and to learn to write themselves out of such impasses. When writing this way becomes a habit, one learns the art of writing oneself into awareness of the complexity of what previously seemed straightforward, obvious, or familiar.

We realized, at last, that the best way to show you the habits of experienced writers at work is to do exactly what we've done here: document just how much work goes into resisting the allure of the familiar and the easily proven.

· · · · ·

So, a different direction.

Certain topics seem to invite predictable writing and thinking. One of the most clichéd topics in high school and college writing curricula is gun control. Given the differences between those who favor gun control and those who favor gun rights, it seems implausible that writers on either side of this debate could introduce anything that would alter where anyone stands on this issue. Pro/con, liberal/conservative, right/wrong. There doesn't appear to be a lot of room for movement.

How do experienced writers, who have made a habit of being genuinely curious, avoid reproducing predictable arguments when writing about long debated topics? To answer this question, let's consider the first few paragraphs of the introduction to *Reducing Gun Violence in America: Informing Policy with Evidence and Analysis*, an edited collection published soon after the mass shooting at Sandy Hook Elementary School in 2012.

The role of guns in violence, and what should be done, are subjects of intense debate in the United States and elsewhere. But certain facts are not debatable. More than 31,000 people died from gunshot wounds in the United States in 2010. Because the victims are disproportionately young, gun violence is one of the leading causes of premature mortality in the United States. In addition to these deaths, in 2010, there were an estimated 337,960 nonfatal violent crimes committed with guns, and 73,505 persons were treated in hospital emergency departments for nonfatal gunshot wounds. The social and economic costs of gun violence in America are also enormous.

Despite the huge daily impact of gun violence, most public discourse on gun policy is centered on mass shootings in public places. Such incidents are typically portrayed as random acts by severely mentally ill individuals which are impossible to predict or prevent. Those who viewed, heard, or read news stories on gun policy might conclude the following: (1) mass shootings, the mentally ill, and assault weapons are the primary concerns; (2) gun control laws disarm law-abiding citizens without affecting criminals' access to guns; (3) there is no evidence that gun control laws work; and (4) the public has no appetite for strengthening current gun laws. Yet all of the evidence in this book counters each of these misperceptions with facts to the contrary.

At first glance, the moves that Daniel W. Webster and Jon S. Vernick, co-authors of the introduction to *Reducing Gun Violence*, make here are likely to seem familiar. They establish the importance of their topic by referencing what they present as undebatable facts. Next, they discuss popular thinking about gun violence and legislation. And then they announce that their book will debunk the four major misperceptions about gun violence in turn.

This description of the way Webster and Vernick build their argument misses their most important move, though: they want to shift the context of the discussion of gun violence away from headline-grabbing mass shootings in order to focus their reader's attention on the high rate of gun violence in the United States. The research they have done documents the undeniable costs of this violence, both in lives lost and in medical expenses for the roughly one hundred thousand people injured or killed by guns in the United States every year. Webster and Vernick then point to one of the problems that limits our ability to discuss workable ways to reduce gun violence: *despite* the prevalence of gun violence in the United States, the only gun violence that gets sustained attention from the media is that which takes the form of a mass shooting.

What Webster and Vernick do next is further evidence of curiosity-driven minds at work on a problem: they detail the conclusions that reasonable people might make from how mass shootings are covered in the media; they *imagine* themselves in the place of such viewers and list the reasons why reducing gun violence seems impossible as a result. They haven't, in other words, produced an unsupportable "most people think" statement; they've made a connection between popular opinions and what mass media focuses on—namely mass shootings. In making this connection, Webster and Vernick have implicitly established a relationship of causality: because most people encounter information about gun violence in the context of mass shootings, they reach certain predictable conclusions about both the means and the possibility of curbing gun violence. Webster and Vernick promise to show how these conclusions no longer hold once the context is shifted from mass shootings to gun violence in general.

Can we imagine someone being persuaded to rethink gun violence as a result of Webster and Vernick's argument? In so doing, do we imagine someone who has thought about the issue a great deal? If this person *is* persuaded, would the change in position be consequential for the person? Does this personal change also have the potential to be consequential on a larger scale? We'd answer all of these questions in the affirmative. In fact, we'd go further and say that asking questions of this sort is a good way to start a conversation about how to distinguish writing that emerges from habits of the creative mind and writing that is done to confirm beliefs the writer already holds: the first kind of writing imagines readers who can consider multiple and conflicting ideas; the second seeks out readers who already agree.

Could a less experienced student writer produce something on gun control that made moves similar to those we found in the opening paragraphs of Webster and Vernick's introduction? We think so, but that writer would have to be genuinely interested in gun control as a question to be understood, rather than as an issue upon which one first takes a stand and then sets out in search of evidence supporting that stand. That student would have to want to spend time doing research that drilled down into questions about gun control, and that student would have to believe that staking out a position on gun control has consequences that extend far beyond the fulfillment of a paper assignment.

If such a student were working in a course that encouraged exploring questions rather than following a formula for putting together an argument, that student would have the chance to experience just how much is involved in understanding a complex issue in depth and what it means to use one's writing to think new thoughts. And this, finally, is why we believe that shifting the teaching of writing from formulas to habits matters. This shift encourages the creation of classroom practices that allow inexperienced writers to cultivate curiosity, to explore in wide-ranging ways, and to engage with the most pressing questions of our time.

Note: All definitions come from merriamwebster.com.

....

Practice Session One

....

Researching

Using the Web as your archive, find an example of a persuasive essay that has been truly influential and that *actually changes your mind* on an issue. See if you can find an example written by a professional journalist or an experienced writer from a newspaper, an important magazine, or an academic journal. Spend at least 30 minutes searching for an essay that meets these criteria.

After you've found a truly persuasive essay, or after you've put in 30 minutes looking for one, take at least 20 minutes to write about your search. What challenges did you encounter? If you found a persuasive essay, was it about a topic that previously mattered to you, or was it about something you hadn't thought much about? What did you learn about persuasive writing as your search progressed? What's the value of doing this exercise?

Practice Session Two

Reading

Select one of the readings included in this book or one of the readings suggested in the Explore section that follows. Read the article or essay and then return to the introductory paragraphs, rereading them with care. After that, spend at least 20 minutes taking notes on how the writer composes the introduction. How does the writer choose to launch the article? How does the writer get the reader interested in the topic at hand? How does the introduction differ from a conventional five-paragraph-essay introduction? Does it share any qualities with the introductions you learned to write in school?

Reflecting

Review the article or essay you read for the Reading Practice Session taking notes about how the writer exercises curiosity; connects ideas, sources, and information in surprising ways; and keeps the reader interested from the beginning of the piece to the end. In other words, explore how the article or essay *works*.

Based on what you've discovered about how the piece you selected is put together, what would you say governed the writer's organizational decisions? Is the writer following a set of rules or a formula that you can identify? Has the writer broken rules you were taught? Spend at least 45 minutes writing about the relationship between the writer's curiosity and the structure he or she has used to organize the article or essay you've read.

EXPLORE

Is there a formula for writing against formula? Probably not. The essays we've suggested here demonstrate, instead, just how malleable the essay's form is. Annie Dillard writes lyrically about witnessing a natural event. James Baldwin reflects fearlessly on what it means to grow up black in America. John Branch uses a host of multimedia resources to help tell the story of a deadly skiing decision. And the reporters at Planet Money use video, taped interviews, and text to show how an ordinary t-shirt is the result of a global production process.

Baldwin, James. "Notes of a Native Son," *Notes of a Native Son*. Boston: Beacon Press, 1955. Print.

Branch, John. "Snow Fall: The Avalanche at Tunnel Creek." *New York Times*. 21 Dec. 2012. Web.

Dillard, Annie. "Total Eclipse," *Teaching a Stone to Talk*. New York: Harper Collins, 1982. 9–29. Print. (Available on Google Books via Preview.)

"Planet Money Makes a T-shirt: The World Behind a Simple Shirt, in Five Chapters." Video. *Planet Money*. National Public Radio. Web.

On Working with the Words of Others

Cite your sources.

It's hard to imagine a research assignment that doesn't include some version of this admonition. If you were to ask your teachers why it's important to provide full information about the sources you've used, they'd likely tell you one of two things: citation is a service to your readers because it allows them to follow up on ideas or information they encounter in your writing, or citation is a way of marking the boundaries between your work and the work of others. These answers aren't wrong, but they both imply that citation is primarily a means for defending yourself from skeptical readers—those who would doubt the quality of your sources and those who would suspect you of plagiarizing.

We acknowledge that documenting sources and preventing plagiarism are both worthy goals, but we fear that discussing citation only in these terms actively discourages students from participating in the most powerful educational experience there is—engaging deeply with the ideas of other thinkers. "To cite" a source means more than following a set of rules about how to list it in a footnote or on a works cited page; "to cite" also refers to the act of quoting, summarizing, or generally making use of material from sources.

We invite you to think of citation as an opportunity to demonstrate what you can *do* with the words of others. To cite sources is to bring other voices, other approaches, and other ideas into your work. It provides the material for you to carry on a conversation with writers whose work you find compelling. While you may have experience using sources as the object of analysis (for instance, when you've been asked to write about a literary text or primary document) or to supply background information, citation can serve your writing in a variety of other ways. It can contribute key ideas or concepts, provide positions or arguments to grapple with, or shift the direction of the conversation. We especially value citation that brings in a new perspective that questions or rejects the most obvious way of thinking, or that turns the issue, question, or problem you are working on so that you can see it from another angle.

With this understanding of citation in mind, every time you cite another writer you should ask: *What work do I want these words or ideas to do for my readers?*

To explore the value of this question, let's take a look at three examples that involve citation and consider what asking this question allows us to see about each writer's project.

. . . . .

1. Fareed Zakaria hosts his own show on CNN, where he discusses foreign policy and international relations. He is the author of bestselling books that consider America's fate in the altered global landscape of the twenty-first century, and he writes for *Time* magazine. On August 10, 2012, he published an editorial in *Time* entitled "The Case for Gun Control: Why Limiting Easy Access to Guns Is Intelligent and American." He was prompted to write, he says, by a mass shooting at a Sikh temple in Oak Creek, Wisconsin, that left seven dead, including the gunman, who committed suicide at the scene.

In his editorial, Zakaria refers to an influential book on the history of gun laws in the United States:

> Adam Winkler, a professor of constitutional law at UCLA, documents the actual history in *Gunfight: The Battle over the Right to Bear Arms in America*. Guns were regulated in the U.S. from the earliest years of the Republic. Laws that banned the carrying of concealed weapons were passed in Kentucky and Louisiana in 1813. Other states soon followed: Indiana in 1820, Tennessee and Virginia in 1838, Alabama in 1839, and Ohio in 1859. Similar laws were passed in Texas, Florida and Oklahoma. As the governor of Texas (Texas!) explained in 1893, the "mission of the concealed deadly weapon is murder. To check it is the duty of every self-respecting, law-abiding man."

What work does Zakaria want this citation of Winkler's work to do for his readers? Zakaria draws his readers' attention to recent scholarship, arguing that gun control in the United States has a history dating back nearly two hundred years. Zakaria clearly identifies both the author of this research and where the research can be found, should his readers care to look more deeply into this history. In referencing and summarizing work of this caliber, Zakaria is displaying his expert credentials: he knows where the best writing on gun control is, and he can succinctly represent the other author's ideas, sparing his readers the work of reading Winkler's 384-page tome on their own. So in this example, the work of citation is analogous to a display of heavy lifting.

That's one way to use citation: to digest and distill information for the reader.

There's one problem with our presenting Zakaria's writing on Winkler as exemplary of this valuable use of citation, however: the heavy lifting on display was done not by Zakaria but by Jill Lepore, whom Zakaria has failed to cite. There's an unmistakable similarity between Zakaria's paragraph and a paragraph in Lepore's April 23, 2012, *New Yorker* article, "Battleground America: One Nation, under the Gun," which she wrote in the aftermath of the shooting death of Trayvon Martin:

> As Adam Winkler, a constitutional-law scholar at U.C.L.A., demonstrates in a remarkably nuanced new book, *Gunfight: The Battle Over the Right to Bear Arms in America,* firearms have been regulated in the United States from the start. Laws banning the carrying of concealed weapons were passed in Kentucky and Louisiana in 1813, and other states soon followed: Indiana (1820), Tennessee and Virginia (1838), Alabama (1839), and Ohio (1859). Similar laws were passed in Texas, Florida, and Oklahoma. As the governor of Texas explained in 1893, the "mission of the concealed deadly weapon is murder. To check it is the duty of every self-respecting, law-abiding man."

When accusations surfaced that Zakaria had used Lepore's work without making clear that he had paraphrased and quoted from her article, CNN and *Time* suspended Zakaria pending a full review of the incident.

This appears on its face to be a clear-cut case of plagiarism. Zakaria never mentions Lepore in his piece, and he doesn't signal in any way that he is presenting her summary of Winkler's book with minor changes. He's representing Lepore's words and work as his own, which is the very definition of plagiarism. Zakaria released a statement the same day the news broke, acknowledging his responsibility for the error: "I made a terrible mistake. It is a serious lapse and one that is entirely my fault. I apologize unreservedly to her [Lepore], to my editors at *Time* and CNN, and to my readers and viewers everywhere." A week later, CNN concluded its review of Zakaria's work and determined that the error was "unintentional" and "an isolated incident." He was immediately reinstated at CNN, and he returned to *Time* after a one-month suspension.

Note that Zakaria was suspended even though his long record of publication establishes beyond a doubt that he knows how to cite in ways that do the heavy lifting for his readers; time and again, he's demonstrated that he knows how to distill long texts into concise summaries. So while we are emphasizing here that we want you to be able to (1) select an appropriately challenging source with which to work, (2) engage with an extended piece of historical scholarship, and (3) capture the author's argument succinctly, Zakaria's example shows just how important it is that you demonstrate, in *every instance*, that you are able to (4) document your sources. No one gets a free pass on that fourth requirement, no matter how long her or his record of publication!

. . . . .

2. For our second example of working with the words of others, we would like to draw your attention to Jonathan Lethem's "The Ecstasy of Influence: A Plagiarism." Early in his essay, Lethem illustrates his thesis that originality and copying go hand in hand during the artistic process by discussing his initial encounter with the John Donne quote that introduces his essay, "All mankind is of one author, and is one volume; when one man dies, one chapter is not torn out of the book, but translated into a better language; and every chapter must be so translated." Lethem tells us that he first came across this quote while watching the film *84 Charing Cross Road*. He then relates a convoluted tale of trying to track down the passage in its original context, turning first to the book and then the play on which the movie was based, before discovering, after many fruitless searches on the Web, that the film had misquoted Donne.

Lethem's story is an elegant example of how the meaning of strings of words (that is, quotations) changes as those strings of words travel through time and across media. There's just one thing about the example, though, as Lethem tells us in the "key" he provides at the end of his essay: "The anecdote [about tracking down the quote] is cribbed, with an elision to avoid appropriating a dead grandmother, from Jonathan Rosen's *The Talmud and the Internet*. I've never seen *84 Charing Cross Road*, nor searched the Web for a Donne quote." As Lethem's key makes clear, he has composed his essay almost entirely of uncited quotations and unattributed ideas to show what his essay has argued—the act of creation always involves copying, building on, modifying, and combining material from other sources. This is what Lethem means by "the ecstasy of influence": all originality depends on the writer having been deeply influenced by the ideas of others.

We are particularly taken with Lethem's description of the writing practice that guided him in "The Ecstasy of Influence," which appears at the end of the essay, in his introduction to the list of his unattributed sources:

> This key to the preceding essay names the source of every line I stole, warped, and cobbled together as I "wrote" (except, alas, those sources I forgot along the way). First uses of a given author or speaker are highlighted in red. Nearly every sentence I culled I also revised, at least slightly—for necessities of space, in order to produce a more consistent tone, or simply because I felt like it.

With his key, Lethem has turned our question on its head: What work does he want his *noncitation* of the words of others to do for his readers? We would say that his noncitation is a performance: since Lethem has subtitled his piece "a plagiarism," and he has provided a closing list of the citations he left uncited in the body of his essay, it's clear he isn't trying to pass off the work of others as his own. Rather, by the time Lethem is done with his key, he has documented that the work of being influenced by the ideas of others requires reading widely and deeply.

· · · · ·

Before moving to our final example, we want to acknowledge the intentionally unconventional character of our first two examples of working with the words of others. We could have pointed to Jill Lepore's distillation of Adam Winkler's book *Gunfight* as a great example of what it means to condense a lengthy text into a concise summary. Instead, we chose to highlight Zakaria's unattributed use of Lepore's writing as an example of what it means to fail to work well with the words of others. And we could have called on any number of prominent examples to further illustrate the perils of plagiarism. But instead we chose Lethem's essay, "The Ecstasy of Influence: A Plagiarism," because it complicates the notion that the process of documenting sources of inspiration or insight could ever be complete. We have started with these examples to encourage you to be thoughtful, and even creative, about working with the words of others. The primary goal of citing others' work shouldn't be to follow the rules of documentation but to extend your own thinking and show your readers that your ideas are grounded in both verifiable facts and an ongoing conversation with sources about the issues and ideas that interest you.

. . . . .

3. For our final example, we'll look at the kind of citation that will most occupy you as a college writer: working with the words of others to complicate and enrich your own understanding of the problem, question, or mystery you've chosen to explore. To do so, we'll turn to perhaps the most generic of research topics: gun control. This was a typical research topic when we were in high school over thirty years ago, and we imagine that it will continue to be a typical research topic thirty years from now. Gun control is seen to be an ideal prompt in traditional writing classrooms, we would say, because it lends itself so easily to for-or-against arguments.

A central point of disagreement in the debate about gun control is what James Madison meant when he wrote the Second Amendment: "A well regulated Militia, being necessary to the security of a free State, the right of the people to keep and bear Arms, shall not be infringed." Did he mean that the people, as a collective, have the right to form militias for their common defense? Or did he mean that individuals have the right to own and carry guns? In our view, it is not a stretch to claim that the argument about the meaning of the Second Amendment and gun control is in part about citation. People on both sides cite the amendment, but neither side can establish, once and for all, what the amendment means. Why? Because all arguments about the amendment's meaning hinge on how one works with Madison's words. And so the for-or-against argument about gun control just gets repeated over and over again, without generating new insights or understandings on either side of the "debate."

A writer who practices curiosity, however, can reject the dead end of the for-or-against assignment. Consider, for example, the article we discussed above (the one Zakaria failed to cite), "Battleground America: One Nation, under the Gun," in which Jill Lepore engages with the question of whether the Second Amendment was originally intended to preserve the right of individuals to own guns. We're particularly interested in this article because of Lepore's adept and highly varied use of citation. As we noted earlier, her summary of Winkler's work is an example of citation as heavy lifting; she does the hard work of condensing a long text into a clear and concise overview. In the exercises at the end of this essay, we ask you to examine how else she works with the words of others, including Madison's. Our goal is for you to be able to use citation as Lepore does, to be able to work with the words of others in the service of exploring and exposing the complexity of a chosen question, problem, or mystery.

Lepore's discussion of the Second Amendment points to a problem all writers face when they work with the words of others. Simply quoting another writer's words isn't enough to make those words do the work you want them to do. There are moments when you have to analyze those words and make a case for what you think they mean. Lepore, a historian who specializes in early US history, mines documents from the country's past, including the Articles of Confederation and the Constitution, to place the Second Amendment in the context of an eighteenth-century debate about whether the states or the newly formed federal government should have the power to maintain militias. In 1776, the Articles of Confederation included the requirement that "every *state* shall always keep up a well regulated and disciplined militia," but in 1787, when the Constitution was signed in Philadelphia, *Congress* was granted the power "to provide for calling forth the Militia to execute the Laws of the Union." When Madison drafted the Bill of Rights in 1789, he was trying to appease those who worried that the Constitution had granted too much power to the federal government.

His concern, Lepore argues, was to address anxieties about a permanent federal army. By citing these original sources, Lepore means to establish that there is a historical ground for arguing that the Second Amendment originally had nothing to do with individual ownership of guns.

But if Lepore's citation of the nation's foundational documents accurately depicts Madison's original intent, how does she then account for the transformation of Madison's original concern with militias and state power into a constitutional defense of private gun ownership? Here, too, Lepore keeps her attention focused on original source material. She points out that even the National Rifle Association—founded in 1871 and now the nation's most influential lobby against gun control—did not interpret the Second Amendment as preserving a personal right to bear arms until the 1970s. What prompted this change? Lepore, citing speeches by Malcolm X and Huey Newton from the 1960s, makes the surprising case that the idea that the Second Amendment guarantees the right of private citizens to own guns was first made by black nationalists and the Black Panther Party for Self-Defense. At that point in time, following the many assassinations of that decade—of President John F. Kennedy, Malcolm X, Robert Kennedy, and Martin Luther King Jr.—the NRA actually supported the Gun Control Act of 1968. Not until 1977, on the cusp of a new conservative movement, did the NRA adopt as its new motto a quote from the Second Amendment: "The Right of the People to Keep and Bear Arms Shall Not Be Infringed." The idea that the amendment protects the rights of individual gun owners only went mainstream during the presidency of Ronald Reagan, after Senator Orrin Hatch and the Subcommittee on the Constitution issued a 1982 report about the Second Amendment entitled "The Right to Keep and Bear Arms."

Can we generalize about the work Lepore wants her many citations to do for the readers of "Battleground America"? Lepore does plenty of heavy lifting, summarizing many important scholarly sources. But what we find to be exemplary is her commitment to working with the words of others who are in the position to complicate her thinking. Throughout the article, Lepore demonstrates her ability to work with primary source material to cast something familiar—in this case, the debate over the Second Amendment—in a new light. Lepore does not, in other words, use citation to simplify the historical record or to flatten an issue into those who stand on one side of the question and those who stand on the other side. Rather, she weaves her many sources together into a sinuous braid supple enough to explain why repeated and horrific acts of gun violence have not yet led to meaningful legislation curbing access to guns.

Practice Session One

Researching

We emphasized the importance of working with primary sources in our essay above. We'd like you to identify the primary sources Jill Lepore cites either in her essay "Battleground America," which is available through the *New Yorker* Web site, or in her essay "The Last Amazon: Wonder Woman Returns," which we've included as a reading in this volume (p. 300). After you've identified all of Lepore's primary sources, select one of the documents she mentions and go find it. If you can't access the source online, try to find it in your library. If you're reading "Battleground America," for instance, you could look at the Constitution, examples of nineteenth-century gun laws, the speech by Malcolm X that Lepore cites, or official documents of the National Rifle Association.

Read the document you've chosen and then spend at least 30 minutes writing about how a more detailed citation from the document could have further complicated Lepore's discussion. If the first document you track down doesn't yield a compelling example, search for other primary source material; once you've found something compelling, complete the assignment.

Reading

Journalists who write for popular magazines or newspapers typically don't provide in-text documentation of page numbers or a list of works cited. And it's rare to come across a footnote in the *New Yorker*, *Harper's*, or the *Atlantic*. Return to the essay you read for the previous exercise and review at least three pages, paying attention to where Lepore is clear about where she found words, ideas, and information from others and where she's not. Spend at least 20 minutes making a list of where she would need to cite her sources if she had written this article for an academic class. Also note how often you were confused or unclear about whether she had taken material from a source.

Reflecting

After reviewing how and where Lepore documents her sources, spend at least 60 minutes writing about the different citation standards of journalism and scholarly writing. Did you find evidence that caused you to trust or to doubt Lepore as a writer? Is there any way to tell whether a citation is accurate or not *without* tracking it down and checking on it yourself?

Practice Session Two

Reading

Now we'd like you to pay attention to the variety of ways writers work with the words of others. Select an essay from the suggested readings in the Explore section that follows, or choose one of the essays included in this volume. Read the essay with care.

Next, spend at least 40 minutes observing, marking, and identifying the many different ways the writer works with sources. You might notice sources used to supply background information, to provide key ideas or concepts, to provide positions or arguments to grapple with, to shift the direction of the conversation, or to serve as the focus of analysis. Where did the writer work with sources in ways that impressed, surprised, or perhaps disappointed you? Were there moments when you felt a citation didn't do the work the writer wanted it to? Did the writer cite sources in ways that you'd like to emulate?

Reflecting

Spend at least 60 minutes writing reflectively about what you've learned from this exercise about working with the words or ideas of others.

EXPLORE

As writers, we are always working with the words of others. Our suggested readings provide examples of ways of doing this work that you might want to give a try. Christopher Chabris questions the words of Malcolm Gladwell, a writer we quote a good deal in *Habits of the Creative Mind*. Zadie Smith argues with a contemporary cultural theorist about the nature of reality.

Sarah Resnick interviews a member of WikiLeaks about the collection and distribution of classified material. And John Jeremiah Sullivan evaluates the success of a half-finished work by a writer he greatly admires.

Chabris, Christopher. "The Trouble with Malcolm Gladwell." *Slate* 8. Oct. 2013. Web.

Smith, Zadie. "The Rise of the Essay." *The Guardian* 20. Nov. 2007. Web.

Resnick, Sarah. "Leave Your Cellphone at Home: Interview with Jacob Applebaum." *n+1* 10. 10 June 2013. Web

Sullivan, John Jeremiah. "Too Much Information." *GQ.* May 2011. Web.

Argument at Work: Michelle Alexander and the Power of Analogy

A decade ago, when legal scholar Michelle Alexander first noticed a bright orange poster stapled to a telephone pole that declared, in bold letters, THE DRUG WAR IS THE NEW JIM CROW, she rejected the statement as preposterous. A Stanford Law School graduate and a former clerk for Supreme Court Justice Harry Blackmun, Alexander had good reason to trust her judgment. She didn't forget that sign, though, and after years of studying how the war on drugs had been carried out, she came to believe "that mass incarceration in the United States had, in fact, emerged as a stunningly comprehensive and well-disguised system of racialized social control that functions in a manner strikingly similar to [the pre–civil rights era, "separate but equal" laws known as] Jim Crow."

Anticipating that some readers of her book *The New Jim Crow: Mass Incarceration in the Age of Colorblindness* will share her initial skepticism about the racist character of the war on drugs, Alexander uses the government's own statistics to show that, although people of all races use and sell drugs at similar rates, "black men have been admitted to prison on drug charges at rates twenty to fifty times greater than those of white men." Over time, mass incarceration leads to mass disenfranchisement, since convicted felons, regardless of their race, lose the right to vote and the right to serve on juries and may also lose access to public housing, student loans, food stamps, and other public benefits. Excluded from the mainstream economy, prisoners who have served their time fall into a status of "permanent second-class citizenship." Given the manifest disparity in rates of incarceration, Alexander argues that "laws prohibiting the use and sale of drugs are facially race neutral, but they are enforced in a highly discriminatory fashion." And this, Alexander goes on to show, has served to create "a racial caste system."

So is the drug war a new incarnation of Jim Crow? An analogy establishes a relationship of similarity, not exact equivalence. The rhetorical strength of such comparisons is realized when they shake us out of our usual ways of thinking, shift our perspectives, make us see a connection that was previously invisible. In this instance, there is evidence that Alexander has produced an argument persuasive enough to get readers who are as skeptical as she once was to reconsider their positions. Bill Frezza, a writer for the conservative magazine *Forbes*, begins his review of Alexander's book thus: "Once in a great while a writer at the opposite end of the political spectrum gets you to look at a familiar set of facts in a new way. Disconcerting as it is, you can feel your foundation shift as your mind struggles to reconcile this new point of view with long held beliefs. Michelle Alexander has done just that in her book, *The New Jim Crow*."

The raw material for Alexander's argument—government statistics on incarceration—is readily available on the Web. Anyone can cite this data, but citation alone doesn't produce a foundation-shifting argument. Alexander drills down into the data and locates her argument in history; she is skeptical of the patterns that emerge, so she tests the connections she has made and allows the results of her research to guide her thinking. In the end, she produces an argument that invites other reasonable skeptics to see the drug war as the reimplementation of Jim Crow–style institutionalized racism.

REFLECTING

....

I f we took away all of the world's reflective surfaces, how would we see ourselves? Through our many tools of self-expression: visual images, music, dance, drama, and, of course, language. In this section, we want you to explore how language can be a reflection of that which might otherwise be invisible—namely, the thoughts in your head and the emotions in your heart. Language doesn't reflect in the ways a mirror does, however. Indeed, what makes writing so challenging is that the writer has to do the work of converting those inner thoughts and feelings into words and sentences that are understandable to others.

What distinguishes humans from all other living creatures is this ability to use language to share our self-reflections. Nowhere is this clearer than in *The Miracle Worker*, which dramatizes Helen Keller's acquisition of language, despite her being deaf, mute, and blind. Can anyone, including Keller herself, represent in language life before language? What is gained by using language to reflect on questions too big to be answered? What is lost by only using language to express what can be proven? When you reflect on what you've written, can you see your work reflect back to you a trace of your mind reflecting on itself?

On the Miracle of Language

What are words for?

We could begin by saying that words are a way to focus the mind, that words make meaning and reflection possible.

But we could also say that words stand in the way of insight; the ceaseless chattering of the inner voice, forever generating judgments and drawing conclusions, must be silenced for new understandings to emerge.

Or we could say that words allow us to formulate ideas and, with these ideas in mind, to make contact with the world and with each other. To this way of thinking, words, organized by syntax, are the component pieces of an essentially human technology, one that enables us to escape the tyranny of the present that rules all other members of the animal kingdom.

Examples abound of the sacred significance we attribute to the acquisition of language. We'll start with two of the most familiar.

Parents eagerly await the moment when their toddler moves from making burbling proto-words to clearly saying what can be counted as the child's first word. The desire to record this moment—to be present when the child points to the night sky and says "moon," or to the snow and says "milk," or to the mother and says "mama"—is the desire to be present at the everyday miracle of language acquisition.

In Genesis, once God has created the heavens and the earth, God places Adam in the garden of Eden and then, to provide Adam with companions, forms "every beast of the field and every bird of the heavens" and brings them "to the man to see what he would call them" (Genesis 2:19). In this account, the first act of the first human is the act of naming.

But when Adam is done naming all the animals that have passed before him, he is still alone, so God fashions another living creature out of Adam's rib to serve as Adam's helper. Once again, Adam's first act upon encountering this new creature is to provide a name for her. And of course, shortly thereafter, Adam and Eve are introduced to language's additional powers to persuade and deceive when the serpent entices Eve to disobey God's command. In the Judeo-Christian tradition, all of human history appears to unfold as a direct result of the first conversation recorded in the Bible.

Our purpose in calling these two very different examples to mind may seem quixotic, but here it is: for the moment, we'd like you to suspend the idea that language is an everyday miracle or a sacred gift. We also want you to pry language loose from the clutches of communication, where it figures as a hammer that gets the job done, and of rhetoric, where it acts as a silver tongue that artfully persuades. Against these visions of language's function, we would like instead to highlight the creative, generative, exploratory powers with which language endows us all.

In *The Miracle Worker*, surely the best-known depiction of language acquisition of the twentieth century, the playwright William Gibson dramatizes the utterly improbable story of how Helen Keller—deaf, blind, and unable to speak—escapes a life of complete social isolation. At the play's opening, Keller's parents have hired the young, inexperienced, formerly blind, and fiercely determined Annie Sullivan to help care for and control their daughter, whose violent behavior has made her all but unmanageable. One of Helen's most distressing habits occurs at mealtimes: refusing to use tableware—or unable to understand how to use it—Helen grabs whatever food is in reach with her bare hands, stuffs what she can in her face, and then casts about for her next handful. And when her frustration at not finding her next mouthful mounts to the boiling point, Helen throws whatever she can get her hands on—tableware, plates, her shoes—until food is once again placed in front of her.

Sullivan decides that the only way to make progress with Helen is to start over and treat her like a very large two-year-old—that is, as a child who is on the developmental threshold of acquiring language. Sullivan signs into Helen's palm all day long, spelling out the words of objects they encounter, repeating them over and over, just as one would do verbally in teaching a toddler to speak. Sullivan also sets about training Helen in appropriate behavior, while struggling to convince Keller's parents that their daughter needs to be punished when she behaves improperly. In the play's climactic scene, Helen, who has learned how to use tableware, regresses and throws a tantrum during the midday meal. In her thrashing about, she spills a pitcher of water, and Sullivan drags her, kicking and writhing, from the room and out to the water pump in the yard. Placing the pitcher in one of Helen's hands, Sullivan begins furiously pumping water into the pitcher, while signing the word *water* one letter at a time, over and over, into Helen's other hand.

How does someone unable to perceive the world through sight or sound grasp the idea of language? As the play tells the story, it occurs in an instant, when Helen, feeling the water from the pump splash on her one hand and the repetition of the same pattern of pressure, traced over and over by Sullivan, in her other palm, connects these two experiences. In the screenplay for the 1962 movie version of his original teleplay, Gibson provides the following instructions to the director and the camera crew for capturing this moment:

And now the miracle happens. We have moved around close to Helen's face, and we see it change, startled, some light coming into it we have never seen there, some struggle in the depths behind it; and her lips tremble, trying to remember something the muscles around them once knew, till at last it finds its way out, painfully, a baby sound buried under the debris of years of dumbness.

Ecstatic at her sudden understanding of the word *water*, Helen signs the word in her own palm, then in Sullivan's, and then falls to the ground, slapping it with one hand and holding her other hand out for instruction. One word leads to another and then another, the irreversible course set in motion. The miracle worker, it turns out, is language itself.

Words make thought possible; they enable us to see things we've never seen and to hear things we've never heard; they even make it possible for us to travel back and forth in time. They give us the power to create and then to ponder abstractions and arguments; they give us the means to discover new ways of understanding the natural world and ourselves. But words don't do any of these things without us. The miracle of our being able to make ourselves known to each other becomes possible only with practice—practice stringing words together into sentences, questions, and paragraphs; practice accommodating the constraints of syntax and convention; practice speaking and writing ourselves into being.

Practice Session

Reflecting

The Miracle Worker dramatizes the power that language has for Helen Keller. While it is tempting to universalize Keller's experience, we think it a better idea to reflect on your own experiences of trying to make your innermost thoughts known to others. What medium do you feel is best for expressing your thoughts? Words? Color? Sound? Touch? Food? Movement?

Our list of possible answers may surprise you, but we want you to reflect on the full range of your expressive experience. When was the moment that you *felt* most fully that you were expressing exactly what you wanted to express in the way you wanted to express it? Write for at least 60 minutes about that moment, doing your best to render the truest representation of your experience at the time.

Reflecting

The power of the water pump scene in *The Miracle Worker* derives in part from all the frustration, rage, and anger that precedes it: the endless hours of instruction that seem to have no payoff; the screaming; the thrown food. Without the miracle at the pump, Helen Keller might have spent the rest of her life unable to communicate her thoughts to others except through physical behavior, in particular gestures of frustration and protest.

When you reflect back on your own experience, when was the moment that you felt most fully *in*capable of making yourself understood? What prevented others from understanding you? What did you do following this experience? Was there a way, at some subsequent moment, to bring about mutual understanding, or are there some experiences that simply cannot be expressed? Write for at least 60 minutes about that moment, doing your best to render the truest representation of your experience at the time.

Writing

When you look at what you wrote in Session One about the moment in which you felt most fully that you were expressing yourself and in Session Two about the moment in which you felt most incapable of expressing yourself, what do you see? What precisely does putting these two examples next to each other reveal to you about how language works? About the nature of communication? About learning and inner experience? Write an essay that speculates about why some efforts to share an understanding succeed and why others fail. Your goal here is neither to argue nor to prove a point—that's not the best use of the evidence of your own experience. Your goal is to use your experience to think in new ways about language, communication, learning, and expression.

EXPLORE

While we may never be able to say, definitively, where language came from, we can ask: What happens to language after it appears? Jared Diamond looks at how spoken language and the written language that represents speech evolve at different rates. Shirley Brice Heath considers the difference between the language practices of children who were read bedtime stories and those who weren't. And historian and essayist Tony Judt, reflecting on a neurological disorder that is slowly robbing him of the ability to make the words in his mind audible to others, considers what happens to the self when language begins to disappear.

Diamond, Jared. "Writing Right." *Discover.* 1 June 1994. Web.

Heath, Shirley Brice. "What No Bedtime Story Means: Narrative Skills at Home and School," *Language in Society.* Vol. 11, No. 1 Apr. 1982. 49–76. Print.

Judt, Tony. "Words." *New York Review of Books.* 15 July 2010. Web.

On Making Thought Visible

Helen Keller (Patty Duke) at the pump, with Anne Sullivan (Anne Bancroft). Still from the 1962 film version of The Miracle Worker.

In "On the Miracle of Language," we considered the most famous teaching scene of the twentieth century: Helen Keller at the pump, Anne Sullivan furiously signing the word *water* in Helen's palm, and Helen's breakthrough of connecting the experience of water pouring over one palm to the signing Sullivan is doing in her other palm.

Our discussion focused on the representation of this moment in William Gibson's *The Miracle Worker*. For the purposes of Gibson's teleplay, Helen's miraculous connection occurs in an instant; it's dramatic, powerful, and visually compelling. Gibson needed to make the workings of Keller's mind visible to his television audience. But as we've continued to think about this play and its influence on how people the world over imagine Helen Keller, we've found ourselves led to another question: Is Gibson's version of this event, composed in the late 1950s, what actually happened at the water pump on that fateful day in 1887? The most well-known representation of learning has got us wondering about the relationship between words and ideas and about whether words or images can ever provide unmediated access to what is going on in another person's mind.

. . . . .

Can we know what actually happened at that pump?

At first, how to answer this question seems obvious: just find out what Helen Keller herself had to say about this transformative moment, and then we'll be done with it. This may seem like a reasonable approach if words make our thoughts visible by simply reporting what we think, in the moment or after the fact. This is what we thought before we began to explore the many different accounts that Keller and her teacher provided of the miracle of Keller's language acquisition. It turns out that there isn't a "true" version of what happened at the pump; rather, there are multiple versions that were put forth at different times to serve different ends.

VERSION ONE: HELEN KELLER'S *THE STORY OF MY LIFE* (1903)

The initial public version of the pump story appears in Keller's first autobiography, *The Story of My Life*, which was published in 1903, when Keller was twenty-three and had just graduated from Radcliffe College. Keller begins her description of the moment thus: Sullivan had taken her outside for a walk, which made Keller "hop and skip with pleasure." They passed someone pumping water; Sullivan placed one of Keller's hands under the water and began signing "w-a-t-e-r" into Keller's other hand, while the unnamed third person continued to pump. Already, the differences between Keller's first-person account and the account in Gibson's teleplay announce themselves: instead of being dragged to the pump in a violent tug of war, Keller is happily walking with her teacher; instead of two people at the pump, there are three.

Here is Keller's description of what happened next:

> I stood still, my whole attention fixed upon the motions of her [Sullivan's] fingers. Suddenly I felt a misty consciousness

as of something forgotten—a thrill of returning thought; and somehow the mystery of language was revealed to me. I knew then that "w-a-t-e-r" meant the wonderful cool something that was flowing over my hand. That living word awakened my soul, gave it light, hope, joy, set it free!

Notice the words and phrases that populate this description: *misty consciousness*; *mystery*; *revealed*; *living word*; *awakened*; *soul*; *light, hope, joy*; *set it free*. A version of the born-again Christian narrative, "I once was lost, but now am found," can be heard in Keller's first description of how she came to language. But Keller's version curiously makes no overt reference to Christ as the source of the "living word" that has awakened her soul; to some readers, it may well seem that Keller is describing a religious conversion without the religion.

Keller continues to draw on the vocabulary of revelation in her description of what happened immediately after her momentous discovery:

As we returned to the house every object which I touched seemed to quiver with life. That was because I saw everything with the strange, new sight that had come to me. On entering the door I remembered the doll I had broken. I felt my way to the hearth and picked up the pieces. I tried vainly to put them together. Then my eyes filled with tears; for I realized what I had done, and for the first time I felt repentance and sorrow.

In this version, the miracle worker is language itself; language has made it possible for blind Helen Keller to "see" and, quickly thereafter, has led her to feel the need to repent for her earlier actions.

We would argue that, at the age of twenty-three, Keller clearly connected her experience of coming to language with what she subsequently learned about the experience of Christian conversion. And if one were to delve deeper into Keller's memoir, one would learn that Keller was exposed to the work of the eighteenth-century Christian theologian Emanuel Swedenborg when she was fourteen and that she, like William Blake, William Butler Yeats, and Ralph Waldo Emerson before her, was drawn to Swedenborg's descriptions of a Christian spirituality that transcended the church-based versions of the religion. So Keller's readers aren't getting a description of what actually happened when she was six; they are getting Keller's rethinking of that experience based on her subsequent experiences learning how to describe a profound change in worldview in a way that is both compelling and recognizable.

That Keller's original version has been shaped to meet her audience's expectations is clear not only in retrospect; it was openly acknowledged at the time by John Macy, who helped Keller write *The Story of My Life*. In an appendix to the volume, Macy offers this observation about the status of the stories that populate Keller's autobiography: to his mind, Keller has not provided "a scientifically accurate record of her life, nor even of the important events. She cannot know in detail how she was taught, and her memory of her childhood is in some cases an idealized memory of what she has learned later from her teacher and others." There is, we would note, nothing exceptional about this: What do you remember about your life at six? How much of your memory of that time is shaped by the stories your parents or siblings tell about you? How much is shaped by photographs and family videos, which are themselves a type of idealized memory?

Perhaps we'll have more luck if we turn to the memories of those who were adults at the time. Anne Sullivan could, in fact, have a truer version of what happened at the pump than Keller does.

VERSION TWO: ANNE SULLIVAN'S CORRESPONDENCE (1887)

The Story of My Life also has in its supplementary materials Anne Sullivan's account of how Keller came to learn how to communicate. In her correspondence with her teachers at the Perkins Institution for the Blind, Sullivan begins her account of the events of March 20, 1887, with this excited declaration: "A miracle has happened! The light of understanding has shone upon my little pupil's mind, and behold, all things are changed!" The miracle that Sullivan goes on to describe, though, is not the miracle of Keller's language acquisition: it is that "the little savage has learned her first lesson in obedience, and finds the yoke easy." Keller has learned to sit still, to be calm. She can make the signs to spell out words, but she confuses *mug* and *milk*, which shows that she "has no idea yet that everything has a name."

Two weeks later, on April 5, Sullivan reports that "something very important has happened. Helen has taken the second great step in her education. She has learned that everything has a name, and that the manual alphabet is the key to everything she wants to know." Sullivan mentions that Keller continued to have problems distinguishing *mug* and *milk*. Sullivan then describes what led her to take Keller outside to the water pump: while washing up in the morning, Keller "wanted to know the name for 'water.' When she wants to know the name of anything, she points to it and pats my hand." Sullivan signs the word, thinking nothing of it at the time, but then later decides to take Keller out to the pump-house, on the hunch that Keller's learning the sign for *water* might help straighten out "the 'mug-milk' difficulty."

Note how Sullivan's correspondence stretches out the sequence of events, placing Keller's acts of learning and discovery in the stream of time. Note, too, that in Sullivan's account, Keller's immersion in the world of signing, which involves weeks of confusion and incomprehension, nevertheless leads to the generation of a question—a question asked before Keller even knows what a question is. The experience of water on the hand. The patting of the palm. In Sullivan's account, Keller is already five weeks into an immersive instructional experience when Sullivan leads her to the pump:

> The word coming so close upon the sensation of cold water rushing over her hand seemed to startle her. She dropped the mug and stood as one transfixed. A new light came into her face. She spelled "water" several times. Then she dropped on the ground and asked for its name and pointed to the pump and the trellis, and suddenly turning round she asked for my name.

For Sullivan, the story at the pump isn't about an instant in time or a revelatory moment of conversion; it's about Sullivan's commitment to weeks of dragging Keller, kicking and screaming, to the threshold of language. Thus, Sullivan's version of the story culminates not in Keller's newly discovered desire to repent but in Keller's desire to learn the name of the person who brought her out of the darkness—her teacher. In the version told by Sullivan, she is the miracle worker.

Given these two versions of the scene at the pump, one might reasonably conclude that we are always the heroes of our own stories: for Keller, the scene at the pump is about her spiritual encounter with an elevated state of consciousness; for Sullivan, it is affirmation of her powers as a teacher. But this conclusion is too simplistic. If we drill down further, we find that not only did Keller's thinking about that scene at the pump continue to change over the course of her lifetime, but Keller came to feel trapped by the power of the story itself because it turned out to be the only story about her that others wanted to hear.

VERSION THREE: HELEN KELLER'S *THE WORLD I LIVE IN* (1908)

Keller first gives voice to this frustration in her second autobiography, *The World I Live In*, which was published just five years after *The Story of My Life*.

> Every book is in a sense autobiographical. But while other self-recording creatures are permitted at least to seem to change the subject, apparently nobody cares what I think of the tariff, the conservation of our natural resources, or the conflicts which revolve about the name of Dreyfus. If I offer to reform the education system of the world, my editorial friends say, "That is interesting. But will you please tell us what idea you had of goodness and beauty when you were six years old?"

In effect, this one story from Keller's childhood was already on its way to being the only story from her life that there was a market for, despite the fact that Keller was the first deaf-blind American to earn a college degree and, was eager to share her thoughts about the virtues of socialism and other matters of global import.

Keenly aware of this conflict between her audience's expectations and her own desires, in *The World I Live In* Keller settles for weaving her thoughts about larger world affairs into the story of her life. This is evident even in the way she retells the story of the pump in her new volume:

> Before my teacher came to me, I did not know that I am. I lived in a world that was a no-world. I cannot hope to describe adequately that unconscious, yet conscious time of nothingness. I did not know that I knew aught, or that I lived or acted or desired. I had neither will nor intellect.

Notice that in this revised account, Keller grants Sullivan a central role in her transformation, but she uses language that foregrounds the transformation as one of the mind, rather than one of the soul or the spirit. Her teacher, represented here iconically rather than by name, gave Keller access to consciousness, to desire, to will, and to the intellect. Keller is still a "self-recording creature," but the self she represents herself as recording has changed; before language, she was incapable of voicing the statement that Descartes asserted is the very foundation of our being: "I think, therefore I am." She was, by her own estimation, not human.

Is this version of what happened at the pump more accurate than either of the previous two versions? Is it possible to remember what life before language was like? Or are the results of any such efforts the product not of memory but of the imagination?

VERSION FOUR: HELEN KELLER'S TEACHER: ANNE SULLIVAN MACY: A TRIBUTE BY THE FOSTER-CHILD OF HER MIND (1955)

More than forty years after the publication of *The World I Live In*, Keller revisited the scene at the pump and revised her telling of the story one final time. Looking back on the version she recorded in *The Story of My Life*, Keller now sees her earliest autobiographical work as having been produced "with the carelessness of a happy, positive young girl," and she regrets that she "failed to stress sufficiently the obstacles and hardships which confronted Teacher" (now capitalized). And so it is with the explicit project of celebrating Anne Sullivan, whom Keller identifies as the foster mother of her mind, that Keller offers her third version of the events at the pump:

> Suddenly Phantom understood the meaning of the word, and her mind began to flutter tiny wings of flame. Caught up in the first joy she had felt since her illness, she reached out eagerly to Annie's ever-ready hand, begging for new words to identify whatever objects she touched. Spark after spark of meaning flew through her mind until her heart was warmed and affection was born. From the well-house there walked two enraptured beings calling each other "Helen" and "Teacher." Surely such moments of delight contain a fuller life than an eternity of darkness.

In this retelling, Phantom, a shadow being without thought, language, or feeling, is transformed into Helen by being given access to the link between words and meaning, after which "her heart was warmed and affection was born." So in this final version of Keller's, a story that once had strong religious overtones gets recast in terms that evoke the pleasures of romance and culminates in the creation of "two enraptured beings" who were joined to one another forever thereafter. But not really forever, since Sullivan had been dead for nearly two decades when Keller published her tribute. Does that fact make this account more true or less so than the previous ones? Are words written in grief or words that seek to repair a past injury more or less likely to express accurately what actually happened?

VERSIONS FIVE AND SIX: WILLIAM GIBSON'S *THE MIRACLE WORKER* (1957) AND *MONDAY AFTER THE MIRACLE* (1982)

As it happens, William Gibson's relationship to the story at the pump also changed over time. As a result of the wild success of *The Miracle Worker*, Gibson's version of Keller's childhood experience has reached a much wider audience than any of the versions Keller herself composed. This is so, we would argue, because of the primacy of the image over the word. To get to Keller's versions or to Sullivan's version, one must commit to the act of reading. To get to Gibson's version, one need only take a seat in the theater or sit before a screen that's broadcasting either the original teleplay, which first appeared on television in 1957 as an episode of the anthology series *Playhouse 90*, or the movie version, which premiered in 1962 and starred Anne Bancroft and Patty Duke in the roles of Sullivan and Keller, respectively, portrayals for which both actors won an Academy Award. The critical and popular success of the film helped to make *The Miracle Worker* a staple of the high school stage, where it has been regularly performed for the past sixty years, cementing in the public consciousness Gibson's version of the moment when Keller acquired language, with a violent struggle leading Keller and Sullivan to the pump, followed by Keller returning to her family for a joyous embrace. This version is highly melodramatic; it's not a record of what actually happened and not a reliable source for understanding how Keller began to make her thoughts visible and thus knowable to others.

As we've alluded to above, Keller struggled throughout her adult life to find an audience for the thoughts and ideas that her miraculous triumph over adversity made possible—thoughts about women's suffrage, pacifism, religion, and world government. Ironically, Gibson himself came to feel trapped by the success of *The Miracle Worker* and by its simplified tale of how the life of a girl with multiple disabilities was transformed by the miracle of language. In 1982, twenty-five years after the original broadcast of his teleplay, Gibson published the play *Monday after the Miracle*, which picks up Keller's story at the time she is attending Radcliffe College and is in the process of writing *The Story of My Life* with the help of Anne Sullivan and John Macy, an English instructor. In the second act, Sullivan, her own eyesight failing, has married Macy, but their relationship is complicated by the fact that Keller, Sullivan's constant companion, is no longer the small, vulnerable child at the pump but is now a grown woman in her mid-twenties.

In the third act, Sullivan and Macy's marriage is in the final stage of collapse, owing to Macy's alcoholism, Sullivan's inability to conceive, their money troubles, and Macy's newfound attraction to Keller. To address the household's financial problems, Sullivan and Keller first go on the lecture circuit and then, in the play's penultimate scene, announce to Macy that they are preparing to join the vaudeville circuit, because there's much more money to be made by performing for audiences that expect to be entertained than by giving lectures to the small groups of educated people interested in Keller's ideas. (Gibson alters the actual timeline of events to create this fictional conflict: Macy and Sullivan split up years before Sullivan and Keller took their show on the road.) When Keller recites her lines from the planned vaudeville act for Macy to critique, he is driven into a rage by her announcing, "My teacher has told you how a word from her hand touched the darkness of my mind. Through love, I found my soul and God and happiness." Macy responds derisively, describing Keller as Sullivan's "trained seal, mouthing platitudes. Found God and happiness, for Christ sake."

Macy then pleads with Keller to leave Sullivan and come to Italy with him: "you can do better—better than the hag-ridden life *you'll* have with her, turning into a tin showpiece. Leave her!" In the darker, more oppressive, and lonelier world Keller and Sullivan inhabit as adults, the miracle of Keller's childhood is now openly mocked, with Macy smashing a bottle of liquor on his typewriter while repeating Keller's lines: "Through love I found my soul and God and happiness." And then, just before he storms out of their lives for good, Macy says to Keller, "you've sucked us empty, angel, you've gutted [Sullivan's] life and mine, and I swear if I could—wipe out the day you were born—"

One could argue that Gibson stages this scene to free both Keller and himself from being frozen in time at the moment Keller learned her first word. If this was Gibson's goal, however, he clearly failed: the critical reception of *Monday after the Miracle* was so negative when it premiered on Broadway in 1982 that the play closed after just one week. Remade into a schlocky "love triangle" TV movie in 1998, *Monday after the Miracle* has essentially been consigned to the dustbin of history.

Is Gibson's second version of Keller's "awakening" more true than his first version? Less true? Completely untrue? What are we to make of the fact that audiences embrace the version of Keller's life that culminates at the water pump and reject the versions of her life that follow her into adulthood?

VERSION SEVEN: ANNE SULLIVAN MACY AND HELEN KELLER ON THE VAUDEVILLE CIRCUIT (1920–1924)

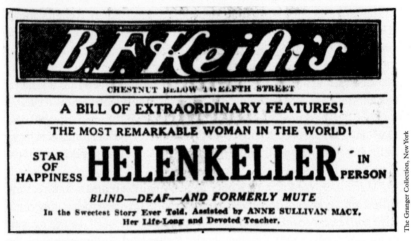

B.F. Keith's

CHESTNUT BELOW TWELFTH STREET

A BILL OF EXTRAORDINARY FEATURES!

THE MOST REMARKABLE WOMAN IN THE WORLD!

STAR OF HAPPINESS **HELENKELLER** IN PERSON

BLIND—DEAF—AND FORMERLY MUTE

In the Sweetest Story Ever Told. Assisted by ANNE SULLIVAN MACY. Her Life-Long and Devoted Teacher.

Evening Public Ledger, *June 5, 1920.*

From our historical vantage point, the vision of Anne Sullivan and Helen Keller performing on the vaudeville stage alongside jugglers, acrobats, magicians, and the physically disabled is likely to seem something Gibson invented for dramatic effect. But, as we drill down further, we discover that Sullivan and Keller did indeed perform on the vaudeville stage from 1920 to 1924, and that each performance began with Sullivan first appearing on stage alone to tell the story of the pump. Then Keller would join her and, to the audience's astonishment, would actually speak the following words (demonstrating that she had learned both sign language *and* how to speak aloud):

> What I have to say is very simple. My teacher has told you how a word from her hand touched the darkness of my mind and I awoke to the gladness of life. I was dumb; now I speak. I owe this to the hands and hearts of others. Through their love I found my soul and God and happiness. Don't you see what it means? We live by each other and for each other. Alone we can do so little. Together we can do so much. Only

love can break down the walls that stand between us and our happiness. . . . I lift up my voice and thank the Lord for love and joy and the promise of life to come.

In her article "'Play[ing] her part correctly': Helen Keller as Vaudevillian Freak," Susan Crutchfield argues that Keller's success on the stage was predicated on her performing the story her audience desired. Instead of explicitly stating her support for socialism, Keller recited a script that masked her politics behind a call for people to work together. In reviewing the contemporary newspaper reports on these performances, Crutchfield concludes that, "Again and again for Keller's vaudeville audience, it is her voice, her physical demonstration of her *ability* to speak rather than what she says, that generates their sense of awe."

Is Keller's vaudeville speech the truest version of the pump story, since it allows her to share a version of her thoughts about what is required to create a better world?

MAKING THOUGHT VISIBLE: A PARADOX

After considering all these versions of Keller at the pump, you're probably tempted to say that there's no way of ever knowing what happened on that fateful day when the water and the word met on Keller's palm for the first time. While that's certainly true, we're interested in the question that is raised by our journey through these many different ways of describing this pivotal moment in Keller's life: Is it ever possible to communicate to another your own experience of thinking?

Everyone who learns how to use language experiences the miracle Keller experienced. But Keller is nearly alone in having been able to credibly claim to remember the miraculous moment when the world of experience shifted from incoherent chaos to a world of nameable objects and actions. We stipulate that this moment is both miraculous and fascinating, but we are nevertheless much more interested in the moments that follow this initial, inexplicable moment of contact—the moments that occur after the mind has matured and there are more words and experiences work with. This is the question that we've written ourselves to as a result of meditating on the many different ways of seeing the story of Helen at the pump: Is it ever possible to describe a new thought coming into being, or must one compose versions of the emergence of new thought that are prepackaged to meet audience expectations? Is the writing one does about one's own thinking always a fiction? Is this so even in academic essays, where one strives to show one's mind at work on a problem?

Practice Session One

Writing

We'd like you to take up the questions with which we've ended our deliberations by considering your own experiences of thinking thoughts that are new to you. While at first blush it may seem that all such experiences are inevitably personal, we encourage you to consider experiences through which you came to think differently about an issue or a topic or a debate and not just those experiences that made you think differently about yourself or others. We want you to choose an example that is important to you, one without which you feel your life would be diminished. Can you make it clear how you came to think this new thought?

The preceding essay gives you a couple of examples of how to go about this task: you can provide a vivid narrative or set of narratives about the experience (as Keller does); or you can provide an evidence-driven account that proceeds via juxtaposition (as we have done). The challenge we invite you to take on is to show, to the best of your ability, not only what the new thought is, but also your own experience of that thought coming into being in your mind.

Practice Session Two

Researching

In the vaudeville performance put on by Keller and Sullivan, Keller would say aloud to the awestruck audience, "I am not dumb now." A century ago, it was common to refer to those who were mute as "dumb," the word then meaning both "incapable of speech" and "unintelligent." But as the example of Keller amply shows, the double meaning of this word reinforced a prejudice against those who, for whatever reason, could not speak. Nearly a century has passed since Keller was performing on the vaudeville circuit, and the language used today to describe any kind of human difference, be it one of ability or sexuality or race, is now much more carefully scrutinized.

Oddly, this concern for the language we use to describe those who differ from ourselves has been dubbed "political correctness." We'd like you to do research into the original use of this term and then explore how this term is used in a contemporary example of your own choosing. (We don't need to provide you with examples because they proliferate in the news media.) When you've collected the information about the term's original meaning and your contemporary example, we'd like you to write an essay about the relationship between thought and language. Is the struggle over language necessarily a struggle over thought?

Practice Session Three

Writing

The most common dodge we come across as writing teachers takes the form of a writer who, after considering a range of conflicting explanations for a given event, concludes that "everyone has a right to his or her own opinion." Translated, we read this statement as meaning, "I don't have a stake in this." We can imagine a reader who considers the seven different versions of the pump scene we've provided above and concludes that everyone has a right to interpret Keller's moment of language acquisition as he or she pleases. We don't think that this is a question of rights, though: by virtue of being language-using creatures, we are all hardwired to interpret. The question is not whether we have a right to interpret as we please, but whether any one interpretation is better than another. If you were writing an essay that explored the relationship between language and thought, which account of Keller's experience would you use, and why? Now write that essay, and see where your writing leads your thinking.

EXPLORE

Tim Bascom's essay, with its explicit focus on how to draw pictures of the thought process, is the perfect companion piece to our own. Clifford Geertz offers one of the best examples we've found of what it means to look at an object from multiple perspectives. Emily Raboteau puzzles over the holiday tradition in Amsterdam of wearing blackface. And Peter Stark finds a way to represent the thoughts of those who are in the process of freezing to death.

Bascom, Tim. "Picturing the Personal Essay: A Visual Guide." *Creative Nonfiction* 49 (Summer 2013). Web.

Geertz, Clifford. "Deep Play: Notes on the Balinese Cockfight." *Daedalus* 101.1 (Winter 1972). 1–37. Print.

Raboteau, Emily. "Who Is Zwarte Piet?" *VQR* 90.1 (Winter 2014). Web.

Stark, Peter. "As Freezing Persons Recollect the Snow—First Chill—Then Stupor—Then the Letting Go: The Cold Hard Facts of Freezing to Death." *Outside Magazine.* Jan. 1997. Web.

On Thinking Unthinkable Thoughts

"To infinity and beyond!"

If you give Buzz Lightyear's familiar rallying cry a moment's thought, you can see that what he's calling for is impossible. It's one of many jokes embedded in the *Toy Story* movies that is meant to entertain the adults in the audience: only a toy superhero would think that there is some point beyond infinity to which one could go.

We may chuckle at Buzz Lightyear's mistake, but do we really understand infinity much better than he does? If you stop and think seriously about what *infinity* means, you'll find yourself thinking that fully comprehending this concept is, by definition, impossible. And yet, while imagining the infinite may be impossible, striving to think this impossible thought has long preoccupied humankind.

The Greek philosopher Zeno used the concept of the infinite to formulate his paradox about the impossibility of movement. In order to get from point A to point B, he reasoned, you must first move half the distance. Call that halfway point C. But to move from point A to point C, you must first move half *that* distance. Call that halfway point D. And so on. Because any distance can be cut in half, the process of dividing never comes to an end—it is, by definition, infinite. If you try to think Zeno's paradox about infinite divisibility to its logical conclusion—that there are an infinite number of steps before one reaches a final destination—you will find yourself driven to conclude that motion of any kind is impossible. And yet we move.

The medieval theologian Saint Anselm defined God as "that than which a greater cannot be conceived." To have a thought equal to the divine being is thus, strictly speaking, impossible, because by definition Saint Anselm's God exceeds any conceivable thought. In this formulation, reasoning inevitably leads to an encounter with reason's limit and then to the point beyond that limit, which Anselm calls faith.

Carl Sagan, astronomer and popularizer of science, spent much of his life trying to promote a fuller understanding of the dimensions of the cosmos. This effort, too, can be understood as an attempt to articulate a vision of the infinite: "We have examined the universe in space and seen that we live on a mote of dust circling a humdrum star in the remotest corner of an obscure galaxy. And if we are a speck in the immensity of space, we also occupy an instant in the expanse of ages."

As these examples are meant to show, to say that thinking the infinite is impossible is not to say that it is not worth attempting. Indeed, we would say that striving to think the infinite is an essential part of the mental training for adulthood. We believe this for many reasons, but the most important one is this: the only way to know the true limits of your thinking is to travel to the edge of your own understanding and peer into the unknown.

Where is that limit?

How will you know when you get there?

....

Practice Session One

....

Reflecting

Spend at least 30 minutes in a quiet place thinking about infinity. Just close your eyes and think. If your thoughts stray, pull them back. Set a timer so you don't interrupt your thoughts to check the time.

When the buzzer rings, write an account of your experience. What, specifically, did you do in your mind to think the infinite? Did you have moments of success, or was your experience an uninterrupted series of failed attempts? How did you feel over the 30 minutes?

Writing

What other thoughts seem unthinkable to you? We've focused on the infinitely big, but what about the infinitely small? What about time? The age of the earth? The smallest fraction of a second? Are the challenges involved with thinking the dimensions of infinity—as an extension of time or space—the same as those that arise when you try to think about infinity in relation to realms of human experience? That is, can you think infinite love? Infinite forgiveness? Infinite patience? Infinite violence? Infinite cruelty?

Write an account of what you learned from this second run at infinity. If you can't think the thought, is the experience of trying a second time qualitatively different from your initial experience? What happens in your mind as you are doing this kind of thinking? What are the consequences of having tried?

Practice Session Two

Researching

We have a former student who interviewed for a job at a major dot-com years ago. He walked in with his résumé and his transcripts documenting his superlative performance as an English major. When he took a seat, the interviewers asked him, "How many golf balls can fit in this room?" Then he was asked to say how many airplanes were in the air at that moment. And finally, he was asked to say how much concrete had been used in constructing the US interstate highway system.

Crazy questions, right? The point of the interview, though, was not to test the candidate's ability to recall information learned in the past; the point was to see how the candidate could think about how to solve problems involving large numbers and several variables.

How would you answer a question of this kind? You're not in an interview situation; you have access to the Internet. Choose one of the questions and describe how you would go about formulating an answer.

EXPLORE

We offer you additional examples of writers contending with the unthinkable. Naomi Alderman writes about science's search for the Higgs Boson particle—a subatomic particle with physical properties that stretch beyond the reach of the human imagination. Wendell Berry asks his readers to imagine the devastating consequences of an economy based on the assumption of limitless growth. Joan Didion meditates on life after the death of her spouse and the experience of a grief without end. Roxane Gay explores the possibility of being privileged and marginalized at the same time. And Naomi Klein covers the worst industrial accident in US history and considers the significance of our inability to contend with the natural disasters we ourselves have caused.

Alderman, Naomi. "The Goddamn Particle." *Granta.* 12 July 2012. Web.

Berry, Wendell. "Faustian Economics." *Harper's Magazine.* May 2008. Web.

Didion, Joan. "After Life." *New York Times.* 25 Sept. 2005. Web.

Gay, Roxane. "Peculiar Benefits." *The Rumpus.* 16 May 2012. Web.

Klein, Naomi. "Gulf Oil Spill: A Hole in the World." *Guardian.* 18 June 2010. Web.

Reflection at Work: Harriet McBryde Johnson and the "Undeniable Reality of Disabled Lives Well Lived"

When Harriet McBryde Johnson was a child, her muscles became too weak to hold up her spine; rather than wear a brace, she let her spine "reshape itself into a deep twisty S-curve." After that, she was "entirely comfortable in [her own] skin." How comfortable? Using her motorized wheelchair to negotiate the streets of Charleston, South Carolina, Johnson earned a law degree and specialized in disability law. Until her death at age fifty, she was also an activist who sought to show the able-bodied majority the necessity of recognizing disability as a natural part of human experience. People with disabilities, she writes, "take constraints that no one would choose and build rich and satisfying lives within them. We enjoy pleasures other people enjoy, and pleasures peculiarly our own. We have something the world needs."

Johnson came to national attention in February 2003 when she published "Unspeakable Conversations" in the *New York Times Magazine*, an article in which she wrote about her face-to-face meeting with the world-renowned philosopher Peter Singer, who maintains that parents and doctors should be allowed to kill severely disabled infants at birth to end their suffering. "He insists he doesn't want to kill me," Johnson writes in the opening sentence of "Unspeakable Conversations." She then goes on to explain Singer's position this way: "He simply thinks it would have been better, all things considered, to have given my parents the option of killing the baby I once was, and to let other parents kill similar babies as they come along and thereby avoid the suffering that comes with lives like mine and satisfy the reasonable preferences of parents for a different kind of child."

Johnson maintains that Singer's philosophical argument is based on a mistaken assumption that the disabled are "worse off" than the able bodied. Against the "terrible purity" of Singer's logic, Johnson offers her own arguments and the counterevidence of her personal experience. She has no trouble arguing in print with what Singer has written;

but when he invites her to speak at Princeton, she has to reflect on new questions. Should she accept the invitation of the man who argues that she could have been justly killed at birth? (She does.) When she meets him, should she shake his hand with the three fingers on her right hand that still function? (She does.) Should she treat him with civility and respect? (She does.) And after spending a day with him, she also has to reflect on the paradox that, while he holds firmly to an argument that underestimates the value and quality of her own life and the lives of similarly disabled people, in person he is respectful, considerate, and free of condescension.

In the end, against the advice of her family, friends, and fellow disability activists, Johnson decides that she cannot categorically dismiss Singer and disability prejudice as "evil." Because she wants "kinship," "community," and "connection," she concludes that she should extend to him and others "basic respect and human sympathy." In that way, she can continue to be a part of the ongoing conversation, giving voice to the "muck and mess and undeniable reality of disabled lives well lived."

MAKING SPACE AND TIME

....

Henry David Thoreau headed off to Walden Pond in 1845 to begin his experiment in self-reliance. One reason he chose Walden Pond was that it was beyond the reach of the mail delivery service. Out there in the relative wilderness, he built his own cabin, planted a garden, watched the seasons change, listened to the birds, and conversed with visitors. He read, reflected on what he'd read, and wrote about his reflections. During his two years away from Concord, Massachusetts, Thoreau was, we could say, living the ideal life of a writer: he was largely self-sufficient; he was free of distractions; he had no concerns about whether there was a market for his writing. (The real story of Thoreau's life on Walden Pond is more complicated, of course.)

Not all writers thrive under these conditions. Some require background music when they are writing; others prefer to work in coffee shops. In this section, we don't assume that the ideal space for writing is far from wherever you are. Rather, we want you to think about consciously choosing places and times to work that will allow you to practice your writing. While Thoreau could focus mainly on a physical location that would work best for him, anyone writing today also has to contend with the pervasiveness of the Internet, which is always just a click away. Making space and time for writing at this moment in history necessarily means seeing the screen you are working on as itself a place. How can you make the screen a place that encourages you to stay focused and thoughtful? What are the benefits of cultivating solitude in our highly connected world? Given that most of what gets written today is destined to appear on a screen, how is this fact changing the activities of writing and reading?

On Creative Places

In 1929, Virginia Woolf famously declared, "A woman must have money and a room of her own if she is to write fiction." Do women writers, or any writers, today face the same challenges? Or has the advent of the Internet age reconfigured those challenges? If Woolf were to publish *A Room of One's Own* today, would she recast her famous insight as, "One must have money and a laptop of one's own, as well as broadband access, if one is to write fiction"? Or would she think "a room of one's own" remains essential, regardless of the technology used to do the writing in that room?

Virginia Woolf

A laptop with broadband access has the potential to connect whoever is sitting at the keyboard with readers around the world, virtual archives richer than any actual archive past writers had access to, and research tools that allow the user to chase an idea wherever it might lead. But as transformative as Internet access is, we would argue that it hasn't eliminated the need that writers of any gender have for solitary time and quiet spaces to do the work of composing and revising. Indeed, because collaborating, getting feedback, and socializing can now all be

done virtually, carving out a place of our own where we can work without intrusion or distraction is significantly harder than it was in Woolf's time. And even if we find a private place to work, there's always another text message, Snapchat, or breaking news story to pull us out of our writing and toss us into the digital sea.

Woolf's writing room certainly had a desk, a chair, books, and a lamp, but not, of course, a computer, a television, or speakers. What about a phone? During Woolf's most prolific writing years, when she lived at 52 Tavistock Square in London, she *did* have a telephone in the house—the number printed on her stationery is "Museum 2621"—but we think it's unlikely the phone was in her writing room. After all, it's not a "room of one's own" if anyone can, on a whim, dial past the closed door and interrupt the writer at her desk.

What does your typical workspace look like? How many distractions are within sight, earshot, or reach when you write?

Our students often insist that their digital devices don't distract them from getting their writing done; many also declare that they work best when they are multitasking. However, in study after study neuroscientists consistently find that people who make such claims don't really know their own minds. The habits of multitasking are so ingrained that we don't recognize when we are distracted; it has become a normal state of being.

Because writing is a complex task, to do it efficiently and well requires the self-discipline to manage the many competing streams of information and entertainment that are now the norm. Making a room of one's own for writing therefore involves not only shutting the door or finding a quiet corner, but also blocking one's access to the Internet, at least for a time, to create the conditions for attention and focus.

. . . . .

Until now, our discussion of creative workplaces has emphasized the solitary practice of writing—away from the hubbub of life, cut off from the demands of social media. But we don't want to suggest that writers should completely isolate themselves from the world. The story of the lone and lonely genius is a familiar one, but there are social elements to the creative process that require the writer to leave the study and engage with the world in all its complexity and detail.

When Virginia Woolf wrote *A Room of One's Own*, she had a home in Bloomsbury, where she lived among a set of relatives and friends—painters, novelists, philosophers, and critics—now known as the Bloomsbury Group. The name "Bloomsbury" might suggest a remote village in the English countryside among green meadows and blossoming gardens, but Bloomsbury is actually a district in central London. Woolf's writing room was in the midst of a lively city.

As part of her work routine, Woolf wandered for hours through the London streets, observing and storing away details of daily life. In her essay "Street Haunting: A London Adventure," Woolf describes the people, sights, and scenes she encountered on a journey to purchase the essential tool of her craft, a pencil. Reflecting on all she'd seen and done on her way to the stationer's shop, Woolf closes her essay thus:

> Walking home through the desolation one could tell oneself the story of the dwarf, of the blind men, of the party in the Mayfair mansion, of the quarrel in the stationer's shop. Into each of these lives one could penetrate a little way, far enough to give oneself the illusion that one is not tethered to a single mind but can put on briefly for a few minutes the bodies and minds of others. One could become a washerwoman, a publican, a street singer. And what greater delight and wonder can there be than to leave the straight lines of personality and deviate into those footpaths that lead beneath brambles and thick tree trunks into the heart of the forest where live those wild beasts, our fellow men?

As this passage makes clear, when Woolf ventured out of the room of her own, she took with her a way of seeing and thinking about the world that she had cultivated and nurtured in private. Her time away from the hustle and bustle of the city didn't deaden her to the pleasures of the company of friends or of the anonymous encounters that accompany movement through a day of errands.

. . . . .

What does our reflection on public encounters, private rooms, and digital distractions mean for you as a writer?

Consider it an essential part of your job as a writer to choose good places to work. Writers need places where they can compose without intrusions, but they also need engagement with the world and with others. They need a computer and Internet access, but they also need to develop the discipline to ward off the distractions that come with Internet access. So when you write, withdraw when you need to; at other times, dive into the fray. Keep in mind, too, that your life as a writer needs to have more dimensions than your screen. The Internet can connect you to information and ideas that you know how to search for, but it can also disconnect you from the less predictable and less containable world around you. To write, you need not just a room of your own, but a community of your own—one that jostles, disrupts, adds to, and opens new vistas for your thinking.

Practice Session One

Researching

Explore your town or campus, looking for places where you could write. Look at libraries, cafés, and places that are quite or bustling with activity and creativity. Find locations where you can attend lectures, films, or concerts. Make a map of places for each of the following elements of a writer's work: encountering the creative work of others; meeting and talking with interesting people; doing research; reading; composing; revising; and editing.

Practice Session Two

Researching

Find or create a quiet space where you can reliably work for long stretches of uninterrupted time. Some people can find a place for solitude within their home; others choose to work elsewhere, such as in a library or even a café, where they are surrounded by other people who are working intently. Ideally, this should be a place where you can write every day. What can you do to make your chosen place even more conducive to composing? What small changes—a seat cushion, some earplugs, a desk nearer to a window—might make it even better? Make the place your own.

For inspiration, take a look at the blog *Writers at Work* and its photographs of writers' workspaces. The essential tools of the trade have long been a writing desk, a chair, books, pen and paper, a typewriter or laptop, and—until recently—cigarettes. What else do you notice in these images, most of them decades (if not centuries) old? After you've spent at least 30 minutes exploring the photographs on *Writers at Work*, take a picture of your own writing space and compare it to the photographs on the blog. Is there a writer's workplace that reminds you of your own?

Practice Session Three

Writing

Spend a week practicing writing in a few promising places. Experiment with small changes: rearrange the furniture; write at different times of the day; write while drinking coffee or tea. Try a few strategies for extending your focused researching and writing time, such as setting timers so that you spend 20 or 30 minutes writing and then take a 5-minute break to stretch, walk, or check text messages. See if you can gradually extend the time between breaks.

Reflecting

After a week, write a reflective essay about what you've learned about the places and practices that best suit your creative work.

EXPLORE

Our essay opened with a discussion of Virginia Woolf's argument that writers need quiet places to work away from distractions. Michael Pollan's book about designing and building his own writing house and the photographs posted on the sites *Writers at Work* and *Writers' Rooms* provide ample evidence that Woolf's argument is true in the main. While writers certainly need temporary retreats, Lemi Ghariokwu and Malcolm Gladwell argue that thinkers of all sorts also need vibrant connections to creative communities—such as the cultural and political life of Lagos, Nigeria, the bustle of New York's West Village, or even a well-designed office building.

Ghariokwu, Lemi. "A Dynasty of Album Cover Art." *Granta*. 4 Oct. 2013. Web.

Gladwell, Malcolm. "Designs for Working." *New Yorker*. 11 Dec. 2000. Gladwell.com. Web.

Pollan, Michael. *A Place of My Own: The Architecture of Daydreams*. New York: Penguin Books, 2008. Print.

Woolf, Virginia. *A Room of One's Own*. New York: Fountain Press, 1929. Print.

Writers at Work. Web.

Writers' Rooms. Guardian. Search "Virginia Woolf writers room" on the *Guardian*'s Web site to see a photograph of Woolf's "writing lodge" at Monk's House, where Woolf wrote most of her novels. Web.

On a Screen of One's Own

Our working assumption is that you do the bulk of your writing on a screen and that you write in many different locations. No matter what brand of computer you are using, the software designers have made default decisions about what should be immediately available to you when you are browsing or writing. Whether you work on a screen that belongs to you or on a shared computer, we encourage you to take the time to personalize your screen in ways that conform to your preferences and that contribute to keeping you focused while you are writing. To this end, we're going to walk you through a set of exercises to help you create a screen of your own.

Practice Session One

A Browser of Your Own

We begin with the browser because this is your portal leading to the vast informational riches on the Web and to the Web's infinite time sinks. (One popular online news source has a recurring piece entitled "Websites You Should Be Wasting Your Time On Right Now!") We want you to think about how best to organize your browser so that it minimizes distractions and reinforces your commitment to being curious and creative. Your browser should, in other words, reflect both your personal choices *and* your creative aspirations.

You need to familiarize yourself with the way that your browser (be it Safari, Firefox, Chrome, Internet Explorer, or some other platform) allows you to control the bookmarks that appear in your toolbar. All browsers work pretty much the same way: there's a button you can click on the browser that allows you to bookmark the page you are looking at; once you click that button, you are given the option of storing your bookmark on the browser toolbar or elsewhere. We're going to trust you to figure out the exact procedures for your particular browser. (You can always search for an instructional video on YouTube.)

What bookmarks should appear in your browser? Where do you want your mind to go when you are doing research? Where do you go when you want to be inspired to think new thoughts? Where do you go when you want to know what's going on in your town? In the United States? In the world?

We recommend the following bookmarks for your toolbar:

- Your school library and/or your local library
- Your school's portal to research journals. (Depending on your school's resources, this may give you access to JSTOR, EBSCOhost, and/or Project MUSE, all of which archive academic articles.)
- Google Scholar
- Google Images
- A range of news sources for you to read regularly. (This will help you develop the habit of being knowledgeable about important current events.) To get started, bookmark a local newspaper, one of the leading national newspapers, and a reputable source for international news.

We also recommend you bookmark Diigo or some other cloud-based archiving program that lets you access your stored bookmarks from any machine connected to the Internet. Placing Diigo's "Diigolet" bookmark on your toolbar will allow you to store (in your Diigo account in the cloud) a bookmark to whatever page you are on at the time that you click the Diigolet button. This is invaluable when you are in the midst of collecting resources: with the click of a button, the link to the resource is saved for your future reference.

After you've populated your toolbar with these resources, the rest is up to you. You might want to add additional bookmarks for sites that:

- contain trustworthy information relevant to your current research;
- inspire you to be a more ambitious thinker;
- provide a public forum for discussing important questions you want to think more about; or
- feature visual art or music that challenges you to see the world differently.

We want the toolbar on your browser to be both immediately useful to you and a standing temptation for you to devote more of your free browsing time to pursuing your higher intellectual and creative goals.

We also want you to make certain that your toolbar doesn't give you immediate access to sites that you know will interrupt your concentration and distract you from your work. It's not that we don't approve of these sites: we know that relaxing is important and that social media can spur intellectual growth and creative energy. But we also know that distraction is built into the screen-based composing and research environment. There's no escaping this while your browser is open, but you can minimize the temptation to multitask (that is, to do two things poorly at the same time) by creating a folder on your toolbar labeled "distractions." In this folder you should put bookmarks to sites you visit regularly that you know break your concentration. You'll know what belongs in the "distractions" folder: for some writers, it will be a link to Facebook; for others, it will be a link to ESPN; and for some, it will be a link to their Twitter feed. When you are writing, you simply need to tell yourself not to click on the "distractions" folder. This is a boundary that only you can patrol.

Note: For those readers who do not have a dedicated screen of their own to personalize, much of what we assign above can be completed in the cloud using the social bookmarking program Diigo. Once you create an account, you can begin to populate your library with the kinds of bookmarks we've described above. Then when you are composing online, accessing your Diigo account will allow you to make the screen you are using function as if it were your own.

Practice Session Two

A Word Processing Toolbar of Your Own (or Not)

Personalizing your word processor is a trickier business, and if you compose using Google Docs, it is actually not a meaningful activity, since Google doesn't give you the option of deciding what appears in its toolbar and what doesn't. We actually recommend using Google Docs over other commercially available word processing programs for this very reason.

It may seem counterintuitive that we prefer a free, stripped-down word processing program to the turbocharged versions, but our reason for doing so is pretty straightforward: open any commercial word processing program, and you will be immediately overwhelmed by all the options available to you. This is because these programs are designed to address every imaginable publishing option, from the single-page memo to the 300-page tabbed report with charts, a table of contents, and an index. The commercial word processing programs are fine if you are working in an office (though we've worked in many offices and have yet to meet anyone who knows how to get the programs to produce documents that actually look the way they want them to). But the tools a writer needs while composing are actually quite few—some ways to change fonts and control the margins, and an easy way to embed charts and images. Google Docs maintains this strict simplicity.

So if you have dependable, ready access to the Internet, we recommend that you create a Google account and begin composing in Google Docs.

If you don't have dependable, ready access to the Internet, or if you would prefer that your work not automatically be stored in the cloud, we recommend that you explore the options for customizing the toolbar on the word processing program you prefer.

What matters here is not which choice you make, but that you make a conscious choice designed to reduce the distractions you face while composing.

EXPLORE

In this essay, we've only scratched the surface of online resources available to help you be more focused and more productive when you've settled in front of your screen to compose. Because the list of potentially invaluable online resources grows and changes by day, we've decided to use this essay's Explore section to recommend three different categories of resources we try to keep up with. First, there are online sources that track new developments in digital technology. Then there are online sources that focus on issues and products that are relevant to conducting online research. And, finally, there are online sources that promote a fuller understanding of copyright in the age of file-sharing and privacy. In each category, we suggest at least one resource primarily focused on practice and another resource primarily concerned with how digital technology has disrupted print-based assumptions about writing, collaborating, and publishing. Recent developments in digital composing:

- Mashable.com is an aggregator site that collects information on digital innovation and social media.
- Reddit.com, self-described as the "front page of the Internet," provides an open forum for the discussion of news stories big and small, culture high and low, and ideas significant and trivial.

- Wired.com is the home page for Wiredmagazine, a print and online journal that covers the ways technology is changing culture, economics, and politics.

Valuable tools for academic research:

- Dropbox.com is the home page for a company that provides free online storage space. Dropbox is ideal for backing up important files and for sharing large files (such as rich images, video clips, and slideshow presentations).
- Profhacker is a collaboratively-written blog on the Chronicle of Higher Education Web site that both explores issues related to moving academic research into the digital realm and evaluates newly released tools and applications that aim to improve the production of academic research.
- Zotero.org is the home page for a free, easy-to-use online tool that you can add to your browser to help you collect, organize, cite, and share your research sources.

Keeping up with copyright:

- Cmsimpact.org is the home page for the Center for Media and Social Impact at American University, a rich repository for information about best practices for complying with the laws governing fair use.
- Creativecommons.org is the home page for Creative Commons, an international organization devoted to rethinking copyright law. It provides a host of legal options for exercising a measure of control over how others may use what you publish on the Web.

On Solitude

When was the last time you spent an extended amount of time alone? Not just without the physical company of others, but also without any virtual company—that is, without those whom you connect with via texts, e-mails, instant messages, Facebook, Snapchat, or Twitter. Time alone is surely among the scarcest resources in our networked times.

The difficulty we face in finding quiet places for reflection would not have surprised the nineteenth century's most famous loner, Henry David Thoreau. He would, however, have been shocked by how connected we are to a virtual world, as opposed to the real world, or ourselves. In 1845, Thoreau wanted more time to think and write than living in Concord, Massachusetts, afforded him, so he took up residence in a small cabin he built himself on the shore of Walden Pond, a little more than a mile outside of town, and lived there for two years, two months, and two days. In the book *Walden*, he describes his experiment living apart from society—"living off the grid," in today's terms—as a decision "to live deliberately, to front only the essential facts of life, and see if I could not learn what it had to teach, and not, when I came to die, discover that I had not lived."

Solitude for Thoreau was not deprivation; it was a choice that allowed time and space for introspection, self-reflection, discovery, and writing. Indeed, one of the topics he reflected on, wrote about, and devoted a chapter of *Walden* to was solitude. For him, the aloneness experienced by someone deep in thought is quite different from physical isolation or social alienation. "A man thinking or working," he writes, "is always alone, let him be where he will. Solitude is not measured by the miles of space that intervene between a man and his fellows." Then Thoreau compares the solitude and sociability of the farmer to that of the college student:

> The really diligent student in one of the crowded hives of Cambridge College is as solitary as a dervish in the desert. The farmer can work alone in the field or the woods all day, hoeing or chopping, and not feel lonesome, because

he is employed; but when he comes home at night he cannot sit down in a room alone, at the mercy of his thoughts, but must be where he can "see the folks," and recreate, and, as he thinks, remunerate himself for his day's solitude; and hence he wonders how the student can sit alone in the house all night and most of the day without ennui and "the blues"; but he does not realize that the student, though in the house, is still at work in *his* field, and chopping in *his* woods, as the farmer in his, and in turn seeks the same recreation and society that the latter does, though it may be a more condensed form of it.

In this passage, Thoreau is sympathetic to the farmer who wants company to escape his thoughts after a long day of laboring alone in the field. But Thoreau wants those who perform physical labor to see that *thinking* is the field in which the student works, and that solitude is an essential condition for carrying out sustained mental labor.

If Thoreau is right, then part of being a student is learning to enjoy working alone. Being alone may not be pleasant or easy at the outset, but the concentration required to learn to play the piano, program a computer, or write an introspective essay requires time apart from interruption or the chatter of others' voices.

What happens when we're alone that can't happen when we're in groups? Psychologist K. Anders Ericsson and his collaborators studied the behavior of a range of experts—violinists, chess players, golfers, even college students who study well—and found that the best performers spend significantly more time practicing in solitude. Only when alone can one do what Ericsson calls "deliberate practice"; only when alone can one focus on monitoring and revising the skills that are, at any given level of achievement, just beyond reach. Deliberate practice can't be casual. It can't be faked. It can be done only by people who are genuinely motivated to strive for some higher level of achievement, experience, performance, or understanding. For Thoreau, that higher goal was experiential: he wanted to find a way "to live deliberately."

When successful writers describe their composing processes, they tend to point to some type of deliberate practice, performed in solitude. Some writers are at their most focused and creative just after they wake.

Toni Morrison, for instance, rises and makes coffee in the early morning when the sky is still dark. She sips her coffee and watches the daylight arrive, and then she is ready to write. Other writers slip off to small cottages or shacks near their homes: this is what Russell Banks and Michael Pollan do and what Virginia Woolf, Roald Dahl, and Thoreau did before them. Most of us, of course, don't have a shack of our own, or even a room of our own, but we can still learn from the examples of generations of writers who have found that some form of solitude—a temporary release from noise, worries, and responsibilities—is essential to gaining access to the mysterious creative powers of the imagination and the intellect.

Getting off the grid is much more difficult now than it was in Thoreau's time. When a computer is one's primary writing tool—and also one's library, news source, shopping mall, and social life—it takes virtually superhuman powers of discipline not to open a browser window and fall into clicking on a link or two to take a break from the hard work of composing. It's not just beginning writers who struggle with this temptation: in the acknowledgments page of her book *NW*, novelist Zadie Smith gives credit to two Internet-blocking applications (one called Freedom, the other SelfControl) for "creating the time" she needed in virtual solitude to complete her work. Given the distractions, old and new, that face every writer, what can you do to create the solitude you need to write? It may seem that the only solution is to unplug and move to a cabin off the grid, but there are other solutions—recall Thoreau's axiom that "solitude is not measured by the miles of space that intervene between a man and his fellows." Your Walden, in other words, can be anywhere: in a coffee shop, in an apartment complex, in a room next to a commuter train line—anywhere.

When Susan Cain was preparing to write *Quiet*, her book about the hidden power of introverts, she decided she'd work best in a home office. She arranged her study with a neat desk, lots of counter space, and natural light. She had all the privacy one could hope for. Perfect for an introvert, right? It turns out that it wasn't the perfect place for Cain; in fact, she couldn't get started. To escape the isolation, Cain found herself carrying her laptop to a neighborhood café to work among other people who were also hunched over their laptops. Why did this place become Cain's primary workplace? The café, she says, was social, yet its casual, come-and-go-as-you-please nature left me free from unwelcome entanglements and able to "deliberately practice" my writing. I could toggle back and forth between observer and social actor as much as I wanted. I could also control my environment. Each day I chose the location of my table—in the center of the room or along the perimeter—depending on whether I wanted to be seen as well as to see. And I had the option to leave whenever I wanted peace and quiet to edit what I'd written that day.

Cain, who treasures being alone, found the kind of solitude she needed, as well as inspiration and stimulation, in a room of other writers. Solitude is not measured by the counter space separating the writer from her fellow coffee drinkers; it is measured in the writer's relationship to her work.

Practice Session One

Reflecting

For two days, observe and take notes about your experiences with solitude. Don't judge; just describe.

When and where do you have the most time during the day for sustained thought and work?

How do you respond to extended time working alone? How do you respond to time alone when you are not working?

What are your typical distractions? Is music a distraction or an aid to focus? Do different kinds of music affect your focus differently?

How often do you make calls, text, tweet, check e-mail, surf the Web, or check Facebook?

What distractions are an unavoidable part of your day?

What other distractions are avoidable?

After you've kept records for two full days, write for at least 30 minutes about your struggles with solitude and distraction when sitting down to write. What changes can you make to free yourself a bit more from typical distractions?

Practice Session Two

Reflecting

For a week, experiment with spending less time online in order to extend the solitary time you have to read, think, and write.

Start by disconnecting from the Internet and turning off your phone for 60 minutes of writing, reading, or other mental labor.

The next day, see if you can extend your time offline. Add 30 minutes or an hour. If you can't resist the Internet's allure, try a free blocking program or application.

It may help if you plan to take a short break every hour, or a slightly longer break every two hours. During each break, you can check e-mail or texts, respond to anything urgent, and then return to work. If you're concerned that people expect immediate responses from you, put an announcement on Facebook and set up an auto-reply message on your e-mail to let folks know when you won't be available. Let them know that you're writing and see how they respond.

After a week of creating space in your day for you to be offline, write for at least 45 minutes about what you've learned about yourself and your online habits and about whether your efforts to limit digital distraction enhanced your writing.

Practice Session Three

Writing

A teacher we know takes the idea of limiting time online to a whole new level. She regularly invites her students to volunteer to spend an entire week offline. Following through on this choice takes a bit of planning, including informing everyone who expects to correspond with you via social media and e-mail that you won't be available. And going offline can be difficult during an academic semester when your work may require you to use digital resources. But if you can manage it, spend at least a day—or, if you can, a week—offline and take notes about your experience. Did you feel free, or anxious, or both? Were you lonely without your virtual connections? What parts of the experiment were hardest, and what parts were easiest? Did you find productive ways to use your extra time?

After experiencing a day or more of a twenty-first-century Walden, write an essay about the experience. Reflect on what you learned about yourself, your attachment to the virtual world, and your comfort with offline solitude. Can you imagine extending or repeating the experiment?

EXPLORE

Time alone to think and compose is essential to writers. In the twenty-first century, when we are rarely without digital connections, the kind of solitude that writers require is difficult to find, unfamiliar, and perhaps even unsettling. In the works we've selected, writers affirm how time alone nurtures thought and creativity. We hear from the sixteenth-century inventor of the essay, Michel de Montaigne, and Walden Pond's nineteenth-century resident, Henry David Thoreau, as well as from contemporary writers Susan Cain and Toni Morrison about the pleasures, challenges, and necessity of solitude.

Cain, Susan. "The Rise of the New Groupthink." *New York Times.* 13 Jan. 2012. Web.

de Montaigne, Michel. "On Solitude." *The Essays of Michel de Montaigne.* Project Gutenberg. Web.

Morrison, Toni. Interview by Elissa Schappell. "Toni Morrison, The Art of Fiction No. 134." *Paris Review.* 128 (Fall 1993). Web.

Thoreau, Henry David. *Walden.* Project Gutenberg. Web.

Curiosity at Work: Alan Lightman and the Mind-Bending Multiverse

In "The Accidental Universe: Science's Crisis of Faith," physicist Alan Lightman reveals his delight in the uncertainty and doubt he finds at the heart of scientific inquiry. Although he revels in the unsolved mysteries of science, he knows that most nonscientists think of science as the solver of all mysteries and the source of hard facts and essential truths:

> The history of science can be viewed as the recasting of phenomena that were once thought to be accidents as phenomena that can be understood in terms of fundamental causes and principles. One can add to the list of the fully explained: the hue of the sky, the orbits of planets, the angle of the wake of a boat moving through a lake, the six-sided patterns of snowflakes, the weight of a flying bustard, the temperature of boiling water, the size of raindrops, the circular shape of the sun. All these phenomena and many more, once thought to have been fixed at the beginning of time or to be the result of random events thereafter, have been explained as *necessary* consequences of the fundamental laws of nature—laws discovered by human beings.

It seems as if Lightman's list could go on for pages, but he interrupts himself to entertain the possibility that "this long and appealing trend may be coming to an end." The era when we could believe that science would provide solid solutions, facts, and truths may be over.

Although scientists have long assumed that we can understand the natural laws governing life and the universe in terms of mathematics and logic, some of the world's premier theoretical physicists now propose that "the fundamental laws of nature do not pin down a single and unique universe." These scientists further speculate that "our universe is only one of an enormous number of universes with wildly varying properties, and that some of the most basic features of our particular universe are indeed mere *accidents*—a random throw of the cosmic dice." In other words, "the *same* fundamental principles from which the laws of nature derive may lead to many *different* self-consistent universes, with many different properties. It is as if you walked into a shoe store, had your feet measured, and found that a size 5 would fit you, a size 8 would also fit, and a size 12 would fit equally well."

Welcome to the "multiverse."

Intrigued? Then read Lightman's "The Accidental Universe." And, after you've finished, track down the vigorous debate that followed its publication. Lightman suggests that the nature of reality is unknowable, unthinkable, and unprovable. If that's the case, what might the future of scientific research look like?

PRACTICING

....

How do you develop a habit? Through practice. But what is practice? When you're a kid practicing handwriting, you learn through repetition. You copy the letters of the alphabet over and over, mastering the block shapes first before moving on to cursive. With both types of writing, you practice certain physical gestures so that you can faithfully reproduce the conventional shape of each letter. This practice requires hand–eye coordination, fine motor control in your dominant hand, and symbol recognition. Once you've practiced these activities enough, you can reproduce all the letters of the alphabet quickly, without conscious thought. Then, in a very limited sense, you know how to write.

What do you practice if you want to become a writer? Aspiring writers are often given two pieces of well-intentioned advice: "write what you know" and "write every day." While we can quibble with this kind of advice, we'd rather have you think about what habits you should be developing through practice (that is, through writing every day). What does it mean to look at the world the way a writer does? What does it mean to read like a writer? What does it mean to ask questions like a writer? In posing these questions, we encourage you to see writing as a way of being curious about the world and your place in it.

On Seeing as a Writer

The very reason I write is so that I might not sleepwalk through my entire life.
—ZADIE SMITH, "FAIL BETTER"

Learning how to draw, as we discussed earlier (pp. 35–40), means learning how to see without naming; this allows the visual, spatial, and synthesizing ways of thinking to guide the hand on the page. Quieting the verbal train of thought allows you to see like an artist, but what if you want to put what you see into words? How do you learn to see as a writer does?

Young children can be intensely observant and curious. They learn about the world by paying attention and asking lots of questions. Once we become adults, many of us stop observing so acutely and constantly—in part because so much of the previously mysterious world is now familiar to us. We go on mental autopilot during routine experiences. We see what we expect to see. And we keep our surprise and wonder in check because both take up time we don't think we have to spare.

To see as a writer does, you need to practice asking questions about what you see. So instead of quieting the verbal activity in your mind, in this process you are training yourself to question the information your eyes are reporting to you. This questioning serves two purposes: it makes you conscious of your own perspective, and it also makes clear that other perspectives are possible. And this, ultimately, is part of what seeing as a writer involves—noticing clashes, subtle tensions, or unexpected connections between differing perspectives.

What do we mean by this? Here's an example of such a conflict, which comes from the opening of an essay by Annie Stiver, a student in one of our creative nonfiction classes:

> Recently, while standing in line for a ticket at the New Brunswick train station, I witnessed a mother nudge her young son, who, after barely noticing his mother's prod, continued to look steadily at a man sitting half-awake on a bench in the corner of the station. After her eyes dropped

and brows narrowed on her son, she clasped his shoulder and bent down to tell him that he is "not supposed to stare at bums." The boy turned his head forward at his mother's instruction, yet as I watched him I noticed his eyes were straining towards the right side of the room where this man was. Eventually, when it was his mother's turn at the ticket machine, the boy immediately turned his head to stare full-on at the man in tattered clothing on the train station bench. I figured that the boy was an infrequent visitor to New Brunswick.

This situation got me thinking about the rate at which children are encouraged not to stare even as they are curiously struck by novel experiences and when confronted with the unexpected. How did it come to be that we are taught not to stare?

A common response is that it's simply not polite to stare. But in those moments of heightened curiosity when we are told to keep our eyes from wandering on another's "business," we are, aside from being polite, affecting our own development and behavior as we repress our individual curiosities and questions about others. What happens when we stare? I would argue that staring goes beyond seeing the "other." Rather, when we stare, we are meant to think about ourselves. Watching the boy staring at the man in the station, I remembered the familiar feeling of when I was his age during unfamiliar and curious encounters with the unknown and unexpected. We're not staring because we want to know that our way of life is more comfortable and reassuring (we can consider this impolite), but sometimes we stare because we feel instinctively that our way of life is not quite right. When this happens, we want to ask, "Why aren't more of us staring?"

This is a great start to a thoughtful essay. Rereading this passage and thinking about the choices the student made as a writer, we see that she began with close, careful observation of the scene in the train station— a mother scolds her young son for staring at a homeless person. The writer had many choices about what perspective to take on this scene, and she chose to pay attention to the tension between what the mother says—that her son is not supposed to stare—and what he does—look again and again. In so doing, the writer stages for her readers an encounter between one perspective (staring is impolite) and another (staring is evidence of curiosity). Rather than arguing that one perspective or the other is the correct one to have on the situation, the writer responds to this common experience of a parent scolding a child with a question that the scene has raised for her:

"How did it come to be that we are taught not to stare?"

The writer pushes past the obvious answer, that it's impolite. There's something more going on here than bad behavior: the child wants to stare. The writer asks another question:

"What happens when we stare?"

Again, the writer rejects the commonplace answer. Staring that involves judgment of others is rude, she concedes, but curious children may be staring for another reason. "I would argue," she writes, "that staring goes beyond seeing the 'other.' Rather, when we stare, we are meant to think about ourselves. . . . Sometimes we stare because we feel instinctively that our way of life is not quite right." And this line of reasoning leads the writer to the question that drives the rest of her essay:

"Why aren't more of us staring?"

As writing teachers, we look at this student's sequence of observations, interpretations, and questions, and we see the habits of a creative mind at work.

> She began with close observation.
>
> She asked lots of questions—and not just questions about the facts (that is, questions starting with the words *what, where,* or *who*), but also questions about cause and significance (questions starting with *how* or *why*).
>
> She recognized a key concept—in this case, staring—and shifted her frame of reference to focus on what's going on when a child stares.

She shifted her perspective away from the straightforward and obvious to think from a different point of view. In this case, she thought about why the child continued to look after having been told not to.

Remembering her own childhood, she realized that a child may stare because her or his usual way of thinking has been unsettled. Staring—or merely looking thoughtfully—can lead to reflection about oneself and one's relationship to others.

This isn't a formula for seeing like a writer; rather, it shows that seeing like a writer means developing the habit of choosing—from what to focus on, to the terms of the description, to the connections made, to the other perspectives entertained. To see as a writer, one doesn't begin by choosing a topic or a theme, both of which are inert, but rather by practicing questioning what one sees, which is a never-ending activity.

Now we'd like you to practice looking from different perspectives at places and the people who inhabit them, with the goal of opening up new and compelling questions about what you see.

Practice Session One

Reflecting (on Public Space)

Begin by selecting a familiar, common space in your community or on your campus, somewhere you've been dozens if not hundreds of times. Visit at a time of day when it's likely to be busy. Observe the space for at least 20 minutes. Take notes on what you see. Notice who uses the space and how they move through it. Move around, exploring different perspectives.

After you've spent 20 or more minutes observing, spend at least 15 minutes writing down questions that your observations have raised for you. How does the space signal that it's public? Is it welcoming and beautiful, or ramshackle and dirty? Is it used by a wide variety of people or by a more homogeneous group? How does the space itself shape the experiences of the people who use it? How does it encourage or enhance some activities and limit others? These questions are just to get you started; they should trigger other questions that are directly related to your observations.

Write a reflective essay that develops out of your observations and a few of your most compelling questions about the place you observed.

Reflecting (on Private Space)

Next, we'd like you to do a similar exercise with a more private place, one that's inside, known or used by few people, and rich in visual detail. (Avoid choosing your own room or any other place that's overly familiar; it's hard to see such places in new ways.) Spend at least 20 minutes observing and taking notes and photographs. Then spend another 15 minutes pondering your experience in the space and writing down questions that your observations have raised. Start with the basics: How does the place signal that it's private? What activities does the space encourage, and what activities does it discourage? Is it possible to have a perspective on this place that is uniquely your own?

Write a reflective essay that develops out of your observations and a few of the most interesting questions you asked about the place you observed. Your goal is to compose a piece that gives your readers a new way to see and understand this private space.

Reflecting (on Natural Space)

Repeat this exercise in a natural, uninhabited, and unlandscaped space. Once again, observe and take notes for at least 20 minutes. Then spend 15 minutes or more developing questions that are grounded in your particular perspective. Coming up with questions about a natural space may be hard at first, but that too is worth pondering. After you've gathered your notes and questions, write another reflective essay that develops out of one or more of your most interesting questions and shows your reader how to see and think about this place in a new way.

Practice Session Two

Reading

In "On Seeing as a Writer," we examine how one of our students started to see as a writer. And we find our evidence in the words she chose to explain her experience in the train station. Select a passage from any of the readings we've included in this book. (This exercise can be done with a reading you've already written about; it can also be done with a reading that is entirely new to you.) What does the passage you've selected reveal about the writer's way of seeing?

Spend at least 30 minutes writing a profile of the writer's way of seeing based on what you can draw from the passage you've read. How is the way of seeing you've identified distinctive?

EXPLORE

In our essay, we ask you to consider the writer's way of seeing the world as something that is learned through practice. Mason Currey's blog, a compendium of the daily routines of writers and other creative people, makes it clear that seeing as a writer isn't a talent one is either born with or not, but a skill that arises from disciplined practice. Patrick Cavanagh asks: are artists and scientists wired to see the world differently? V. S. Ramachandran, looking at three cases of brain damaged patients, concludes that the ability to make abstractions, which all healthy brains have, arises because the essence of mental activity is the ceaseless making of connections via metaphor. And, finally, Joan Didion's famous riposte to George Orwell provides an electrifying account of how her acts of attention led her to turn to writing.

Cavanagh, Patrick. "The Artist as Neuroscientist." *Nature* 434 (March 17, 2005). 301–7. Print.

Currey, Mason. *Daily Routines: How Writers, Artists, and Other Interesting People Organize Their Days.* Blog.

Didion, Joan. "Why I Write." *New York Times Book Review.* 5 December 1976. Web.

Ramachandran, V. S. "Three Clues to Understanding Your Brain." TED. March 2007. Web.

On Reading as a Writer

In our writing classes, we have a couple of mantras about reading that we repeat throughout the semester:

> In order to learn how to write, you have to learn how to read as a writer.
>
> There's only one way to learn how to read well, and that's by rereading.

These mantras are connected. To read as a writer means to pay close attention to the choices other writers make. This kind of reading requires attending to lots of things at once—what the writer says, how she organizes her ideas, what types of sources she works with, and how she addresses her readers. Such multifocal reading can only be accomplished by rereading. The first time through a challenging work, you might only be able to focus on what it says; after you know how the writer gets from point A to point Z, then you can attend more carefully to the choices the writer has made along the way. As your understanding of the entire piece comes together, you can assess what works, what doesn't, and why.

If you were in a history class and were assigned Susan Sontag's essay "Looking at War," your teacher would expect you to read the essay as a student, which would entail being able to identify Sontag's thesis and to evaluate the evidence she provides to support her thesis. But if you were in one of our classes, where the focus is on becoming a writer, we would ask you to read differently: we would ask you to attend not only to Sontag's thesis and to the evidence Sontag provides in its support but also to how she presents and develops her ideas. So instead of expecting you to mark Sontag's main points with a highlighter, we would encourage you to slow down so that you can make connections, puzzle over references, and think about how the details contribute to the overarching effect of the piece.

Sontag begins her essay (which we've included as a reading in this book) by telling her readers about Virginia Woolf's *Three Guineas*, a

book-length essay that Woolf wrote while the Spanish Civil War was in progress. Sontag explains that Woolf framed her essay as a long-delayed response to a letter from a London lawyer who had asked her, "How in your opinion are we to prevent war?" While Woolf has sympathy for his cause, she calls into question the idea that she and the lawyer belong to the same collective "we." Even though they are both members of the same privileged social class, as a woman Woolf was denied the kind of education and professional experience that the lawyer, a man, took for granted. Woolf suggests that the two of them will only be able to find common ground by looking at photographs of war's atrocities, which are, in her view, "simply statements of fact addressed to the eye."

> However different the education, the traditions behind us, our sensations are the same; and they are violent. You, Sir, call them "horror and disgust." We also call them horror and disgust. And the same words rise to our lips. War, you say, is an abomination; a barbarity; war must be stopped at whatever cost. And we echo your words.

For Sontag, the key words in this passage from Woolf's essay are, surprisingly, "us," "our," and "we." These tiny words might seem hardly worthy of comment, but Sontag wants her readers to see what work they do in the passage she's cited. Reading as a writer, Sontag notices that, when Woolf imagines herself looking with the lawyer at photographs of the war, she uses the pronoun "our" to show that the photographs evoke the same emotional responses in both of them. They agree that the images reveal war to be an abomination and a barbarity. But this alliance between them is temporary. In the final sentences quoted above, Woolf has shifted the meaning of "we" and "our." They no longer refer to Woolf and the lawyer, but to Woolf and other women. "We" *women* "echo your words." Woolf has become the voice for what she believes is a universal female opposition to war, an opposition triggered by a shared revulsion to the realities of war as depicted in photographs.

After writing several paragraphs explicating *Three Guineas*, Sontag suddenly rejects Woolf's argument. "Who believes today," Sontag asks,

"that war can be abolished? No one, not even pacifists." Why does Sontag start her own essay in this curious way? If Woolf's position is wrong, why tell her readers about it at all?

Starting her essay with Woolf allows Sontag to get three common assumptions about war and photography on the table for consideration: (1) that women are unified in opposition to war; (2) that photographs are "statements of fact"; and (3) that seeing photographs of war's brutal effects will bring about an end to war. Seventy-five years after Woolf published *Three Guineas*, Sontag sees no evidence to support the contention that women naturally oppose war, and she sees no reason to stipulate that photographs present self-evident truths. To the contrary, Sontag sets out to argue that documentary photographs of war have never given rise to a political consensus against war and will never do so. Reading Woolf's essay led Sontag to formulate her own question: If it's not the function of war photography to bring about the end of war, what *is* its function?

Our discussion of Sontag's use of Woolf's essay models the importance of both reading as a writer and rereading. These practices attune us to the choices writers make as they shape their ideas and their readers' experience.

. . . . .

We have a third mantra we repeat to our students:

Read in slow motion.

When we teach writing, we know it's more valuable for students who are learning to read as writers to read and reread a brief selection with great care than it is for them to race through a much longer text in search of some highlighter-worthy main point. Reading in slow motion means looking up unfamiliar terms, names, historical events, and images. We encourage our students to track down some of the author's sources and to read those sources as writers, which means having them explore the connections the author has made to or between those sources. We do this because we want our students to see that whatever they're reading is connected to a much larger network of meaning.

If you read Sontag's "Looking at War" in slow motion, for example, and track down the text of *Three Guineas*, you'll discover something surprising: far from being a treatise on war photography, Woolf's 144-page book includes just two paragraphs on the subject. This fact makes Sontag's decision to begin her essay with a discussion of Woolf's work curious in a different way. Is her presentation of Woolf's position a distortion? Is Sontag setting Woolf up to make her own argument look more compelling than it actually is?

After slow reading, we've decided that Sontag learned more from Woolf than she lets on. The difference between Woolf's style and Sontag's is striking: Woolf makes her arguments through stories, while Sontag makes hers with ideas, drawing on the work of preeminent thinkers in history, art, and political theory. And yet, despite her predilection for ideas over stories, Sontag arrives, late in her argument, at the idea that photographs can only "haunt us," while "narratives can make us understand." The passage that Sontag cites from *Three Guineas* at the opening of her own essay is, we realize in retrospect, a narrative. Although Sontag rejects Woolf's idea that war photography can create solidarity for peace, she recognizes that Woolf's mode of writing may well be better suited to generating insights than a discussion of abstract ideas would be.

Seeing how Sontag has used Woolf in the opening of "Looking at War" helps us to see the significance of Sontag's decision to conclude her essay by narrating a story told by a photograph. Jeff Wall's 13-by-7.5-foot photograph *Dead Troops Talk (A vision after an ambush of a Red Army patrol, near Moqor, Afghanistan, winter 1986)* shows thirteen Russian soldiers clustered on a desolate, rocky landscape. It may look at first like a documentary photograph, but it's actually a fictional scene of postbattle carnage. The men in the photograph are actors on a studio set, playing the parts of soldiers. These soldiers, it seems, have died from gruesome injuries, but most of them appear alive to each other and are talking and laughing. Sontag describes them as indifferent to the world of the living: "one could fantasize that the soldiers might turn and talk to us. But no, no one is looking out of the picture at the viewer. . . . These dead are supremely uninterested in the living. . . . Why should they seek our gaze? What would they have to say to us?"

The collective "us" at the end of Sontag's essay is not Woolf's female collective "we." Rather, at the end of "Looking at War," Sontag arrives at a new "we": "this 'we' is everyone who has never experienced anything like what [the soldiers] went through." This "we," Sontag argues, can never fully understand what this photograph depicts: "We don't get it. We truly can't imagine what it was like. We can't imagine how dreadful, how terrifying war is—and how normal it becomes. Can't understand, can't imagine." Only by reading in slow motion can we appreciate that Sontag makes her point about how little most of us know of war by translating Wall's photograph into a story. This story does not try to teach us what it's like to be in a war; instead, it teaches us that without actual experience of war, we can never know how it feels or understand its horrors.

Reading as writers, we can appreciate the arc of Sontag's essay and the elegance of her argument without being compelled to reach the same conclusions. And in fact, this is exactly how Sontag responded to Woolf's *Three Guineas*: she admired the way Woolf shifted the meaning of "we" in a single paragraph and Woolf's ability to seamlessly embed a story in her larger argument, but Sontag didn't feel bound by this admiration to agree with Woolf. Rather, she did what writers do who wish to engage fully with the ideas of another: she wrote an essay of her own.

Practice Session One

Reading

You can use any serious text to practice reading and rereading as a writer. For now, we recommend that you read Sontag's "Looking at War" (p. 321). Start by reading the essay from beginning to end and marking key moments in Sontag's argument. Next, read the essay again, paying attention *as a writer* to how Sontag phrases and organizes her ideas, what types of sources she uses, how and where she presents major points, and how she addresses her readers. Take notes in the margins.

What's striking about how Sontag chose to approach her topic? What parts drew you in? Are there parts of the essay that confuse you, or parts where you don't know enough about photographs or history to follow her argument?

Were there any points or turns of phrase that impressed you, or sections you found yourself rereading with appreciation?

Having read Sontag's essay as a writer, identify one of the significant choices Sontag made when she composed her essay, and then spend at least 30 minutes writing about that choice. As you write, quote specific passages from Sontag's work to help your reader see what you find meaningful about how Sontag writes as well as what she writes.

Researching

Next you'll return to Sontag's work to practice a specific kind of rereading—reading in slow motion.

Sontag wrote about photographs throughout her career. Despite her enduring fascination with images, she did not include photographs in books such as *On Photography* or *Regarding the Pain of Others.* "Looking at War" is an exception to Sontag's usual practice: when the essay was originally published in the *New Yorker*, it included photographs; now that it is on the *New Yorker* Web site, the images are no longer part of the essay. (The imageless version is the one we've included in this book.)

The experience of reading "Looking at War" without reproductions of the photographs obviously differs from the experience of reading the text with the images. It's important to consider why Sontag typically chose *not* to reproduce photographs in her essays about photography. But it's also important to know that you are not bound by her decisions—or by the decisions of any writer. Indeed, when reading as a writer, you are always considering both what the writer says and what the writer *doesn't* say, what the writer directs you to look at and what the writer *doesn't* draw your attention to.

Working with "Looking at War," use the Web to track down the photographs Sontag references. Seek out the highest-resolution images you can find. Look at them with care. Learn about their context by reading what others have written about them. Then return to Sontag's essay and consider what additional sources might deepen your understanding of her argument. Search more; read more. Keep track of which sources you turn to and why.

Writing

Now that you've reread "Looking at War" in slow motion, write an essay about how slow reading altered your understanding of Sontag's work. It's likely that your research enhanced your reading of Sontag's work significantly. It's also

likely that new questions or confusions arose. Again, as you write, quote specific passages from Sontag's work and your sources to show what you find meaningful about what is said and how it is said.

Practice Session Two

Writing

What happens if we shift the focus from photographs to paintings? The Colombian artist Fernando Botero has created over fifty paintings that are inspired by the globally circulated images of human rights abuses committed by members of the United States Army at Abu Ghraib, in 2003. Search the Web for the highest-resolution versions of Botero's paintings you can find. Conduct your research *as a writer*, taking notes that will allow you to write an essay that is in conversation with Sontag's "Looking at War." Write an essay about the value of painting images of war in the age of digital photography.

EXPLORE

"Annotation Tuesday!" is a regular feature on *Nieman Storyboard* in which writers are interviewed about how they composed a particular essay or article. As the interviewers move through the pieces paragraph by paragraph, the writers explain their choices, often in surprising ways. We invite you to browse the archives of "Annotation Tuesday!" on the *Nieman Storyboard* Web site. We recommend, in particular or search for the interviews with writers Buzz Bissinger, Leslie Jamison, and Rachel Kaadzi Ghansa listed below.

"Annotation Tuesday! Buzz Bissinger and 'The Killing Trail.'" Interview by Elon Green. *Nieman Storyboard*. 28 Jan. 2014. Web.

"Annotation Tuesday! Leslie Jamison and the Imprisoned Ultradistance Runner." Interview by Elon Green. *Nieman Storyboard*. 2 July 2013. Web.

"Annotation Tuesday! Rachel Kaadzi Ghansa and 'If He Hollers Let Him Go.'" Interview by Elon Green. *Nieman Storyboard*. 7 Oct. 2014. Web.

On Self-Curation

....

The word *curate* has an interesting etymological history. According to the *Oxford English Dictionary*, *curate* entered the English language in the mid-fourteenth century as a noun signifying someone "entrusted with the cure of souls: a spiritual pastor." This nominal form of the word is linked to earlier adjectival forms in medieval Latin (*cūrātus*) and Italian (*curato*) and to the French noun *curé*, all of which denoted "having a cure or charge."

Some six hundred years later, *curate* made its first appearance as a verb in an English dictionary. And notice what happens to the meaning of the word when it moves from being used as a noun or an adjective to being used as a transitive verb: "to act as curator of (a museum, exhibits, etc.); to look after and preserve." So, for a very long time, a curate was a religious occupation; in the twentieth century, it became a secular activity.

Self-curation does not yet appear in the *Oxford English Dictionary* or *Merriam-Webster* or the *Cambridge Dictionary*. Nevertheless, if you search the Web for the term (with the hyphen), you'll find that this as-yet-unofficial word is currently in circulation and that it is used most frequently to refer to the conscious management of one's online life. Fancifully, we might define *self-curation* thus: "to act as curator of one's own online life; to look after and preserve an archive of one's digital existence."

We first came across the term while reading Dana Spiotta's wonderful novel *Stone Arabia*. The principle that guides the life of Nik Worth, brother of the novel's narrator, is "Self-curate or disappear." The mystery at the heart of the novel is twofold: first, what Nik has actually done is self-curate *and* disappear; and second, the self Nik has curated is an entirely fictional one. Not wanting to be remembered as an unsuccessful crank living on the margins of society, Nik spent two decades fabricating the documents, the personal journals, and the history of a forward-looking, deeply thoughtful musician. And then he left without a word. All his sister Denise can do while she waits for word from him is to make her way through the fictional journals in hopes of piecing together some understanding of what Nik had done with his life.

Nik's relationship to self-curation is pathological: he fabricates reviews of performances that never happened; he creates but never releases CDs by his fictional persona and then records the public reception of music that only he has ever heard. But Spiotta shows over the course of her novel that self-curation, understood more generally as the conscious act of placing oneself in a larger narrative, is an activity we all participate in, to a greater or lesser degree. Ada, Denise's estranged daughter, self-curates via her blog, where she foregrounds her work in documentary film. And Denise herself tries to fit the artifacts Nik has left behind into a narrative of her own life that she can understand.

In the Age of Paper, self-curation was a largely private affair. One kept a journal, perhaps, or collected shells or stamps or firearms or first editions or autographs or whatever. Now that we live in the Age of the Screen, self-curation is a largely public affair: there is the self or the selves that an individual maintains via social media; the blogging self; the photo- or video-posting self; the reviewing self. These are selves over which a person has some measure of control. And then there is the self as represented by others—via social media, via the news, via public documents.

What do you know about yourself as currently represented on the Web? Is that the version of yourself you would voluntarily give others access to? There's a practical reason for making that distinction: once something associated with your name, your face, or your work appears on the Web, it is potentially on the Web forever. Were you identified doing a keg stand on a friend's Facebook page? Did you post a comment on a local news site railing against something you now support? Have you had a run-in with the law? Any one of these events could function as a "digital tattoo" for you, ensuring that there's a public record of some past embarrassment available to anyone who is interested in digging it up. Self-curation is a practical way to counter the negative effects of the digital tattoo.

While there are good practical reasons to self-curate, we're more interested in the creative benefits that come with self-curation. If you take control of your online presence, you have the opportunity to represent yourself as a multifaceted individual with a range of interests. By self-curating as a writer, you make it that much easier for potential readers to find your work. And by making your work public, you create the opportunity to have the kind of readers all writers want—those who read voluntarily.

Practice Session One

Researching

What happens when you do a Google search on your name? Do you get different results if you use Dogpile? Twitter? Facebook? Pinterest? Photobucket? Your high school's home page? Do a thorough search and document all the information about you that is publicly available on the Web. Your final dossier should include images where appropriate. Spend at least 20 minutes writing about the results of your research: What does the uncurated version of yourself, as represented on the Web, look like?

Reflecting

What would you like people who search for you to find? What would best represent you as a thinker? A writer? A creative person? An artist? If you were to design a self-curated site, what would it include?

Spend at least 45 minutes sketching out what such a site would look like by hand or using the graphing feature on your word processing platform. Another option is to actually create a self-curated site. Regardless of which option you choose to do, you'll need to decide what tabs you would like to appear in your home page's navigation bar. Are you a writer who works in more than one genre? Have you made videos? Taken striking photographs? Started a graphic novel? Are you involved in other projects or activities that you could represent on your site? We are particularly interested in you designing a site that represents you as someone whose creativity expresses itself in production rather than consumption, so we ask that you restrict your listing of favorite books, musicians, and artists to the "About" tab on your site.

Practice Session Two

Researching

What happens when you do a Google search on a contemporary visual artist or writer you admire? Do you get different results if you use Dogpile? Twitter? Facebook? Pinterest? Photobucket? Spend at least 30 minutes doing a thorough search and document all the information about the artist or writer you've chosen that is publicly available on the Web. (Don't choose a celebrity, a sports star, or a politician; these figures always bring gossip, scandals, and excitable fans in their wake.) Then spend an additional 20 minutes writing about the results of your search. What does the uncurated version of the writer's or artist's self look like?

Researching

Seek out the official site or sites for the contemporary visual artist or writer you elected to research. Then take at least 45 minutes to write an essay on the difference between the official, curated self and the version of that self that emerged during your open-ended search. Drawing on your research, discuss what the artist or writer you've chosen to study might do on his or her self-curated site to engage with whatever additional unauthorized material you've discovered circulating outside the site.

Practice Session Three

Researching

It is now common journalistic practice to head straight to the Web in the immediate aftermath of a tragedy to see what social media can tell us about the possible victims or the possible perpetrators in the unfolding event. This practice has tended to have catastrophic results, as the pressure to be first on the scene with news has created a fertile ground for jumping to unfounded conclusions. This happened, for instance, after the tragedy in Sandy Hook and after the Boston Marathon bombing. In both cases, an innocent person was linked to the atrocity and was then quickly "convicted" online on the basis of material that was later revealed to be erroneous.

Choose a recent event that has been in the headlines and spend at least 45 minutes investigating what role social media has played in both the coverage and the interpretation of the event. Why do some responses to the event get picked up, shared, and repeated, while others are ignored? Take extensive notes, tracking key moments in the coverage of the chosen event. When you're done with your research, create a timeline that represents what you've learned about the role social media played in shaping popular understandings of the event.

Writing

If you were to curate a site dedicated to the event you selected, what would you include? Write an essay on self-curation, the digital tattoo, and social media as they relate to the event you've chosen to research. Your piece should include your design for a site that would provide a richer understanding both of the event and of its coverage.

EXPLORE

Our suggested readings all focus on understanding how social media has changed human behavior. Ann Friedman provides a trenchant analysis of LinkedIn, the self-proclaimed largest professional network on the Web. Ariel Levy examines the role that Twitter played in the handling of the Steubenville rape trial. And Clay Shirky looks at the ways that social media is changing how citizens and their elected officials engage with each other.

Friedman, Ann. "All LinkedIn with Nowhere to Go." *The Baffler* 23 (2013). Web.

Levy, Ariel. "Trial by Twitter." *New Yorker*. 5 Aug. 2013. Web.

Shirky, Clay. "How Social Media Can Make History." TED. June 2009. Web.

Creativity at Work: Twyla Tharp and the Paradox of Habitual Creativity

The film *Amadeus* annoys dancer Twyla Tharp because it portrays Wolfgang Amadeus Mozart as a born genius. "Of course, this is hogwash," Tharp writes in her book, *The Creative Habit*. Then in large red letters she asserts, **"There are no 'natural' geniuses."**

Tharp has done her research. She knows that Mozart's father, Leopold, who was himself a composer and a musician, recognized his son's musical interest and nurtured the boy's ability by teaching him to play at a very young age. She also knows that Mozart had a strong work ethic, even as a child. And she knows that he complained in a letter to a friend that people mistakenly thought he composed without struggle; the truth was that making beautiful music took time and effort.

Tharp uses Mozart's story to begin her book about creative habits because she wants to be clear about her project: "More than anything, this book is about preparation: **In order to be creative you have to know how to prepare to be creative.**"

She understands the allure of thinking that creativity is the birthright of a lucky few, but her experience as a dancer and choreographer, as well as with the creative people who have surrounded her all her life, has shown her that creativity can be learned and that it can be taught. "There's a paradox," she writes,

> in the notion that creativity should be a habit. We think of creativity as a way of keeping everything fresh and new, while habit implies routine and repetition. That paradox intrigues me because it occupies the place where creativity and skill rub up against each other.
>
> It takes skill to bring something you've imagined into the world. . . . No one is born with that skill. It is developed through exercise, through repetition, through a blend of learning and reflection that's both painstaking and rewarding. And it takes time.

Tharp reminds her readers that Mozart, who certainly had a gift and a passion for music, composed *twenty-four* symphonies before he wrote a work that would endure: Symphony no. 25 in G Minor, which serves as the opening score for *Amadeus*.

What can we learn from the examples of Mozart and Tharp? Tharp distills her ideas in this simple statement: "Creativity is a habit; and the best creativity is a result of good work habits." So practice every day. Make a ritual of your practice. "The routine," Tharp writes, "is as much a part of the creative process as the lightning bolt of inspiration, maybe more."

PLANNING AND REPLANNING

....

When you undertake a writing project, one of the early steps in the process is to make an outline. The value of doing so seems self-evident: an outline, with its schematic representation of the argument you hope to make, shows you where you plan to go and keeps you on track so you don't get lost in a thicket of irrelevant details. But, the risk in the outline-driven approach is that anything that threatens to pull the project away from its predetermined destination can be dismissed as irrelevant: potential connections won't get explored, new information won't be pursued, and unsettling insights will be ignored.

In this section, we recommend curiosity-driven approach to planning that assumes replanning is an inevitable and essential part of the writing process. This doesn't necessarily mean abandoning the outline, so much as it means assuming that the outline is likely to get revised as the writing project develops. It means thinking of structure as malleable rather than inevitable; it means anticipating the possibility that revision will yield unforeseen insights that require starting the planning process over again from scratch; it means acknowledging that the failure of the original outline may well be proof that learning has occurred. The creative mind always has a plan, but that plan always includes planning on replanning.

On Structure

John McPhee, the author of twenty-nine books and a staff writer for the *New Yorker* since 1965, is one of the most prolific and influential writers of contemporary nonfiction—which he prefers to call "factual writing." He's written books about subjects as diverse as the geography of the western United States (*Annals of the Former World*); efforts to contain natural destruction caused by lava, water, and mountainside debris flow (*The Control of Nature*); people who work in freight transportation (*Uncommon Carriers*); and even a rogue American professor whose covert actions played a central role in preserving dissident Soviet art (*The Ransom of Russian Art*). While we admire McPhee's work, we draw your attention to him here because McPhee may well be the best writing teacher on the planet. His former students, who collectively have published over 430 books, include David Remnick, a Pulitzer Prize winner and editor-in-chief of the *New Yorker*; Richard Stengel and Jim Kelly, each of whom has served as managing editor of *Time*; Eric Schlosser, author of *Fast Food Nation*; and Richard Preston, author of *The Hot Zone*.

Why are McPhee's students so successful?

One reason is how McPhee trains them to think about structure. In a *New Yorker* essay simply titled "Structure," McPhee offers lessons about writing and its organization that were previously reserved for the small number of Princeton University students lucky enough to get a seat in one of his seminars. He begins the essay by describing the crisis of confidence he faced early in his career when he settled in to write a long article about the Pine Barrens of New Jersey, which he'd been researching for eight months. "I had assembled enough material to fill a silo," he recalls, "and now I had no idea what to do with it." He spent two weeks lying on his back on a picnic table, stymied by panic, unable to see a way to organize his thoughts. Finally, he realized that an elderly native of the Pine Barrens, Fred Brown, had connections to most of the topics he wanted to discuss, so McPhee decided he could begin the essay by describing his first encounter with Brown and then connect each theme to various forays he and Brown made together. Having solved his structure problem, McPhee got off the picnic table and began to write. "Structure," he says, "has preoccupied me in every project I have undertaken since."

For four decades, McPhee has taught his students that structure should be "strong, sound, and artful" and that it is possible to "build a structure in such a way that it causes people to want to keep turning pages." Nonfiction, in other words, can be as absorbing as a good novel if the structure is right. To teach his students how to find the right structure, McPhee compares preparing to write to preparing to cook.

> The approach to structure in factual writing is like return-
> ing from a grocery store with materials you intend to cook
> for dinner. You set them out on the kitchen counter, and
> what's there is what you deal with, and all you deal with.
> If something is red and globular, you don't call it a tomato
> if it's a bell pepper.

In other words, to plan the structure of a piece of writing, you have to gather all the pieces of your research and lay them out so you can see them at a glance. And as you figure out the structure, you can only work with the facts in front of you.

Before he had a computer, McPhee would type all of his notes, study them, separate them into piles so that his facts were literally in front of him. Then, he would distill them into a set of several dozen index cards. On each card he would write two or three code words that indicated to him a component of the story he wanted to tell. The codes might refer to a location (UNY for upstate New York) or to an event or anecdote ("Upset Rapid"). His office furniture at the time included "a standard sheet of plywood—thirty-two square feet—on two sawhorses." He would scatter his index cards face up on the plywood, anchoring a few pieces and moving the others around until he figured out how to organize the work in ways that were both strong and artful.

Rebecca Skloot, author of *The Immortal Life of Henrietta Lacks*, regularly uses McPhee's essay "Travels in Georgia" to teach structure to her writing students. She shows her students that, if you map the narrative of "Travels in Georgia," you can see that it spirals in time: McPhee begins in the middle of the story, goes forward briefly, and then loops backward in time. By the middle of the essay, McPhee has brought his account back to where it started, and from that point on, he moves the narrative steadily forward in time. Skloot explains that McPhee calls this "the lowercase *e* structure," and she promises that once you recognize it, you'll see it everywhere—in movies, novels, and *New Yorker* articles. (Skloot's exercise teaches her students to read as writers, a topic discussed in our essay "On Reading as a Writer."

Like McPhee, Skloot has a story about grappling for a long time with a writing task. In her case, though, she had to figure out how to organize ten years of research that she had collected for her book. She struggled because she was writing about multiple time periods and had three different narratives: the story of Henrietta Lacks, an African American woman who developed cervical cancer and died at the age of thirty-one in 1951; the story of Lacks's cancer cells, which were cultured without Lacks's consent and continue to be used to this day in medical research; and the story of Lacks's family, especially her daughter, Deborah, who for much of her life did not know that her mother's cells were alive in medical labs all over the world.

Skloot's breakthrough in organizing her research into a readable book came when she was watching *Hurricane*, a movie about the boxer Hurricane Carter, who was falsely convicted of a triple homicide in 1966. Skloot saw that the film braided three different narratives together: the story of Carter's conviction; the story of Carter's twenty years in prison; and the story of how a Brooklyn teen and three Canadian activists successfully lobbied to have Carter's case reopened. She wrote notes about the film's scenes on colored-coded index cards—one color for each of the three storylines—and laid them out on her bed according to where the scenes occurred in the film. Then she placed the color-coded index cards for the three strands of her own book on top of the cards for *Hurricane*. She saw that the film jumped more quickly between the three strands of narrative than her book manuscript did, and that the rapidity of those jumps helped sustain the momentum of each line of the intertwined narrative. When Skloot finally realized how to weave together the pieces of her own narrative, she photographed the rows of colored index cards for posterity. (See this photograph on next page.)

For Skloot to structure her ten years of research as a braided narrative, she had to throw a lot of material away, just as McPhee did when he was sorting the siloful of material he'd collected for his article on the

Rebecca Skloot's note cards for *The Immortal Life of Henrietta Lacks*, arranged on her bed.

Pine Barrens. Neither Skloot nor McPhee thought that time spent collecting unused research was wasted, however. McPhee's former student Eric Schlosser recalled how McPhee taught him that deciding what *not* to include is a crucial and often unrecognized step in defining structure. McPhee told him, "Your writing should be like an iceberg." What ends up on the printed page is just the tip of the iceberg, while beneath the surface is all the research, reading, and writing that was done to generate the final product. The reader may not be able to see that work, but it's there—the hidden substructure of the writer's visible work.

. . . . .

In school, the operating assumption is often that there is one structure with which students should work: introduction, body, conclusion. Note that this approach *begins* by prescribing an organizing structure, no matter what the subject or project is, whereas the examples from McPhee and Skloot show the structure emerging *after* the research process is finished or well underway. In line with these examples, we think that the best time for you to make decisions about structure is *after* you've formulated the question you want to answer, the problem or puzzle you want to solve, or the idea you want to explore, and *after* you've taken time to do substantial research. Once you've gathered your materials, then you can experiment. You can move the ideas around on paper or on digital index cards, testing out possibilities. You can consider whether there's an organic order to your project. You can think about how different parts of your essay seem connected and about how you can best make those connections meaningful to your readers. Then, when you've mapped a possible structure, step back and think carefully about what you see.

Imagine that your index cards define a path readers will follow as you guide them through the development of your thoughts, and consider these questions:

- What shape is the path? Is it straight and simple because you're writing a descriptive essay ("there's this and that and the other thing")? Given the assignment or your ambitions, is this structure sufficient?

- Does the path of your project take interesting turns? Is there a step that takes your thoughts in a new direction? Are there turns that might pivot on a qualifying word or phrase such as *but, however,* or *on the other hand*?

- Does the path turn more than once? Does it double back on itself? Does it have a "lowercase *e* structure"? Does it braid three or more strands together?

- Is there a fork in the path? Is there a moment where you entertain multiple options?

- Are there gaps? Does the path abruptly change direction or miss a step between a given section and the one that follows?

- Are there pieces or ideas that don't fit anywhere? Does it make sense to include the material as a digression that eventually leads back to the main path? Would a digression contribute to the essay's overall project?

- Is there a dead end, a place where the path hits a brick wall or goes off a cliff? If so, can you use this dead end to rethink how you've addressed your essay's question or problem?

After remapping the path of your project, step back even further and consider whether the structure you've now laid out is "strong, sound, and artful." We also recommend asking the following questions:

- Where do you see evidence of your curiosity? Your creativity? Your skill at making connections between sources and ideas? Your depth of knowledge? Your mastery of detail?

- If these aren't evident, how could you rework your project? Should you do more research? Formulate a different question or problem?

- Are there places where you ignored information that would have complicated the structure or the path? Are there places where you chose the easier route?

Practice Session One

Researching

We recently discovered the *Nieman Storyboard* Web site, which we recommend for a number of reasons. It not only gathers notable examples of narrative journalism but also includes a series of "Essays on Craft" in which experienced journalists explain how they have moved a story from initial idea to final publication. In addition, there's a series called "Why's This So Good?" in which writers discuss what they value in the work of a fellow writer. You can't go wrong on *Nieman Storyboard*. Explore the site for at least 20 minutes. Then select at least three essays that intrigue you and read them.

Practice Session Two

Reading

If you search on *Nieman Storyboard*, you'll find Adam Hochschild's piece on John McPhee's craft, "'Why's This So Good?' No. 61: John McPhee and the Archdruid." What McPhee calls "structure," Hochschild calls "engineering." Hochschild explains: "A key secret of McPhee's ability to make us care about his vast and improbable range of subject matter lies in his engineering. From the pilings beneath the foundations to the beams that support the rooftop observation deck, he is the master builder of literary skyscrapers."

As you read the essay about McPhee, pay attention to Hochschild's descriptions of the structure of his favorite works. For example, Hochschild describes *Encounters with the Archdruid* as having been built using a structure that McPhee described as:

$$\frac{ABC}{D}$$

After you've read Hochschild's essay once through, spend at least 30 minutes reviewing his descriptions of four of McPhee's other works: a profile of Thomas Hoving; the book *Levels of the Game*; and the articles "In Search of Marvin Gardens" and "A Forager." Make simple sketches to represent the structure of each of these four works.

Practice Session Three

Reading

Select and read any one of the readings included in this book or, if you prefer, an article from the "Notable Narratives" section of *Nieman Storyboard*. Then spend at least 30 minutes making a detailed map of the essay's structure using any medium you like—a computer graphics program, pen and pencil, crayon and cardboard, or index cards on a bedspread. The map you make should highlight what surprised or impressed you about the writer's structural choices.

Practice Session Four

Writing

Go through your personal archive of papers you've written and select at least three of them. Then make a map or sketch of the structure of each one. Once you're done, step back and think about the relationship between the maps or sketches you generated for this exercise and the ones you generated for Practice Sessions Two and Three above. Your own essays will probably be shorter than Hochschild's essay or the other essays on *Nieman Storyboard*, but what other differences are there between the structure of your writing and the structure of essays by professional writers? Write an essay that uses the maps of your own writing and those you made for the previous exercises as material for speculating about the relationship between structure and thought.

EXPLORE

David Dobbs describes the structure of Michael Lewis's essay about the Greek financial crisis as "an agile manipulation of a standard trip-to-Oz story form." It can be hard to step back and see the structure of a piece of writing as a whole, but Dobbs's comparison seems obvious after the fact. To help you develop a sense for structure, we invite you to read Lewis's essay alongside Dobbs's analysis, or to read McPhee's "Structure" as well as his interview in the *Paris Review*. While Dobbs and McPhee are concerned with the big picture, the manuscript pages on Joyce Carol Oates's blog provide a more detailed picture of how a fiction writer invents and refines the shape of a novel by making sketches of towns, charts of characters, and lists of scenes and their arrangement.

Dobbs, David. "'Why's This So Good?' No. 15: Michael Lewis' Greek Odyssey." *Nieman Storyboard*. 11 Oct. 2011. Web.

Lewis, Michael. "Beware of Greeks Bearing Bonds." *Vanity Fair*. Oct. 2010. Web.

McPhee, John. "John McPhee, The Art of Nonfiction No. 3." Interview by Peter Hessler. *Paris Review*. 192 Spring 2010. Web.

McPhee, John. "Structure." *New Yorker*. 14 Jan. 2014. Web.

Oates, Joyce Carol. "Manuscripts," "Research and Bibliography." *Celestial Timepiece: The Joyce Carol Oates Home Page*. Web.

On Revising

Every writing lesson in *Habits of the Creative Mind* is implicitly connected to revision. We've repeatedly encouraged you to look and look again. (Another name for the act of reseeing is "revision.") We showed you how being curious requires that you peer around corners, disappear down rabbit holes, and explore the unknown in order to replace old assumptions or confusions with new knowledge and understanding. We showed you that creative habits of mind include being able to reflect on (that is, to resee) how you express yourself and even how you think. In a multitude of ways, reseeing and revising are fundamental practices for writers.

So why include a separate essay on revision? Two reasons, really. First, people who take writing seriously know that writing *is* revising. Indeed, the claim that "there is no such thing as good writing, only good rewriting" is so widely acknowledged by writers that it has been attributed to Robert Graves, Louis Brandeis, Isaac Bashevis Singer, William Zinsser, and Roald Dahl. Second, we know that revision is not a single stage in the writing process but a range of practices that occur throughout the writing process. The distinction is worth driving home, we've found, because many students mistakenly believe that revising is simply correcting errors and tidying up unclear sentences that a teacher marked in an essay draft. In our view this is copyediting, not revision, and it misrepresents true revision.

As writers, we know that rethinking, reseeing, and rewriting can happen at any step in producing a work of writing. In fact, before we drafted the opening paragraphs of *this* essay, we composed two different preliminary outlines and two different introductions. When we determined that neither of those versions worked, we scrapped them and started over. This example isn't an anomaly; writers regularly spiral back to rethink what they've done, entirely abandoning earlier work and beginning all over again. Moments of revision can occur as soon as you've thought your first thought or written your first word; they can occur just when you think you're writing your final sentence; and they can occur anywhere between those two points.

If revision isn't correcting grammatical mistakes and isn't a single step in a linear process, then what is it? We'd like to help you resee revision by offering descriptions and examples of a variety of ways of returning to the writing you've already completed with the goal of improving it. You won't use all of these practices every time you rewrite, but you're quite likely to use more than one as you work over what you've written.

RETHINKING

As essayists and academic writers, when we contemplate a new project, we spend a lot of time reading, exploring, researching, learning, and thinking before we begin a formal draft. And yet, after composing the first pages or even the entire first draft, we may still find our work unsatisfactory because, in the process of writing about our chosen topic, we have begun to question our original position. Rethinking motivates us to revise globally—to rework our ideas rather than tinker away at surface corrections.

What's the difference between rethinking and tinkering? It's difficult to point to a published example of the former because rethinking typically occurs before publication and thus remains hidden from readers. But writer and blogger Ta-Nehisi Coates makes a practice of rethinking his opinions in public, so we'll look at a moment when he felt obligated to acknowledge that new events had shifted his perspective.

Coates's essay "Fear of a Black President" contends with a paradox at the heart of President Obama's first term in office: "As a candidate, Barack Obama said we needed to reckon with race and with America's original sin, slavery. But as our first black president, he has avoided mention of race almost entirely." To illustrate how constraining this paradox is, Coates looks at a rare public statement on race by Obama in which the president puts that topic—and his own race—at the center of the nation's attention.

On March 23, 2012, Obama was asked to comment on the shooting death of an unarmed black teenager, Trayvon Martin, that had occurred a month earlier in Florida. George Zimmerman, a member of a neighborhood watch patrol, claimed to have shot Martin in self-defense when the young man responded violently to being detained. Obama briefly addressed the uproar that followed Martin's death, saying: "When I think about this boy, I think about my own kids, and I think every parent in America should be able to understand why it is absolutely imperative that we investigate every aspect of this, and that everybody pulls together—federal, state, and local—to figure out exactly how this tragedy happened." Obama closed with the following statement: "But my main message is to the parents of Trayvon Martin. If I had a son, he'd look like Trayvon. I think they are right to expect that all of us as Americans are going to take this with the seriousness it deserves, and that we're going to get to the bottom of exactly what happened." As mild, measured, and brief as Obama's comments were, a media frenzy ensued. Radio shock jocks and cable TV pundits accused the president of lighting the match that could start a race war. Far from finding Obama's response incendiary, Coates details in "Fear of a Black President" his own frustration with Obama for making such moderate comments and for avoiding an open discussion of race.

As strong as his criticism of Obama was in "Fear of a Black President," Coates displayed his commitment to rethinking in a blog post he wrote after Obama responded to the news that George Zimmerman had been acquitted of second-degree murder and manslaughter charges on July 19, 2013. In this instance, Coates says, Obama spoke *as* an African American and *for* African Americans to explain their suffering over the verdict. We think it's worth quoting Obama's statement in full.

> You know, when Trayvon Martin was first shot I said that this could have been my son. Another way of saying that is Trayvon Martin could have been me 35 years ago. And when you think about why, in the African American community at least, there's a lot of pain around what happened here, I think it's important to recognize that the African American community is looking at this issue through a set of experiences and a history that doesn't go away.
>
> There are very few African American men in this country who haven't had the experience of being followed when they were shopping in a department store. That includes me. There are very few African American men who haven't had the experience of walking across the street and hearing the locks click on the doors of cars. That happens to me—at least before I was a senator. There are very few African Americans who haven't had the experience of getting on an elevator

and a woman clutching her purse nervously and holding her breath until she had a chance to get off. That happens often.

And I don't want to exaggerate this, but those sets of experiences inform how the African American community interprets what happened one night in Florida. And it's inescapable for people to bring those experiences to bear. The African American community is also knowledgeable that there is a history of racial disparities in the application of our criminal laws—everything from the death penalty to enforcement of our drug laws. And that ends up having an impact in terms of how people interpret the case.

Coates's blog post, "Considering the President's Comments on Racial Profiling," praises Obama for having the courage to speak out personally about the experience of racism: "No president has ever done this before. It does not matter that the competition is limited. The impact of the highest official in the country directly feeling your pain, because it is his pain, is real. And it is happening now." Coates's willingness to change his mind and express his gratitude sets him apart from many other political-opinion journalists. He's committed to presenting himself as an avid learner, and he refuses the pundit's pretense of certainty.

When you're writing for school, it may seem that you don't have the opportunity that Coates has as a blogger to rethink and rewrite; once a paper is handed in, there's usually no going back. But the truth is that every time you sit down to write, you have the opportunity to seek out new information that will complicate or alter what you were thinking before you started writing. This is the lesson we'd like you to take from Coates's work: in order to begin the process of rethinking what you've written, you need to seek out new information and be open to questioning everything, even your own certainties.

RESTRUCTURING

Often first drafts make sense to the writer, but the logic behind what has been written isn't yet clear enough for a reader to follow. This can be caused by gaps in the research or argument; lack of attention to what readers need to know and when they need to know it; too much information or too many ideas about one topic and not enough about another; or the lack of good transitions. These problems can be addressed through revision that focuses on structure.

The history of F. Scott Fitzgerald's *The Great Gatsby* reveals what a difference structural revisions can make. Fitzgerald sent the manuscript of his novel to his editor, Maxwell Perkins, who immediately saw that it was brilliant but flawed. First of all, the character of Gatsby was too physically vague. "The reader's eyes can never quite focus upon him, his outlines are dim," he wrote to Fitzgerald. "Now everything about Gatsby is more or less a mystery . . . , and this may be somewhat of an artistic intention, but I think it is mistaken." Fitzgerald's reply indicates that defining Gatsby's character was something he hadn't been able to accomplish in the first draft: "*I myself didn't know what Gatsby looked like or was engaged in* & you felt it." Perkins's second complaint about Fitzgerald's presentation of Gatsby was that the character's whole history—his apprenticeship on Dan Cody's yacht, his time in the army, his romance with Daisy, and his past as an "Oxford man"—all tumbled out in one long monologue in the penultimate chapter.

What to do? Perkins suggested that Fitzgerald reorganize the *whole* novel: "you can't avoid the biography altogether. I thought you might find ways to let the truth of some of his claims like 'Oxford' and his army career come out bit by bit in the course of actual narrative." Fitzgerald followed this advice, weaving bits of Gatsby's past more gracefully into earlier chapters. The result? *The Great Gatsby*, first published in 1925, has now sold over twenty-five million copies and is widely considered an enduring example of the Great American Novel.

Notice that Perkins's advice about revising *Gatsby* focused on creating a better experience for the reader. Notice, too, that Fitzgerald couldn't see what *The Great Gatsby* needed until he got the feedback that made it possible for him to view the novel through the eyes of another. (we discuss how to provide and how to respond to such feedback on p. 216)

The Post-Draft Outline

While outside feedback is essential to the revision process, there is a way to defamiliarize your own writing to the point that you can make its implicit structure explicit and, simultaneously, produce a map that can direct your revisions. The way to do this is to produce a "post-draft outline," so called because, instead of making it before you begin to write your draft, you make it after the draft is completed.

The process for making a post-draft outline is straightforward: sequentially number every paragraph in your draft, and then write a one-sentence statement about the main idea or point in each paragraph. When you're done, you'll be able to see the structure of your draft as a whole, which you can then use in a variety of ways to help you assess the quality of the experience you've created for your reader.

1. Your outline gives you a snapshot of the path your draft has taken. To develop this snapshot, read the sentences of your post-draft outline in order, and then read the post-draft outline again, this time thinking through the following questions (which also appear in our essay "On Structure" on pp. 200–05):

- Is the path a straight line? Does it proceed by a series of *and* connections (that is, there's this and this and this)?

- Does the path turn? Is there a paragraph that qualifies what has gone before or takes the conversation in a new direction? Are there sentences or paragraphs that pivot—or could pivot—on a qualifying word or phrase such as *but, however,* or *although*?

- Does the path turn more than once? Does it double back on itself?

- Is there a fork in the path? Is there a moment where more than one option is entertained?

- Is there a paragraph that pivots on words or phrases such as *or, perhaps,* or *what if*? that introduce more than one possible outcome or position?

- Are there gaps? Does the path abruptly change direction or miss a step between a given paragraph and the one that follows?

- Are there digressions, places where there's a loop off the path that eventually returns to the main path? If the answer is yes, does each digression contribute to the essay's overall project? (Don't assume the answer to this last question is no. In restructuring, some digressions can become central to the newly organized draft.)

- Is there a dead end, a place where the path hits a brick wall or goes off a cliff, never to return? (Again, don't assume that this is necessarily a bad thing; in restructuring, there are times when dead ends can be repurposed to improve your handling of your essay's question or problem.)

After you have a sense of the path you took in your draft you can begin to sketch plans for structural revision.

2. Before you begin to rewrite, return to the draft and reassess it as a snapshot of your mind at work on a problem.

- Where is your curiosity in evidence? Your creativity? Your skill at putting original sources into conversation? Your interest in language? Your mastery of detail? How can these be made more evident in revision?

- Spend some time thinking about what you've left out of your draft. Are there places in the draft where you ignored ideas or information that would have complicated the journey? Where you chose to go where you were expected to go instead of where your thinking was pointing you? What can you do now to introduce ideas and information that would make your essay more interesting?

- Could anyone else have written the draft, or is it obvious to you that it's *yours*? How can you make the essay even more your own?

By using the post-draft outline in this way, you'll be serving as your own Maxwell Perkins: you'll assess both what your draft is and what it might become through structural revision.

LETTING GO

Cutting sentences and paragraphs, or cutting everything and starting over from scratch: has there ever been a writer who enjoys this part of the writing process? Has there ever been a writer of note who could skip the cross-out, the toss, the "Ctrl-A, Delete"? No. But the difference between beginning writers and experienced writers is that experienced writers have practiced encountering the newly blank screen; they know that the blinking cursor can be set in motion once again and that there are always more words out there somewhere. Beginning writers, without much practice starting over, tend to fear the blank screen and to see deleted work as wasted time rather than as an unavoidable part of letting the mind work on a problem.

To encourage our students to see letting go as a habit of creative minds, we tell a story about going to hear Nobel Prize–winning writer Toni Morrison read from a work in progress. Morrison approached the lectern, paused, and then told the audience that the year before she'd completed well over a hundred pages of the novel's manuscript, but that she stood before us that night to read from the forty or so pages she had left. What had happened? Revision happened. Morrison had set out in one direction and then had to spend a year peeling off pages and pages of what she'd written until she found work that met her standards.

The Morrison anecdote can be read as an extension of the quote we opened this essay with: "there is no such thing as good writing, only good rewriting," and all good rewriting involves letting go. We hear this idea repeated in Colette's definition of an author: "Put down every-thing that comes into your head and then you're a writer. But an author is one who can judge his own stuff's worth, without pity, and destroy most of it." Novelist Anne Lamott makes this point about letting go in perhaps its bluntest form in her popular book *Bird by Bird*, where she asserts that all good writers write "shitty first drafts," drafts that they know will be thrown away. "This," she says, "is how they end up with good second drafts and terrific third drafts."

While Lamott's specific recommendations may not apply to all writing or to all writers, we believe there's real value in her advice to view draft after draft as practice, as work that may never see the light of day but that is valuable nonetheless. If you give yourself sufficient time to use writing to help yourself think, knowing that you are going to get rid of most of it before anyone else sees it, then maybe, as Lamott writes, you'll find "something in the very last line of the very last paragraph on page six that you just love, that is so beautiful or wild that you now know what you're supposed to be writing about, more or less, or in what direction you might go—but there was no way to get to this without first getting through the first five and a half pages."

GETTING FEEDBACK

Most writers don't publish until after they've gotten feedback from friends, colleagues, and editors. We think that getting feedback from people whose work you admire is probably *the most important revision practice of all.*

To acheive this Kerry Walk, a teacher we admire, recommends that cover letters accompany all drafts submitted for feedback. If you were to compose such a cover letter, Walk would advise you to state:

- the main question or problem your writing seeks to address;
- the idea or point you feel you've made most successfully;
- the idea or point you feel you need help with;
- your number one concern about your paper that you'd like your reader to answer for you; and
- any questions you have about how or where to start your revision.

The advantage of a cover letter of this kind is that it gives your reader a clear sense of how you see your draft and where you think it needs work. Your reader need not agree with your assessment, but the letter gives your reader a way to gauge his or her response to what you've written and to adjust that response accordingly.

TAKING A BREAK

The best way to see your writing with fresh eyes is to set your draft aside—for a day if that's all you have, or for longer if possible. When you pick it up again, you'll be able to see more clearly what's working and what's not. And the feedback you've received, which may have caught you off guard at first, may now seem more reasonable. The point is to give yourself time to reenergize, so that you don't resort to tinkering on the edges of your writing when you really need to be rethinking and restructuring your first draft.

Prolific writer Neil Gaiman explains taking a break also allows you to return to your work as a reader, instead of as its writer. Once a draft is done, he advises, "put it away until you can read it with new eyes. . . . Put it in a drawer and write other things. When you're ready, pick it up and read it as if you've never read it before. If there are things you aren't satisfied with as a reader, go in and fix them as a writer: that's revision." By "fix them as a writer," he means rethinking, restructuring, letting go of what's not working, getting feedback, writing again, polishing—doing whatever it takes to move the writing forward.

Practice Session One

Reflecting

Spend at least 20 minutes reflecting on your experiences with revision and your thoughts about trying new approaches. What is your typical approach to revision? Which of the strategies that we describe in this essay have you tried before? Which approach seems easiest for you? Which approach seems most challenging or unsettling?

Now commit to setting aside the time you need to practice revision in new ways. Make a resolution to try at least three of these strategies—rethinking, restructuring, post-draft outlining, letting go, getting feedback, taking a break—before handing in your next paper. Which three do you think you'll try?

Practice Session Two

Researching

Do an online image search for "manuscript revisions." You'll get many pages of results. Explore, clicking on images of manuscripts that call out to you and visiting the pages where they are embedded. Look for examples from writers you admire. Then spend at least 30 minutes examining several images carefully, taking notes on how various writers revise. What can you learn about writing and revision by looking at marked-up manuscript pages?

Writing

Write an essay that examines three or more of the manuscript revisions you find most interesting. Explain what you've learned from these specific examples about various processes for revising.

Practice Session Three

Writing

Take a final draft that you wrote recently and see if you can cut it by at least 25 percent without losing the main argument or ideas. After you've cut your original piece by a quarter, compare the original version to the shorter, revised one. What's better about the more concise version? What's better about the longer one?

Then try cutting the shortened version by 25 percent again. What happens to your argument or ideas this time?

Practice Session Four

Revising

If you have a draft you're presently working on, follow the advice in "Getting Feedback" and find a tutor, teacher, or fellow student who agrees to give you feedback. Spend at least 20 minutes writing a one-page, single-spaced cover letter that explains your concerns about the draft. Give this letter to your reader with a copy of the draft, and schedule a meeting to discuss his or her feedback.

After you've received your reader's feedback, figure out what kind of revision the feedback suggests is most necessary: Should you try rethinking, restructuring, letting go, or a combination of strategies? Then revise.

EXPLORE

The word *revision* refers to many practices—from rethinking and restructuring to polishing sentences. For Adrienne Rich, revision is a process of reading and writing—reseeing texts from the past to make new thoughts, stories, and poems possible. Other forms of revision, especially sentence-level editing, have become essential elements of writing due to advances in technology. Craig Fehrman describes the typewriters emergence as a writing tool at the beginning of the twentieth century. You can see examples of famous writers' manuscript revisions at the *Bad Penny Review* and the *Paris Review* Web sites. At the *Paris Review*, we recommend looking at the work of Salman Rushdie and Joan Didion.

Fehrman, Craig. "Revising Your Writing Again? Blame the Modernists." *Boston Globe*. 30 June 2013. Web.

Rich, Adrienne. "When We Dead Awaken: Writing as Re-vision." *College English* 34.1 (October 1972). 18–30. Print.

"Murdering Your Darlings: Writers' Revisions." *A Bad Penny Review*. Web.

"Interviews." *Paris Review*. Web.
    (To get to the manuscript files, first select an interview; then click on the "view a manuscript page" button in the menu under the title. Zoom in on the pages to read them.)

On Learning from Failure

When we watch children building a sandcastle on a summer beach, we see creativity in action. The process seems so simple. The castle grows and becomes more elaborate—with moats, towers, turrets, and carefully laid rows of shells—until late in the day it's abandoned, to be reclaimed by the tide before morning. If we watch more closely, however, we can see that the activity of building is more than just adding more and more pieces.

When we look again we notice how often things go wrong. An unexpected wave knocks down an hour's worth of building. A toddler wanders over from a neighboring beach blanket and causes more destruction. The sand dries and walls crumble. Unless disagreements and exhaustion take over, we also see the kids recover from failures. They experiment to figure out how to build a better moat to stay the tide. The toddler is distracted by collecting shells. A bucket brigade creates a pile of wetter sand. Or the construction project is moved up or down the beach to a better location. When children are at play, often enough they react to failures as opportunities for invention. They're not afraid of failure, because the stakes are low. The point is simply to have fun.

However, once we become adults, we're likely to avoid situations where the prospect of failure is high. Whether at work or school, most of us fear tackling a complex problem in front of our peers because of the possible consequences of failing: i.e. embarrassment, shame, a lower grade, a demotion. This fear of failure stifles creativity and innovation.

Not all people respond to fear of failure in the same way, though. In fact, creative people tend to have an attitude toward failure that's more like the kids on the beach than like a typical adult trying to solve a problem at work or a student trying to figure out what the teacher wants him to say. In *What the Best College Students Do*, Ken Bain argues that what sets the best students apart from the rest is their willingness to acknowledge failures, to explore them, and to learn from them. Unlike less creative people, they didn't deny their mistakes or get defensive about errors.

Where does this ability to bounce back from failure come from? To answer this question, Bain points to a study that compared two groups of ten-year-olds who were each given a series of puzzles. The first eight problems required the students to make real effort, but the challenges matched the students' age and education level. The next four problems were designed to be too hard for the students to solve. Over the first eight problems, there were no differences in how the groups performed; both groups talked about the problems as they worked through them, had fun, and came up with roughly the same number of correct solutions. On the second set of problems, however, the groups' reactions differed greatly from each other. The first group got frustrated, complained, and tried to change the rules; they started to make surprisingly poor choices, shifted their focus away from the problems, and gave up. By contrast, the second group continued to encourage each other, tested different approaches, and seemed to thrive on the challenge, even though they couldn't solve the hard problems either.

What caused the divergent responses? The students were grouped by researchers based on their attitudes toward intelligence. The first group had a fixed view of intelligence and the second group believed, conversely, that with effort you could become smarter. (As shorthand, we call members of the first group the "knowers" and members of the second group the "learners.") When the knowers faced failure, they looked for an escape route, because their failures called their intelligence into question; they went into mental tailspins, reverting to strategies that might be expected from preschoolers. The learners didn't take failure personally. Because they believed they could develop intelligence, working on the problems was its own reward. Even if they never found solutions, they valued learning things along the way.

Obviously, we can't just snap our fingers and change ingrained beliefs and patterns of behavior. And we can't change the fact that in some situations, when the stakes are immediate and high, it's nearly impossible to sustain an impersonal attitude toward failure. We believe, however, that it is possible to cultivate more creative attitudes toward failure through practice, and one of the most important locations for such practice in school assignments where time is allowed for experimentation and revision—such as the writing assignments (which we call "practice sessions") provided throughout *Habits of the Creative Mind*.

You've probably noticed that these practice sessions ask open questions or pose messy problems that can't be responded to simply with facts or by following a formula to a right answer.

In our writing classes, we encourage students to pursue what interests them, and we're thrilled when they set aside their fears and egos and risk exploring really knotty problems. In the end, even if their efforts come to naught, these students tend to learn from their mistakes. They figure out what went wrong and decide what they'll do differently the next time.

When we learn from failure, we discover that practice never ends.

Practice Session One

Reflecting

As a thought experiment, look back at what kind of student you were in middle school and in high school. Then imagine what school would have been like for you if grades hadn't mattered to parents or college admissions committees. Would you have taken more risks as a writer and learner, or would you have worked less?

Then set aside at least 30 minutes to reflect on the kind of school that could foster an environment in which students, including you, would be willing both to work hard and to "fail big." At your college, are there classes, teachers, or majors that encourage or even require students to take creative and intellectual risks?

Practice Session Two

Reading

In "Fail Better," an essay about writing, Zadie Smith identifies the cliché as a small-scale example of literary failure. "What is a cliché," she asks, "except language passed down by Das Mann [the Man], used and shop-soiled by so many before you, and in no way the correct jumble of language for the intimate part of your vision you meant to express? With a cliché you have pandered to a shared understanding, you have taken a short-cut, you have represented what was pleasing and familiar rather than risked what was true and strange." This isn't the usual definition of failure, but it's a useful way of thinking about how to write well. While there are occasions when settling for the pleasing, familiar, and expected is the polite thing to do, success for a writer seeking new thoughts means having written something unfamiliar, unexpected, even unsettling—productively unsettling.

We'd like you to choose one of the readings we've included in this book and look for passages in which the writer is productively disruptive, rather than pleasing and familiar.

Then spend at least 40 minutes reflecting in writing about three passages from the reading that you think are particularly risky. Was the writer's risk worthwhile? Did the writer succeed or fail in Zadie Smith's terms? How about in your terms?

Practice Session Three

Reflecting

We imagine it would be pretty straightforward to ask you to write about a time when you learned from failure. So instead of asking you to write up an account of a moral or educational failure that ends in self-improvement—"and ever afterwards, I was a better person"—we'd like you to write about a time when you failed to understand a concept or idea. What were the consequences of your failure? What rewards, if any, followed from overcoming that failure?

EXPLORE

We know how failure feels: we're disappointed in ourselves and ashamed of disappointing others. Catherine Tice describes the regret and loss that has accompanied her failure to become a musician. When the British daily newspaper the *Guardian* asked seven writers to reflect on failure, however, few of them expressed regret. Most wrote about failure as an inherent part of writing, inseparable from creativity. While even these writers fall into platitudes about failure as opportunity, together their comments suggest a more nuanced view: it's possible to fail *well*—to learn from failure, to make use of it, and to continue to work. Learning from failure also concerns Paul Tough, who wonders whether schools that protect students from failure in the short term ultimately set them up for failure in the long term.

"Falling Short: Seven Writers Reflect on Failure." *Guardian.* 22 June 2013. Web.

Tice, Catherine. "A Brief History of a Musical Failure." *Granta.* 2 Oct. 2013.

Tough, Paul. "What If the Secret to Success Is Failure?" *New York Times Magazine.* 18 Sept. 2011. Web.

Curiosity at Work: Alison Bechdel and the Layered Complexity of the Graphic Narrative

When Alison Bechdel began publishing her comic strip, *Dykes to Watch Out For*, in 1983, the possibility of anyone becoming a graphic memoirist—that is, someone who tells her life story using words and images—wasn't on anyone's radar. In the 1980s, the comic form was restricted largely to "the funnies" in the newspapers and to serialized stories about superheroes sold on rotating racks in convenience stores. The readers of these stories were assumed to be mostly, if not exclusively, teenage boys. A young woman just out of college composing a comic strip that followed the lives of feminists, lesbians, and gays? Not exactly a foolproof plan for success.

And yet Bechdel, inspired by Howard Cruse's *Gay Comix*, was convinced that she could use the comic form in a new way and that she could reach a different demographic with different reading interests. While she didn't set out to produce a strip that would steadily gain popularity and influence, this is exactly what Bechdel ended up doing, by dint of her ability to unite her meticulously drawn characters (some of whom were suggested to her by her avid fans) with compelling lines of narrative that crisscrossed the genres of political commentary, melodrama, and humor. (Bechdel has described the strip as "half op-ed column and half endless, serialized Victorian novel.") And this unlikely project earned Bechdel a living and numerous awards during the twenty-five years she kept *Dykes to Watch Out For* in syndication.

Bechdel's breakout work as a graphic memoirist came in 2006 when she used her cartooning skills to tell her own coming-of-age story *Fun Home: A Family Tragicomic* (the title is a play on the fact that Bechdel grew up above a funeral home). The mystery that resides at the center of *Fun Home* is her father's apparent suicide, which occurred shortly after Bechdel left home for college. Told from the dual perspective of Bechdel as a child moving into adolescence and contending with her eccentric family in rural Pennsylvania, and Bechdel as a mature, successful cartoonist reflecting on the past, *Fun Home* provided Bechdel with a means of exploring her past that simply wasn't available to her in the comic strip form.

Bechdel's sustained attention to detail, which is evident in every cell and every word of her narrative, allows her to see all of the players in this tragicomic tale in their complex humanity: her father, who was a mortician, fastidious home restorer, strict disciplinarian, and guardian of a secret life; her mother, who was an actress, distant and miserable; her brothers; the townspeople; her first female lover in college; and herself. In an interview, Bechdel described how the graphic narrative allowed her to reproduce the multiple perspectives that are ever-present in real life: "Every moment that we're living and having experiences, we're bringing to bear all of the other experiences that we've had. This is what is exciting to me about graphic narrative, that you're able to do a layered complexity that I couldn't imagine doing with just writing."

An instant success, *Fun Home* was followed in 2012 by *Are You My Mother? A Comic Drama*, Bechdel's equally incisive exploration of her mother's life in the time before and after Bechdel's father's mysterious death. In 2014, Bechdel received a MacArthur "genius" grant in recognition of her ongoing work "changing our notions of the contemporary memoir and expanding the expressive potential of the graphic form."

ARGUING

....

I n college, it often seems that *writing* and *arguing* are treated as synonyms. Teachers ask their students to write arguments that present interesting claims supported by evidence. But how do good, thoughtful arguments come into being? Does the act of writing move a preformulated argument from your brain to the screen? Or is an argument created through the act of writing? The distinction matters: if argument comes first, then writing is simply transcription. If writing comes first, then the argument emerges through the process of engaging with and responding to writing—one's own and the writing of others.

While it would certainly be more convenient if writing simply recorded our already-formulated thoughts, we know as writers and as teachers of writing that the best arguments emerge over time—after one has read, thought, reflected, drafted, revised, started over, and reconsidered. Thus, in this section we invite you to think of an argument as a compelling idea that emerges over the course of an intellectual journey. We also invite you to imagine your mental life as a drama in which there's action, excitement, and passion that can motivate your writing. And we show how three influential scholarly arguments are driven by curiosity. The emphasis throughout is on producing writing that matters.

On Argument as Journey

....

When professors assign papers in college classes, they typically expect their students to hand in essays that make an argument. What they mean by "an argument," however, isn't always clear to the students. Many of our students arrive in our classes believing that writing an argument is like participating in a debate: they pick a side (their thesis); they gather evidence to support the side they've chosen; and they write as if trying to show that they are right and the other side is wrong. Winning, or getting a good grade, is the goal—not thoughtfulness, not discovery, not learning.

There are contexts within which this type of writing is entirely appropriate: a legal brief, for example, or a letter of complaint. But if you listen to pundits on cable news, follow congressional debates, or read the comment sections of online news sources, you'll see that such oppositional argumentation has become the norm in contemporary culture. In these venues, pushing ideas to their extremes, stirring up the emotions of one's allies and enemies, and scoring points with a pithy phrase or sound bite are more common than the reasoned exchange of ideas.

Because we have not found that practicing argument-as-debate leads to good academic writing—or to good journalism or good literary nonfiction—we propose, in its place, practicing argument as journey. What's the difference? In practicing argument as journey, you begin with the goal of answering a question or solving a problem (that's your destination); you ponder possible trajectories; you do research and rethink your plan; you learn more and more; you write, make mistakes, and head off in new and unanticipated directions; you make discoveries; you define a clearer purpose and path; you figure out how you want to answer your central question or solve your problem. Finally, the finished essay takes your readers on a journey to new ideas.

We'd like to walk you through an extended example of the argument as journey by looking at Elizabeth Kolbert's *Field Notes from a Catastrophe*, a book about global climate change. When Kolbert chose this topic, she knew she was stepping into contentious territory. Some people see climate change as an empirically verifiable threat to the future of life on this planet and others dismiss it as a false claim based in bad or inconclusive science. In the scientific community, the consensus is clear: global warming is a fact and it is caused by human activity—especially our reliance on burning carbon-based fuels such as coal, oil, wood, and natural gas. There is no such consensus in politics. Indeed as the scientific community has made it harder to deny that global warming is a fact, nonscientists of every stripe have shifted their doubt to the role humans play in changing the earth's climate. Given this political context, the project of writing about climate change poses a real challenge for Kolbert: if the National Academy of Sciences, which has been issuing warnings about impending environmental disaster since 1979, hasn't been able to convince people of the reality and danger of climate change and that humans have caused it, what could Kolbert—or any writer, for that matter—possibly say that would change readers' minds?

We admire *Field Notes from a Catastrophe* both because Kolbert sets out to see for herself the effects of climate change on the environment and because she takes her readers with her on a journey that is both physical and metaphysical. She seeks to examine evidence of climate change and also to contemplate why we have been so reluctant to acknowledge and act on signs of impending disaster. She begins by traveling above the Arctic Circle because the signs of warming are so striking there.

Kolbert visits the Alaskan village of Shishmaref, on an island off the coast of the Seward Peninsula, where native villagers once drove snowmobiles twenty miles out on the ice to hunt seals. By the time she gets there, the ice around the island is so soft that using snowmobiles is no longer safe, so the hunters use boats. The village, only twenty-two feet above sea level, has become so vulnerable to storm surges that the residents have decided to give up their way of life and relocate. Farther inland, near Fairbanks, Kolbert sees the effects of melting permafrost. Areas of ground that have been frozen since the beginning of the last glacial cycle are now threatened by thaw. Where the permafrost has been disturbed by the construction of buildings or roads, the land is especially vulnerable to warming; in some neighborhoods, foundations are degrading and houses are collapsing.

Kolbert then visits Iceland during the summer-melt season and meets members of the Icelandic Glaciological Society, who regularly survey the size of the country's three hundred or so glaciers. Though glaciers in Iceland continued to grow in the 1970s and 1980s, even as North American glaciers were shrinking, in the 1990s they, too, began to retreat. There have been glaciers on Iceland for two million years, Kolbert writes, but climate models predict that by the end of the next century there will be no more ice left to measure in Iceland.

Kolbert also travels to a research station on the Greenland ice sheet where scientists study ice cores drilled from the glacier. "A hundred and thirty-eight feet down," Kolbert writes, "there is snow that fell during the time of the American Civil War; 2,500 feet down, snow from the time of the Peloponnesian Wars, and, 5,350 feet down, snow from the days when the cave painters of Lascaux were slaughtering bison. At the very bottom, 10,000 feet down, there is snow that fell on central Greenland before the start of the last ice age, more than a hundred thousand years ago." Today, however, scientists at the research station are observing and measuring the gradual contraction of this massive glacier, which contains eight percent of the world's fresh water supply. If the Greenland ice sheet melts—and it is shrinking by twelve cubic miles each year—the consequences will be more than the loss of the history it contains. The ice sheet, Kolbert reports, contains enough water to raise sea levels around the world by twenty-three feet.

As Kolbert describes her physical journey, she also takes her readers on a journey through the science of climate change. Chapter by chapter, she carefully and clearly tells her readers how science explains the role humans have played in bringing about current warming trends and what these changes indicate about the future of the planet. After her account of Shishmaref, for instance, Kolbert summarizes the first major study of global warming, completed in 1979 by the National Academy of Sciences. A panel evaluated early studies on the effects of adding carbon dioxide to the atmosphere and concluded that continued increases in carbon dioxide would cause climate changes. They knew then that there was "no reason to believe that these changes [would] be negligible." If we had taken their warning seriously thirty years ago, we might have lessened the impact of climate change.

Later Kolbert explains why we should be concerned about the melting of perennial sea ice, which, unlike seasonal ice that forms and melts each year, remains frozen year-round. Back in 1979, perennial sea ice covered 1.7 billion acres—about the size of the continental United States. By the time Kolbert was writing her book in 2005, that area had shrunk by 250 million acres, an area about the combined size of Texas, New York, and Georgia. Why does this matter? Ice reflects sunlight away from the earth, while the dark open water of the ocean absorbs its heat. The more the perennial ice melts, exposing open ocean water, the more heat gets retained by the ocean, which then melts even more ice: the system feeds on itself, and the pace of warming speeds up. Small changes in the average temperature of ocean water, in other words, can lead to big changes in climate.

Having explained the science of the greenhouse effect and how industrialization—with its coal-burning factories, railroads, and power stations—started the process of global warming, Kolbert moves in her third chapter to discuss a contemporary symposium on climate change she attended in Iceland. None of the scientists at the symposium doubt that humans are responsible for warming the Earth's atmosphere. So Kolbert's journey through the science leads her and her readers to a *certainty* that too many politicians willingly deny: human consumption of carbon-based fuels has dramatically raised the level of carbon dioxide in the atmosphere and the consequences are changing life on earth.

Kolbert's journey does not end when she leaves the Arctic. She goes to England to see how climate change threatens the survival of butterflies and toads—and up to a quarter of the Earth's species. She learns how droughts long-ago caused the disappearance of ancient civilizations. She visits the Netherlands, where existing dikes will not hold back rising seawaters, so companies are manufacturing floating "amphibious" homes. She also travels to Burlington, Vermont, where a grassroots campaign to reduce greenhouse gas emissions by ten percent affirms the possibilities of local action, and also its limits. After all, whatever the residents of this small city accomplish is quickly offset by the rest of the world's continued expansion of energy use. Kolbert closes her book by arguing that humans have launched the planet into a new geological era. We should recognize, she says, that the Holocene, the epoch that began at the end of the Pleistocene about 11,700 years ago, is now over. We are in the dawn of the "Anthropocene," a "new age . . . defined by one creature—man—who [has] become so dominant that he [is] capable of altering the planet on a geological scale."

It's obvious throughout *Field Notes from a Catastrophe* that Kolbert thinks we must end our destructive addiction to fossil fuels, but she knows this argument has been made before to little effect. So she doesn't use her book to tell us what to do. Instead, the journey she takes us on makes the argument that the problem is so far along and so deeply entrenched in human behavior that it may not be solvable. When Kolbert arrives at the conclusion that we have entered the Anthropocene, it's clear that her readers have to choose what to do now. Denial, disbelief, or despair is always an option, but if we have been affected by reading Kolbert's book, we may at least be willing to accept responsibility for the problem we've created, and we may decide that trying to halt the pace or lessen the effect of the catastrophe is surely better than doing nothing at all. Indeed, if we're capable of causing disaster on a global scale, we may also be smart, creative, and lucky enough to come up with ways to ameliorate the consequences of this disaster. If we're truly lucky, we may even manage to delay the end of the Anthropocene era.

Practice Session One

Reading

We've just described how Elizabeth Kolbert takes a physical journey that she then transforms into an intellectual journey for her readers. Now we'd like you to choose one of the three readings included in this book and follow the author's intellectual journey. After you've read through the piece once, set aside at least 40 minutes to review it and take more detailed notes about how the journey unfolds. Pay attention to the sources—the people and texts the author cites. Step back and look at the decisions the author made about how to organize the text.

Then draw a map of the journey. When did it move straight ahead? When did you encounter turns of thought? Did the author send you off on digressions? Did they still feel like digressions after you'd followed them to their conclusions?

Reflecting

Spend at least 30 minutes writing reflectively about your own journey as a reader of the essay you selected. After reading and then reviewing the article, how far have you traveled intellectually? Were there places where your own thinking diverged from the path the author provided? Did reading the piece allow you to think about its central problem or question in a new way? Did it change your mind?

....

Practice Session Two

....

Research Essay

After reading our description of *Field Notes from a Catastrophe*, you now have a sense of Kolbert's view of the environmental challenges we face. The world we know will change radically during our lifetimes and, as a consequence of our collective choices and actions, may eventually become a planet that is uninhabitable by humans. The facts are menacing and disturbing, and they raise an important question: Can we construct rational hope in the face of climate change, and if so, how?

To compose an essay that offers a thoughtful answer to this question, you will first need to do additional reading. If you go out to the Web, you will find more on climate change than any single person could read in a lifetime. How do you separate what's worth considering from what's not? How do you determine what's compelling? We'd like you to spend at least 60 minutes searching online for a fact or a set of facts about climate change that you find both powerful and worthy of further consideration.

Write up a discussion of the facts you've uncovered. What makes the facts you're presenting more convincing than other facts regarding climate change? In completing your write-up, you are likely to need to do more reading, since facts only become convincing when placed in context.

Speculative Essay

Thinking seriously about climate change inevitably affects one's sense of the future. Given the evidence you've uncovered in your limited research, would you say that it is possible to construct a rational hope about the future? What compelling evidence would you point to that either supports or undermines the grounds for rational hope? In composing your response, stick to evidence that you find persuasive: this isn't an invitation to trade in generalities about "human nature"; it's an opportunity to consider the relationship between evidence, reason, and the future. Take your reader on a journey that reveals your mind at work on this problem.

EXPLORE

Writers we admire often begin their work with a question about why an event occurred, how an idea came into being, or how a problem might be resolved; then they lead their readers through facts, analysis, and ideas to arrive at their own answers. The list below offers examples of such complex journeys. Brian Cathcart guides us through a London murder case while pondering race and injustice. Ta-Nehisi Coates considers the evolution of racism in the United States, from slavery to Jim Crow and from segregation to racist housing policies, asking whether a discussion about financial reparations might bring about necessary change. Joan Didion reflects on how a set of fixed political opinions led to the US invasions of Iraq and Afghanistan. Venkatesh Rao invites readers to consider how having resources to waste serves creativity. And Rebecca Solnit walks us through the collapsed city of Detroit where she finds hope in how nature quickly reclaims the landscape.

Cathcart, Brian. "The Case of Stephen Lawrence." *Granta.* 6 Jan. 2012. Web.

Coates, Ta-Nehisi. "The Case for Reparations." *Atlantic.* 21 May 2014. Web.

Didion, Joan. "Fixed Opinions, or the Hinge of History." *New York Review of Books.* 16 Jan. 2003. Web.

Rao, Venkatesh. "Waste, Creativity, and Godwin's Corollary for Technology." *Ribbonfarm.* 23 Aug. 2012. Web.

Solnit, Rebecca. "Detroit Arcadia." *Harper's Magazine.* July 2007. Web.

On the Theater of the Mind

If you do a search on the phrase "theater of the mind," you'll find it has been used in two ways. Starting in 1956, "theater of the mind" was used by those wishing to argue that listening to radio dramas required more brainpower than watching dramas on the newer medium of television. Radio dramas, the argument went, are superior to television dramas because they take place not in the sound studio where the voice actors and sound effects people convene, but in the imaginations of the listening audience. The phrase is now used more generally to describe what happens when words, whether read or heard, and/or images, whether seen or described, create a dramatic scene in the mind of the beholder. And so one could say that advertising, which has long made the programming on radio and television possible, is convened in the theater of the mind, where it continuously prods audiences to imagine the better life that comes from consumption. Indeed, this search exercise itself demonstrates just how much advertising dominates the theater of the mind: the top search results for this phrase are not links to definitions or discussions of the debate over whether radio is superior to television or vice versa; they are for the sixth studio album by the hip-hop artist Ludacris, which happens to be named . . . *Theater of the Mind*.

We'd like to hijack the phrase "theater of the mind" and use it for an entirely different purpose. We grant that words and images can create a virtual theater *in* the mind. What we're interested in, though, is considering what becomes possible when you think of the flow of thoughts in your mind as participating in an open-ended drama that quietly plays out as you think through and about the ideas that are most important to you. It's a drama not just *in* your mind but *of* your mind. And you can use your writing to make the theater of your mind available for others to experience. Indeed, we'd say that this is one way to define the practice of creativity. When you write, you also shape an experience in the minds of your readers; your words stage the unfolding of an idea or an argument or a narrative.

When scientific and philosophic treatises were presented as dialogues, it was easier to see that there are dramatic, comedic, and even tragic aspects to the exchange of ideas. Galileo's use of the telescope, for example, shows how a new technology can generate new information that, under the right circumstances, triggers an internal dialogue—in the theater of the mind—that in turn leads to a whole new way of thinking and seeing.

In 1609, with the aid of one of the world's first telescopes, Galileo began to collect evidence suggesting that the earth was not at the center of what we now call the solar system. He first published his results as a scientific treatise in 1610. In 1632, in his book *The Dialogue Concerning the Two Chief World Systems*, Galileo presented his argument for a sun-centered model of the universe as a dialogue between three fictional characters: Salviati, a scholar whose research supports the idea that the sun is at the center of the universe; Simplicio, who believes that the earth is at the center of the universe, an idea initially presented by Aristotle and Ptolemy more than a thousand years earlier; and Sagredo, an intelligent bystander who asks questions as Salviati and Simplicio debate the merits of the two diametrically opposed models. Galileo used the form of the dialogue to make his own thinking process accessible to the greatest number of readers, most of whom were not involved in studying the heavens. He staged what would otherwise be an arcane discussion about measuring the movements of celestial bodies as a dialogue for a general audience, one that serves up humor and insults along with explanations of the significance of his discovery of craters on the moon. With his dialogue, Galileo made it possible for his readers to imagine that the sun was at the center of the universe regardless of what the Bible said or what the Church held. While Galileo's 1610 treatise presented the same fundamental threat to the Catholic Church's worldview, it was the publication of *The Dialogue* that led to Galileo's trial for heresy in 1633, where he was forced to recant his argument for the heliocentric universe and was then sentenced to house arrest for the remainder of his life.

Were you expecting a happier ending?

Our second example comes from ancient Greece. Plato, Socrates's prolific student, presented his teacher's philosophical reflections as a series of dialogues. Here, too, one finds the exchange of ideas depicted not as the dispassionate, orderly laying out of the steps that lead to some deep truth but as a wayward back-and-forth between Socrates, who is forever searching after the Good, and one or more interlocutors, who are inevitably shown to know much less than they claim to know. In *The Republic*, the Platonic dialogue that explores whether or not the State has the power to produce good, law-abiding citizens, Socrates tells a story about the difference between the world as it is seen by average people and the world as it is seen by those who seek the truth.

Socrates asks his listeners to imagine a cave in which prisoners are chained to the ground, their gaze fixed on the cave wall before them. Behind them there is a fire, and between the fire and the prisoners is a pathway traveled by people carrying life-size cutouts of various objects. The fire casts shadows of the objects on the wall, and the prisoners, because they can't turn their heads, take these moving shadows to be reality. This, Socrates would have his listeners believe, is how unthinking people experience life: they mistake shadows for reality; they are prisoners to illusions.

Continuing his story, Socrates imagines a prisoner who breaks free of his chains, turns and sees the fire and the cutouts, and then walks from the cave into the sunlight. The former prisoner now sees things as they are, and he returns to the cave to tell the prisoners what he has seen. For Socrates, the freed prisoner is akin to the philosopher, and the return to the cave is the beginning of the philosopher's educational mission, which Socrates defines as turning the prisoners toward the light of the fire.

> Then education is the craft concerned with doing this very thing, this turning around, and with how the soul can most easily and effectively be made to do it. It isn't the craft of putting sight into the soul. Education takes for granted that sight is there but that it isn't turned the right way or looking where it ought to look, and it tries to redirect it appropriately.

With Socrates's allegory of the cave, we get a nested set of theaters of the mind: there's the theater in the prisoner's mind, which is inhabited by shadows; there's the theater in the philosopher's mind, where one encounters reality; and there's Plato's theater of the mind, which stages this moment when Socrates uses a story to illustrate his view of education as the process of turning from the illusory to the real.

What we find compelling about the Allegory of the Cave and *The Dialogue Concerning the Two Chief World Systems* is that they make visible what would otherwise go unnoticed—namely, that there is a drama to the life of the mind that gets expressed in the movement from confusion to clarity, a drama that gets felt in the weight and heft of the process of changing one's mind. While the dramas that played out in the theater of Galileo's mind and the theater of Socrates's mind proved to be of global significance, we all experience a true change of mind, like a genuine change of heart, as life changing, even though the significance of the change extends no further than our own worldview.

Writing plays a central role in the theater of the mind because it makes it possible for us to see our own thoughts and then to reflect on what happens when we move those thoughts out into the world. As it happens this is why Socrates so distrusted writing: unlike an embodied dialogue between a teacher and a student, with writing there's no one there but ourselves to test the veracity of our thoughts as we express them. Despite Socrates's argument against writing, his student Plato wrote a series of dialogues featuring Socrates that have been read, discussed, and argued over for the past two thousand years. Why? Because the questions Socrates poses in Plato's dialogues cut to the very essence of what it means to be human. Indeed, for Socrates, it is the ongoing engagement with the theater of one's mind, where questions about how to live a good life are posed and reposed, that separates us from all the other animals. This sentiment, succinctly captured in Socrates's oft-quoted declaration in *The Apology* that "the unexamined life is not worth living," is, we would argue, more accurately rendered as "a life lived without ongoing self-examination is not a human life." The drama of the theater of the mind commences as soon as the question "What do I think?" is given serious consideration.

Practice Session One

Reflecting

There's a quick way to test how the idea of the theater of the mind, as we've defined it, can be of use to you: write a description of the most dramatic moment you've experienced in the realm of thought. In the theater of the mind, one deals with ideas—friendship, citizenship, truth, faith, integrity, or success, for example—and the drama is in the development of a revised understanding of the idea at the center of one's self-examination. We are not asking you to write a story about how winning an award improved your self-confidence or how an act of shoplifting led to feelings of guilt. The assignment is to focus squarely on the redefinition of an *idea* and to lead your readers through your thought process to show them why the shift in definition *matters*.

Practice Session Two

Reading

There's a maxim in argumentation that goes like this: tell them what you're going to say; say it; tell them that you said it. This is argumentation through repetition. In the context of the current discussion, we'd say that this kind of argumentation contains no drama; there's nothing for the reader to do in the theater of the mind other than accept or reject the point that is being argued.

This is not the case for any of the readings we've included at the end of this volume. Choose one of the readings and observe, as you read, how the writer tries to create a theater of the mind for the readers, encouraging them to think in new ways about the topic at hand.

Set aside at least 30 minutes to take notes about places where the writer dramatizes the evolution of ideas, perhaps by refining the argument, shifting directions, or introducing new and surprising information.

Writing

After you've read and reviewed the article, draft an essay that describes how the writer moves your thinking along from the beginning of the article to the end. Is there a drama to this movement? What has the writer done to get you to shift your thinking? Does he or she succeed?

Revising

And now for the real challenge: revise the essay you wrote in the previous exercise so that it compellingly demonstrates your experience reading the piece you've chosen and contending with its implications. In other words, create for your reader the drama of your engagement with the writer's ideas.

EXPLORE

One of the pleasures of reading and writing is exploring the theater of other people's minds. In the *Invisibilia* podcast "The Secret History of Thoughts," you can hear the "ghost boy," who spent thirteen years in a vegetative state, describe what it was like to live entirely inside his mind. Leslie Jamison discusses how her experiences as a medical actor—i.e., playing sick for doctors in training—transformed her understanding of empathy. Cheryl Strayed offers advice to a beginning writer, Elissa Bassist, about how to overcome the internal fears that prevent getting down to work. In an interview two years later, Strayed speaks with Bassist, who has completed the book she feared she would never write.

Bassist, Elissa, and Cheryl Strayed. "How to Write Like a Mother#^@%&."
   Creative Nonfiction. #47, Winter 2013. Web.

Jamison, Leslie. "The Empathy Exams: A Medical Actor Writes Her Own
   Script." *The Believer.* Feb. 2014. Web.

"The Secret History of Thoughts." *NPR Invisibilia.* 9 Jan. 2015. Podcast.

Strayed, Cheryl. "Write Like a Motherfucker." *The Rumpus.* 19 Aug. 2010. Web.

On Curiosity at Work in the Academy

Throughout this book, we've included short entries about "Curiosity at Work"—examples of how curiosity inspires creative thought and expression. In these brief essays, we emphasize the work of contemporary nonfiction writers because they do such a good job of posing compelling questions about the world. If you're a student learning to write for school, however, you may be wondering how to connect what this book teaches you about writers' habits of mind to the kinds of papers you are asked to write for classes in particular academic disciplines. We think the best way to address that connection is to show you examples of curiosity at work in academic writing so you can see how academic articles and books emerge from the very habits of mind we've been discussing.

Academic writing differs from journalistic writing and general nonfiction in important ways. Scholarly articles and books explicitly join conversations taking place in particular branches of knowledge, and they focus on questions that are of interest to others in the same discipline; philosophers ask different kinds of questions than psychologists or anthropologists or historians ask. The various fields of study also differ from each other in their methods of research, the kinds of evidence used, and the traditions that govern how arguments, ideas, evidence, and sources are presented.

Despite these differences, academic writing has much in common with nonfiction written by generalists. Each of the three academic works we discuss below begins with the author expressing curiosity about a difficult problem, puzzle, or paradox that can be addressed through research. While the authors present their work according to the conventions of their respective academic fields, they are all motivated by a desire to advance understanding about complex issues. Reviewing these examples will make it easier for you to see three of the main moves academics make in launching their writing projects. Each writer identifies an important problem, puzzle, or paradox; joins an ongoing discussion about the problem, puzzle, or paradox; and establishes the key words in that conversation. This description may suggest that we think academic writing follows a formula. But we'd say that these writers *begin* with curiosity. The conventions become useful later as the writers shape what they've discovered for an audience of specialized readers.

. . . . .

One of the most influential articles in the field of political theory is Michael Walzer's "Political Action: The Problem of Dirty Hands," which appeared in *Philosophy & Public Affairs* in 1973. (The full article can easily be found online.) In the introduction to his essay, Walzer immediately signals that he's joining an ongoing conversation. His first paragraph explains that he's interested in a disagreement about moral dilemmas that has already been addressed by three fellow philosophers—Thomas Nagel, Richard B. Brandt, and R. M. Hare. They disagree about "whether or not a man can ever face, or ever has to face, a moral dilemma, a situation where he must choose between two courses of action *both of which it would be wrong for him to undertake*" (emphasis added). More specifically, they're concerned about whether it's possible for a leader to govern "innocently." In other words, can a political leader resolve moral dilemmas without ever having to choose a course of action that is immoral?

Nagel thinks that, because dilemmas arise in which each possible course of action is morally wrong, a leader cannot govern innocently. Brandt argues that logical reasoning can be used to resolve such dilemmas and thus a leader can remain innocent. Hare agrees, arguing dilemmas of this kind can and should be resolved at a higher level of moral discourse.

Walzer is not satisfied with any of these answers. In the third paragraph of his article, he writes:

> My own answer is no, I don't think I could govern innocently; nor do most of us believe that those who govern us are innocent—as I shall argue below—even the best of them. But this does not mean that it isn't possible to do the right thing while governing. It means that a particular act of government (in a political party or in the state) may be exactly the right thing to do in utilitarian terms and yet leave the man who does it guilty of a moral wrong. The innocent man, afterwards, is no longer innocent. If on the other hand

he remains innocent . . . , he not only fails to do the right thing (in utilitarian terms), he may also fail to measure up to the duties of his office (which imposes on him a considerable responsibility for consequences and outcomes).

If you have trouble understanding what Walzer is saying the first time through, try reading this passage again, slowly, and look up the terms that are unfamiliar to you. If you look up *utilitarianism*, for example, you'll find that it is the principle of the greatest good for the greatest number. A utilitarian evaluates choices on the basis of how useful they are; the *right* choice to a utilitarian is one that is beneficial for more people.

With this definition in mind, you might assume that calculating the greatest good for the greatest number is a straightforward business, but Walzer thinks that making a utilitarian decision could be simultaneously the right course of action and a morally wrong one. For example, suppose a political leader could serve the greater good of his or her country by sacrificing the lives of bystanders to kill the head of a terrorist organization. Even if the political leader makes the "right" utilitarian choice to kill bystanders for the greater good of the country, she or he has still committed the immoral act of killing innocent people and now has dirty hands. If the leader refuses to commit this immoral act on behalf of the greater good and lets the terrorist live, then the leader has put his or her own citizens at risk. With this choice, the leader commits a different moral wrong and also has dirty hands.

Six pages into the article, Walzer fully lays out the paradox that leaders "who act for us and in our name are often killers, or seem to become killers too quickly and too easily." Even "good and decent people" who choose politics as a vocation, he writes,

> are then required to learn the lesson Machiavelli first set out to teach: "how not to be good." Some of them are incapable of learning; many more profess to be incapable. But they will not succeed unless they learn, for they have joined the terrible competition for power and glory; they have chosen to work and struggle as Machiavelli says, among "so many who are not good." They can do no good themselves unless they win the struggle, which they are unlikely to do unless they are willing and able to use the necessary means. So we

are suspicious even of the best of winners. It is not a sign of our perversity if we think them only more clever than the rest. They have not won, after all, because they were good, or not only because of that, but also because they were not good. No one succeeds in politics without getting his hands dirty. This is conventional wisdom again, and again I don't mean to insist that it is true without qualification. I repeat it only to disclose the moral dilemma inherent in the convention. For sometimes it is right to try to succeed, and then it must also be right to get one's hands dirty. But one's hands get dirty from doing what it is wrong to do. And how can it be wrong to do what is right? Or, how can we get our hands dirty by doing what we ought to do?

As this last paragraph shows, Waltzer doesn't rush to resolve the moral puzzle that fascinates him. Rather than being satisfied with the conclusion that successful leaders must have dirty hands, he continues to generate more and more questions: If having dirty hands is inevitable, when should dirty-handed leaders be held accountable? Does holding leaders accountable then dirty the hands of citizens in turn? Does everyone end up with dirty hands? Walzer concludes his essay without having answered any of these questions definitively. And yet, forty years after it was written, "Political Action: The Problem of Dirty Hands" is still being cited by scholars and taught in politics classes. Why? For two reasons: because Walzer's article presents the complex puzzle of "doing bad to do good" with remarkable clarity; and because Walzer's way of engaging with this puzzle is so lively and original that readers from across the political spectrum feel invited to join with him as he wrestles with the unsolvable challenge of leadership.

. . . . .

Edward Said's influential book *Orientalism* begins by making the same series of moves we saw Walzer's "Political Action" make above: in the introduction to *Orientalism*, Said joins an ongoing conversation about culture; he works to unsettle key terms; and he argues that we should understand a complicated puzzle in a new way. The introduction opens with Said staging his response to the following: "On a visit to Beirut during the terrible civil war of 1975–1976 a French journalist wrote regretfully of the gutted downtown area that 'it had once seemed to belong to . . . the Orient of Chateaubriand and Nerval.'" The jounalist saw only what his own country had lost. The distortions of this view of Beirut inspired Said to write a book about how the East has been seen through Western eyes.

We'd like you to read the first two paragraphs of *Orientalism* and observe how Said's curiosity about the journalist's sentence leads him to intellectually creative thoughts. It will help you understand Said's project if you know that Chateaubriand and Nerval were nineteenth-century French writers who wrote extensively about their travels to the Middle East and, more specifically, about their time in Beirut.

On a visit to Beirut during the terrible civil war of 1975–1976 a French journalist wrote regretfully of the gutted downtown area that "it had once seemed to belong to . . . the Orient of Chateaubriand and Nerval." He was right about the place, of course, especially so far as a European was concerned. The Orient was almost a European invention, and had been since antiquity a place of romance, exotic beings, haunting memories and landscapes, remarkable experiences. Now it was disappearing; in a sense it had happened, its time was over. Perhaps it seemed irrelevant that Orientals themselves had something at stake in the process, that even in the time of Chateaubriand and Nerval Orientals had lived there, and that now it was they who were suffering; the main thing for the European visitor was a European representation of the Orient and its contemporary fate, both of which had a privileged communal significance for the journalist and his French readers.

Americans will not feel quite the same about the Orient, which for them is much more likely to be associated very differently with the Far East (China and Japan, mainly). Unlike the Americans, the French and the British—less so the Germans, Russians, Spanish, Portuguese, Italians, and

Swiss—have had a long tradition of what I shall be calling *Orientalism*, a way of coming to terms with the Orient that is based on the Orient's special place in European Western experience. The Orient is not only adjacent to Europe; it is also the place of Europe's greatest and richest and oldest colonies, the source of its civilizations and languages, its cultural contestant, and one of its deepest and most recurring images of the Other. In addition, the Orient has helped to define Europe (or the West) as its contrasting image, idea, personality, experience. Yet none of this Orient is merely imaginative. The Orient is an integral part of European *material* civilization and culture. Orientalism expresses and represents that part culturally and even ideologically as a mode of discourse with supporting institutions, vocabulary, scholarship, imagery, doctrines, even colonial bureaucracies and colonial styles. . . .

You may need to read this passage more than once and look up terms that are unfamiliar to you to understand Said's project. You could look carefully, for instance, at what Said does with the term "the Orient." For over a century, the term seemed to be culturally neutral, but Said draws our attention to how it is deeply embedded in a Western cultural perspective that casts the East as both in service to and inferior to the West. The ways the West perceives the East, he says, have far-reaching effects. The European idea of "the Orient" is embedded in the European languages, patterns of thought, and institutional structures. If we return to the journalist's description of the "gutted downtown" of Beirut that "had once seemed to belong to . . . the Orient of Chateaubriand and Nerval," we can now see what Said wants us to see—namely, the nostalgia of a Frenchman who cannot appreciate Beirut as an Eastern city and who regrets that it no longer reflects the influence of its French colonizers. With this brief example, Said takes the first step in his journey to establish that the idea of "the Orient" is a European invention. His intellectual journey ultimately inspired a generation of scholars to document the ways that European and Americans have represented Middle Eastern, African, and Asian societies and cultures over time.

. . . . .

The two examples of academic writing we've offered so far are both focused on abstract concepts, "Orientalism" and "the problem of dirty hands," and they both address how ideas and narratives shape the way we think about politics, power, culture, and cultural difference. Our third example, from the field of sociology, is less abstract, though it too examines the power of cultural narratives. "Fetal Alcohol Syndrome: The Origins of a Moral Panic," by Elizabeth M. Armstrong and Ernest L. Abel, examines the growing concern in the 1990s about fetal alcohol syndrome (FAS) as a public health issue. The writers of this article are very direct: they begin by defining fetal alcohol syndrome and then quickly cite six articles to demonstrate that they are entering an ongoing scholarly conversation about the prevalence and danger of fetal alcohol syndrome. Although their prose is unadorned, they make clear in their introduction that they've uncovered an unexpected and serious problem.

> Fetal alcohol syndrome (FAS) is a pattern of anomalies occurring in children born to alcoholic women (Jones and Smith, 1973). The main features of this pattern are pre- and/or postnatal growth retardation, characteristic facial abnormalities, and central nervous system dysfunction, including mental retardation (Stratton *et al.*, 1996). Despite the pervasiveness of alcohol and drunkenness in human history (Abel, 1997), FAS went largely unrecognized until 1973, when it was characterized as a "tragic disorder" by Jones and Smith, the Seattle physicians who discovered it (Jones and Smith, 1973). By the 1990s, FAS had been transformed in the United States from an unrecognized condition to a moral panic characterized as a "major public health concern" (e.g. Stratton *et al.*, 1996) and a "national health priority" (Egeland *et al.*, 1998). In this paper, we trace this evolution, paying special attention to the ways in which this moral panic has inflated fear and anxiety about the syndrome beyond levels warranted by evidence of its prevalence or impact. To acknowledge that the current level of concern about FAS is exaggerated is not to suggest that the syndrome does not exist. One of us

(E. L. A.) has spent his entire professional career researching and writing about FAS and continues to be actively
engaged in its prevention.

Armstrong and Abel are curious about a paradox in the history of fetal
alcohol syndrome: although the syndrome was unknown before 1973,
in the space of twenty years, fetal alcohol syndrome went from being
invisible to being the focus of a "moral panic." They want to understand how and why the syndrome became an urgent "public health
priority."

In the pages that follow the introduction, the authors reinterpret
evidence that was available to everyone at the time and yet was routinely oversimplified and misunderstood by others caught up in the
moral panic. They point out, for example, that highly visible prevention efforts, such as the placement of warning labels on alcohol
bottles, "are doomed to fail" because all pregnant women are not,
in fact, equally at risk of giving birth to children with fetal alcohol
syndrome. If, as the authors say, "a small proportion of women of
child-bearing age, especially those who are most disadvantaged by
poverty, bear the greatest burden of risk for FAS," then the real public health concern should be identifying and helping those women
who are most at risk.

This is what it means to be creative as an academic: you show your
readers how to understand a problem in a new way. Armstrong and
Abel have recast a seemingly intractable public health crisis so that new
ways of responding to it become imaginable.

. . . . .

These three examples of curiosity at work in the academy offer just a
glimpse of how academics share their curiosity about the ways of the
world with others. Academic writing poses special challenges to readers
who are new to a topic or a field of study, but if you know to look for
the problem, question, puzzle, or paradox that the writer is grappling
with, if you can spot where the writer is joining an ongoing conversation with other scholars, and if you figure out how to define key terms
and concepts, you'll be able to get your bearings, even if the language
and subject matter at first seem entirely unfamiliar.

Practice Session One

Reading

Above we've presented examples of two kinds of curiosity-driven scholarly projects: Armstrong and Abel seek to resolve a puzzle, and Walzer and Said explore the complexity of an abstraction. For this exercise, we want you to think about other roles that curiosity can play in scholarly writing.

Begin by selecting a scholarly essay to read. You can work with one of the five articles listed in the Explore section (p. 250), or your teacher may suggest other readings. You may even be able to read an article written by one of your teachers.

Read the essay you've chosen from beginning to end, marking key moments in the argument. Then read the essay again; most academic articles need to be read more than once to be fully understood. As you reread, pay attention to how the scholar organizes ideas, works with sources, presents major points, and addresses readers. Take notes in the margins about the key moments you marked.

After you've read and reread the article with care, take at least 30 minutes to write out answers to the following questions: How did the scholar introduce his or her topic? Where did the writing draw you in? Are there parts of the essay that confused you, or sections where you didn't know enough about the topic or the sources to follow the argument? What parts of the article were particularly clear? Were there passages that prompted you to think new thoughts?

Writing

Write an essay that reflects on how curiosity gets announced and pursued in the article you've read. Make certain to quote specific passages where you feel the focus of the scholar's curiosity is made clear. What is the status of that curiosity at the end of the article? Have the author's questions been resolved, or have they led to other questions?

Practice Session Two

Reading

All of your teachers will have other examples of academic writing they admire. Ask some of them to recommend a few favorite academic articles, chapters, or books. Choose one and read it with an eye toward understanding the curiosity that drives the scholar's project, following the steps in the Reading section of Practice Session One: read, reread, take notes, reflect, and write. Why do you think your teacher recommended that piece of writing? Can you offer an explanation for why it has been influential?

EXPLORE

Zora Neale Hurston once wrote, "research is formalized curiosity." Although some academic prose seems dry and airless, many scholarly writers put their passion and curiosity on display. Hurston's fellow anthropologist, Ruth Behar, challenges her field to recognize ethnography as an art that engages the imagination. Douglas Hofstadter wonders about the importance of analogy in thinking, and proposes that analogy *is* cognition. Anne Harrington also examines how scientists think about thinking; she questions the assumption that neuroscience alone can account for "moral choice, existential passion, and social contracts." David Bartholomae and Shirley Brice Heath both raise questions about how teachers evaluate learning. Bartholomae insists that we rethink our assumptions about how college students learn to write academic essays, and Heath points out how strange it is that teachers judge academic ability with formulaic essays when, by design, these essays curtail "creativity, the pursuit of alternative answers, and the power of collaborative thinking in academic life."

Bartholomae, David. "Inventing the University." *When a Writer Can't Write: Studies in Writer's Block and Other Composing-Process Problems.* Ed. Mike Rose. New York: Guilford, 1985. 134–65. Print.

Behar, Ruth. "Ethnography in a Time of Blurred Genres." *Anthropology and Humanism* 32.2 (2007). 145–55. Web.

Harrington, Anne. "How to House a Mind Inside a Brain: Lessons from History." *EMBO Reports* 8, no. S1 (2007). Web.

Heath, Shirley Brice. "Rethinking the Sense of the Past: The Essay as Legacy of the Epigram." *Theory and Practice in the Teaching of Writing: Rethinking the Discipline.* Ed. Lee Odell. Carbondale: Southern Illinois UP, 1993. 105–31. Print.

Hofstadter, Douglas R. "Analogy as the Core of Cognition." Stanford Presidential Lectures in the Humanities and Arts. Web.

Argument at Work: Sonia Sotomayor and Principled Openness

On August 8, 2009, Sonia Sotomayor, who was born and raised in a working-class Puerto Rican family in the Bronx, was sworn in as the first Latina member of the United States Supreme Court. Since then, Sotomayor has written a coming-of-age memoir, *My Beloved World* (simultaneously published in Spanish as *Mi mundo adorado*), in which she describes her early years living in public housing with an alcoholic father and a distant mother, her studies at Princeton University and Yale Law School, and the steps early in her career that put her on a path to the Supreme Court.

Sotomayor credits many mentors and friends for contributing to her success, but her memoir also makes it clear that her success is due to her intellectual habits of mind, which were evident before she graduated from Cardinal Spellman High School. As a member of that school's forensics club, Sotomayor discovered that she loved vigorous argument. She enjoyed arguing not because she was always certain of her position but because she took pleasure in the sport of rhetorical sparring and in testing her ideas against challenges.

She recalls that her manner of using argument as a tool for learning—as opposed to sticking to her original position no matter what new information and ideas she encountered—didn't always inspire the affection or admiration of her competitors. At a forensics meet during her junior year of high school, she encountered an especially hostile opponent who accused her of never being willing to take a strong stand and of thinking too much about how her position depended on context. Sotomayor thought it was valuable to be open to persuasion, but her fellow debater found it a mark of weakness because Sotomayor's position on an issue was never predictable. She accused Sotomayor of being without principles.

Sotomayor writes in her memoir's epilogue that she grappled with that accusation for decades. She concedes that she would be at fault if she truly lacked principles and had no moral center. She counts among her core values "integrity, fairness, and the avoidance of cruelty." At the same time, she reasons, "if you held to principle so passionately, so inflexibly, indifferent to the particulars of circumstance—the full range of what human beings, with all their flaws and foibles, might endure or create—if you enthroned principle above even reason, weren't you then abdicating the responsibilities of a thinking person?" Her practice as a Supreme Court justice is built on this habitual questioning and curiosity, on an openness to individual difference and a willingness to learn. She concludes: "Concern for individuals, the imperative of treating them with dignity and respect for their ideas and needs, regardless of one's own views—these too are surely principles and as worthy as any of being deemed inviolable. To remain open to understandings—perhaps even to principles—as yet not determined is the least that learning requires, its barest threshold."

DIVERGING

Two roads diverged in a wood, and I—
I took the one less traveled by,
And that has made all the difference.

Could we have chosen a more clichéd opening for our essays on divergence than these lines from Robert Frost's "The Road Not Taken"? No, probably not, but we chose them anyway, because the poem contains a surprise that many readers miss. Every person who quotes Frost with a self-congratulatory "and that has made all the difference" fails to recognize that "The Road Not Taken" actually pokes fun at people who tell such stories. Frost diverges from the expected because his poem about divergence is actually about the failure to diverge. He invites us to recognize how rarely people chart new paths.

Writing that's worth reading, like Frost's poem, offers its readers something new, something surprising, something unexpected. So to become a writer whose work is worth reading, you need to practice diverging from the tired, the familiar, and the conventional—from the roads always taken. We encourage you to cultivate habits of questioning and experimentation. Go ahead: ask "what if?" and see where your curiosity takes you.

The essays in this section invite divergent thinking while also diverging from one another. "The pen is mightier than the sword" is a commonplace, but is it true? Does laughter have a role in the serious business of academic writing? Are conventions something you can play with? In each essay, we invite you to consider what is made possible when you veer from the common path.

On Writing's Magical Powers

One of the most familiar claims about the power of writing is that "the pen is mightier than the sword." This saying conjures a world where ideas are more powerful than brute force and the work of writing outlasts the work of fighting. For an example we can turn to *The Iliad*: if it weren't for Homer's words having been put down in writing, the individual acts of treason or heroism in the Trojan War, and perhaps even the outcome of the war itself, would have been lost to the passage of time.

While we, too, believe that writing matters, we think the claim that "the pen is mightier than the sword" that just doesn't ring true. Examples of words perishing completely in the face of brute force abound. Take the burning of the library of Alexandria, which is said to have occurred anywhere from fifteen hundred to two thousand years ago—the exact date is unknown because no writing contemporaneous with the event has survived to the present day. More recently, there was the looting of the National Museum in Baghdad in the aftermath of the 2003 American invasion of Iraq. Despite the fact that museum officials published impassioned pleas in advance of the invasion warning of this imminent cultural catastrophe, irreplaceable antiquities that recorded the earliest moments of human expression are now gone forever.

The more we thought about the relationship between language and power, the harder it became for us to come up with examples that supported the fanciful idea that the pen is indeed mightier than the sword. And that got us to wondering where this phrase came from. Our research yielded some surprising results.

To begin with, it turns out that the phrase "the pen is mightier than the sword" first appeared in a historical drama entitled *Richelieu; or, The Conspiracy*, written by Edward Bulwer-Lytton and published in 1839. In the second act of the play, Bulwer-Lytton has Cardinal Richelieu, Louis XIII's minister of state, discover a plot to remove Richelieu from power. Outraged, Richelieu has his servant Joseph bring him his two-handed broadsword. Looking the blade over and finding a familiar notch on its edge, Richelieu recalls an earlier battle at Rochelle, where he brought the sword down on a helmeted English soldier and "shore him to the waist!" This same sword, which Richelieu remembers as being like "a toy—a feather" when he was young, is suddenly too heavy for the old man to lift. Collapsing into a chair, Richelieu says disconsolately, "a child could / Slay Richelieu now." Reminded by his servant that he has other weapons at his command, Richelieu takes up a pen and declares: "Beneath the rule of men entirely great / The pen is mightier than the sword."

The original context changes the meaning, doesn't it?

The pen is not *always* mightier than the sword, as the cliché would have us believe. Rather, the pen can become mightier than the sword when it is used under the rule of men—such as Richelieu—who are "entirely great." *Entirely* great? Yes, that's what the line from the play actually says.

And what about when the pen is used by people with less power?

The conclusion of the play answers this hypothetical question decisively. Richelieu triumphs because he has gained possession of a secret message meant for those who are conspiring against him. The writers and the intended recipients of this message, having been betrayed by the pen, face a range of dire fates—banishment, imprisonment, death. And Richelieu? He remains in power. Thus the pen really is mightier than the sword, if the pen is in the hands of someone with the power to destroy those who are less powerful.

While we were looking into this, we also discovered that "the pen is mightier than the sword" isn't the only phrase of Bulwer-Lytton's that history has preserved. Bulwer-Lytton's words, uncited, appear in Charles Schulz's classic depiction of the struggling writer:

PEANUTS © 1993 Peanuts Worldwide LLC. Dist. by Universal UCLICK. Reprinted with permission. All rights reserved.

It turns out that the first sentence of Snoopy's ever-unfinished novel is a truncated version of the opening sentence of Bulwer-Lytton's three-volume novel *Paul Clifford* (1830), which begins:

> It was a dark and stormy night; the rain fell in torrents, except at occasional intervals, when it was checked by a violent gust of wind which swept up the streets (for it is in London that our scene lies), rattling along the house-tops, and fiercely agitating the scanty flame of the lamps that struggled against the darkness.

The passage of time obviously hasn't been kind to Bulwer-Lytton. Though he was a prolific, best-selling author during the nineteenth century, his works go unread today, and, as we've seen here, the two pieces of his writing that do remain in circulation do so without referencing his name. Indeed, were it not for San Jose State University's annual Bulwer-Lytton Fiction Contest, in which writers the world over compete to produce the worst opening line to an unwritten novel, it is doubtful that Bulwer-Lytton's name would be raised anywhere other than in scholarly discussions of nineteenth-century literary production. However, because of the Bulwer-Lytton contest, the author of the statement "the pen is mightier than the sword" lives on as a punch line to a long-standing joke among writers, his name synonymous with prose that is pretentious, overblown, contorted, and clichéd.

One could conclude, after looking at the arc of Bulwer-Lytton's career, tracking from respected author to punch line, that whatever might his pen had was largely, perhaps even completely, out of his hands. But it turns out that what holds true for Bulwer-Lytton holds true for all writers. It doesn't matter who is holding the pen or typing at the keyboard; the writing device still produces writing that is susceptible to being misread, misunderstood, or misinterpreted. Why? Because writing is always at the mercy of its readers.

To say that there is no writing mighty enough to control how it is read is not to say, however, that writing has *no* power. The writing you do has the power to change you and to change your relationship to the world. Indeed, this is why we think writing is so important; it allows you to explore the inner workings of your mind, the world, and your place in the world. We don't believe that using your writing to conduct such explorations will make *anything* possible. But, we do believe it will better prepare you, day by day, to live in and with a world of ever-unfolding possibilities.

Practice Session One

Writing

At the end of "On Writing's Magical Powers," we assert that writing is capable of changing you and your relationship to the world. That sounds good, but is it true? Have you ever had an experience of this kind with writing—either writing as activity or writing as end product? Do you know someone who has?

If you have had such an experience, write an account of it, and if you can, cite the writing that had this effect. Be as specific as possible about how the writing—the process, the product, or both—changed you and your relationship to the world.

If you are writing about someone else's experience, begin by interviewing your acquaintance, finding out as much as you can about how writing—either as activity or as end product—worked its magic. Then write up an account of your interviewee's experience. Cite from both the interview and the writing that was transformative.

In your account, reflect on whether the experience you've described is reproducible. Can it be practiced? Can it be learned? Are there conditions that have to be in play for it to be possible?

Practice Session Two

Researching

Conventional wisdom has it that aspiring writers should avoid clichés . . . like the plague! But for this exercise, we invite you to do as we've done in "On Writing's Magical Powers." Choose a saying, a phrase, or a slogan that gets repeated habitually in your environment. Research the origins of your selection. Where does your exploration lead you? Spend at least 30 minutes writing about what your selection means now and what it meant originally.

EXPLORE

Writing's magical powers allow us to make meaning out of chaos. Mark Bowden discusses a scientist's effort to collect data on his every bodily function in the finest detail. Geoff Dyer ponders three instances where his criminal activities escaped detection. Mac McClelland contemplates the horrific consequences of a relative's mental illness. In all of these pieces, the authors seek to make sense of the past in order to better understand the present.

Bowden, Mark. "The Measured Man." *Atlantic*. July 2012. Web.

Dyer, Geoff. "My Secret Life of Crime." *Guardian*. 30 June 2009. Web.

McClelland, Mac. "Schizophrenic. Killer. My Cousin." *Mother Jones*. May/June 2013. Web.

On Laughter

"So, two writing teachers walk into a bar."

Could a joke that starts this way ever be funny?

What about this joke:

"How many writing teachers does it take to screw in a light bulb?"

Or a joke that begins,

"This writing teacher shows up at the Pearly Gates . . ."?

It all depends, right?

And not just on whatever the next line is, but also on the context—on who's telling the joke, how they're telling it, where they're telling it, and why they're telling it—and, of course, on who's listening and/or watching and/or reading the joke. Humor is, we would argue, the most contextually dependent and the most contextually sensitive of all the possible speech acts.

This is one reason why humor is the least likely of the habits of the creative mind to be taught in school: since it involves playing with audience expectations, it has the potential to both fail (that is, not to be funny) and to offend (that is, to violate the audience's values) at the same time. Another reason humor has no formal place in education is because it just seems inherently less serious and less important than other forms of communication. We want to argue, though, that humor (in terms of having a sense of humor and of having the ability to be humorous) can play a central role in the creative process. How? When you successfully disrupt audience expectations by saying something surprising—perhaps by making connections between things that seem disconnected, or by pointing out an incongruity, or by unsettling typical ways of thinking about and seeing the world—you make it possible for your audience to shift perspectives, to see things in a new way. In our view, practicing being funny is a way to practice seeing a situation from multiple perspectives; it's also a way to practice gauging just how flexible your audience's expectations are.

Sometimes you will be wrong in your estimation of how much your audience will bend. One of us once made a joke in a paper in graduate school, and in the margin of the paper, next to the joke, the teacher wrote: "Humor has no place in academic discourse."

No place? Really?

It is true that academic research on humor is unlikely to produce riotous laughter. It's also true that the tone and style of academic writing in general tends to fall somewhere on a spectrum that extends from the dispassionate to the gravely serious. But here's the thing: no government, religion, or tradition—not even the hallowed tradition of academic discourse—is powerful enough to completely suppress the desire to laugh. And there is *no* situation about which someone somewhere isn't prepared to make a joke.

We can imagine the incredulous response to our claim that a joke can be made in or about *any* situation. We've presented this statement dispassionately, as a fact. Now let's test it.

How about death? Can death be funny? Can the certainty of our own mortality evoke laughter?

In *Romeo and Juliet*, Shakespeare's well-known and (some would say) quite silly play about star-crossed lovers, Romeo's best friend, the witty Mercutio, ends up being stabbed during a standoff with a rival clan. When Romeo tries to determine whether his friend has been injured during the brandishing of swords, Mercutio won't give him a straight answer:

> Ask for me to-morrow, and you shall find me a grave man.

A *grave* man? *Really?*

Yes, Shakespeare really does have his character make a joke about his own death while he is dying. Not only that, Shakespeare has Mercutio resort to a pun, which some define as the lowest form of humor, to both tell and not tell Romeo about the seriousness of his injury. Moments later, Mercutio exits and, we later learn, does indeed die of his wound. *Exeunt*, pursued by a pun.

But, you object, this is just a play. It's not real life. Real people wouldn't crack a joke when Death is *really* at their door, would they?

On August 3, 2012, the comedian Tig Notaro walked onto the stage of the Largo, a comedy club in Los Angeles, and said to the audience:

> Good evening. Hello. I have cancer. How are you? Hi, how are you? Is everybody having a good time? I have cancer.

> How are you? Ah, it's a good time. Diagnosed with cancer.
> [Sighs] It feels good. Just diagnosed with cancer. Oh, God.

There was some uncomfortable laughter. Notaro repeated herself. More laughter followed, but it was the laughter of disbelief, of nervousness, of uncertainty. She can't be serious, can she? This seems beyond the pale, making jokes at the expense of people who really do have cancer—who would make light of such a thing?

As the routine continued, the audience slowly realized that Notaro was *both* telling the truth *and* joking about her diagnosis. She repeatedly paused to speak directly to audience members who didn't know how to respond to what she was telling them: a man who was laughing too much; a woman who was deeply troubled by what she was hearing.

> It's OK. It's going to be OK. [Pause] It might not be OK. But I'm just saying, it's OK. You're going to be OK. [Pause] I don't know what's going on with me.

Louis CK was the headliner that night and was standing just offstage during Notaro's performance. Here's an excerpt from his description of what it was like to be there:

> I can't really describe it but I was crying and laughing and listening like never in my life. Here was this small woman standing alone against death and simply reporting where her mind had been. . . .
>
> The show was an amazing example of what comedy can be. A way to visit your worst fears and laugh at them. Tig took us to a scary place and made us laugh there. Not by distracting us from the terror but by looking right at it and just turning to us and saying, "Wow. Right?" She proved that everything is funny. And has to be. And she could only do this by giving us her own death as an example. So generous.

Louis CK is a comedian, of course, so one could argue that his response isn't typical. To him it was "one of the greatest standup performances" ever, but what about the audience? Did the audience members ever get over being disturbed by the fact that Notaro was entertaining them with her immediate experience of having death at her door?

We invite you to listen to the entire thirty-minute show and judge for yourself.

At this point, Notaro, Louis CK, and Shakespeare have probably convinced you that one can joke about one's own death; but that's different, you might say, from making a joke about a situation in which *others* have suffered and died. Surely no one would do that, at least not right away.

How much time has to pass before awful, unbearable, or unthinkable events can be redeployed in the service of comedy? What is the etiquette when one is making a joke that references the deaths of others? How soon is too soon?

In *The Aristocrats,* a documentary we admire, the filmmakers set out to understand the history of one particularly vulgar and offensive joke that comedians tell each other. The trigger for the documentary? The editors of the *Onion* and many comedy headliners were attending a roast of Hugh Hefner at the Friars Club in New York City on November 4, 2001; the event was being filmed by Comedy Central for future broadcast. Then this happened:

The comic Gilbert Gottfried took his turn at the podium and made a joke that alluded to 9/11. There was a nervous response, some boos, and then shouts of "too soon!" With the ruins of the Twin Towers still being sifted through for human remains at the time, Gottfried had clearly crossed the invisible line of his audience's expectations about what constituted an appropriate topic for the occasion.

Gottfried's response?

He shifted gears and went straight into a joke known to all professional comics, a set piece that can be infinitely expanded between the setup (a family enters a talent agency) and the punch line ("We call the act, 'The Aristocrats'!"). Soon enough, the room was filled with laughter; someone on the stage laughed so hard he fell out of his chair. Gottfried reminded everyone in the room that comedy's function is to make it possible to laugh in response to that which is surprising, incongruous, or dissonant, and that this necessarily includes laughing at the unimaginably horrific things that humans do to one another.

In the documentary about this joke (which includes footage of Gottfried's Friars Club appearance), no one gets hurt. There are no vivid scenes of murder or rape or humiliation. There's no nudity and no simulation of sex acts. There isn't, in other words, any of the kind of visual material that is common fare in movie theaters, tv shows, and music videos. All there is to see is comic after comic telling the same vulgar, obscene joke, though the language and the shape of the joke change with each telling. And after hearing this joke told over and over, we come to understand that the best jokes help us to see incongruities in the world and in ourselves, to make sense of nonsense, and to connect things that seem unconnectable. Or to put this another way, jokes give us access to the powers of the imagination in all of its unruliness.

But what about in the realm of the essay? Does humor have any place in writing that is research driven? Investigative? Exploratory? Thoughtful? We believe that humor provides a vital role in the deliberative process: when one line of thinking leads to an impasse, the introduction of humor can serve to open up access to another plane of thought, one in which the impasse gets reframed as the occasion for laughter. But we don't want to argue the point; we want you to be the judge.

In "Fear of a Black President," Ta-Nehisi Coates gives a number of examples of how, prior to Barack Obama's election to the presidency, the idea of a black president had a long history of being joked about by black comics. Coates then offers an interpretation of the function of these jokes, after which Coates makes a joke that riffs on his own interpretation:

> Just beneath the humor [about the impossibility of a black president] lurked a resonant pain, the scars of history, an aching doubt rooted in the belief that "they" [white people] would never accept us [black people]. And so in our Harlems and Paradise Valleys, we invoked a black presidency the way a legion of 5-foot point guards might invoke the dunk—as evidence of some great cosmic injustice, weighty in its import, out of reach.
>
> And yet Spud Webb lives.

This last line, we maintain, is a joke Coates introduces to move his deliberation on the significance of Obama's election forward, from what was once generally believed to be a laughable impossibility to what is now a fact. His reference to Spud Webb enables this forward movement, but the joke Coates makes and the forward motion it is meant to produce only succeed if the reader knows both that Spud Webb had a distinguished career as a professional basketball player, despite being only five feet seven inches tall, and that he was such a good dunker that he won the NBA Slam Dunk Contest in 1986. The first set of jokes about black presidents and short dunkers alleviates the pain of an impossible situation; then there's the reality of Obama's election; after that, Coates reminds us of Spud Webb, which makes a joke about the jokers' sense of what is impossible. In this way, Coates shows how humor, deftly deployed, unsettles complacency, points out inconsistencies, and plays with audience expectations, all to shake us out of our usual patterns of thought so that we can see things differently. When the function of humor is understood in this way, it's hard to see how humor wouldn't have a central place in curiosity-driven, creative work.

Practice Session One

Reading

In the preceding essay, we've offered one example of how humor can be used in a piece of nonfiction prose to advance an argument—an example taken from Ta-Nehisi Coates's "Fear of a Black President" (p. 274). Now we'd like you to go through Coates's entire essay and pull out moments where you believe he is being humorous. The humor need not be a knee-slappingly funny joke to warrant attention: indeed, we'd like you to be able to tease out instances in which his use of humor occurs at the level of word choice or manifests itself as a nuanced phrase or transition. [This exercise may also be profitably done with Jill Lepore's "*The Last Amazon: Wonder Woman Returns*" (p. 300) or any of the readings in the Explore section on page 266.]

Once you have found at least three instances of humor in one of the readings, spend 60 minutes or more writing a piece that explains how the humor works in each of the examples you've selected. After you've completed your analysis, reflect on what it has revealed to you about the author's habits of mind. Is there a pattern that emerges from your examples? Do your examples support the hypothesis that humor can play a more significant role in the creative process than just lightening the mood?

Practice Session Two

Revising

We believe that humor has heuristic value during the writing process. We encounter a problem and can't think our way out of it; what can we do? What if, when this happens—as it must, because all writing involves getting stuck—we opted to make some sort of contextual joke, like the one Ta-Nehisi Coates made when he introduced Spud Webb? What would happen next?

For this exercise, take one of the pieces you wrote for a different section of this book, a piece in which you got blocked or stalled or repeated yourself at one or more points, and see what happens when you introduce a contextual joke at one of those moments in the piece. Then write for at least 30 minutes beyond the point where you've introduced the contextual joke. Where do you end up?

When you are happy with the results of your effort, go back and try your hand at turning the contextual joke into a more conventional transitional sentence or paragraph.

Practice Session Three

Writing

While humor is rare in academic writing, it is one of the primary modes for communicating online. What is its function in this other medium?

Drawing together your favorite memes and viral videos, put together a working file of the humorous material that you've encountered in your online life. Feel free to include text exchanges, Facebook posts, tweets, snapchats—whatever best represents the various functions that humor plays for you and your community of friends. Then explore what the evidence you've collected suggests about the values and expectations of this group of people. Finally, write an essay that explains the various functions humor plays in your online community.

Practice Session Four

Writing

For this exercise, we've adapted one of the essay prompts from the University of Chicago's 2013 application: Write out your favorite joke and then explain the joke without ruining it.

EXPLORE

Our suggested readings all show that laughter and insight can occur at the same time. Alice Dreger confronts the reality that there are people who hire dwarves for entertainment. Tig Notaro goes onstage and does a standup routine about having just been diagnosed with breast cancer. Walker Percy wonders how nonsensical versions of familiar metaphors still manage to convey meaning. And David Sedaris reflects on the jokes people tell in public.

Dreger, Alice. "Lavish Dwarf Entertainment." *Bioethics Forum.* 25 Mar. 2008. Web.

Notaro, Tig. "Too Soon?" *This American Life.* 5 Oct. 2012. Podcast.

Percy, Walker. "Metaphor as Mistake." *Sewanee Review* 66.1 (Winter 1958). 79–99. Web.

Sedaris, David. "The Learning Curve." *Me Talk Pretty One Day*. New York: Little, Brown, 2000. 83–96. Print.

On Playing with Conventions

Public speeches are, by definition, governed by convention. Take graduation speeches. They all more or less follow this predictable arc: the opening joke, the personal anecdote, praise for students' achievements, warnings about the challenges to come, and wise final words of encouragement about achieving success with integrity. Everybody in the audience knows that life after graduation is not that simple, but graduations are celebratory occasions, so it just doesn't do to point out the magnitude of the problems graduates are likely to face or the difficulties they will have in traveling the road ahead.

When the conventions are so rigid, is creativity possible? We've worked with many beginning creative writers who believe that all constraints, guidelines, and requirements are disabling intrusions; we even had a student who refused to read anyone else's work, published or unpublished, on the grounds that such exposure would taint the purity of his own writing. But thinking of creativity as the evasion of conventions is a mistake; creativity, we maintain, is better thought of as a way of playing with and within conventions.

David Foster Wallace's 2005 commencement speech at Kenyon College illustrates this creative play beautifully. Wallace began conventionally enough, with a parable about how much the young still have to learn:

> There are these two young fish swimming along and they happen to meet an older fish swimming the other way, who nods at them and says, "Morning, boys. How's the water?" And the two young fish swim on for a bit, and then eventually one of them looks over at the other and goes, "What the hell is water?"

Given the occasion, Wallace acknowledged that his audience was likely to see the point of the parable as introducing the moment when the "wise old fish" behind the podium shared his wisdom with the "younger fish" in the audience: "the most obvious, important realities are often the ones that are hardest to see and talk about." Wallace didn't sound much like a wise elder when he told the graduating seniors and their families that he wanted to talk about "the value of the totally obvious." That's an odd topic for a commencement speech, but Wallace insisted that his unconventional choice made sense. "In the day-to-day trenches of adult existence," he said, "banal platitudes can have a life-or-death importance."

Life-or-death importance?

Coming from a more conventional writer, those words might have served only as a laugh line, an over-the-top exaggeration. But Wallace wasn't kidding. He was utterly, disarmingly sincere. Having posed the problem of our numbness to our own lives and surroundings, as well as our tendency "to be deeply and literally self-centered, and to see and interpret everything through this lens of self," he challenged his audience to consider other options:

> Twenty years after my own graduation, I have come gradually to understand that the liberal arts cliché about teaching you how to think is actually shorthand for a much deeper, more serious idea: learning how to think really means learning how to exercise some control over how and what you think. It means being conscious and aware enough to choose what you pay attention to and to choose how you construct meaning from experience. Because if you cannot exercise this kind of choice in adult life, you will be totally hosed.

In other words, we can put our brains on their default settings and glide along thinking we are the center of the universe, or we can be deliberate about how we think and what we pay attention to. Choosing to pay attention takes practice and effort. It is, Wallace stated at the end of his address, "unimaginably hard to do this, to stay conscious and alive in the adult world day in and day out." And this means, he concluded, that "yet another grand cliché turns out to be true: your education really *is* the job of a lifetime." The ultimate value of an education, he continued,

> has almost nothing to do with knowledge, and everything to do with simple awareness; awareness of what is so real and essential, so hidden in plain sight all around us, all the time, that we have to keep reminding ourselves over and over:

"This is water."

"This is water."

When Wallace sat down to write this commencement speech, he knew the basic conventions of the genre, but in order to write a *good* speech, a *memorable* speech, he needed the habits of a curious and creative mind. He gave the families of the Kenyon graduates what they came for by hitting most of the marks of a conventional graduation speech—the parable, the words of wisdom, and so on. But he also invited his audience to join him in conscious reflection about the artificiality of those conventions when they are deployed without creativity, and about the authenticity that can be generated when those same conventions are used to say something unexpected. He asked all those present to contemplate the possibility that the adult lives these graduates were about to commence could well become so consuming in their dull everydayness that experience might stop being meaningful.

Wallace didn't end his speech on this ominous note, though: this is a commencement speech, after all. Instead, almost in spite of himself, he offered the audience some wise advice—that it's possible to become aware again of what's real and essential, and that reacquiring and maintaining this awareness never stops being work. Or to put it another way, he encouraged his audience to practice the habits of the creative mind, day in and day out, while knowing that the practice never ends.

. . . . .

David Foster Wallace's speech is worth reading and listening to in full, so we'd like you to find a copy of *This Is Water* at the library, or find transcripts and audio files of the speech online. We recommend reading the transcript while following along with Wallace's voice on a recording before you move on to the practice sessions on the next page.

Practice Session One

Reading

In our discussion of convention, we said that thinking of creativity as the evasion of conventions is a mistake, and that creativity is better thought of as a way of playing with conventions. In this practice session we want you to explore how Wallace plays with, rather than evades, conventions. Listen to the speech—ideally with a transcript in hand—and find at least five specific examples, other than the ones we've discussed above, of Wallace playing with conventions.

Then take at least 30 minutes to write about how his play with words, style, ideas, and the tradition of the commencement speech contributes to your experience as a reader. Note: At times you may not like Wallace's playfulness, so feel free to write about the full range of ways his approach to convention contributes to your experience.

Practice Session Two

Reflecting

Wallace's commencement speech points out that it's conventional for adults to be governed by an inner monologue that ends up preventing them from thinking new thoughts. For this practice session we'd like you to set aside three 15-minute periods over a span of several days during which you consciously try to silence your automatic inner monologue and practice being aware of your surroundings—the people around you, the scene unfolding before you, the questions or ideas you might normally tune out. After you've practiced awareness over the three 15-minute periods, spend at least 30 minutes writing about what you saw, heard, or sensed that was new to you.

Writing

Wallace says in his speech that, when we are no longer numb to our surroundings, we have the opportunity to make choices about the meaning of our experience. After reviewing your notes from the "Reflecting" practice session, write a meditative essay that makes your experience of paying attention meaningful. We invite you to play with conventions of thought and form as you write. We don't want you to imitate Wallace's voice—just his habits of mind.

EXPLORE

Throughout this book, we've identified many examples of writing that plays with convention, and below we offer a short reading list of inventive book-length contemporary works. Alison Bechdel uses the relatively new form graphic novel to tell an utterly nontraditional coming-of-age story. Junot Díaz's narrator blends English with untranslated Spanish and Dominican slang and mixes high and low cultural references to tell a new migration story. David Shields and Rebecca Solnit both experiment with nonfiction form: Shields explores the relationship of fiction and nonfiction in 618 numbered paragraphs and Solnit recreates the essay as a collage of analogies.

Bechdel, Alison. *Fun Home.* New York: Houghton Mifflin, 2006. Print.

Díaz, Junot. *The Brief Wonderful Life of Oscar Wao.* New York: Riverhead, 2007. Print.

Shields, David. *Reality Hunger: A Manifesto.* New York: Knopf, 2010. Print.

Solnit, Rebecca. *The Faraway Nearby.* New York: Penguin, 2014. Print.

Creativity at Work: James McBride's Serious Humor

When militant abolitionist John Brown and eighteen followers raided a federal armory in Harpers Ferry, Virginia, in 1859, their intention was to steal weapons and arm local slaves. Instead, Brown and his men were besieged by troops, and he was arrested, tried for treason, and hanged. He died unrepentant, insisting that he was right to fight the sin of slavery with violence. Although many echoed Robert E. Lee's dismissal of Brown as a "fanatic or madman," he became an international hero, praised by Henry David Thoreau, Ralph Waldo Emerson, and even Victor Hugo for his courage and integrity. To this day, historians remain divided about whether Brown was insane, visionary, or America's first domestic terrorist.

Brown's story has been retold many times, but novelist and memoirist James McBride felt something vital about Brown was lost in the accounts that focus on whether Brown was a visionary or a madman, so he set out "to find a way to do him differently." How, McBride wondered, might Brown have appeared to a young slave—as a madman, a visionary leader, or both? To explore this question, McBride invented 12-year-old Kansas Territory slave Henry Shackleford and, at the beginning of *The Good Lord Bird,* has him become a fugitive slave after a violent confrontation between Brown and Shackleford's owner. Should Henry go with the unpredictable Brown, who has mistaken him for a girl and has nicknamed him "Onion," or should he return to the predictable insanity of slavery? Shackleford sticks with Brown and provides running commentary on Brown's Abolitionist efforts that is surprisingly, even shockingly, humorous.

Indeed, the unexpected homor in *The Good Lord Bird* prompted a *New York Times* reviewer to ask whether the novel shows that we have "come so far from historical horrors that we freely jest about them." McBride said in interviews that he did, in fact, want to write a novel that would allow people to laugh at things they had difficulty talking about—in particular, the history of slavery in the United States. This is one of humor's important cultural functions; we can recognize

historical injustices and other horrors through comedy, even when we can't yet face them directly. So when McBride tells Brown's familiar story in an irreverent way, the humor serves a deeper purpose: even as we laugh at Brown, an odd figure and the unlikeliest of heroes, we also come to understand that he was right to recognize slavery as an injustice that had to be abolished at any cost.

READINGS

FEAR OF A BLACK PRESIDENT

Ta-Nehisi Coates

Ta-Nehisi Coates is a writer, senior editor, and blogger at *The Atlantic*, one of the nation's oldest and most respected magazines. Coates uses his blog to think publicly about politics, history, and race, and moderates a comment section that keeps the conversation—and his thinking—going. His post, "I Might Be Charlie," is exemplary in this regard. Coates was in Paris when a massacre occurred at the offices of the satirical magazine *Charlie Hebdo*. He wrote about how the people around him were making sense of the tragedy, while he didn't yet feel qualified to voice an opinion. In an effort to understand the meaning of the terrorist act and the subsequent outpouring of patriotism, Coates turned to history; he discussed Algeria's war for independence from France and the sustained practice of racism in Europe. Near the end of his post, he wrote: "I don't yet know how all of this connects to the events we are seeing today. But I proceed from the working theory that all nations like to begin the story with the chapter that most advantages them and the job of the writer is to resist this instinct."

The irony of President Barack Obama is best captured in his comments on the death of Trayvon Martin, and the ensuing fray. Obama has pitched his presidency as a monument to moderation. He peppers his speeches with nods to ideas originally held by conservatives. He routinely cites Ronald Reagan. He effusively praises the enduring wisdom of the American people, and believes that the height of insight lies

in the town square. Despite his sloganeering for change and progress, Obama is a conservative revolutionary, and nowhere is his conservative character revealed more than in the very sphere where he holds singular gravity—race.

Part of that conservatism about race has been reflected in his reticence: for most of his term in office, Obama has declined to talk about the ways in which race complicates the American present and, in particular, his own presidency. But then, last February, George Zimmerman, a 28-year-old insurance underwriter, shot and killed a black teenager, Trayvon Martin, in Sanford, Florida. Zimmerman, armed with a 9 mm handgun, believed himself to be tracking the movements of a possible intruder. The possible intruder turned out to be a boy in a hoodie, bearing nothing but candy and iced tea. The local authorities at first declined to make an arrest, citing Zimmerman's claim of self-defense. Protests exploded nationally. Skittles and Arizona Iced Tea assumed totemic power. Celebrities—the actor Jamie Foxx, the former Michigan governor Jennifer Granholm, members of the Miami Heat—were photographed wearing hoodies. When Representative Bobby Rush of Chicago took to the House floor to denounce racial profiling, he was removed from the chamber after donning a hoodie mid-speech.

The reaction to the tragedy was, at first, trans-partisan. Conservatives either said nothing or offered tepid support for a full investigation—and in fact it was the Republican governor of Florida, Rick Scott, who appointed the special prosecutor who ultimately charged Zimmerman with second-degree murder. As civil-rights activists descended on Florida, *National Review,* a magazine that once opposed integration, ran a column proclaiming "Al Sharpton Is Right." The belief that a young man should be able to go to the store for Skittles and an iced tea and not be killed by a neighborhood-watch patroller seemed uncontroversial.

By the time reporters began asking the White House for comment, the president likely had already given the matter considerable thought. Obama is not simply America's first black president—he is the first president who could credibly teach a black-studies class. He is fully versed in the works of Richard Wright and James Baldwin, Frederick Douglass and Malcolm X. Obama's two autobiographies are deeply concerned with race, and in front of black audiences he is apt to cite

important but obscure political figures such as George Henry White, who served from 1897 to 1901 and was the last African American congressman to be elected from the South until 1970. But with just a few notable exceptions, the president had, for the first three years of his presidency, strenuously avoided talk of race. And yet, when Trayvon Martin died, talk Obama did:

> When I think about this boy, I think about my own kids, and I think every parent in America should be able to understand why it is absolutely imperative that we investigate every aspect of this, and that everybody pulls together— federal, state, and local—to figure out exactly how this tragedy happened. . . .
>
> But my main message is to the parents of Trayvon Martin. If I had a son, he'd look like Trayvon. I think they are right to expect that all of us as Americans are going to take this with the seriousness it deserves, and that we're going to get to the bottom of exactly what happened.

The moment Obama spoke, the case of Trayvon Martin passed out of its national-mourning phase and lapsed into something darker and more familiar—racialized political fodder. The illusion of consensus crumbled. Rush Limbaugh denounced Obama's claim of empathy. *The Daily Caller*, a conservative Web site, broadcast all of Martin's tweets, the most loutish of which revealed him to have committed the unpardonable sin of speaking like a 17-year-old boy. A white-supremacist site called Stormfront produced a photo of Martin with pants sagging, flipping the bird. *Business Insider* posted the photograph and took it down without apology when it was revealed to be a fake.

Newt Gingrich pounced on Obama's comments: "Is the president suggesting that if it had been a white who had been shot, that would be okay because it wouldn't look like him?" Reverting to form, *National Review* decided the real problem was that we were interested in the deaths of black youths only when nonblacks pulled the trigger. John Derbyshire, writing for *Taki's Magazine*, an iconoclastic libertarian publication, composed a racist advice column for his children inspired by the Martin affair. (Among Derbyshire's tips: never help black people

in any kind of distress; avoid large gatherings of black people; cultivate black friends to shield yourself from charges of racism.)

The notion that Zimmerman might be the real victim began seeping out into the country, aided by PR efforts by his family and legal team, as well as by various acts of stupidity—Spike Lee tweeting Zimmerman's address (an act made all the more repugnant by the fact that he had the wrong Zimmerman), NBC misleadingly editing a tape of Zimmerman's phone conversation with a police dispatcher to make Zimmerman seem to be racially profiling Martin. In April, when Zimmerman set up a Web site to collect donations for his defense, he raised more than $200,000 in two weeks, before his lawyer asked that he close the site and launched a new, independently managed legal-defense fund. Although the trial date has yet to be set, as of July the fund was still raking in up to $1,000 in donations daily.

But it would be wrong to attribute the burgeoning support for Zimmerman to the blunders of Spike Lee or an NBC producer. Before President Obama spoke, the death of Trayvon Martin was generally regarded as a national tragedy. After Obama spoke, Martin became material for an Internet vendor flogging paper gun-range targets that mimicked his hoodie and his bag of Skittles. (The vendor sold out within a week.) Before the president spoke, George Zimmerman was arguably the most reviled man in America. After the president spoke, Zimmerman became the patron saint of those who believe that an apt history of racism begins with Tawana Brawley and ends with the Duke lacrosse team.

The irony of Barack Obama is this: he has become the most successful black politician in American history by avoiding the radioactive racial issues of yesteryear, by being "clean" (as Joe Biden once labeled him)—and yet his indelible blackness irradiates everything he touches. This irony is rooted in the greater ironies of the country he leads. For most of American history, our political system was premised on two conflicting facts—one, an oft-stated love of democracy; the other, an undemocratic white supremacy inscribed at every level of government. In warring against that paradox, African Americans have historically been restricted to the realm of protest and agitation. But when President Barack Obama pledged to "get to the bottom of exactly what happened," he was not protesting or agitating. He was not appealing

to federal power—he was employing it. The power was black—and, in certain quarters, was received as such.

No amount of rhetorical moderation could change this. It did not matter that the president addressed himself to "every parent in America." His insistence that "everybody [pull] together" was irrelevant. It meant nothing that he declined to cast aspersions on the investigating authorities, or to speculate on events. Even the fact that Obama expressed his own connection to Martin in the quietest way imaginable—"If I had a son, he'd look like Trayvon"—would not mollify his opposition. It is, after all, one thing to hear "I am Trayvon Martin" from the usual placard-waving rabble-rousers. Hearing it from the commander of the greatest military machine in human history is another.

By virtue of his background—the son of a black man and a white woman, someone who grew up in multiethnic communities around the world—Obama has enjoyed a distinctive vantage point on race relations in America. Beyond that, he has displayed enviable dexterity at navigating between black and white America, and at finding a language that speaks to a critical mass in both communities. He emerged into national view at the Democratic National Convention in 2004, with a speech heralding a nation uncolored by old prejudices and shameful history. There was no talk of the effects of racism. Instead Obama stressed the power of parenting, and condemned those who would say that a black child carrying a book was "acting white." He cast himself as the child of a father from Kenya and a mother from Kansas and asserted, "In no other country on Earth is my story even possible." When, as a senator, he was asked if the response to Hurricane Katrina evidenced racism, Obama responded by calling the "ineptitude" of the response "color-blind."

Racism is not merely a simplistic hatred. It is, more often, broad sympathy toward some and broader skepticism toward others. Black America ever lives under that skeptical eye. Hence the old admonishments to be "twice as good." Hence the need for a special "talk" administered to black boys about how to be extra careful when relating to the police. And hence Barack Obama's insisting that there was no racial component to Katrina's effects; that name-calling among children somehow has the same import as one of the oldest guiding principles of American policy—white supremacy. The election of an

African American to our highest political office was alleged to demonstrate a triumph of integration. But when President Obama addressed the tragedy of Trayvon Martin, he demonstrated integration's great limitation—that acceptance depends not just on being twice as good but on being half as black. And even then, full acceptance is still withheld. The larger effects of this withholding constrict Obama's presidential potential in areas affected tangentially—or seemingly not at all—by race. Meanwhile, across the country, the community in which Obama is rooted sees this fraudulent equality, and quietly seethes.

Obama's first term has coincided with a strategy of massive resistance on the part of his Republican opposition in the House, and a record number of filibuster threats in the Senate. It would be nice if this were merely a reaction to Obama's politics or his policies—if this resistance truly were, as it is generally described, merely one more sign of our growing "polarization" as a nation. But the greatest abiding challenge to Obama's national political standing has always rested on the existential fact that if he had a son, he'd look like Trayvon Martin. As a candidate, Barack Obama understood this.

"The thing is, a *black man* can't be president in America, given the racial aversion and history that's still out there," Cornell Belcher, a pollster for Obama, told the journalist Gwen Ifill after the 2008 election. "However, an extraordinary, gifted, and talented young man who happens to be black can be president."

Belcher's formulation grants the power of anti-black racism, and proposes to defeat it by not acknowledging it. His is the perfect statement of the Obama era, a time marked by a revolution that must never announce itself, by a democracy that must never acknowledge the weight of race, even while being shaped by it. Barack Obama governs a nation enlightened enough to send an African American to the White House, but not enlightened enough to accept a black man as its president.

. . . . .

Before Barack Obama, the "black president" lived in the African American imagination as a kind of cosmic joke, a phantom of all that could never be. White folks, whatever their talk of freedom and liberty, would not allow a black president. They could not tolerate Emmett's

boyish gaze. Dr. King turned the other cheek, and they blew it off. White folks shot Lincoln over "nigger equality," ran Ida Wells out of Memphis, beat Freedom Riders over bus seats, slaughtered Medgar in his driveway like a dog. The comedian Dave Chappelle joked that the first black president would need a "Vice President Santiago"—because the only thing that would ensure his life in the White House was a Hispanic president-in-waiting. A black president signing a bill into law might as well sign his own death certificate.

And even if white folks could moderate their own penchant for violence, we could not moderate our own. A long-suffering life on the wrong side of the color line had denuded black people of the delicacy necessary to lead the free world. In a skit on his 1977 TV comedy show, Richard Pryor, as a black president, conceded that he was "courting an awful lot of white women" and held a press conference that erupted into a riot after a reporter requested that the president's momma clean his house. More recently, the comedian Cedric the Entertainer joked that a black president would never have made it through Monicagate without turning a press conference into a battle royal. When Chappelle tried to imagine how a black George W. Bush would have justified the war against Saddam Hussein, his character ("Black Bush") simply yelled, "The nigger tried to kill my father!"

Thus, in hard jest, the paradoxes and problems of a theoretical black presidency were given voice. Racism would not allow a black president. Nor would a blackness, forged by America's democratic double-talk, that was too ghetto and raw for the refinement of the Oval Office. Just beneath the humor lurked a resonant pain, the scars of history, an aching doubt rooted in the belief that "they" would never accept us. And so in our Harlems and Paradise Valleys, we invoked a black presidency the way a legion of 5-foot point guards might invoke the dunk—as evidence of some great cosmic injustice, weighty in its import, out of reach.

And yet Spud Webb lives.

When presidential candidate Barack Obama presented himself to the black community, he was not to be believed. It strained credulity to think that a man sporting the same rigorously managed haircut as Jay-Z, a man who was a hard-core pickup basketball player, and who was married to a dark-skinned black woman from the South Side,

could coax large numbers of white voters into the booth. Obama's blackness quotient is often a subject of debate. (He himself once joked, while speaking to the National Association of Black Journalists in 2007, "I want to apologize for being a little bit late, but you guys keep on asking whether I'm black enough.") But despite Obama's post-election reluctance to talk about race, he has always displayed both an obvious affinity for black culture and a distinct ability to defy black America's worst self-conceptions.

The crude communal myth about black men is that we are in some manner unavailable to black women—either jailed, dead, gay, or married to white women. A corollary myth posits a direct and negative relationship between success and black culture. Before we actually had one, we could not imagine a black president who loved being black. In *The Audacity of Hope,* Obama describes his first kiss with the woman who would become his wife as tasting "of chocolate." The line sounds ripped from *Essence* magazine. That's the point.

These cultural cues became important during Obama's presidential run and beyond. Obama doesn't merely evince blackness; he uses his blackness to signal and court African Americans, semaphoring in a cultural dialect of our creation—crooning Al Green at the Apollo, name-checking Young Jeezy, regularly appearing on the cover of black magazines, weighing the merits of Jay-Z versus Kanye West, being photographed in the White House with a little black boy touching his hair. There is often something mawkish about this signaling—like a Virginia politico thickening his southern accent when talking to certain audiences. If you've often been the butt of political signaling (Sister Souljah, Willie Horton), and rarely the recipient, these displays of cultural affinity are powerful. And they are all the more powerful because Obama has been successful. Whole sections of America that we had assumed to be negrophobic turned out in support of him in 2008. Whatever Obama's other triumphs, arguably his greatest has been an expansion of the black imagination to encompass this: the idea that a man can be culturally black and many other things also—biracial, Ivy League, intellectual, cosmopolitan, temperamentally conservative, presidential.

It is often said that Obama's presidency has given black parents the right to tell their kids with a straight face that they can do anything. This is a function not only of Obama's election to the White House but of the way his presidency broadcasts an easy, almost mystic, blackness to the world. The Obama family represents our ideal imagining of ourselves—an ideal we so rarely see on any kind of national stage.

What black people are experiencing right now is a kind of privilege previously withheld—seeing our most sacred cultural practices and tropes validated in the world's highest office. Throughout the whole of American history, this kind of cultural power was wielded solely by whites, and with such ubiquity that it was not even commented upon. The expansion of this cultural power beyond the private province of whites has been a tremendous advance for black America. Conversely, for those who've long treasured white exclusivity, the existence of a President Barack Obama is discombobulating, even terrifying. For as surely as the iconic picture of the young black boy reaching out to touch the president's curly hair sends one message to black America, it sends another to those who have enjoyed the power of whiteness.

· · · · ·

In America, the rights to own property, to serve on a jury, to vote, to hold public office, to rise to the presidency have historically been seen as belonging only to those people who showed particular integrity. Citizenship was a social contract in which persons of moral standing were transformed into stakeholders who swore to defend the state against threats external and internal. Until a century and a half ago, slave rebellion ranked high in the fevered American imagination of threats necessitating such an internal defense.

In the early years of our republic, when democracy was still an unproven experiment, the Founders were not even clear that all white people should be entrusted with this fragile venture, much less the bestial African. Thus Congress, in 1790, declared the following:

> All free white persons who have, or shall migrate into the United States, and shall give satisfactory proof, before a magistrate, by oath, that they intend to reside therein, and shall take an oath of allegiance, and shall have resided in the United States for one whole year, shall be entitled to all the rights of citizenship.

In such ways was the tie between citizenship and whiteness in America made plain from the very beginning. By the 19th century, there was, as Matthew Jacobson, a professor of history and American studies at Yale, has put it, "an unquestioned acceptance of whiteness as a prerequisite for naturalized citizenship." Debating Abraham Lincoln during the race for a US Senate seat in Illinois in 1858, Stephen Douglas asserted that "this government was made on the white basis" and that the Framers had made "no reference either to the Negro, the savage Indians, the Feejee, the Malay, or an other inferior and degraded race, when they spoke of the equality of men."

After the Civil War, Andrew Johnson, Lincoln's successor as president and a unionist, scoffed at awarding the Negro the franchise:

> The peculiar qualities which should characterize any people who are fit to decide upon the management of public affairs for a great state have seldom been combined. It is the glory of white men to know that they have had these qualities in sufficient measure to build upon this continent a great political fabric and to preserve its stability for more than ninety years, while in every other part of the world all similar experiments have failed. But if anything can be proved by known facts, if all reasoning upon evidence is not abandoned, it must be acknowledged that in the progress of nations Negroes have shown less capacity for government than any other race of people. No independent government of any form has ever been successful in their hands. On the contrary, wherever they have been left to their own devices they have shown a constant tendency to relapse into barbarism.

The notion of blacks as particularly unfit for political equality persisted well into the 20th century. As the nation began considering integrating its military, a young West Virginian wrote to a senator in 1944:

> I am a typical American, a southerner, and 27 years of age. . . . I am loyal to my country and know but reverence to her flag, BUT I shall never submit to fight beneath that

banner with a negro by my side. Rather I should die a thousand times, and see Old Glory trampled in the dirt never to rise again, than to see this beloved land of ours become degraded by race mongrels, a throw back to the blackest specimen from the wilds.

The writer—who never joined the military, but did join the Ku Klux Klan—was Robert Byrd, who died in 2010 as the longest-serving US senator in history. Byrd's rejection of political equality was echoed in 1957 by William F. Buckley Jr., who addressed the moral disgrace of segregation by endorsing disenfranchisement strictly based on skin color:

The central question that emerges—and it is not a parliamentary question or a question that is answered by merely consulting a catalog of the rights of American citizens, born Equal—is whether the White community in the South is entitled to take such measures as are necessary to prevail, politically and culturally, in areas in which it does not predominate numerically? The sobering answer is Yes—the White community is so entitled because, for the time being, it is the advanced race.

Buckley, the founder of *National Review*, went on to assert, "The great majority of the Negroes of the South who do not vote do not care to vote and would not know for what to vote if they could."

The idea that blacks should hold no place of consequence in the American political future has affected every sector of American society, transforming whiteness itself into a monopoly on American possibilities. White people like Byrd and Buckley were raised in a time when, by law, they were assured of never having to compete with black people for the best of anything. Blacks used inferior public pools and inferior washrooms, attended inferior schools. The nicest restaurants turned them away. In large swaths of the country, blacks paid taxes but could neither attend the best universities nor exercise the right to vote. The best jobs, the richest neighborhoods, were giant set-asides for whites—universal affirmative action, with no pretense of restitution.

Slavery, Jim Crow, segregation: these bonded white people into a broad aristocracy united by the salient fact of unblackness. What Byrd saw in an integrated military was the crumbling of the ideal of whiteness, and thus the crumbling of an entire society built around it. Whatever the saintly nonviolent rhetoric used to herald it, racial integration was a brutal assault on whiteness. The American presidency, an unbroken streak of nonblack men, was, until 2008, the greatest symbol of that old order.

Watching Obama rack up victories in states like Virginia, New Mexico, Ohio, and North Carolina on Election Night in 2008, anyone could easily conclude that racism, as a national force, had been defeated. The thought should not be easily dismissed: Obama's victory demonstrates the incredible distance this country has traveled. (Indeed, William F. Buckley Jr. later revised his early positions on race; Robert Byrd spent decades in Congress atoning for his.) That a country that once took whiteness as the foundation of citizenship would elect a black president is a victory. But to view this victory as racism's defeat is to forget the precise terms on which it was secured, and to ignore the quaking ground beneath Obama's feet.

During the 2008 primary, the *New Yorker*'s George Packer journeyed to Kentucky and was shocked by the brazen declarations of white identity. "I think he would put too many minorities in positions over the white race," one voter told Packer. "That's my opinion." That voter was hardly alone. In 2010, Michael Tesler, a political scientist at Brown University, and David Sears, a professor of psychology and political science at UCLA, were able to assess the impact of race in the 2008 primary by comparing data from two 2008 campaign and election studies with previous surveys of racial resentment and voter choice. As they wrote in *Obama's Race: The 2008 Election and the Dream of a Post-Racial America*:

> No other factor, in fact, came close to dividing the Democratic primary electorate as powerfully as their feelings about African Americans. The impact of racial attitudes on individual vote decisions . . . was so strong that it appears to have even outstripped the substantive impact of racial attitudes on Jesse Jackson's more racially charged campaign for the nomination in 1988.

Seth Stephens-Davidowitz, a doctoral candidate in economics at Harvard, is studying how racial animus may have cost Obama votes in 2008. First, Stephens-Davidowitz ranked areas of the country according to how often people there typed racist search terms into Google. (The areas with the highest rates of racially charged search terms were West Virginia, western Pennsylvania, eastern Ohio, upstate New York, and southern Mississippi.) Then he compared Obama's voting results in those areas with John Kerry's four years earlier. So, for instance, in 2004 Kerry received 50 percent of the vote in the media markets of both Denver and Wheeling (which straddles the Ohio–West Virginia border). Based on the Democratic groundswell in 2008, Obama should have received about 57 percent of the popular vote in both regions. But that's not what happened. In the Denver area, which had one of the nation's lowest rates of racially charged Google searching, Obama received the predicted 57 percent. But in Wheeling, which had a high rate of racially charged Google searching, Obama's share of the popular vote was only 48 percent. Of course, Obama also picked up some votes because he is black. But, aggregating his findings nationally, Stephens-Davidowitz has concluded that Obama lost between 3 and 5 percentage points of the popular vote to racism.

After Obama won, the longed-for post-racial moment did not arrive; on the contrary, racism intensified. At rallies for the nascent Tea Party, people held signs saying things like Obama Plans White Slavery. Steve King, an Iowa congressman and Tea Party favorite, complained that Obama "favors the black person." In 2009, Rush Limbaugh, bard of white decline, called Obama's presidency a time when "the white kids now get beat up, with the black kids cheering 'Yeah, right on, right on, right on.' And of course everybody says the white kid deserved it—he was born a racist, he's white." On *Fox & Friends*, Glenn Beck asserted that Obama had exposed himself as a guy "who has a deep-seated hatred for white people or the white culture. . . . This guy is, I believe, a racist." Beck later said he was wrong to call Obama a racist. That same week he also called the president's health-care plan "reparations."

One possible retort to this pattern of racial paranoia is to cite the Clinton years, when an ideological fever drove the right wing to derangement, inspiring militia movements and accusations that the president had conspired to murder his own lawyer, Vince Foster. The

upshot, by this logic, is that Obama is experiencing run-of-the-mill political opposition in which race is but a minor factor among much larger ones, such as party affiliation. But the argument assumes that party affiliation itself is unconnected to race. It pretends that only Toni Morrison took note of Clinton's particular appeal to black voters. It forgets that Clinton felt compelled to attack Sister Souljah. It forgets that whatever ignoble labels the right wing pinned on Clinton's health-care plan, "reparations" did not rank among them.

Michael Tesler, following up on his research with David Sears on the role of race in the 2008 campaign, recently published a study assessing the impact of race on opposition to and support for health-care reform. The findings are bracing. Obama's election effectively racialized white Americans' views, even of health-care policy. As Tesler writes in a paper published in July in the *American Journal of Political Science,* "Racial attitudes had a significantly greater impact on health care opinions when framed as part of President Obama's plan than they had when the exact same policies were attributed to President Clinton's 1993 health care initiative."

While Beck and Limbaugh have chosen direct racial assault, others choose simply to deny that a black president actually exists. One in four Americans (and more than half of all Republicans) believe Obama was not born in this country, and thus is an illegitimate president. More than a dozen state legislatures have introduced "birther bills" demanding proof of Obama's citizenship as a condition for putting him on the 2012 ballot. Eighteen percent of Republicans believe Obama to be a Muslim. The goal of all this is to delegitimize Obama's presidency. If Obama is not truly American, then America has still never had a black president.

White resentment has not cooled as the Obama presidency has proceeded. Indeed, the GOP presidential-primary race featured candidates asserting that the black family was better off under slavery (Michele Bachmann, Rick Santorum); claiming that Obama, as a black man, should oppose abortion (Santorum again); or denouncing Obama as a "food-stamp president" (Newt Gingrich).

The resentment is not confined to Republicans. Earlier this year, West Virginia gave 41 percent of the popular vote during the Democratic primary to Keith Judd, a white incarcerated felon (Judd actually defeated

Obama in 10 counties). Joe Manchin, one of West Virginia's senators, and Earl Ray Tomblin, its governor, are declining to attend this year's Democratic convention, and will not commit to voting for Obama.

It is often claimed that Obama's unpopularity in coal-dependent West Virginia stems from his environmental policies. But recall that no state ranked higher on Seth Stephens-Davidowitz's racism scale than West Virginia. Moreover, Obama was unpopular in West Virginia before he became president: even at the tail end of the Democratic primaries in 2008, Hillary Clinton walloped Obama by 41 points. A fifth of West Virginia Democrats openly professed that race played a role in their vote.

What we are now witnessing is not some new and complicated expression of white racism—rather, it's the dying embers of the same old racism that once rendered the best pickings of America the exclusive province of unblackness. Confronted by the thoroughly racialized backlash to Obama's presidency, a stranger to American politics might conclude that Obama provoked the response by relentlessly pushing an agenda of radical racial reform. Hardly. Daniel Gillion, a political scientist at the University of Pennsylvania who studies race and politics, examined the Public Papers of the Presidents, a compilation of nearly all public presidential utterances—proclamations, news-conference remarks, executive orders—and found that in his first two years as president, Obama talked less about race than any other Democratic president since 1961. Obama's racial strategy has been, if anything, the opposite of radical: he declines to use his bully pulpit to address racism, using it instead to engage in the time-honored tradition of black self-hectoring, railing against the perceived failings of black culture.

His approach is not new. It is the approach of Booker T. Washington, who, amid a sea of white terrorists during the era of Jim Crow, endorsed segregation and proclaimed the South to be a land of black opportunity. It is the approach of L. Douglas Wilder, who, in 1986, not long before he became Virginia's first black governor, kept his distance from Jesse Jackson and told an NAACP audience: "Yes, dear Brutus, the fault is not in our stars, but in ourselves. . . . Some blacks don't particularly care for me to say these things, to speak to values. . . . Somebody's got to. We've been too excusing." It was even, at times, the approach of Jesse Jackson himself, who railed against "the rising use of drugs, and babies making babies, and violence . . . cutting away our opportunity."

The strategy can work. Booker T.'s Tuskegee University still stands. Wilder became the first black governor in America since Reconstruction. Jackson's campaign moved the Democratic nominating process toward proportional allocation of delegates, a shift that Obama exploited in the 2008 Democratic primaries by staying competitive enough in big states to rack up delegates even where he was losing, and rolling up huge vote margins (and delegate-count victories) in smaller ones.

And yet what are we to make of an integration premised, first, on the entire black community's emulating the Huxtables? An equality that requires blacks to be twice as good is not equality—it's a double standard. That double standard haunts and constrains the Obama presidency, warning him away from candor about America's sordid birthmark.

· · · · ·

Another political tradition in black America, running counter to the one publicly embraced by Obama and Booker T. Washington, casts its skepticism not simply upon black culture but upon the entire American project. This tradition stretches back to Frederick Douglass, who, in 1852, said of his native country, "There is not a nation on the earth guilty of practices more shocking and bloody than are the people of the United States at this very hour." It extends through Martin Delany, through Booker T.'s nemesis W. E. B. Du Bois, and through Malcolm X. It includes Martin Luther King Jr., who at the height of the Vietnam War called America "the greatest purveyor of violence in the world today." And it includes Obama's former pastor, he of the famous "God Damn America" sermon, Jeremiah Wright.

The Harvard Law professor Randall Kennedy, in his 2011 book, *The Persistence of the Color Line: Racial Politics and the Obama Presidency*, examines this tradition by looking at his own father and Reverend Wright in the context of black America's sense of patriotism. Like Wright, the elder Kennedy was a veteran of the US military, a man seared and radicalized by American racism, forever remade as a vociferous critic of his native country: in virtually any American conflict, Kennedy's father rooted for the foreign country.

The deep skepticism about the American project that Kennedy's father and Reverend Wright evince is an old tradition in black America.

Before Frederick Douglass worked, during the Civil War, for the preservation of the Union, he called for his country's destruction. "I have no love for America," he declaimed in a lecture to the American Anti-Slavery Society in 1847. "I have no patriotism. . . . I desire to see [the government] overthrown as speedily as possible and its Constitution shivered in a thousand fragments."

Kennedy notes that Douglass's denunciations were the words of a man who not only had endured slavery but was living in a country where whites often selected the Fourth of July as a special day to prosecute a campaign of racial terror:

> On July 4, 1805, whites in Philadelphia drove blacks out of the square facing Independence Hall. For years thereafter, blacks attended Fourth of July festivities in that city at their peril. On July 4, 1834, a white mob in New York City burned down the Broadway Tabernacle because of the antislavery and antiracist views of the church's leaders. Firefighters in sympathy with the arsonists refused to douse the conflagration. On July 4, 1835, a white mob in Canaan, New Hampshire, destroyed a school open to blacks that was run by an abolitionist. The antebellum years were liberally dotted with such episodes.

Jeremiah Wright was born into an America of segregation—overt in the South and covert in the North, but wounding wherever. He joined the Marines, vowing service to his country, at a time when he wouldn't have been allowed to vote in some states. He built his ministry in a community reeling from decades of job and housing discrimination, and heaving under the weight of drugs, gun violence, and broken families. Wright's world is emblematic of the African Americans he ministered to, people reared on the anti-black-citizenship tradition—poll taxes, states pushing stringent voter-ID laws—of Stephen Douglas and Andrew Johnson and William F. Buckley Jr. The message is "You are not American." The countermessage—God damn America—is an old one, and is surprising only to people unfamiliar with the politics of black life in this country. Unfortunately, that is an apt description of large swaths of America.

Whatever the context for Wright's speech, the surfacing of his remarks in 2008 was utterly inconvenient not just for the Obama campaign but for much of black America. One truism holds that black people are always anxious to talk about race, eager to lecture white people at every juncture about how wrong they are and about the price they must pay for past and ongoing sins. But one reason Obama rose so quickly was that African Americans are war-weary. It was not simply the country at large that was tired of the old Baby Boomer debates. Blacks, too, were sick of talking about affirmative action and school busing. There was a broad sense that integration had failed us, and a growing disenchantment with our appointed spokespeople. Obama's primary triumphs in predominantly white states gave rise to rumors of a new peace, one many blacks were anxious to achieve.

And even those black Americans who embrace the tradition of God Damn America do so not with glee but with deep pain and anguish. Both Kennedy's father and Wright were military men. My own father went to Vietnam dreaming of John Wayne, but came back quoting Malcolm X. The poet Lucille Clifton once put it succinctly:

> They act like they don't love their country
> No
> what it is
> is they found out
> their country don't love them.

In 2008, as Obama's election became imaginable, it seemed possible that our country had indeed, at long last, come to love us. We did not need our Jeremiah Wrights, our Jesse Jacksons, our products of the polarized '60s getting in the way. Indeed, after distancing himself from Wright, Obama lost almost no black support.

Obama offered black America a convenient narrative that could be meshed with the larger American story. It was a narrative premised on Crispus Attucks, not the black slaves who escaped plantations and fought for the British; on the 54th Massachusetts, not Nat Turner; on stoic and saintly Rosa Parks, not young and pregnant Claudette Colvin; on a Christlike Martin Luther King Jr., not an avenging Malcolm X. Jeremiah Wright's presence threatened to rupture that comfortable narrative by symbolizing that which makes integration impossible—black rage.

From the "inadequate black male" diatribe of the Hillary Clinton supporter Harriet Christian in 2008, to Rick Santelli's 2009 rant on CNBC against subsidizing "losers' mortgages," to Representative Joe Wilson's "You lie!" outburst during Obama's September 2009 address to Congress, to John Boehner's screaming "Hell no!" on the House floor about Obamacare in 2010, politicized rage has marked the opposition to Obama. But the rules of our racial politics require that Obama never respond in like fashion. So frightening is the prospect of black rage given voice and power that when Obama was a freshman senator, he was asked, on national television, to denounce the rage of Harry Belafonte. This fear continued with demands that he keep his distance from Louis Farrakhan and culminated with Reverend Wright and a presidency that must never betray any sign of rage toward its white opposition.

Thus the myth of "twice as good" that makes Barack Obama possible also smothers him. It holds that African Americans—enslaved, tortured, raped, discriminated against, and subjected to the most lethal homegrown terrorist movement in American history—feel no anger toward their tormentors. Of course, very little in our history argues that those who seek to tell bold truths about race will be rewarded. But it was Obama himself, as a presidential candidate in 2008, who called for such truths to be spoken. "Race is an issue that I believe this nation cannot afford to ignore right now," he said in his "More Perfect Union" speech, which he delivered after a furor erupted over Reverend Wright's "God Damn America" remarks. And yet, since taking office, Obama has virtually ignored race.

Whatever the political intelligence of this calculus, it has broad and deep consequences. The most obvious result is that it prevents Obama from directly addressing America's racial history, or saying anything meaningful about present issues tinged by race, such as mass incarceration or the drug war. There have been calls for Obama to take a softer line on state-level legalization of marijuana or even to stand for legalization himself. Indeed, there is no small amount of inconsistency in our black president's either ignoring or upholding harsh drug laws that every day injure the prospects of young black men—laws that could have ended his own, had he been of another social class and arrested for the marijuana use he openly discusses. But the intellectual argument doubles as the counterargument. If the fact of a black president is enough to racialize the wonkish world of health-care reform, what havoc would the Obama touch wreak upon the already racialized world of drug policy?

The political consequences of race extend beyond the domestic. I am, like many liberals, horrified by Obama's embrace of a secretive drone policy, and particularly the killing of American citizens without any restraints. A president aware of black America's tenuous hold on citizenship, of how the government has at times secretly conspired against its advancement—a black president with a broad sense of the world—should know better. Except a black president with Obama's past is the perfect target for right-wing attacks depicting him as weak on terrorism. The president's inability to speak candidly on race cannot be bracketed off from his inability to speak candidly on everything. Race is not simply a portion of the Obama story. It is the lens through which many Americans view all his politics.

But whatever the politics, a total submission to them is a disservice to the country. No one knows this better than Obama himself, who once described patriotism as more than pageantry and the scarfing of hot dogs. "When our laws, our leaders, or our government are out of alignment with our ideals, then the dissent of ordinary Americans may prove to be one of the truest expressions of patriotism," Obama said in Independence, Missouri, in June 2008. Love of country, like all other forms of love, requires that you tell those you care about not simply what they want to hear but what they need to hear.

But in the age of the Obama presidency, expressing that kind of patriotism is presumably best done quietly, politely, and with great deference.

· · · · ·

This spring I flew down to Albany, Georgia, and spent the day with Shirley Sherrod, a longtime civil-rights activist who embodies exactly the kind of patriotism that Obama esteems. Albany is in Dougherty County, where the poverty rate hangs around 30 percent—double that of the rest of the state. On the drive in from the airport, the selection of vendors—payday loans, title loans, and car dealers promising no credit check—evidenced the statistic.

When I met Sherrod at her office, she was working to get a birthday card out to Roger Spooner, whose farm she'd once fought to save. In July 2010, the conservative commentator Andrew Breitbart posted video clips on his Web site of a speech Sherrod had delivered to the NAACP the previous March. The video was edited so that Sherrod, then an official at the US Department of Agriculture, appeared to be bragging about discriminating against a white farmer and thus enacting a fantasy of racial revenge. The point was to tie Obama to the kind of black rage his fevered enemies often impute to him. Fearing exactly that, Sherrod's supervisors at the USDA called her in the middle of a long drive and had her submit her resignation via BlackBerry, telling her, "You're going to be on *Glenn Beck* tonight."

Glenn Beck did eventually do a segment on Sherrod—one in which he attacked the administration for forcing her out. As it turned out, the full context showed that Sherrod was actually documenting her own turn *away* from racial anger. The farmer who was the subject of the story came forward, along with his wife, and explained that Sherrod had worked tirelessly to help the family. The farmer was Roger Spooner.

Sherrod's career as an activist, first in civil rights and then later in the world of small farmers like Roger Spooner, was not chosen so much as thrust upon her. Her cousin had been lynched in 1943. Her father was shot and killed by a white relative in a dispute over some cows. There were three witnesses, but the grand jury in her native Baker County did not indict the suspect. Sherrod became an activist with the Student Nonviolent Coordinating Committee, registering voters near her hometown. Her husband, Charles Sherrod, was instrumental in leading the Albany Movement, which attracted Martin Luther King Jr. to town. But when Stokely Carmichael rose to lead SNCC and took it in a black-nationalist direction, the Sherrods, committed to nonviolence and integration, faced a weighty choice. Carmichael himself had been committed to nonviolence, until the killings and beatings he encountered as a civil-rights activist took their toll. Sherrod, with a past haunted by racist violence, would have seemed ripe for recruitment to the nationalist line. But she, along with her husband, declined, leaving SNCC in order to continue in the tradition of King and nonviolence.

Her achievements from then on are significant. She helped pioneer the farm-collective movement in America, and cofounded New Communities—a sprawling 6,000-acre collective that did everything from growing crops to canning sugar cane and sorghum. New Communities folded in 1985, largely because Ronald Reagan's USDA refused to sign off on a loan, even as it was signing off on money for smaller-scale white farmers. Sherrod went on to work with Farm Aid. She befriended Willie Nelson, held a fellowship with the Kellogg Foundation, and was shortlisted for a job in President Clinton's Agriculture Department. Still, she remained relatively unknown except to students of the civil-rights movement and activists who promoted the rights of small farmers. And unknown she would have remained, had she not been very publicly forced out of her position by the administration of the country's first black president.

Through most of her career as an agriculture activist, Sherrod had found the USDA to be a barrier to the success of black farmers. What hurt black farms the most were the discriminatory practices of local officials in granting loans. Sherrod spent years protesting these practices. But then, after the election of Barack Obama, she was hired by the USDA, where she would be supervising the very people she'd once fought. Now she would have a chance to ensure fair and nondiscriminatory lending practices. Her appointment represented the kind of unnoticed but significant changes Obama's election brought.

But then the administration, intimidated by a resurgent right wing specializing in whipping up racial resentment, compelled Sherrod to resign on the basis of the misleading clips. When the full tape emerged, the administration was left looking ridiculous.

And cowardly. An e-mail chain later surfaced in which the White House congratulated Agriculture Secretary Tom Vilsack's staff for getting ahead of the news cycle. None of them had yet seen the full tape. That the Obama administration would fold so easily gives some sense of how frightened it was of a protracted fight with any kind of racial subtext, particularly one that had a subtext of black rage. Its enemies understood this, and when no black rage could be found, they concocted some. And the administration, in a panic, knuckled under.

Violence at the hands of whites robbed Shirley Sherrod of a cousin and a father. White rage outlined the substantive rules of her life: Don't

quarrel with white people. Don't look them in the eye. Avoid Route 91 after dark. White racism destroyed New Communities, a fact validated by the nearly $13 million the organization received in the class-action suit it joined alleging racial discrimination by the local USDA officials granting loan applications. (Which means that her being forced out by Vilsack was the second time the USDA had wronged her directly.) And yet through it all, Sherrod has hewed to the rule of "twice as good." She has preached nonviolence and integration. The very video that led to her dismissal was of a speech aimed at black people, warning them against the dangers of succumbing to rage.

Driving down a sparse country road, Sherrod and I pulled over to a grassy footpath and stepped out at the spot where her father had been shot and killed in 1965. We then drove a few miles into Newton, and stopped at a large brick building that used to be the courthouse where Sherrod had tried to register to vote a few months after her father's death but had been violently turned back by the sheriff; where a year later Sherrod's mother pursued a civil case against her husband's killer. (She lost.) For this, Sherrod's mother enjoyed routine visits from white terrorists, which abated only after she, pregnant with her dead husband's son, appeared in the doorway with a gun and began calling out names of men in the mob.

When we got back into the car, I asked Sherrod why she hadn't given in to rage against her father's killers and sided with Stokely Carmichael. "It was simple for me," she said. "I really wanted to work. I wanted to win."

I asked Sherrod if she thought the president had a grasp of the specific history of the region and of the fights waged and the sacrifices made in order to make his political journey possible. "I don't think he does," Sherrod said. "When he called me [shortly after the incident], he kept saying he understood our struggle and all we'd fought for. He said, 'Read my book and you'll see.' But I *had* read his book."

In 2009, Sergeant James Crowley arrested Henry Louis Gates Jr., the eminent professor of African American studies at Harvard, at his front door in Cambridge, for, essentially, sassing him. When President Obama publicly asserted the stupidity of Crowley's action, he was so besieged that the controversy threatened to derail what he hoped would be his signature achievement—health-care reform. Obama, an African

American male who had risen through the ranks of the American elite, was no doubt sensitive to untoward treatment at the hands of the police. But his expounding upon it so provoked right-wing rage that he was forced away from doing the kind of truth-telling he'd once lauded. "I don't know if you've noticed," Obama said at the time, "but nobody's been paying much attention to health care."

Shirley Sherrod has worked all her life to make a world where the rise of a black president born of a biracial marriage is both conceivable and legal. She has endured the killing of relatives, the ruination of enterprises, and the defaming of her reputation. Crowley, for his actions, was feted in the halls of American power, honored by being invited to a "beer summit" with the man he had arrested and the leader of the free world. Shirley Sherrod, unjustly fired and defamed, was treated to a brief phone call from a man whose career, in some profound way, she had made possible. Sherrod herself is not immune to this point. She talked to me about crying with her husband while watching Obama's Election Night speech. In her new memoir, *The Courage to Hope*, she writes about a different kind of tears: when she discussed her firing with her family, her mother, who'd spent her life facing down racism at its most lethal, simply wept. "What will my babies say?" Sherrod cried to her husband, referring to their four small granddaughters. "How can I explain to my children that I got fired by the first black president?"

· · · · ·

In 2000, an undercover police officer followed a young man named Prince Jones from suburban Maryland through Washington, D.C., into northern Virginia and shot him dead, near the home of his girlfriend and 11-month-old daughter. Jones was a student at Howard University. His mother was a radiologist. He was also my friend. The officer tracking Prince thought he was on the trail of a drug dealer. But the dealer he was after was short and wore dreadlocks—Prince was tall and wore his hair cropped close. The officer was black. He wore dreadlocks and a T-shirt, in an attempt to look like a drug dealer. The ruse likely worked. He claimed that after Prince got out of his car and confronted him, he drew his gun and said "Police"; Prince returned to his car and repeatedly rammed the officer's unmarked car with his own vehicle. The story sounded wildly at odds with the young man I knew. But even if it was

accurate, I could easily see myself frightened by a strange car following me for miles, and then reacting wildly when a man in civilian clothes pulled out a gun and claimed to be a cop. (The officer never showed a badge.)

No criminal charges were ever brought against Carlton Jones, the officer who killed my friend and rendered a little girl fatherless. It was as if society barely blinked. A few months later, I moved to New York. When 9/11 happened, I wanted nothing to do with any kind of patriotism, with the broad national ceremony of mourning. I had no sympathy for the firefighters, and something bordering on hatred for the police officers who had died. I lived in a country where my friend— twice as good—could be shot down mere footsteps from his family by agents of the state. God damn America, indeed.

I grew. I became a New Yorker. I came to understand the limits of anger. Watching Barack Obama crisscross the country to roaring white crowds, and then get elected president, I became convinced that the country really had changed—that time and events had altered the nation, and that progress had come in places I'd never imagined it could. When Osama bin Laden was killed, I cheered like everyone else. God damn al-Qaeda.

When trans-partisan mourning erupted around Trayvon Martin, it reinforced my conviction that the world had changed since the death of Prince Jones. Like Prince, Trayvon was suspected of being a criminal chiefly because of the color of his skin. Like Prince's, Trayvon's killer claimed self-defense. Again, with little effort, I could see myself in the shoes of the dead man. But this time, society's response seemed so very different, so much more heartening.

Then the first black president spoke, and the Internet bloomed. Young people began "Trayvoning"—mocking the death of a black boy by photographing themselves in hoodies, with Skittles and iced tea, in a death pose.

In a democracy, so the saying goes, the people get the government they deserve. Part of Obama's genius is a remarkable ability to soothe race consciousness among whites. Any black person who's worked in the professional world is well acquainted with this trick. But never has it been practiced at such a high level, and never have its limits been so obviously exposed. This need to talk in dulcet tones, to never be angry

regardless of the offense, bespeaks a strange and compromised integration indeed, revealing a country so infantile that it can countenance white acceptance of blacks only when they meet an Al Roker standard.

And yet this is the uncertain foundation of Obama's historic victory—a victory that I, and my community, hold in the highest esteem. Who would truly deny the possibility of a black presidency in all its power and symbolism? Who would rob that little black boy of the right to feel himself affirmed by touching the kinky black hair of his president?

I think back to the first time I wrote Shirley Sherrod, requesting an interview. Here was a black woman with every reason in the world to bear considerable animosity toward Barack Obama. But she agreed to meet me only with great trepidation. She said she didn't "want to do anything to hurt" the president.

THE LAST AMAZON: WONDER WOMAN RETURNS

Jill Lepore

Jill Lepore is a professor of American History at Harvard University and a regular contributor to the *New Yorker*; she is one of a small number of academics who have found a way to write for a general audience. Lepore is a prolific and highly regarded writer, with seven books published to date, ranging from a trilogy on the political history of early America to *The Secret History of Wonder Woman*. What's Lepore's secret? In a handout about writing for students in one of her history classes, she makes a point that will sound familiar to readers of *Habits of the Creative Mind*: "Every argument worth making begins with a question." Lepore knows how to ask good questions and, even more importantly, she doesn't back away when the questions yield unexpected answers. She retells American history in ways that reveal the gaps and absences in the received wisdom and she has found a wide audience because the writing she produces is governed by respect for opposing points of view.

The Wonder Woman Family Museum occupies a one-room bunker beneath a two-story house on a hilly street in Bethel, Connecticut. It contains more than four thousand objects. Their arrangement is higgledy-piggledy. There are Wonder Woman lunchboxes, face masks, coffee mugs, a Frisbee, napkins, record-players, T-shirts, bookends, a trailer-hitch cover, plates and cups, pencils, kites, and, near the floor, a pressed-aluminum cake mold, her breasts like cupcakes. A cardboard stand holds Pez dispensers, red, topped with Wonder Woman's head. Wonder Woman backpacks hang from hooks; sleeping bags are rolled up on a shelf. On a ten-foot-wide stage whose backdrop depicts ancient Greece—the Parthenon atop the Acropolis—Hippolyte, queen of the Amazons, a life-size mannequin wearing sandals and a toga, sits on a throne. To her left stands her daughter, Princess Diana, a mannequin dressed as Wonder Woman: a golden tiara on top of a black wig; a red bustier embossed with an American eagle, its wings spread to form the letters "WW"; a blue miniskirt with white stars; bracelets that can stop bullets; a golden lasso strapped to her belt; and, on her feet, super-kinky knee-high red boots. Nearby, a Wonder Woman telephone rests on a glass shelf. The telephone is unplugged.

Superman debuted in 1938, Batman in 1939, Wonder Woman in 1941. She was created by William Moulton Marston, a psychologist with a PhD from Harvard. A press release explained, "'Wonder Woman' was conceived by Dr. Marston to set up a standard among children and young people of strong, free, courageous womanhood; to combat the idea that women are inferior to men, and to inspire girls to self-confidence and achievement in athletics, occupations and professions monopolized by men" because "the only hope for civilization is the greater freedom, development and equality of women in all fields of human activity." Marston put it this way: "Frankly, Wonder Woman is psychological propaganda for the new type of woman who should, I believe, rule the world."

The house in Bethel belongs to Marston's oldest son, Moulton Marston. He's eighty-six. Everyone calls him Pete. "I started it six or seven years ago when I had so much Wonder Woman stuff lying around," he says. A particular strength of the collection is its assortment of Wonder Woman dolls, action figures, and statuary. They come in every size, in ceramic, paper, rubber, plastic, and cloth; jointed, inflatable, and bobble-headed. Most are posed standing, legs astride, arms akimbo, fists clenched, half sassy, half badass. In a corner, blue eye-shadowed, pouty-lipped Wonder Woman Barbie dolls, tiaras missing, hair unkempt, have been crammed into a Wonder Woman wastebasket.

Many of the objects in the Wonder Woman Family Museum date to the nineteen-seventies, when DC Comics, which owns Superman, Batman, and Wonder Woman, was newly affiliated with Warner Bros. Between 1975 and 1979, Warner Bros. produced a Wonder Woman TV series, starring Lynda Carter, a former beauty queen. Since 1978, Warner Bros. has made six Superman films and eight Batman films, but, to the consternation of Wonder Woman fans, there has never been a Wonder Woman film. This is about to change. Last December, Warner Bros. announced that Wonder Woman would have a role in an upcoming Superman-and-Batman film, and that, in a three-movie deal, Gal Gadot, a lithe Israeli model, had signed on to play the part. There followed a flurry of comments about her anatomical insufficiency for the role.

"It's been said that you're too skinny," an interviewer told Gadot on Israeli television. "Wonder Woman is large-breasted."

"Wonder Woman is Amazonian," Gadot said, smiling coyly. "And historically accurate Amazonian women actually had only one breast." (They cut off the other one, the better to wield a bow.)

The film, being shot this summer and fall in Detroit and Chicago, is a sequel to last year's *Man of Steel*, directed by Zack Snyder, with Henry Cavill as Superman. For the new film, Ben Affleck was cast as Batman. One critic tweeted this suggestion for a title: "BATMAN VS. SUPERMAN WITH ALSO SOME WONDER WOMAN IN THERE SO SIT DOWN LADIES WE'RE TREATING YOU FINE: THE MOVIE." Warner Bros. has yet to dispel this impression. In May, the company announced that the film would be called *Batman v. Superman: Dawn of Justice*.

"You can talk all you want about other superhero movies, but it's Batman and Superman, let's just be honest," Snyder said in an interview with *USA Today* in July. "I don't know how you get bigger than that."

The much cited difficulties regarding putting Wonder Woman on film—Wonder Woman isn't big enough, and neither are Gal Gadot's breasts—aren't chiefly about Wonder Woman, or comic books, or superheroes, or movies. They're about politics. Superman owes a debt to science fiction, Batman to the hardboiled detective. Wonder Woman's debt is to feminism. She's the missing link in a chain of events that begins with the woman-suffrage campaigns of the nineteen-tens and ends with the troubled place of feminism a century later. Wonder Woman is so hard to put on film because the fight for women's rights has gone so badly.

. . . . .

"In the days of ancient Greece, many centuries ago, we Amazons were the foremost nation in the world," Hippolyte explains to her daughter in "Introducing Wonder Woman," the character's début, in a 1941 issue of *All-Star Comics*. "In Amazonia, women ruled and all was well." Alas, that didn't last: men conquered and made women slaves. The Amazons escaped, sailing across the ocean to an uncharted island where they lived in peace for centuries until, one day, Captain Steve Trevor, a US Army officer, crashed his plane there. "A man!" Princess Diana cries when she finds him. "A man on Paradise Island!" After rescuing him, she flies him in her invisible plane to "America, the last citadel of democracy, and of equal rights for women!"

Wonder Woman's origin story comes straight out of feminist utopian fiction. In the nineteenth century, suffragists, following the work of anthropologists, believed that something like the Amazons of Greek myth had once existed, a matriarchy that predated the rise of patriarchy. "The period of woman's supremacy lasted through many centuries," Elizabeth Cady Stanton wrote in 1891. In the nineteen-tens, this idea became a staple of feminist thought. The word *feminism*, hardly ever used in the United States before 1910, was everywhere by 1913. The suffrage movement had been founded on a set of ideas about women's supposed moral superiority. Feminism rested on the principle of equality. Suffrage was a single, elusive political goal. Feminism's demand for equality was far broader. "All feminists are suffragists, but not all suffragists are feminists," as one feminist explained. They shared an obsession with Amazons.

In 1913, Max Eastman, a founder of the New York Men's League for Woman Suffrage and the editor of the *Masses*, published *Child of the Amazons and Other Poems*. In the title poem, an Amazonian girl falls in love with a man but can't marry him until "the far age when men shall cease / Their tyranny, Amazons their revolt." The next year, Inez Haynes Gillmore, who, like Mary Woolley, the president of Mount Holyoke College, had helped found college suffrage leagues, published a novel called *Angel Island*, in which five American men are shipwrecked on a desert island that turns out to be inhabited by "super-humanly beautiful" women with wings, who, by the end of the novel, walk "with the splendid, swinging gait of an Amazon."

Gillmore and Max Eastman's sister Crystal were members of Heterodoxy, a group of Greenwich Village feminists. So was Charlotte Perkins Gilman. In 1915, Gilman published *Herland*, in which women live free from men, bearing only daughters, by parthenogenesis. (On Paradise Island, Queen Hippolyte carves her daughter out of clay.) In these stories' stock plots, men are allowed to live with women only on terms of equality, and, for that to happen, there has to be a way for the men and women to have sex without the women getting pregnant all the time. The women in Gilman's utopia practice what was called "voluntary motherhood." "You see, they were Mothers, not in our sense of helpless involuntary fecundity," Gilman wrote, "but in the sense of Conscious Makers of People." At the time, contraception was illegal. In 1914, Margaret Sanger, another Greenwich Village feminist who attended meetings of Heterodoxy, started a magazine called the *Woman Rebel*, in which she coined the phrase *birth control* and insisted that "the right to be a mother regardless of church or state" was the "basis of Feminism."

In 1917, when motion pictures were still a novelty and the United States had only just entered the First World War, Sanger starred in a silent film called *Birth Control*; it was banned. A century of warfare, feminism, and cinema later, superhero movies—adaptations and updates of mid-twentieth-century comic books whose plots revolve around anxieties about mad scientists, organized crime, tyrannical super-states, alien invaders, misunderstood mutants, and world-ending weapons—are the super-blockbusters of the last superpower left standing. No one knows how Wonder Woman will fare onscreen: there's hardly ever been a big-budget superhero movie starring a female superhero. But more of the mystery lies in the fact that Wonder Woman's origins have been, for so long, so unknown. It isn't only that Wonder Woman's backstory is taken from feminist utopian fiction. It's that, in creating Wonder Woman, William Moulton Marston was profoundly influenced by early-twentieth-century suffragists, feminists, and birth-control advocates and that, shockingly, Wonder Woman was inspired by Margaret Sanger, who, hidden from the world, was a member of Marston's family.

. . . . .

Marston entered Harvard College, as a freshman, in 1911. That fall, the Harvard Men's League for Woman Suffrage invited the British militant Emmeline Pankhurst to give a lecture; the Harvard Corporation banned her from speaking on campus. The news made headlines all over the United States. "IS HARVARD AFRAID OF MRS. PANKHURST?" one newspaper asked. (The answer was yes.) Undaunted, Pankhurst spoke in Harvard Square. "The most ignorant young man, who knows nothing of the needs of women, thinks himself a competent legislator, because he is a man," Pankhurst told the crowd, eying the Harvard men. In 1915, Marston married Elizabeth Holloway, who'd just graduated from

Mount Holyoke, where she studied Greek, read Sappho, and became a feminist. Her hero was Mary Woolley, who lived for fifty-five years with Jeannette Marks, an English professor and an ardent suffragist. "Feminism is not a prejudice," Woolley explained. "It is a principle." In 1916, Jeannette Rankin became the first woman elected to Congress, and Margaret Sanger and her sister Ethel Byrne, both nurses, opened the first birth-control clinic in the United States, in Brooklyn. (Sanger and Byrne founded what later became Planned Parenthood.) Byrne was arrested and, inspired by Pankhurst and her followers, went on a hunger strike that nearly killed her. In a statement to the press, she called attention to the number of women who die during abortions. "With the Health Department reporting 8,000 deaths a year in the State from illegal operations on women, one more death won't make much difference, anyway," she said. Against Byrne's wishes, Sanger, hoping to save her sister's life, made a deal with the governor of New York; he issued a pardon for Byrne on the condition that Sanger promise that her sister would never again participate in the birth-control movement.

Marston graduated from Harvard Law School in 1918; Holloway graduated from Boston University's law school the same year. (Harvard Law School did not admit women.) Women finally gained the right to vote in 1920. That year, in her book *Woman and the New Race*, Sanger wrote, "The most far-reaching development of modern times is the revolt of woman against sex servitude," and promised that contraception would "remake the world." Marston finished his PhD at Harvard in 1921, after a stint of service during the First World War. His research had to do with emotions. His dissertation concerned the detection of deception, as measured by changes in blood pressure. (Marston is often credited with inventing the lie-detector test, which is why Wonder Woman carries a magic lasso that makes anyone she ropes tell the truth.) He was also interested in another preoccupation of psychologists: sex, sexual difference, and sexual adjustment. Lewis Terman, who helped develop the IQ test, also helped create a test to measure "masculinity" and "femininity": its purpose was to identify deviance. According to the behaviorist John B. Watson, feminism itself was a form of deviance. "Most of the terrible women one must meet, women with the blatant views and voices, women who have to be noticed, who shoulder one about, who can't take life quietly, belong to this large percentage of women who have never made a sex adjustment," Watson wrote in the *Nation*. Marston's research ran in a different direction. In "Sex Characteristics of Systolic Blood Pressure Behavior," published in the *Journal of Experimental Psychology*, he reported on a series of tests that he and Holloway had conducted on ten men and ten women at Harvard between 1919 and 1921, while Holloway was pursuing a graduate degree in psychology at Radcliffe. They'd tried to get their subjects upset, and then they'd tried to arouse them. He believed his study demonstrated that women are more emotional than men and that women's emotions are often rooted in their sexuality ("there being a far greater number of adequate stimuli to sex-emotion in the female organism"). He also found out he really liked studying sex.

He then embarked on an academic career. Gaining the right to vote had by no means automatically led to political equality. The Equal Rights Amendment, drafted by Alice Paul, was first introduced to Congress in 1923. At the time, women were denied the right to serve on juries in thirty-one states. At American University, Marston and Holloway conducted a series of experiments whose findings, he said, demonstrated that women are more reliable jurors than men: "They were more careful, more conscientious and gave much more impartial consideration to all the testimony than did the male juries." Marston was fired from American University, after he was arrested for fraud, in connection with some business dealings. (All the charges were later dropped.) He next taught at Tufts, where, in 1925, he fell in love with one of his students: Ethel Byrne's daughter Olive.

At Tufts, Marston and Olive Byrne conducted research together. Byrne took him to her sorority, Alpha Omicron Pi, where freshmen pledges were required to dress up like babies and attend a "Baby Party." Marston later described it: "The freshmen girls were led into a dark corridor where their eyes were blindfolded, and their arms were bound behind them." Then the freshmen were taken into a room where juniors and seniors compelled them to do various tasks, while sophomores hit them with long sticks. "Nearly all the sophomores reported excited pleasantness of captivation emotion throughout the party," Marston reported. (Marston's interest in what he called "captivation emotion" informs the bondage in Wonder Woman.)

Beginning in 1925, Marston, Holloway, Byrne, and a librarian named Marjorie Wilkes Huntley, whom Marston had met during the war, attended regular meetings at the Boston apartment of Marston's aunt, Carolyn Keatley. Keatley believed in the teachings contained in a book called *The Aquarian Gospel of Jesus the Christ*, by a preacher named Levi H. Dowling. She thought that she was living in the dawn of the Age of Aquarius, the beginning of a new astrological age, an age of love: the New Age. Minutes for the meetings held at Keatley's apartment describe a sexual "clinic," involving Love Leaders, Mistresses (or Mothers), and Love Girls. A Love Leader, a Mistress, and their Love Girl form a Love Unit, a perfect constellation. There is much in the minutes about sex itself; e.g., "During the act of intercourse between the male and his Mistress, the male's love organ stimulates the inner love organs of the Mistress, and not the external love organs," but "if anyone wishes to develop the consciousness of submission, he or she must keep the sexual orgasm in check, and thus permit the nervous energy to flow freely and uninterruptedly into the external genital organs." There is also much in the minutes about Marston's theory of dominance and submission; females, "in their relation to males, expose their bodies and use various legitimate methods of the Love sphere to create in males submission to them, the women mistresses or Love leaders, in order that they, the Mistresses, may submit in passion to the males."

In 1926, Olive Byrne, then twenty-two, moved in with Marston and Holloway; they lived as a threesome, "with love making for all," as Holloway later said. Olive Byrne is the mother of two of Marston's four children; the children had three parents. "Both Mommies and poor old Dad" is how Marston put it.

Holloway said that Marston, Holloway, and Byrne's living arrangements began as an idea: "A new way of living has to exist in the minds of men before it can be realized in actual form." It had something to do with Sanger's *Woman and the New Race*. Holloway tried to explain what she'd taken away from reading it: "The new race will have a far greater love capacity than the current one and I mean physical love as well as other forms." And it had something to do with what Havelock Ellis, a British doctor who was one of Margaret Sanger's lovers, called "the erotic rights of women." Ellis argued that the evolution of marriage as an institution had resulted in the prohibiting of female sexual pleasure, which was derided as wanton and abnormal. Erotic equality, he insisted in 1918, was no less important than political equality, if more difficult to achieve. "The right to joy cannot be claimed in the same way as one claims the right to put a voting paper in a ballot box," he wrote. "That is why the erotic rights of women have been the last of all to be attained."

But there was more to it. For Holloway, the arrangement solved what, in the era of the New Woman, was known as the "woman's dilemma": hardly a magazine was sold, in those years, that didn't feature an article that asked, "Can a Woman Run a Home and a Job, Too?" The modern woman, Crystal Eastman explained in the *Nation*, "wants some means of self-expression, perhaps, some way of satisfying her personal ambitions. But she wants a husband, home and children, too. How to reconcile these two desires in real life, that is the question." You can find more or less the very same article in almost any magazine today— think of Anne-Marie Slaughter's 2012 essay, "Why Women Still Can't Have It All"—which is a measure of just how poorly this question has been addressed. A century ago, though, it was new. Between 1910 and 1920, Virginia MacMakin Collier reported in 1926, in *Marriage and Careers*, the percentage of married women working had nearly doubled, and the number of married women in the professions had risen by forty per cent. "The question, therefore, is no longer, should women combine marriage with careers, but how?"

Here's how. Marston would have two wives. Holloway could have her career. Byrne would raise the children. No one else need ever know.

. . . . .

The scandal of Marston's family arrangements, which, inevitably, became known to his close colleagues, cost him his academic career. This kind of thing happens all the time in Wonder Woman. "What are you doing here?" Dean Sourpuss, of Holliday College, asks Professor Toxino. "You know you're not welcome at this college!" In the nineteen-twenties, Marston barely held any appointment longer than a year, and, with each move, he climbed another step down the academic ladder. At American University, he'd been a full professor and the chair of the

Psychology Department. Tufts appointed him an untenured assistant professor. In 1928, while he was teaching at Columbia—on a one-year appointment, as a lecturer—he published a book called *Emotions of Normal People*, as part of a series called the International Library of Psychology, Philosophy and Scientific Method. (Other contributors to the series included Wittgenstein, Piaget, and Adler.) Its chief argument is that much in emotional and sexual life that is generally regarded as abnormal and is therefore commonly hidden actually inheres within the very structure of the nervous system. The work of the clinical psychologist, Marston argued, is to provide patients with an "emotional re-education": "People must be taught that the love parts of themselves, which they have come to regard as abnormal, are completely normal."

Marston's interests in deception, sex, and emotion fed a long-standing interest in film. He'd worked his way through Harvard by selling screenplays. In 1915, after the Edison Company held a nation-wide talent search among American college students, promising a hundred dollars to the author of the best movie scenario submitted by a student at one of ten colleges—Harvard, Yale, Columbia, Cornell, Princeton, and the Universities of California, Chicago, Michigan, Pennsylvania, and Wisconsin—Marston won. The resulting film, *Jack Kennard, Coward*, played at scattered theatres across the country, in some places sharing a billing with Charlie Chaplin. In 1916, Marston's undergraduate adviser, Hugo Münsterberg, who ran Harvard's Psychological Laboratory, published a psychological theory of cinema. (Münsterberg, who vehemently opposed both the suffrage and the feminist movements, is the inspiration for Wonder Woman's arch-nemesis, Doctor Psycho.) In 1928, when it became clear to Marston that his academic career was doomed, he returned to his earlier interest in the movies. Working with Byrne, who was, at the time, pursuing a PhD in psychology at Columbia, he conducted a series of experiments at the Embassy Theatre, in New York. He invited reporters and photographers to watch as he seated an audience of six chorus girls—three blondes and three brunettes—in the front row. The experiment was captured on newsreel footage: "Dr. William Marston tests his latest invention: the Love Meter." Marston and Byrne hooked the girls up to blood-pressure cuffs and recorded their level of excitement as they watched the romantic climax of M-G-M's 1926 silent film *Flesh and the Devil*, starring Greta Garbo. Marston claimed his findings proved that brunettes are more easily aroused than blondes. Columbia did not renew Marston's appointment. Essentially, he was blacklisted. "He might fit very well in some places," the Harvard psychologist Edwin Boring wrote in a fainthearted letter of recommendation, "but in the average, normal, general department of psychology he would probably remain separated in his work, and even at times open to the charge of sensationalism."

. . . . .

In the summer of 1928, Carl Laemmle, the head of Universal Studios, placed a notice in the pages of the *Saturday Evening Post*:

> Wanted—A Psychologist
>
> Somewhere in this country there is a practical psychologist—accomplished in the science of the mind—who will fit into the Universal organization. He can be of real help in analyzing certain plot situations and forecasting how the public will react to them. As moving pictures are reaching out more and more for refinements, such a mental showman will have great influence on the screens of the world.

"Carl Laemmle Digs the 'Doc,' " *Variety* reported five months later, announcing that Universal had hired Marston, "Who Went Through Harvard Three Times Without Quitting." Marston, Holloway, Byrne, and baby Pete moved to Los Angeles. Marston was supposed to help with casting, story editing, and setting up camera shots, and, in general, to "apply psychology wherever psychology is needed." In one experiment, he showed Universal's 1929 film *The Love Trap* to a thousand college students, omitting the final scene. He wanted to know whether audiences could handle movies that end with unfinished business.

Meanwhile, Marston and his friend Walter Pitkin, who had taught at the Columbia School of Journalism, wrote a book about how to write a screenplay for the talkies. Much of *The Art of Sound Pictures*, published in 1929, is dedicated to explaining, point by point and state by state, what could pass the censors, and what couldn't. Branding—"Scene showing branding iron in fire, if application of it is not shown"—was OK in New York, Ohio, and Virginia, not allowed in Pennsylvania, Maryland, or Kansas. Sex—"Man and woman (married or unmarried) walking toward bedroom, indicating contemplated intimacy, if they are not shown after the door closes on them"—depended on action. Homosexuality—"Action of characters, indicating they are perverted, as scene showing women kissing each other, if shown in long shot"—was not usually allowed.

Marston and Pitkin also founded a production company, Equitable Pictures. Pitkin scratched out a story idea for a film whose plot was to revolve "Around Bill Marston's thesis: How can a woman love & yet make a living? How be economically independent & also erotically independent?" It would be called either *Brave Woman* or *Giddy Girl*. (The Giddy Girls was the stage name of Billy and Charlie Byrne, Olive Byrne's uncles; they were female impersonators on the vaudeville circuit.) Equitable Pictures was incorporated in October of 1929, days before the stock market collapsed. It folded. A woman, one woman, who could be both economically and erotically independent would have to wait out the Depression. She'd have to have been a superhero, anyway. And superheroes hadn't quite been invented yet.

Marston spent most of the nineteen-thirties unemployed, supported by Holloway, who worked for Metropolitan Life Insurance, while Olive Byrne raised their four children in a sprawling house they called Cherry Orchard, in Rye, New York. Byrne also wrote for *Family Circle*, using the pen name Olive Richard. Her first article, a cover story from 1935, was a profile of Marston. In the story, she pretends they're strangers. She goes to visit him. Marston attaches a blood-pressure cuff to Byrne's arm—the machine that, in the experiments they conducted together, Byrne usually took charge of:

"Tell me what you did last evening—truth or lie, just as you like."

I thought for a minute. Then I decided to be clever. I'd mix truth and falsehood and see if he could tell which was which.

Byrne at once hid everything about her life and, like Marston, almost compulsively exposed it. But, plainly, she adored him. He was undignified and funny and warm. She found him wonderful:

> This noted scientist is the most genuine human being I've met. He isn't fat—that is, in the ordinary way. He's just enormous all over. We walked through the garden and about the grounds. The doctor asked me about my work and myself, and I told him more in 15 minutes than I'd tell my most intimate friend in a week. He's the kind of person to whom you confide things about yourself you scarcely realize.

Margaret Sanger visited Cherry Orchard, and Olive Byrne brought the children—her two sons, Byrne and Donn, and Holloway's two children, Pete and Olive Ann—to visit Sanger at Sanger's house in Fishkill. (The kids called Sanger Aunt Margaret.) Sanger knew about the family intrigue and was untroubled by it. The children knew less. "The whys and wherefores of the family arrangements were never discussed with the kids—ever," Pete says.

The kids called Holloway Keets or Keetie, for "cutie," and Olive Byrne Dots or Dotsie, for "docile."

"What are Mommies, Daddies, and Keeties for anyway?" Olive Ann, at the age of three, asked Olive Byrne.

"I can't quite say myself," she replied quietly.

In 1937, the year the American Medical Association finally endorsed contraception, Marston held a press conference in which he predicted that women would one day rule the world. He also offered a list, "in the order of the importance of their contributions to humanity," of six surpassingly happy and influential people: Margaret Sanger was No. 2, just after Henry Ford and just before FDR. The story was picked up by the Associated Press, wired across the continent, and printed in newspapers from Topeka to Tallahassee. "WOMEN WILL RULE 1,000 YEARS HENCE!" the Chicago *Tribune* announced. The Los Angeles *Times* reported, "FEMININE RULE DECLARED FACT."

In 1940, M. C. Gaines, who published Superman, read an article in *Family Circle* by Olive Byrne. She'd been worried by reading in the papers that comic books were dangerous, and that Superman was a

Fascist. "With terrible visions of Hitlerian justice in mind," she wrote in *Family Circle*, "I went to Dr. Marston."

"Do you think these fantastic comics are good reading for children?" she asked.

Mostly, yes, Marston said. They are pure wish fulfillment: "And the two wishes behind Superman are certainly the soundest of all; they are, in fact, our national aspirations of the moment—to develop unbeatable national might, and to use this great power, when we get it, to protect innocent, peace-loving people from destructive, ruthless evil."

Gaines decided to hire Marston as a consultant. Marston convinced Gaines that what he needed, to counter the critics, was a female superhero. The idea was for her to become a member of the Justice Society of America, a league of superheroes that held its first meeting in *All-Star Comics No. 3*, in the winter of 1940: "Each of them is a hero in his own right, but when the Justice Society calls, they are only members, sworn to uphold honor and justice!" Wonder Woman's début appeared in December, 1941, in *All-Star Comics No. 8*. On the eve of the Second World War, she flew her invisible plane to the United States to fight for peace, justice, and women's rights. To hide her identity, she disguised herself as a secretary named Diana Prince and took a job working for US Military Intelligence. Her gods are female, and so are her curses. "Great Hera!" she cries. "Suffering Sappho!" she swears. Her "undermeaning," Marston explained, concerned "a great movement now under way—the growth in power of women." Drawn by an artist named Harry G. Peter, who, in the nineteen-tens, had drawn suffrage cartoons, she looked like a pinup girl. She's Eleanor Roosevelt; she's Betty Grable. Mostly, she's Margaret Sanger.

In the spring of 1942, Gaines included a one-page questionnaire in *All-Star Comics*. "Should WONDER WOMAN be allowed, even though a woman, to become a member of the Justice Society?" Of the first eighteen hundred and one questionnaires returned, twelve hundred and sixty-five boys and three hundred and thirty-three girls said yes; a hundred and ninety-seven boys, and just six girls, said no. Wonder Woman joined the Justice Society. She was the only woman. Gardner Fox, who wrote the Justice Society stories, made her the society's secretary. In the summer of 1942, when all the male superheroes head off to war, Wonder Woman stays behind to answer the mail. "Good luck boys," she calls out to them. "I wish I could be going with you!" Marston was furious.

In May, 1942, FDR created the Women's Army Auxiliary Corps. A hundred and fifty thousand women joined the Army, filling jobs that freed more men for combat. The corps "appears to be the final realization of woman's dream of complete equality with men," Sanger wrote in the New York *Herald-Tribune*. But she was dismayed that the government didn't provide contraceptives for WAACs and adopted a policy of dismissing any woman who got pregnant. "This new women's Army is a great thing, a real test of the woman's movement," she said. "Never before has the fight for woman's equality narrowed down to the real issue, sex."

In 1943, Marston wrote a Wonder Woman story called "Battle for Womanhood." It opens with Mars, the god of war, angry that so many American women are helping with the war effort.

"There are eight million American women in war activities—by 1944 there will be eighteen million!" one of Mars' female slaves reports, dragging a ball and chain.

"If women gain power in *war* they'll escape man's domination completely!" Mars thunders. "They will achieve a horrible independence! . . . If women become warriors like the Amazons, they'll grow stronger than men and put an end to war!"

He commands the Duke of Deception to put a stop to it. The Duke enlists the aid of Doctor Psycho, who, by means of tools he's developed in his psychological laboratory, conjures a trick in which George Washington rises from the dead and addresses a spellbound audience.

"I have a message for you—a warning!" Washington says. "*Women* will lose the war for America! Women should not be permitted to have the responsibilities they now have! Women must not make shells, torpedoes, airplane parts—they must not be trusted with war secrets or serve in the armed forces. *Women will betray their country through weakness* if not treachery!"

Wonder Woman, watching from the side, cries out, "He's working for the Axis!" To defeat Doctor Psycho, she breaks into his laboratory, dropping in through a skylight. Captured, she's trapped. Doctor Psycho locks her in a cage. Eventually, she's rescued by her best friend, Etta Candy, after which she frees Psycho's wife, Marva, whom he has blindfolded and chained to a bed.

"Submitting to a cruel husband's domination has ruined my life!" an emancipated Marva cries. "But what can a weak girl do?"

"Get strong!" Wonder Woman urges. "Earn your own living—join the WAACs or WAVES and fight for your country!"

At the end of 1943, Wonder Woman reports to Hippolyte, "Women are gaining power in the man's world!" Hippolyte shows Wonder Woman what lies ahead: Etta Candy will be awarded an honorary degree and become Professor of Public Health at Wonder Woman College, and Diana Prince will be President of the United States.

In 1944, Wonder Woman became the only superhero, aside from Superman and Batman, to make the jump from the pages of a comic book to daily newspaper syndication as a comic strip. Marston had so much work to do, writing Wonder Woman stories, that he hired an assistant, nineteen-year-old Joye Hummel. She'd been a student in a psychology class he taught at the Katharine Gibbs School. (Hummel, now ninety, still has the exam that Marston gave in class. It reads as though it were written by Sheryl Sandberg. Question No. 6: "Advise Miss F. how to overcome her fear of talking with the company Vice President who is in charge of her Division and whom she has plenty of opportunities to contact if she chooses; also tell Miss F. why these contacts are to her advantage.") To help Hummel write Wonder Woman, the family gave her copies of Marston's *Emotions of Normal People* and Sanger's *Woman and the New Race*.

By the end of the Second World War, the number of American women working outside the home had grown by sixty per cent; three-quarters of these women were married, and a third were mothers of young children. Three-quarters of the working women hoped to keep their jobs, but they were told to make room for men returning from military service. If they didn't quit, they were forced out: their pay was cut, and factories stopped providing child care.

Marston died in 1947. "Hire me," Holloway wrote to DC Comics. Instead, DC hired Robert Kanigher, and Wonder Woman followed the hundreds of thousands of American women workers who, when peace came, were told that their labor threatened the stability of the nation. Kanigher made Wonder Woman a babysitter, a fashion model, and a movie star. She gave advice to the lovelorn, as the author of a lonely-hearts newspaper advice column. Her new writer also abandoned a regular feature, "The Wonder Women of History"—a four-page centerfold in every issue, containing a biography of a woman of achievement. He replaced it with a series about weddings, called "Marriage à la Mode."

"You, Daughter, must become the women's leader," the Duke of Deception tells Lya, in a Wonder Woman story written by Kanigher. "You must persuade them that they don't want any political rights and that everything I dictate they vote for." Lya smiles, and says, "That'll be easy!"

In the nineteen-fifties, women went home. Women's rights went underground. And homosexuals were persecuted. Is there a "quick test like an X-ray that discloses these things?" US Senator Margaret Chase Smith asked in hearings about homosexuality in 1950. At the State Department, a former FBI officer was put in charge of purging the civil service of homosexuals by administering lie-detector tests, based on Marston's research. Those who failed were required to resign. Between 1945 and 1956, a thousand accused homosexuals employed by the State Department and five thousand employed by the federal government lost their jobs. Marston, Holloway, and Byrne had led a closeted life. It had its costs.

· · · · ·

In 1948, Holloway went back to her job at Metropolitan Life. Byrne found another kind of employment. "I am working for our local 'Maternal Health Center' clinic," she wrote to Margaret Sanger, "and am most amused when they speak of you. Somehow they think you are a contemporary of Florence Nightingale." It was as if Sanger had lived in another century. Byrne tried to explain to people at the clinic that Sanger was alive and well, but she never told anyone that she was Sanger's niece.

In the nineteen-fifties, Sanger turned her attention to the question of how she would be remembered. She'd been sorting through her papers, preparing them for the Library of Congress and for Smith College, deciding which papers to keep, and which to throw away. In 1951, at the age of seventy-two, Sanger sold the rights to a film based on her autobiography. She then wrote a letter to Ethel Byrne, claiming that the scriptwriter wished to make a slight alteration to the facts of the founding of the birth-control movement, regarding the trials the two women had faced in 1917. In the film, Sanger told her sister, "I should be the Hunger Strikee." Ethel Byrne would not be mentioned. Sanger asked her sister to sign a release stating that she agreed that the film would not "portray me or any part of my life" and that, in the film, it would appear "that Mrs. Sanger engaged in the famous hunger strike instead of myself." Ethel Byrne thought the release was "the funniest thing in the world," according to Olive. She never signed it. The film was never made.

In much the same way that Sanger wished she could erase from the historical record the fact that Ethel Byrne, and not she, had gone on a hunger strike, she also wanted to keep well hidden her ties to the comic-book superhero created by William Moulton Marston. Maybe she found the association embarrassing or thought it was unimportant. But, more likely, never mentioning it was among the things that Sanger did to help keep Olive Byrne's family arrangements secret, in order to avoid scandal for Olive and the children, and harm to Sanger's cause. Whatever the reason, in no part of the story of Sanger's life, as she told it, did she ever mention Wonder Woman.

. . . . .

Holloway and Byrne lived together for the rest of their lives. In the fifties and sixties, they often stayed in Tucson, taking care of Sanger. Byrne worked as Sanger's secretary. In 1961, Byrne's son Donn married one of Sanger's granddaughters; she became Margaret Sanger Marston. In 1965, when the Supreme Court effectively legalized contraception, in *Griswold v. Connecticut*, Byrne wrote to Justice William O. Douglas, who had written the opinion for the 7-2 majority, "I am sure Mrs. Sanger, who is very ill, would rejoice in this pronouncement which crowns her 50 years of dedication to the liberation of women." Sanger died the next year.

In 1972, the editors of *Ms.* put Wonder Woman on the cover of the first regular issue, bridging the distance between the feminism of the nineteen-tens and the feminism of the nineteen-seventies with the Wonder Woman of the nineteen-forties, the feminism of their childhoods. "Looking back now at these Wonder Woman stories from the '40s," Gloria Steinem wrote, "I am amazed by the strength of their feminist message."

Ms. was meant to be an organ for a revived feminist movement, begun in 1963 with the publication of Betty Friedan's *Feminine Mystique* and the passage of the Equal Pay Act. The National Organization for Women was founded in 1966. In 1969, Ellen Willis and Shulamith Firestone started the Redstockings of the Women's Liberation Movement. Firestone's manifesto, *The Dialectic of Sex: The Case for Feminist Revolution*, was published the next year, along with Kate Millett's *Sexual Politics* and Robin Morgan's *Sisterhood Is Powerful*. A revolution was being waged, too, in the world of magazines. In March, 1970, forty-six women working at *Newsweek* sued the magazine for discrimination. At the *Ladies' Home Journal*, more than a hundred women staged an eleven-hour sit-in; their demands included day care, a female senior editorial staff, and a special issue of the magazine to be called the *Women's Liberated Journal*.

The revolution also came to comics. In July, 1970, the Women's Liberation Basement Press, in Berkeley, launched an underground comic book called *It Aint Me Babe*. Its first issue featured Wonder Woman on its cover marching in a parade with female comic characters, protesting stock plots. In a story called "Breaking Out," Veronica ditches Archie for Betty, Supergirl tells Superman to get lost, Petunia Pig tells Porky Pig to cook his own dinner, and, when Iggy tells Lulu she can't be in his parade ("No girls allowed!"), she walks away, saying, "Fuck this shit!"

A nationwide Women's Strike for Equality was held on August 26, 1970, the fiftieth anniversary of the passage of the Nineteenth Amendment. Joanne Edgar helped organize the work stoppage at Facts on File. Patricia Carbine went on strike at *Look*. A year later, Edgar became a founding editor of *Ms.*, Carbine its publisher.

"Hello, I'm Elizabeth Marston and I know all about Wonder Woman," Holloway said when she walked into the offices of *Ms.*, in the spring of 1972. She was nearly eighty, as pale as paper and as thin as bone. In Virginia, where she was living with Olive Byrne, who was sixty-eight, she'd got a letter from Joanne Edgar, telling her that *Ms.* was planning to run a cover story about Wonder Woman. Holloway flew to New York. She met the magazine's writers and editors and artists. "All were on the young side, very much in earnest," she reported to Marjorie Wilkes Huntley. "I told them I was 100% with them in what they are trying to do and to 'charge ahead!'" Huntley sent in a money order for a subscription, signing herself, at the age of eighty-two, "Marjorie Wilkes Huntley (Ms.)."

But Holloway never told Edgar, or anyone else, about Olive Byrne. In 1974, when a Berkeley PhD student writing a dissertation about Wonder Woman asked Holloway about Wonder Woman's bracelets, Holloway replied in a letter, "A student of Dr. Marston's wore on each wrist heavy, broad silver bracelets, one African and the other Mexican. They attracted his attention as symbols of love binding so that he adopted them for the Wonder Woman strip." The bracelets were Olive Byrne's. Olive Byrne had at that point been living with Holloway for forty-eight years.

At the beginning of 1972, when the editors of *Ms.* were planning their Wonder Woman issue, the women's movement seemed on the verge of lasting success. On March 22, 1972, the Equal Rights Amendment passed the Senate, nearly a half century after it had been introduced. In June, Congress also passed Title IX, assuring that "No person in the United States shall, on the basis of sex, be excluded from participation in, be denied the benefits of, or be subjected to discrimination under any education program or activity receiving federal financial assistance." The year 1972 was a legislative watershed. "We put sex-discrimination provisions into everything," Bella Abzug said. "There was no opposition. Who'd be against equal rights for women?"

A lot of people. In 1972, Wonder Woman was named a "Symbol of Feminist Revolt"; the next year, the Supreme Court legalized abortion. But the aftermath of *Roe v. Wade* didn't bolster the feminist movement; it narrowed it. If 1972 was a legislative watershed, 1973 marked the beginning of a drought. The movement stalled. Wages never reached parity; social and economic gains were rolled back; political and legal victories seemingly within sight were never achieved. Then, too, the movement was divided, bitterly and viciously, radicals attacking liberals and liberals attacking radicals. In May, 1975, the Redstockings held a press conference and issued a sixteen-page report purporting to reveal that Gloria Steinem was a CIA agent, that *Ms.* was both a capitalist manifesto and part of a CIA strategy to destroy the women's movement, and that Wonder Woman was a symbol of nothing so much as feminism betrayed. "Wonder Woman also reflects the anti-people attitude of the 'liberal feminists' and matriarchists who look to mythical and supernatural heroines and 'models' while ignoring or denigrating the achievements and struggles of down-to-earth women," they charged. "It leads to the 'liberated woman,' individualist line that denies the need for a movement, and implies that when women don't make it, it's their own fault." Steinem rebutted the allegations. "Although it seems bizarre to have to write this obvious sentence," she wrote, "let me state that I am not now nor have I ever been an employee of the Central Intelligence Agency."

Wonder Woman ran for President in a comic book written by Marston in 1943; she ran for President on the cover of *Ms.* in 1972. She'll run again; she's never won. The Equal Rights Amendment never became law; in 1982, the deadline for its ratification expired. A century after Sanger started the *Woman Rebel*, even the fight for birth control isn't over.

· · · · ·

Last March, I went to see *Captain America: The Winter Soldier*, with Byrne Holloway Marston. He's named for all three of his parents. He's eighty-three. He's a retired obstetrician. He's also a movie buff. He's optimistic about Gal Gadot, though he thinks that Jennifer Lawrence would have made a tip-top Wonder Woman. "She's good enough to soften it up," he says.

Captain America and Wonder Woman are about the same age. He made his début in 1940. They've aged differently, the Boy Scout and the bombshell. Captain America is so hard to update that Marvel decided to have him frozen in 1945 and awakened in 2011. A guy he meets while out for a run on the Washington Mall asks him what's different about now versus 1945. "No polio is good," he says.

Warner Bros. is unlikely to release a film in which Wonder Woman is frozen in time in 1941, in order to call attention to what's changed for women, and what's not, when she's defrosted. She'd have to take stock, and what could she say about what women have got? Breast pumps and fetal rights instead of paid maternity leave and equal rights? Longer hours instead of equal pay? Aphrodite, aid me! Lean in? Are you *kidding*? Batman vs. Superman? Suffering Sappho.

Sitting in the dark, I asked Byrne Marston what he thought he would do if he were writing Wonder Woman into the script for *Dawn of Justice*.

"God, I don't know," he said. He stretched out his legs. "I'd go back to the origins."

LOOKING AT WAR

Susan Sontag

Susan Sontag was an essayist, a novelist, a critic, a filmmaker, a theater director, and an intellectual gadfly. She wrote passionately and imperiously about photography, art, popular culture, illness, politics, theater, war, and human rights. What connects these disparate subjects? From the beginning of Sontag's career to its end, she never tired of examining the ethics of representing suffering and the danger of indifference to the suffering of others. In *Against Interpretation* and *On Photography* she warned that modern perceptions are dulled by the overproduction and distribution of images. In *Illness as Metaphor* and *AIDS and Its Metaphors*, she argued that popular accounts of illness perpetuate destructive stigmas. And Sontag did not limit her interests to the sheltered realms of the library and the gallery; she visited war zones in Vietnam, Israel, and Sarajevo. Although Sontag's life and work were driven by a capacious curiosity, a reader could come away from her essays feeling that she reveled in certainties, not ambiguities; answers, not questions. Sontag's primary goal as a writer was to instill intellectual habits of mind in her readers; she wanted her work to shake them and say, "be serious, be passionate, wake up."

In June, 1938, Virginia Woolf published *Three Guineas*, her brave, unwelcomed reflections on the roots of war. Written during the preceding two years, while she and most of her intimates and fellow-writers were rapt by the advancing Fascist insurrection in Spain, the book was couched as a tardy reply to a letter from an eminent lawyer in London who had asked, "How in your opinion are we to prevent war?" Woolf begins by observing tartly that a truthful dialogue between them may not be possible. For though they belong to the same class, "the educated class," a vast gulf separates them: the lawyer is a man and she is a woman. Men make war. Men (most men) like war, or at least they find "some glory, some necessity, some satisfaction in fighting" that women (most women) do not seek or find. What does an educated—that is, privileged, well-off—woman like her know of war? Can her reactions to its horrors be like his?

Woolf proposes they test this "difficulty of communication" by looking at some images of war that the beleaguered Spanish government has been sending out twice a week to sympathizers abroad. Let's see "whether when we look at the same photographs we feel the same things," she writes. "This morning's collection contains the photograph of what might be a man's body, or a woman's; it is so mutilated that it might, on the other hand, be the body of a pig. But those certainly are dead children, and that undoubtedly is the section of a house. A bomb has torn open the side; there is still a bird-cage hanging in what was presumably the sitting room." One can't always make out the subject, so thorough is the ruin of flesh and stone that the photographs depict. "However different the education, the traditions behind us," Woolf says to the lawyer, "we"—and here women are the "we"—and he might well have the same response: "War, you say, is an abomination; a barbarity; war must be stopped at whatever cost. And we echo your words. War is an abomination; a barbarity; war must be stopped."

Who believes today that war can be abolished? No one, not even pacifists. We hope only (so far in vain) to stop genocide and bring to justice those who commit gross violations of the laws of war (for there are laws of war, to which combatants should be held), and to stop specific wars by imposing negotiated alternatives to armed conflict. But protesting against war may not have seemed so futile or naïve in the nineteenthirties. In 1924, on the tenth anniversary of the national mobilization in Germany for the First World War, the conscientious objector Ernst Friedrich published *War Against War!* (*Krieg dem Kriege!*), an album of more than a hundred and eighty photographs that were drawn mainly from German military and medical archives, and almost all of which were deemed unpublishable by government censors while the war was on. The book starts with pictures of toy soldiers, toy cannons, and other delights of male children everywhere, and concludes with pictures taken in military cemeteries. This is photography as shock therapy. Between the toys and the graves, the reader has an excruciating photo tour of four years of ruin, slaughter, and degradation: wrecked and plundered churches and castles, obliterated villages, ravaged forests, torpedoed passenger steamers, shattered vehicles, hanged conscientious objectors, naked personnel of military brothels, soldiers in death agonies after a poison-gas attack, skeletal Armenian children.

Friedrich did not assume that heartrending, stomach-turning pictures would speak for themselves. Each photograph has an impassioned caption in four languages (German, French, Dutch, and English), and the wickedness of militarist ideology is excoriated and mocked on every page. Immediately denounced by the German government and by veterans' and other patriotic organizations—in some cities the police raided bookstores, and lawsuits were brought against public display of the photographs—Friedrich's declaration of war against war was acclaimed by left-wing writers, artists, and intellectuals, as well as by the constituencies of the numerous antiwar leagues, who predicted that the book would have a decisive influence on public opinion. By 1930, *War Against War!* had gone through ten editions in Germany and been translated into many languages.

In 1928, in the Kellogg-Briand Pact, fifteen nations, including the United States, France, Great Britain, Germany, Italy, and Japan, solemnly renounced war as an instrument of national policy. Freud and Einstein were drawn into the debate four years later, in an exchange of letters published under the title "Why War?" *Three Guineas*, which appeared toward the close of nearly two decades of plangent denunciations of war and war's horrors, was at least original in its focus on what was regarded as too obvious to be mentioned, much less brooded over: that war is a man's game—that the killing machine has a gender, and it is male. Nevertheless, the temerity of Woolf's version of "Why War?" does not make her revulsion against war any less conventional in its rhetoric, and in its summations, rich in repeated phrases. Photographs of the victims of war are themselves a species of rhetoric. They reiterate. They simplify. They agitate. They create the illusion of consensus.

Woolf professes to believe that the shock of such pictures cannot fail to unite people of good will. Although she and the lawyer are separated by the age-old affinities of feeling and practice of their respective sexes, he is hardly a standard-issue bellicose male. After all, his question was not, What are your thoughts about preventing war? It was, How in your opinion are we to prevent war? Woolf challenges this "we" at the start of her book, but after some pages devoted to the feminist point she abandons it.

"Here then on the table before us are photographs," she writes of the thought experiment she is proposing to the reader as well as to the spectral lawyer, who is eminent enough to have KC, King's Counsel, after his name—and may or may not be a real person. Imagine a spread of loose photographs extracted from an envelope that arrived in the morning mail. They show the mangled bodies of adults and children. They show how war evacuates, shatters, breaks apart, levels the built world. A bomb has torn open the side of a house. To be sure, a cityscape is not made of flesh. Still, sheared-off buildings are almost as eloquent as body parts (Kabul; Sarajevo; East Mostar; Grozny; sixteen acres of Lower Manhattan after September 11, 2001; the refugee camp in Jenin). Look, the photographs say, *this* is what it's like. This is what war *does*. And *that*, that is what it does, too. War tears, rends. War rips open, eviscerates. War scorches. War dismembers. War *ruins*. Woolf believes that not to be pained by these pictures, not to recoil from them, not to strive to abolish what causes this havoc, this carnage, is a failure of imagination, of empathy.

But surely the photographs could just as well foster greater militancy on behalf of the Republic. Isn't this what they were meant to do? The agreement between Woolf and the lawyer seems entirely presumptive, with the grisly photographs confirming an opinion already held in common. Had his question been, How can we best contribute to the defense of the Spanish Republic against the forces of militarist and clerical fascism?, the photographs might have reinforced a belief in the justness of that struggle.

. . . . .

The pictures Woolf has conjured up do not in fact show what war—war in general—does. They show a particular way of waging war, a way at that time routinely described as "barbaric," in which civilians are the target. General Franco was using the tactics of bombardment, massacre, torture, and the killing and mutilation of prisoners that he had perfected as a commanding officer in Morocco in the nineteen-twenties. Then, more acceptably to ruling powers, his victims had been Spain's colonial subjects, darker-hued and infidels to boot; now his victims were compatriots. To read in the pictures, as Woolf does, only what confirms a general abhorrence of war is to stand back from an engagement with Spain as a country with a history. It is to dismiss politics.

For Woolf, as for many antiwar polemicists, war is generic, and the images she describes are of anonymous, generic victims. The pictures sent out by the government in Madrid seem, improbably, not to have been labeled. (Or perhaps Woolf is simply assuming that a photograph should speak for itself.) But to those who are sure that right is on one side, oppression and injustice on the other, and that the fighting must go on, what matters is precisely who is killed and by whom. To an Israeli Jew, a photograph of a child torn apart in the attack on the Sbarro pizzeria in downtown Jerusalem is first of all a photograph of a Jewish child killed by a Palestinian suicide bomber. To a Palestinian, a photograph of a child torn apart by a tank round in Gaza is first of all a photograph of a Palestinian child killed by Israeli ordnance. To the militant, identity is everything. And all photographs wait to be explained or falsified by their captions. During the fighting between Serbs and Croats at the beginning of the recent Balkan wars, the same photographs of children killed in the shelling of a village were passed around at both Serb and Croat propaganda briefings. Alter the caption: alter the use of these deaths.

Photographs of mutilated bodies certainly can be used the way Woolf does, to vivify the condemnation of war, and may bring home, for a spell, a portion of its reality to those who have no experience of war at all. But someone who accepts that in the world as currently divided war can become inevitable, and even just, might reply that the photographs supply no evidence, none at all, for renouncing war—except to those for whom the notions of valor and of sacrifice have been emptied of meaning and credibility. The destructiveness of war—short of total destruction, which is not war but suicide—is not in itself an argument against waging war, unless one thinks (as few people actually do) that violence is always unjustifiable, that force is always and in all circumstances wrong: wrong because, as Simone Weil affirms in her sublime essay on war, "The Iliad, or, The Poem of Force," violence turns anybody subjected to it into a thing. But to those who in a given situation see no alternative to armed struggle, violence can exalt someone subjected to it into a martyr or a hero.

In fact, there are many uses of the innumerable opportunities that a modern life supplies for regarding—at a distance, through the medium of photography—other people's pain. Photographs of an atrocity may give rise to opposing responses: a call for peace; a cry for revenge; or simply the bemused awareness, continually restocked by photographic information, that terrible things happen. Who can forget the three color pictures by Tyler Hicks that the *New York Times* ran on November 13, 2001, across the upper half of the first page of its daily section devoted to America's new war? The triptych depicted the fate of a wounded Taliban soldier who had been found in a ditch by some Northern Alliance soldiers advancing toward Kabul. First panel: the soldier is being dragged on his back by two of his captors—one has grabbed an arm, the other a leg—along a rocky road. Second panel: he is surrounded, gazing up in terror as he is pulled to his feet. Third panel: he is supine with arms outstretched and knees bent, naked from the waist down, a bloodied heap left on the road by the dispersing military mob that has just finished butchering him. A good deal of stoicism is needed to get through the newspaper each morning, given the likelihood of seeing pictures that could make you cry. And the disgust and pity that pictures like Hicks's inspire should not distract from asking what pictures, whose cruelties, whose deaths you are *not* being shown.

II

Awareness of the suffering that accumulates in wars happening elsewhere is something constructed. Principally in the form that is registered by cameras, it flares up, is shared by many people, and fades from view. In contrast to a written account, which, depending on its complexity of thought, references, and vocabulary, is pitched at a larger or smaller readership, a photograph has only one language and is destined potentially for all.

In the first important wars of which there are accounts by photographers, the Crimean War and the American Civil War, and in every other war until the First World War, combat itself was beyond the camera's ken. As for the war photographs published between 1914 and 1918, nearly all anonymous, they were—insofar as they did convey something of the terrors and devastation endured—generally in the epic mode, and were usually depictions of an aftermath: corpse-strewn or lunar landscapes left by trench warfare; gutted French villages the war had passed through. The photographic monitoring of war as we know it had to wait for a radical upgrade of professional equipment: lightweight cameras, such as the Leica, using 35-mm film that could be exposed thirty-six times before the camera needed to be reloaded. The Spanish Civil War was the first war to be witnessed ("covered") in the modern sense: by a corps of professional photographers at the lines of military engagement and in the towns under bombardment, whose work was immediately seen in newspapers and magazines in Spain and abroad. Pictures could be taken in the thick of battle, military censorship permitting, and civilian victims and exhausted, begrimed soldiers studied up close. The war America waged in Vietnam, the first to be witnessed day after day by television cameras, introduced the home front to a new intimacy with death and destruction. Ever since, battles and massacres filmed as they unfold have been a routine ingredient of the ceaseless flow of domestic, small-screen entertainment. Creating a perch for a particular conflict in the consciousness of viewers exposed to dramas from everywhere requires the daily diffusion and rediffusion of snippets of footage about the conflict. The understanding of war among people who have not experienced war is now chiefly a product of the impact of these images.

Non-stop imagery (television, streaming video, movies) surrounds us, but, when it comes to remembering, the photograph has the deeper bite. Memory freeze-frames; its basic unit is the single image. In an era of information overload, the photograph provides a quick way of apprehending something and a compact form for memorizing it. The photograph is like a quotation, or a maxim or proverb. Each of us mentally stocks hundreds of photographs, subject to instant recall. Cite the most famous photograph taken during the Spanish Civil War, the Republican soldier "shot" by Robert Capa's camera at the same moment he is hit by an enemy bullet, and virtually everyone who has heard of that war can summon to mind the grainy black-and-white image of a man in a white shirt with rolled-up sleeves collapsing backward on a hillock, his right arm flung behind him as his rifle leaves his grip—about to fall, dead, onto his own shadow.

It is a shocking image, and that is the point. Conscripted as part of journalism, images were expected to arrest attention, startle, surprise. As the old advertising slogan of *Paris Match*, founded in 1949, had it: "The weight of words, the shock of photos." The hunt for more dramatic—as they're often described—images drives the photographic enterprise, and is part of the normality of a culture in which shock has become a leading stimulus of consumption and source of value. "Beauty will be convulsive, or it will not be," André Breton proclaimed.

He called this aesthetic ideal "surrealist," but, in a culture radically revamped by the ascendancy of mercantile values, to ask that images be jarring, clamorous, eye-opening seems like elementary realism or good business sense. How else to get attention for one's product or one's art? How else to make a dent when there is incessant exposure to images, and overexposure to a handful of images seen again and again? The image as shock and the image as cliché are two aspects of the same presence. Sixty-five years ago, all photographs were novelties to some degree. (It would have been inconceivable to Virginia Woolf—who did appear on the cover of *Time* in 1937—that one day her face would become a much reproduced image on T-shirts, book bags, refrigerator magnets, coffee mugs, mouse pads.) Atrocity photographs were scarce in the winter of 1936–37: the depiction of war's horrors in the photographs Woolf discusses in *Three Guineas* seemed almost like clandestine knowledge. Our situation is altogether different. The ultra-familiar, ultra-celebrated image—of an agony, of ruin—is an unavoidable feature of our camera-mediated knowledge of war.

. . . . .

Photography has kept company with death ever since cameras were invented, in 1839. Because an image produced with a camera is, literally, a trace of something brought before the lens, photographs had an advantage over any painting as a memento of the vanished past and the dear departed. To seize death in the making was another matter: the camera's reach remained limited as long as it had to be lugged about, set down, steadied. But, once the camera was emancipated from the tripod, truly portable, and equipped with a range finder and a variety of lenses that permitted unprecedented feats of close observation from a distant vantage point, picture-taking acquired an immediacy and authority greater than any verbal account in conveying the horror of mass-produced death. If there was one year when the power of photographs to define, not merely record, the most abominable realities trumped all the complex narratives, surely it was 1945, with the pictures taken in April and early May in Bergen-Belsen, Buchenwald, and Dachau, in the first days after the camps were liberated, and those taken by Japanese witnesses such as Yosuke Yamahata in the days following the incineration of the populations of Hiroshima and Nagasaki, in early August.

Photographs had the advantage of uniting two contradictory features. Their credentials of objectivity were inbuilt, yet they always had, necessarily, a point of view. They were a record of the real—incontrovertible, as no verbal account, however impartial, could be (assuming that they showed what they purported to show)—since a machine was doing the recording. And they bore witness to the real, since a person had been there to take them.

The photographs Woolf received are treated as windows on the war: transparent views of what they show. It was of no interest to her that each had an "author"—that photographs represent the view of someone—although it was precisely in the late nineteen-thirties that the profession of bearing individual witness to war and war's atrocities with a camera was forged. Before, war photography had mostly appeared in daily and weekly newspapers. (Newspapers had been printing photographs since 1880.) By 1938, in addition to the older popular magazines that used photographs as illustrations—such as *National Geographic* and *Berliner Illustrierte Zeitung*, both founded in the late nineteenth century—there were large-circulation weekly magazines, notably the French *Vu*, the American *Life*, and the British *Picture Post*, devoted entirely to pictures (accompanied by brief texts keyed to the photos) and "picture stories" (four or five pictures by the same photographer attached to a story that further dramatized the images); in a newspaper, it was the photograph—and there was only one—that accompanied the story.

In a system based on the maximal reproduction and diffusion of images, witnessing requires star witnesses, renowned for their bravery and zeal. War photographers inherited what glamour going to war still had among the anti-bellicose, especially when the war was felt to be one of those rare conflicts in which someone of conscience would be impelled to take sides. In contrast to the 1914–18 war, which, it was clear to many of the victors, had been a colossal mistake, the second "world war" was unanimously felt by the winning side to have been a necessary war, a war that had to be fought. Photojournalism came into its own in the early nineteen-forties—wartime. This least controversial of modern wars, whose necessity was sealed by the full revelation of Nazi infamy in Europe, offered photojournalists a new legitimacy. There was little place for the left-wing dissidence that had informed much of the serious use of photographs in the interwar period, including Friedrich's *War Against War!* and the early work of Robert Capa, the most celebrated figure in a generation of politically engaged photographers whose work centered on war and victimhood.

In 1947, Capa and a few friends formed a cooperative, the Magnum Photo Agency. Magnum's charter, moralistic in the way of the founding charters of other international organizations and guilds created in the immediate postwar period, spelled out an enlarged, ethically weighted mission for photojournalists: to chronicle their own time as fair-minded witnesses free of chauvinistic prejudices. In Magnum's voice, photography declared itself a global enterprise. The photographer's beat was "the world." He or she was a rover, with wars of unusual interest (for there were many wars) a favorite destination.

The memory of war, however, like all memory, is mostly local. Armenians, the majority in diaspora, keep alive the memory of the Armenian genocide of 1915; Greeks don't forget the sanguinary civil war in Greece that raged through most of the second half of the nineteen-forties. But for a war to break out of its immediate constituency and become a subject of international attention it must be regarded as something of an exception, as wars go, and represent more than the clashing interests of the belligerents themselves. Apart from the major world conflicts, most wars do not acquire the requisite fuller meaning. An example: the Chaco War (1932–35), a butchery engaged in by Bolivia (population one million) and Paraguay (three and a half million) that took the lives of a hundred thousand soldiers, and which was covered by a German photojournalist, Willi Ruge, whose superb closeup battle pictures are as forgotten as that war. But the Spanish Civil War, in the second half of the nineteen-thirties, the Serb and Croat wars against Bosnia in the mid-nineties, the drastic worsening of the Israeli-Palestinian conflict that began in 2000—these relatively small wars were guaranteed the attention of many cameras because they were invested with the meaning of larger struggles: the Spanish Civil War because it was a stand against the Fascist menace, and was understood to be a dress rehearsal for the coming European, or "world," war; the Bosnian war because it was the stand of a small, fledgling European country wishing to remain multicultural as well as independent against the dominant power in the region and its neo-Fascist program of ethnic cleansing; and the conflict in the Middle East because the United States supports the State of Israel. Indeed, it is felt by many who champion the Palestinian side that what is ultimately at stake, by proxy, in the struggle to end the Israeli domination of the territories captured in 1967 is the strength of the forces opposing the juggernaut of American-sponsored globalization, economic and cultural.

The memorable sites of suffering documented by admired photographers in the nineteen-fifties, sixties, and early seventies were mostly in Asia and Africa—Werner Bischof's photographs of famine victims in India, Don McCullin's pictures of war and famine in Biafra, W. Eugene Smith's photographs of the victims of the lethal pollution of a Japanese fishing village. The Indian and African famines were not just "natural" disasters: they were preventable; they were crimes of the greatest magnitude. And what happened in Minamata was obviously a crime; the Chisso Corporation knew that it was dumping mercury-laden waste into the bay. (Smith was severely and permanently injured by Chisso goons who were ordered to put an end to his camera inquiry.) But war is the largest crime, and, starting in the mid-sixties, most of the best-known photographers covering wars set out to show war's "real" face. The color photographs of tormented Vietnamese villagers and wounded American conscripts that Larry Burrows took and *Life* published, starting in 1962, certainly fortified the outcry against the American presence in Vietnam. Burrows was the first important photographer to do a whole war in color—another gain in verisimilitude and shock.

In the current political mood, the friendliest to the military in decades, the pictures of wretched hollow-eyed GIs that once seemed subversive of militarism and imperialism may seem inspirational. Their revised subject: ordinary American young men doing their unpleasant, ennobling duty.

III

The iconography of suffering has a long pedigree. The suffering most often deemed worthy of representation is that which is understood to be the product of wrath, divine or human. (Suffering brought on by natural causes, such as illness or childbirth, is scantily represented in the history of art; that brought on by accident virtually not at all—as if there were no such thing as suffering by inadvertence or misadventure.)

The statue group of the writhing Laocoön and his sons, the innumerable versions in painting and sculpture of the Passion of Christ, and the immense visual catalog of the fiendish executions of the Christian martyrs—these are surely intended to move and excite, to instruct and exemplify. The viewer may commiserate with the sufferer's pain—and, in the case of the Christian saints, feel admonished or inspired by model faith and fortitude—but these are destinies beyond deploring or contesting.

It seems that the appetite for pictures showing bodies in pain is almost as keen as the desire for ones that show bodies naked. For a long time, in Christian art, depictions of Hell offered both of these elemental satisfactions. On occasion, the pretext might be a Biblical decapitation story (Holofernes, John the Baptist) or massacre yarn (the newborn Hebrew boys, the eleven thousand virgins) or some such, with the status of a real historical event and of an implacable fate. There was also the repertoire of hard-to-look-at cruelties from classical antiquity—the pagan myths, even more than the Christian stories, offer something for every taste. No moral charge attaches to the representation of these cruelties. Just the provocation: Can you look at this? There is the satisfaction at being able to look at the image without flinching. There is the pleasure of flinching.

To shudder at Goltzius's rendering, in his etching *The Dragon Devouring the Companions of Cadmus* (1588), of a man's face being chewed off his head is very different from shuddering at a photograph of a First World War veteran whose face has been shot away. One horror has its place in a complex subject—figures in a landscape—that displays the artist's skill of eye and hand. The other is a camera's record, from very near, of a real person's unspeakably awful mutilation; that and nothing else. An invented horror can be quite overwhelming. (I, for one, find it difficult to look at Titian's great painting of the flaying of Marsyas, or, indeed, at any picture of this subject.) But there is shame as well as shock in looking at the closeup of a real horror. Perhaps the only people with the right to look at images of suffering of this extreme order are those who could do something to alleviate it—say, the surgeons at the military hospital where the photograph was taken—or those who could learn from it. The rest of us are voyeurs, whether we like it or not.

In each instance, the gruesome invites us to be either spectators or cowards, unable to look. Those with the stomach to look are playing a role authorized by many glorious depictions of suffering. Torment, a canonical subject in art, is often represented in painting as a spectacle, something being watched (or ignored) by other people. The implication is: No, it cannot be stopped—and the mingling of inattentive with attentive onlookers underscores this.

The practice of representing atrocious suffering as something to be deplored, and, if possible, stopped, enters the history of images with a specific subject: the sufferings endured by a civilian population at the hands of a victorious army on the rampage. It is a quintessentially secular subject, which emerges in the seventeenth century, when contemporary realignments of power become material for artists. In 1633, Jacques Callot published a suite of eighteen etchings titled *The Miseries and Misfortunes of War*, which depicted the atrocities committed against civilians by French troops during the invasion and occupation of his native Lorraine in the early sixteen-thirties. (Six small etchings on the same subject that Callot had executed prior to the large series appeared in 1635, the year of his death.) The view is wide and deep; these are scenes with many figures, scenes from a history, and each caption is a sententious comment in verse on the various energies and dooms portrayed in the images. Callot begins with a plate showing the recruitment of soldiers; brings into view ferocious combat, massacre, pillage, and rape, the engines of torture and execution (strappado, gallows tree, firing squad, stake, wheel), and the revenge of the peasants on the soldiers; and ends with a distribution of rewards. The insistence in plate after plate on the savagery of a conquering army is startling and without precedent, but the French soldiers are only the leading malefactors in the orgy of violence, and there is room in Callot's Christian humanist sensibility not just to mourn the end of the independent Duchy of Lorraine but to record the postwar plight of destitute soldiers who squat on the side of the road, begging for alms.

Callot had his successors, such as Hans Ulrich Franck, a minor German artist who, in 1643, toward the end of the Thirty Years' War, began making what would be (by 1656) a suite of twenty-five etchings depicting soldiers killing peasants. But the preeminent concentration on the horrors of war and the vileness of soldiers run amok is Goya's, in the early nineteenth century. *The Disasters of War*, a numbered sequence of eighty-three etchings made between 1810 and 1820 (and first published, except for three plates, in 1863, thirty-five years after his death), depicts the atrocities perpetrated by Napoleon's soldiers, who invaded Spain in 1808 to quell the insurrection against French rule. Goya's images move the viewer close to the horror. All the trappings of the spectacular have been eliminated: the landscape is an atmosphere, a darkness, barely sketched in. War is not a spectacle. And Goya's print series is not a narrative: each image, captioned with a brief phrase lamenting the wickedness of the invaders and the monstrousness of the suffering they inflicted, stands independent of the others. The cumulative effect is devastating.

The ghoulish cruelties in *The Disasters of War* are meant to awaken, shock, wound the viewer. Goya's art, like Dostoyevsky's, seems a turning point in the history of moral feelings and of sorrow—as deep, as original, as demanding. With Goya, a new standard for responsiveness to suffering enters art. (And new subjects for fellow-feeling: for example, the painting of an injured laborer being carried away from a construction site.) The account of war's cruelties is constructed as an assault on the sensibility of the viewer. The expressive phrases in script below each image comment on the provocation. While the image, like all images, is an invitation to look, the caption, more often than not, insists on the difficulty of doing just that. A voice, presumably the artist's, badgers the viewer: Can you bear this? One caption declares, "*No se puede mirar*" ("One can't look"). Another says, "*Esto es malo*" ("This is bad"). "*Esto es peor*" ("This is worse"), another retorts.

The caption of a photograph is traditionally neutral, informative: a date, a place, names. A reconnaissance photograph from the First World War (the first war in which cameras were used extensively for military intelligence) was unlikely to be captioned "Can't wait to overrun this!" or the X-ray of a multiple fracture to be annotated "Patient will probably have a limp!" It seems no less inappropriate to speak for the photograph in the photographer's voice, offering assurances of the image's veracity, as Goya does in *The Disasters of War*, writing beneath one image, "*Yo lo vi*" ("I saw this"). And beneath another, "*Esto es lo verdadero*" ("This is the truth"). Of course the photographer saw it. And, unless there's been some tampering or misrepresenting, it is the truth.

Ordinary language fixes the difference between handmade images like Goya's and photographs through the convention that artists "make" drawings and paintings while photographers "take" photographs. But the photographic image, even to the extent that it is a trace (not a construction made out of disparate photographic traces), cannot be simply a transparency of something that happened. It is always the image that someone chose; to photograph is to frame, and to frame is to exclude. Moreover, fiddling with the picture long antedates the era of digital photography and Photoshop manipulations: it has always been possible for a photograph to misrepresent. A painting or drawing is judged a fake when it turns out not to be by the artist to whom it had been attributed. A photograph—or a filmed document available on television or the Internet—is judged a fake when it turns out to be deceiving the viewer about the scene it purports to depict.

That the atrocities perpetrated by Napoleon's soldiers in Spain didn't happen exactly as Goya drew them hardly disqualifies *The Disasters of War*. Goya's images are a synthesis. Things *like* this happened. In contrast, a single photograph or filmstrip claims to represent exactly what was before the camera's lens. A photograph is supposed not to evoke but to show. That is why photographs, unlike handmade images, can count as evidence. But evidence of what? The suspicion that Capa's *Death of a Republican Soldier*—recently retitled *The Falling Soldier*, in the authoritative compilation of Capa's work—may not show what it has always been said to show continues to haunt discussions of war photography. Everyone is a literalist when it comes to photographs.

· · · · ·

Images of the sufferings endured in war are so widely disseminated now that it is easy to forget that, historically, photographers have offered mostly positive images of the warrior's trade, and of the satisfactions of starting a war or continuing to fight one. If governments had their way, war photography, like much war poetry, would drum up support for soldiers' sacrifices. Indeed, war photography begins with such a mission, such a disgrace. The war was the Crimean War, and the photographer, Roger Fenton, invariably called the first war photographer, was no less than that war's "official" photographer, having been sent to the Crimea in early 1855 by the British government, at the instigation of Prince Albert. Acknowledging the need to counteract the alarming printed accounts of the dangers and privations endured by the British soldiers dispatched there the previous year, the government invited a well-known professional photographer to give another, more positive impression of the increasingly unpopular war.

Edmund Gosse, in *Father and Son*, his memoir of a mid-nineteenth-century English childhood, relates how the Crimean War penetrated even his stringently pious, unworldly family, which belonged to an evangelical sect called the Plymouth Brethren: "The declaration of war with Russia brought the first breath of outside life into our Calvinist cloister. My parents took in a daily newspaper, which they had never done before, and events in picturesque places, which my Father and I looked out on the map, were eagerly discussed." War was, and still is, the most irresistible—and picturesque—news, along with that invaluable substitute for war, international sports. But this war was more than news. It was bad news. The authoritative, pictureless London newspaper to which Gosse's parents had succumbed, the *Times*, attacked the military leadership whose incompetence was responsible for the war's dragging on, with so much loss of British life. The toll on the soldiers from causes other than combat was horrendous—twenty-two thousand died of illnesses; many thousands lost limbs to frostbite during the long Russian winter of the protracted siege of Sebastopol—and several of the military engagements were disasters. It was still winter when Fenton arrived in the Crimea for a four-month stay, having contracted to publish his photographs (in the form of engravings) in a less venerable and less critical weekly paper, the *Illustrated London News*, exhibit them in a gallery, and market them as a book upon his return home.

Under instructions from the War Office not to photograph the dead, the maimed, or the ill, and precluded from photographing most other subjects by the cumbersome technology of picture-taking, Fenton went about rendering the war as a dignified all-male group outing. With each image requiring a separate chemical preparation in the darkroom and a long exposure time, he could photograph British officers in open-air staff meetings or common soldiers tending the cannons only after asking them to stand or sit together, follow his directions, and hold still. His pictures are tableaux of military life behind the front lines; the war—movement, disorder, drama—stays off-camera. The one photograph Fenton took in the Crimea that reaches beyond benign documentation is *The Valley of the Shadow of Death*, whose title evokes the consolation offered by the Biblical Psalmist as well as the disaster in which six hundred British soldiers were ambushed on the plain above Balaklava—Tennyson called the site "the valley of Death" in his memorial poem, "The Charge of the Light Brigade." Fenton's memorial photograph is a portrait of absence, of death without the dead. It is the only photograph that would not have needed to be staged, for all it shows is a wide rutted road, studded with rocks and cannonballs, that curves onward across a barren rolling plain to the distant void.

A bolder portfolio of after-the-battle images of death and ruin, pointing not to losses suffered but to a fearsome British triumph over the enemy, was made by another photographer who had visited the Crimean War. Felice Beato, a naturalized Englishman (he was born in Venice), was the first photographer to attend a number of wars: besides being in the Crimea in 1855, he was at the Sepoy Rebellion (what the British call the Indian Mutiny) in 1857–58, the Second Opium War in China, in 1860, and the Sudanese colonial wars in 1885. Three years after Fenton made his anodyne images of a war that did not go well for England, Beato was celebrating the fierce victory of the British Army over a mutiny of native soldiers under its command, the first important challenge to British rule in India. Beato's *Ruins of Sikandarbagh Palace*, an arresting photograph of a palace in Lucknow that has been gutted by bombardment, shows the courtyard strewn with the rebels' bones.

The first full-scale attempt to document a war was carried out a few years later, during the American Civil War, by a firm of Northern photographers headed by Mathew Brady, who had made several official portraits of President Lincoln. The Brady war pictures—most were shot by Alexander Gardner and Timothy O'Sullivan, although their employer was invariably credited with them—showed conventional subjects, such as encampments populated by officers and foot soldiers, towns in war's way, ordnance, ships, and also, most famously, dead Union and Confederate soldiers lying on the blasted ground of Gettysburg and Antietam. Though access to the battlefield came as a privilege extended to Brady and his team by Lincoln himself, the photographers were not commissioned, as Fenton had been. Their status evolved in rather typical American fashion, with nominal government sponsorship giving way to the force of entrepreneurial and freelance motives.

The first justification for the brutally legible pictures of a field of dead soldiers was the simple duty to record. "The camera is the eye of history," Brady is supposed to have said. And history, invoked as truth beyond appeal, was allied with the rising prestige of a certain notion of subjects needing more attention, known as realism, which was soon to have a host of defenders among novelists as well as photographers. In the name of realism, one was permitted—required—to show unpleasant, hard facts. Such pictures also convey "a useful moral" by showing "the blank horror and reality of war, in opposition to its pageantry," as Gardner wrote in a text accompanying O'Sullivan's picture of fallen Confederate soldiers, their agonized faces clearly visible. "Here are the dreadful details! Let them aid in preventing another such calamity falling upon the nation." But the frankness of the most memorable pictures in an album of photographs by Gardner and other Brady photographers, which Gardner published after the war, did not mean that he and his colleagues had necessarily photographed their subjects as they found them. To photograph was to compose (with living subjects, to pose); the desire to arrange elements in the picture did not vanish because the subject was immobilized, or immobile.

. . . . .

Not surprisingly, many of the canonical images of early war photography turn out to have been staged, or to have had their subjects tampered with. Roger Fenton, after reaching the much shelled valley near Sebastopol in his horse-drawn darkroom, made two exposures from the same tripod position: in the first version of the celebrated photograph he was to call *The Valley of the Shadow of Death* (despite the title, it was not across this landscape that the Light Brigade made its doomed charge), the cannonballs are thick on the ground to the left of the road; before taking the second picture—the one that is always reproduced—he oversaw the scattering of cannonballs on the road itself. A picture of a desolate site where a great deal of dying had indeed recently taken place, Beato's *Ruins of Sikandarbagh Palace*, involved a more thorough theatricalization of its subject, and was one of the first attempts to suggest with a camera the horrific in war. The attack occurred in November, 1857, after which the victorious British troops and loyal Indian units searched the palace room by room, bayoneting the eighteen hundred surviving Sepoy defenders who were now their prisoners and throwing their bodies into the courtyard; vultures and dogs did the rest. For the photograph he took in March or April, 1858, Beato constructed the courtyard as a deathscape, stationing some natives by two pillars in the rear and distributing human bones about the foreground.

At least they were old bones. It's now known that the Brady team rearranged and displaced some of the recently dead at Gettysburg; the picture titled *The Home of a Rebel Sharpshooter, Gettysburg* in fact shows a dead Confederate soldier who was moved from where he had fallen on the field to a more photogenic site, a cove formed by several boulders flanking a barricade of rocks, and includes a prop rifle that Gardner leaned against the barricade beside the corpse. (It seems not to have been the special rifle a sharpshooter would have used, but a common infantryman's rifle; Gardner didn't know this or didn't care.)

Only starting with the Vietnam War can we be virtually certain that none of the best-known photographs were setups. And this is essential to the moral authority of these images. The signature Vietnam War horror photograph, from 1972, taken by Huynh Cong Ut, of children from a village that has just been doused with American napalm running down the highway, shrieking with pain, belongs to the universe of photographs that cannot possibly be posed. The same is true of the well-known pictures from the most widely photographed wars since.

That there have been so few staged war photographs since the Vietnam War probably should not be attributed to higher standards of journalistic probity. One part of the explanation is that it was in Vietnam that television became the defining medium for showing images of war, and the intrepid lone photographer, Nikon or Leica in hand, operating out of sight much of the time, now had to compete with, and endure the proximity of, TV crews. There are always witnesses to a filming. Technically, the possibilities for doctoring or electronically manipulating pictures are greater than ever—almost unlimited. But the practice of inventing dramatic news pictures, staging them for the camera, seems on its way to becoming a lost art.

IV

Central to modern expectations, and modern ethical feeling, is the conviction that war is an aberration, if an unstoppable one. That peace is the norm, if an unattainable one. This, of course, is not the way war has been regarded throughout history. War has been the norm and peace the exception.

Descriptions of the exact fashion in which bodies are injured and killed in combat is a recurring climax in the stories told in the *Iliad*. War is seen as something men do, inveterately, undeterred by the accumulation of suffering it inflicts; to represent war in words or in pictures requires a keen, unflinching detachment. When Leonardo da Vinci gives instructions for a battle painting, his worry is that artists will lack the courage or the imagination to show war in all its ghastliness: "Make the conquered and beaten pale, with brows raised and knit, and the skin above their brows furrowed with pain . . . and the teeth apart as with crying out in lamentation. . . . Make the dead partly or entirely covered with dust . . . and let the blood be seen by its color flowing in a sinuous stream from the corpse to the dust. Others in the death agony grinding their teeth, rolling their eyes, with their fists clenched against their bodies, and the legs distorted." The concern is that the images won't be sufficiently upsetting: not concrete, not detailed enough.

Pity can entail a moral judgment if, as Aristotle suggests, pity is considered to be the emotion that we owe only to those enduring undeserved misfortune. But pity, far from being the natural twin of fear in the dramas of catastrophic misfortune, seems diluted—distracted—by fear, while fear (dread, terror) usually manages to swamp pity. Leonardo is suggesting that the artist's gaze be, literally, pitiless. The image should appall, and in that *terribilità* lies a challenging kind of beauty.

That a gory battlescape could be beautiful—in the sublime or awesome or tragic register of the beautiful—is a commonplace about images of war made by artists. The idea does not sit well when applied to images taken by cameras: to find beauty in war photographs seems heartless. But the landscape of devastation is still a landscape. There is beauty in ruins. To acknowledge the beauty of photographs of the World Trade Center ruins in the months following the attack seemed frivolous, sacrilegious. The most people dared say was that the photographs were "surreal," a hectic euphemism behind which the disgraced notion of beauty cowered. But they *were* beautiful, many of them—by veteran photographers such as Gilles Peress, Susan Meiselas, and Joel Meyerowitz and by many little-known and nonprofessional photographers. The site itself, the mass graveyard that had received the name Ground Zero, was, of course, anything but beautiful. Photographs tend to transform, whatever their subject; and as an image something may be beautiful—or terrifying, or unbearable, or quite bearable—as it is not in real life.

Transforming is what art does, but photography that bears witness to the calamitous and the reprehensible is much criticized if it seems "aesthetic"; that is, too much like art. The dual powers of photography—to generate documents and to create works of visual art—have produced some remarkable exaggerations about what photographers ought or ought not to do. These days, most exaggeration is of the puritanical kind. Photographs that depict suffering shouldn't be beautiful, as captions shouldn't moralize. In this view, a beautiful photograph drains attention from the sobering subject and turns it toward the medium itself, inviting the viewer to look "aesthetically," and thereby compromising the picture's status as a document. The photograph gives mixed signals. Stop this, it urges. But it also exclaims, What a spectacle!

Take one of the most poignant images from the First World War: a column of English soldiers blinded by poison gas—each rests his hand on the shoulder of the man ahead of him—stumbling toward a dressing station. It could be an image from one of the searing movies made about the war—King Vidor's *The Big Parade*, of 1925, or G. W. Pabst's *Westfront 1918*, Lewis Milestone's *All Quiet on the Western Front*, and Howard Hawks's *Dawn Patrol*, all from 1930. The way in which still photography finds its perfection in the reconstruction of battle scenes in the great war movies has begun to backfire on the photography of war. What assured the authenticity of Steven Spielberg's much admired re-creation of the Omaha Beach landing on D Day in *Saving Private Ryan* (1998) was that it was based on, among other sources, the photographs taken with immense bravery by Robert Capa during the landing. But a war photograph seems inauthentic, even though there is nothing staged about it, when it looks like a still from a movie. Sebastião Salgado, a photographer who specializes in world misery (including but not restricted to the effects of war), has been the principal target of the new campaign against the inauthenticity of the beautiful. Particularly with the seven-year project he calls *Migrations: Humanity in Transition*, Salgado has come under steady attack for producing spectacular, beautifully composed big pictures that are said to be "cinematic."

The sanctimonious Family of Man–style rhetoric that accompanies Salgado's exhibitions and books has worked to the detriment of the pictures, however unfair this may be. The pictures have also been sourly treated in response to the highly commercialized situations in which, typically, Salgado's portraits of misery are seen. But the problem is in the pictures themselves, not the way they are exhibited: in their focus on the powerless, reduced to their powerlessness. It is significant that the powerless are not named in the captions. A portrait that declines to name its subject becomes complicit, if inadvertently, in the cult of celebrity that has fueled an insatiable appetite for the opposite sort of photograph: to grant only the famous their names demotes the rest to representative instances of their occupations, their ethnicities, their plights. Taken in thirty-five countries, Salgado's migration pictures group together, under this single heading, a host of different causes and kinds of distress. Making suffering loom larger, by globalizing it, may spur people to feel they ought to "care" more. It also invites them to feel that the sufferings and misfortunes are too vast, too irrevocable, too epic to be much changed by any local, political intervention. With a subject conceived on this scale, compassion can only flounder—and make abstract. But all politics, like all history, is concrete.

It used to be thought, when candid images were not common, that showing something that needed to be seen, bringing a painful reality closer, was bound to goad viewers to feel—feel more. In a world in which photography is brilliantly at the service of consumerist manipulations, this naïve relation to poignant scenes of suffering is much less plausible. Morally alert photographers and ideologues of photography are concerned with the issues of exploitation of sentiment (pity, compassion, indignation) in war photography, and how to avoid rote ways of arousing feeling.

Photographer-witnesses may try to make the spectacular *not* spectacular. But their efforts can never cancel the tradition in which suffering has been understood throughout most of Western history. To feel the pulse of Christian iconography in certain wartime or disaster-time photographs is not a sentimental projection. It would be hard not to discern the lineaments of the Pietà in W. Eugene Smith's picture of a woman in Minamata cradling her deformed, blind, and deaf daughter, or the template of the Descent from the Cross in several of Don McCullin's pictures of dying American soldiers in Vietnam.

. . . . .

The problem is not that people remember through photographs but that they remember only the photographs. This remembering through photographs eclipses other forms of understanding—and remembering. The concentration camps—that is, the photographs taken when the camps were liberated, in 1945—are most of what people associate with Nazism and the miseries of the Second World War. Hideous deaths (by genocide, starvation, and epidemic) are most of what people retain of the clutch of iniquities and failures that have taken place in postcolonial Africa.

To remember is, more and more, not to recall a story but to be able to call up a picture. Even a writer as steeped in nineteenth-century and early-modern literary solemnities as W. G. Sebald was moved to seed his lamentation-narratives of lost lives, lost nature, lost cityscapes with photographs. Sebald was not just an elegist; he was a militant elegist. Remembering, he wanted the reader to remember, too.

Harrowing photographs do not inevitably lose their power to shock. But they don't help us much to understand. Narratives can make us understand. Photographs do something else: they haunt us. Consider one of the most unforgettable images of the war in Bosnia, a photograph of which the *New York Times* foreign correspondent John Kifner wrote, "The image is stark, one of the most enduring of the Balkan wars: a Serb militiaman casually kicking a dying Muslim woman in the head. It tells you everything you need to know." But of course it doesn't tell us everything we need to know.

From the identification supplied by the photographer, Ron Haviv, we learn that the photograph was taken in the town of Bijeljina in April, 1992, the first month of the Serb rampage through Bosnia. From behind, we see a uniformed Serb soldier, a youthful figure with sunglasses perched on the top of his head, a cigarette between the second and third fingers of his raised left hand, rifle dangling in his right hand, right leg poised to kick a woman lying face down on the sidewalk between two other bodies. The photograph doesn't tell us that she is Muslim, but she is not likely to have been labeled in any other way, or why would she and the two others be lying there, as if dead (why "dying"?), under the gaze of some Serb soldiers? In fact, the photograph tells us very little—except that war is hell, and that graceful young men with guns are capable of kicking in the head overweight older women lying helpless, or already killed.

The pictures of Bosnian atrocities were seen soon after they took place. Like pictures from the Vietnam War, such as Ron Haberle's documents of the massacre by a company of American soldiers of some five hundred unarmed civilians in the village of My Lai in March, 1968, they became important in bolstering indignation at this war which had been far from inevitable, far from intractable; and could have been stopped much sooner. Therefore one could feel an obligation to look at these pictures, gruesome as they were, because there was something to be done, right now, about what they depicted. Other issues are raised when the public is invited to respond to a dossier of hitherto unknown pictures of horrors long past.

An example: a trove of photographs of black victims of lynching in small towns in the United States between the eighteen-nineties and the nineteen-thirties, which provided a shattering, revelatory experience for the thousands who saw them in a gallery in New York in 2000. The lynching pictures tell us about human wickedness. About inhumanity. They force us to think about the extent of the evil unleashed specifically by racism. Intrinsic to the perpetration of this evil is the shamelessness of photographing it. The pictures were taken as souvenirs and made, some of them, into postcards; more than a few show grinning spectators, good churchgoing citizens, as most of them had to be, posing for a camera with the backdrop of a naked, charred, mutilated body hanging from a tree. The display of the pictures makes us spectators, too.

What is the point of exhibiting these pictures? To awaken indignation? To make us feel "bad"; that is, to appall and sadden? To help us mourn? Is looking at such pictures really necessary, given that these horrors lie in a past remote enough to be beyond punishment? Are we the better for seeing these images? Do they actually teach us anything? Don't they rather just confirm what we already know (or want to know)?

All these questions were raised at the time of the exhibition and afterward when a book of the photographs, *Without Sanctuary,* was published. Some people, it was said, might dispute the need for this grisly photographic display, lest it cater to voyeuristic appetites and perpetuate images of black victimization—or simply numb the mind. Nevertheless, it was argued, there is an obligation to "examine"—the more clinical "examine" is substituted for "look at"—the pictures. It was further argued that submitting to the ordeal should help us understand such atrocities not as the acts of "barbarians" but as the reflection of a belief system, racism, that by defining one people as less human than another legitimatizes torture and murder. But maybe they *were* barbarians. Maybe *this* is what barbarians look like. (They look like everybody else.)

That being said, whom do we wish to blame? More precisely, whom do we believe we have the right to blame? The children of Hiroshima and Nagasaki were no less innocent than the young African-American men (and a few women) who were butchered and hanged from trees in small-town America. More than a hundred thousand German civilians, three-fourths of them women, were incinerated in the RAF fire bombing of Dresden on the night of February 13, 1945; seventy-two thousand civilians were killed by the American bomb dropped on Hiroshima. The roll call could be much longer. Again, whom do we wish to blame? What atrocities from the incurable past do we think we are obliged to see?

Probably, if we are Americans, we think that it would be "morbid" to go out of our way to look at pictures of burned victims of atomic bombing or the napalmed flesh of the civilian victims of the American war on Vietnam but that we have some kind of duty to look at the lynching pictures—if we belong to the party of the right-thinking, which on this issue is now large. A stepped-up recognition of the monstrousness of the slave system that once existed, unquestioned by most, in the United States is a national project of recent decades that many Euro-Americans feel some tug of obligation to join. This ongoing project is a great achievement, a benchmark of civic virtue. But acknowledgment of American use of disproportionate firepower in war (in violation of one of the cardinal laws of war) is very much not a national project. A museum devoted to the history of America's wars that included the vicious war the United States fought against guerrillas in the Philippines from 1899 to 1902 (expertly excoriated by Mark Twain), and that fairly presented the arguments for and against using the atomic bomb in 1945 on the Japanese cities, with photographic evidence that showed what those weapons did, would be regarded—now more than ever—as an unpatriotic endeavor.

V

Consider two widespread ideas—now fast approaching the stature of platitudes—on the impact of photography. Since I find these ideas formulated in my own essays on photography, the earliest of which was written thirty years ago, I feel an irresistible temptation to quarrel with them.

The first idea is that public attention is steered by the attentions of the media—which means images. When there are photographs, a war becomes "real." Thus, the protest against the Vietnam War was mobilized by images. The feeling that something had to be done about the war in Bosnia was built from the attentions of journalists: "the CNN effect," it was sometimes called, which brought images of Sarajevo under siege into hundreds of millions of living rooms night after night for more than three years. These examples illustrate the determining influence of photographs in shaping what catastrophes and crises we pay attention to, what we care about, and ultimately what evaluations are placed on these conflicts.

The second idea—it might seem the converse of what has just been described—is that in a world saturated, even hypersaturated, with images, those which should matter to us have a diminishing effect: we become callous. In the end, such images make us a little less able to feel, to have our conscience pricked.

In the first of the six essays in *On Photography*, which was published in 1977, I argued that while an event known through photographs certainly becomes more real than it would have been if one had never seen the photographs, after repeated exposure it also becomes less real. As much as they create sympathy, I wrote, photographs shrivel sympathy. Is this true? I thought it was when I wrote it. I'm not so sure now. What is the evidence that photographs have a diminishing impact, that our culture of spectacle neutralizes the moral force of photographs of atrocities?

The question turns on a view of the principal medium of the news, television. An image is drained of its force by the way it is used, where and how often it is seen. Images shown on television are, by definition, images of which, sooner or later, one tires. What looks like callousness has its origin in the instability of attention that television is organized to arouse and to satiate, by its surfeit of images. Image-glut keeps attention light, mobile, relatively indifferent to content. Image-flow precludes a privileged image. The whole point of television is that one can switch channels, that it is normal to switch channels: to become restless, bored. Consumers droop. They need to be restimulated, jump-started, again and again. Content is no more than one of these stimulants. A more reflective engagement with content would require a certain intensity of awareness—just what is weakened by the expectations brought to images disseminated by the media. The leaching out of content is what contributes most to the deadening of feeling.

The argument that modern life consists of a menu of horrors by which we are corrupted and to which we gradually become habituated is a founding idea of the critique of modernity—a tradition almost as old as modernity itself. In 1800, Wordsworth, in the Preface to *Lyrical Ballads*, denounced the corruption of sensibility produced by "the great national events which are daily taking place, and the increasing accumulation of men in cities, where the uniformity of their occupations produces a craving for extraordinary incident, which the rapid communication of intelligence hourly gratifies." This process of over-stimulation acts "to blunt the discriminating powers of the mind" and "reduce it to a state of almost savage torpor."

Wordsworth singled out the blunting of mind produced by "daily" events and "hourly" news of "extraordinary incident." (In 1800!) Exactly what kind of events and incidents was discreetly left to the reader's imagination. Some sixty years later, another great poet and cultural diagnostician—French, and therefore as licensed to be hyperbolic as the English are prone to understate—offered a more heated version of the same charge. Here is Baudelaire writing in his journal in the early eighteen-sixties: "It is impossible to glance through any newspaper, no matter what the day, the month or the year, without finding on every line the most frightful traces of human perversity. . . . Every newspaper, from the first line to the last, is nothing but a tissue of horrors. Wars, crimes, thefts, lecheries, tortures, the evil deeds of princes, of nations, of private individuals; an orgy of universal atrocity. And it is with this loathsome appetizer that civilized man daily washes down his morning repast."

Newspapers did not yet carry photographs when Baudelaire wrote. But this doesn't make his accusatory description of the bourgeois sitting down with his morning newspaper to breakfast with an array of the world's horrors any different from the contemporary critique of how much desensitizing horror we take in every day, via television as well as the morning paper. Newer technology provides a non-stop feed: as many images of disaster and atrocity as we can make time to look at.

Since *On Photography* was published, many critics have suggested that the agonies of war—thanks to television—have devolved into a nightly banality. Flooded with images of the sort that once used to shock and arouse indignation, we are losing our capacity to react. Compassion, stretched to its limits, is going numb. So runs the familiar diagnosis. But what is really being asked for here? That images of carnage be cut back to, say, once a week? More generally, that we work toward an "ecology of images," as I suggested in *On Photography*? But there *isn't* going to be an ecology of images. No Committee of Guardians is going to ration horror, to keep fresh its ability to shock. And the horrors themselves are not going to abate.

· · · · ·

The view proposed in *On Photography*—that our capacity to respond to our experiences with emotional freshness and ethical pertinence is being sapped by the relentless diffusion of vulgar and appalling images—might be called the conservative critique of the diffusion of such images. I call this argument "conservative" because it is the sense of reality that is eroded. There is still a reality that exists independent of the attempts to weaken its authority. The argument is in fact a defense of reality and the imperiled standards for responding to it more fully. In the more radical—cynical—spin on this critique, there is nothing to defend, for, paradoxical as it may sound, there is no reality anymore. The vast maw of modernity has chewed up reality and spat the whole mess out as images. According to a highly influential analysis, we live in a "society of spectacle." Each thing has to be turned into a spectacle to be real—that is, interesting—to us. People themselves become images: celebrities. Reality has abdicated. There are only representations: media.

Fancy rhetoric, this. And very persuasive to many, because one of the characteristics of modernity is that people like to feel they can anticipate their own experience. (This view is associated in particular with the writings of the late Guy Debord, who thought he was describing an illusion, a hoax, and of Jean Baudrillard, who claims to believe that images, simulated realities, are all that exists now; it seems to be something of a French specialty.) It is common to say that war, like everything else that seems to be real, is *médiatique*. This was the diagnosis of several distinguished French day-trippers to Sarajevo during the siege, among them André Glucksmann: that the war would be won or lost not by anything that happened in Sarajevo, or Bosnia generally, but by what happened in the media. It is often asserted that "the West" has increasingly come to see war itself as a spectacle. Reports of the death of reality—like the death of reason, the death of the intellectual, the death of serious literature—seem to have been accepted without much reflection by many who are attempting to understand what feels wrong, or empty, or idiotically triumphant in contemporary politics and culture.

To speak of reality becoming a spectacle is a breathtaking provincialism. It universalizes the viewing habits of a small, educated population living in the rich part of the world, where news has been converted into entertainment—a mature style of viewing that is a prime acquisition of the "modern," and a prerequisite for dismantling traditional forms of party-based politics that offer real disagreement and debate. It assumes that everyone is a spectator. It suggests, perversely, unseriously, that there is no real suffering in the world. But it is absurd to identify "the world" with those zones in the rich countries where people have the dubious privilege of being spectators, or of declining to be spectators, of other people's pain, just as it is absurd to generalize about the ability to respond to the sufferings of others on the basis of the mind-set of those consumers of news who know nothing at first hand about war and terror. There are hundreds of millions of television watchers who are far from inured to what they see on television. They do not have the luxury of patronizing reality.

VI

Is there an antidote to the perennial seductiveness of war? And is this a question a woman is more likely to pose than a man? (Probably yes.)

Could one be mobilized actively to oppose war by an image (or a group of images), as one might be enrolled among the opponents of capital punishment by reading, say, Dreiser's *An American Tragedy* or Turgenev's "The Execution of Troppmann," an account of a night spent with a notorious criminal who is about to be guillotined? A narrative seems likely to be more effective than an image. Partly it is a question of the length of time one is obliged to look, and to feel. No photograph, or portfolio of photographs, can unfold, go further, and further still, as does *The Ascent* (1977), by the Ukrainian director Larisa Shepitko, the most affecting film about the horror of war I know.

Among single antiwar images, the huge photograph that Jeff Wall made in 1992 entitled *Dead Troops Talk (A vision after an ambush of a Red Army patrol, near Moqor, Afghanistan, winter 1986)* seems to me exemplary in its thoughtfulness, coherence, and passion. The antithesis of a document, the picture, a Cibachrome transparency seven and a half feet high and more than thirteen feet wide and mounted on a light box, shows figures posed in a landscape, a blasted hillside, that was constructed in the artist's studio. Wall, who is Canadian, was never in Afghanistan. The ambush is a made-up event in a conflict he had read about. His imagination of war (he cites Goya as an inspiration) is in the tradition of nineteenth-century history painting and other forms of history-as-spectacle that emerged in the late eighteenth and early nineteenth centuries—just before the invention of the camera—such as tableaux vivants, wax displays, dioramas, and panoramas, which made the past, especially the immediate past, seem astonishingly, disturbingly real.

The figures in Wall's visionary photo-work are "realistic," but, of course, the image is not. Dead soldiers don't talk. Here they do.

Thirteen Russian soldiers in bulky winter uniforms and high boots are scattered about a pocked, blood-splashed pit lined with loose rocks and the litter of war: shell casings, crumpled metal, a boot that holds the lower part of a leg. The soldiers, slaughtered in the Soviet Union's own late folly of a colonial war, were never buried. A few still have their helmets on. The head of one kneeling figure, talking animatedly, foams with his red brain matter. The atmosphere is warm, convivial, fraternal. Some slouch, leaning on an elbow, or sit, chatting, their opened skulls and destroyed hands on view. One man bends over another, who lies on his side in a posture of heavy sleep, perhaps encouraging him to sit up. Three men are horsing around: one with a huge wound in his belly straddles another, who is lying prone, while the third, kneeling, dangles what might be a watch before the laughing man on his stomach. One soldier, helmeted, legless, has turned to a comrade some distance away, an alert smile on his face. Below him are two who don't seem quite up to the resurrection and lie supine, their bloodied heads hanging down the stony incline.

Engulfed by the image, which is so accusatory, one could fantasize that the soldiers might turn and talk to us. But no, no one is looking out of the picture at the viewer. There's no threat of protest. They're not about to yell at us to bring a halt to that abomination which is war. They are not represented as terrifying to others, for among them (far left) sits a white-garbed Afghan scavenger, entirely absorbed in going through somebody's kit bag, of whom they take no note, and entering the picture above them (top right), on the path winding down the slope, are two Afghans, perhaps soldiers themselves, who, it would seem from the Kalashnikovs collected near their feet, have already stripped the dead soldiers of their weapons. These dead are supremely uninterested in the living: in those who took their lives; in witnesses—or in us. Why should they seek our gaze? What would they have to say to us? "We"— this "we" is everyone who has never experienced anything like what they went through—don't understand. We don't get it. We truly can't imagine what it was like. We can't imagine how dreadful, how terrifying war is—and how normal it becomes. Can't understand, can't imagine. That's what every soldier, and every journalist and aid worker and independent observer who has put in time under fire and had the luck to elude the death that struck down others nearby, stubbornly feels. And they are right.

ACKNOWLEDGMENTS (continued)

Council of Writing Program Administrators. Bulleted list of points taken verbatim from p. 1 of "Framework for Success in Postsecondary Writing." Council of Writing Program Administrators. Wpacouncil.org. Reprinted by permission.

Frost, Robert. Excerpt from "The Road Not Taken." The Poetry of Robert Frost. Copyright © 1969 Holt, Rhinehart & Winston, Inc.

Lepore, Jill. "The Last Amazon," originally published in The New Yorker (Sept. 22, 2014), adapted from The Secret History of Wonder Woman by Jill Lepore. Copyright © 2014 by Jill Lepore. Used by permission of Alfred A. Knopf, an imprint of the Knopf Doubleday Publishing Group, a division of Penguin Random House LLC. All rights reserved.

Said, Edward W. "Introduction" from Orientalism. Copyright © 1978 by Edward W. Said. Used by permission of Pantheon Books, an imprint of the Knopf Doubleday Publishing Group, a division of Penguin Random House LLC. All rights reserved.

Sontag, Susan. "Looking at War." Excerpt from Regarding the Pain of Others. Copyright © 2003 by Susan Sontag. Reprinted by permission of Farrar, Straus and Giroux, LLC.

Walzer, Michael. Excerpt 1 from "Political Action: The Problem of Dirty Hands." Philosophy and Public Affairs 2.2 (1973): 160–180. Philosophy & Public Affairs by Blackwell Publishing, Inc. Reproduced with permission of Blackwell Publishing, Inc. in the format Republish in a book via Copyright Clearance Center.

Webster, Daniel W., and Jon S. Vernick, eds. Foreword by Michael R. Bloomberg. Reducing Gun Violence in America: Informing Policy with Evidence and Analysis. pp. xxv–xxviii. Copyright © 2013 The Johns Hopkins University Press. Reprinted with permission of Johns Hopkins University Press.

WORKS CITED

"About the Project." 7 Billion Others. The GoodPlanet Foundation, n.d. Web. 27 Dec. 2013.

Abumrad, Jad, and Robert Krulwich. "An Equation for Good." Radiolab. WNYC. 15 Dec. 2010. Podcast. 21 Dec. 2013.

Alexander, Michelle. The New Jim Crow: Mass Incarceration in the Age of Color Blindness. New York: New Press, 2010. Print.

The Aristocrats. Dir. Paul Provenza. Think Film Company, 2005. Film.

Armstrong, Elizabeth M., and Ernest L. Abel. "Fetal Alcohol Syndrome: The Origins of a Moral Panic." Alcohol and Alcoholism 35.3 (May 2000): 276–82. Web. 29 Dec. 2013.

Arthus-Bertrand, Yann. 6 Billion Others: Portraits of Humanity from Around the World. New York: Abrams, 2009. Print.

———. Earth from Above. 3rd ed. New York: Abrams, 2005. Print.

Bain, Ken. What the Best College Students Do. Cambridge, MA: Harvard UP, 2012. Print.

———. What the Best College Teachers Do. Cambridge, MA: Harvard UP, 2004. Print.

Bechdel, Alison. "Comics Reporter Interview #1—Alison Bechdel." Interview by Tom Spurgeon. Comicsreporter.com. The Comics Reporter, 18 Dec. 2012. Web. 8 Nov. 2014.

———. Fun Home: A Family Tragicomic. New York: Mariner, 2006. Print.

———. MacArthur Fellow Biography. MacArthur Foundation. Web. 8 Nov 2014.

---. Quoted in Dwight Garner. "The Days of Their Lives: Lesbians Star in Funny Pages." Books of the Times. *New York Times*, 2 Dec. 2008. Web. 8 Nov. 2014.

Berger, John. "Why Look at Animals?" *About Looking*. New York: Random, 2011. Print.

Berthoff, Ann E. *Forming/Thinking/Writing: The Composing Imagination*. Montclair, NJ: Boynton/Cook, 1982. Print.

Blake, William. "Auguries of Innocence." *The Poetry Foundation*. Web. 16 Jan. 2014.

Bulwer-Lytton, Edward. *Paul Clifford. Gutenberg.org*. Project Gutenberg, 6 Nov. 2012. Web. 16 Jan. 2014.

---. *Richelieu, or, The Conspiracy: A Play in Five Acts. Openlibrary.org*. Web. 16 Jan. 2014.

The Bulwer-Lytton Fiction Contest. English Dept. San Jose State U, n.d. Web. 16 Jan. 2014.

Burke, Kenneth. *The Philosophy of Literary Form*. U of California. Berkeley: UP of California, 1941. Print.

Cain, Susan. *Quiet: The Power of Introverts in a World That Can't Stop Talking*. New York: Crown, 2012. Print.

Capote, Truman. *In Cold Blood*. New York: Random, 1965. Print.

---. "The Story Behind a Nonfiction Novel." Interview by George Plimpton. *New York Times*, 16 Jan. 1966. Web. 21 Dec. 2013.

Carroll, Lewis. *Alice's Adventures in Wonderland. Gutenberg.org*. Project Gutenberg, 8 Mar. 1994. Web. 18 Dec. 2013.

CK, Louis. "About Tig Notaro." *Louis CK*, 5 Oct. 2012. Web. 24 Jan. 2014.

Coates, Ta-Nehisi. "Considering the President's Comments on Racial Profiling." *Theatlantic.com*. Atlantic Monthly Group, 19 July 2013. Web. 27 Dec. 2013.

---. "Fear of a Black President." *Theatlantic.com*. Atlantic Monthly Group, 22 Aug. 2012. Web. 27 Dec. 2013.

Colette. Quoted in Emily Temple. "'My Pencils Outlast Their Erasers': Great Writers on the Art of Revision." *Theatlantic.com*. Atlantic Monthly Group, 14 Jan. 2013. Web. 27 Dec. 2013.

Crutchfield, Susan. "Play[ing] Her Part Correctly: Helen Keller as Vaudevillian Freak." *Disability Studies Quarterly* 25.3 (2005): n.pag. Web. 17 Jan. 2013.

Csikszentmihalyi, Mihaly. *Creativity: Flow and the Psychology of Discovery and Invention*. New York: Harper, 1996. Print.

Delbanco, Andrew. *College: What It Was, Is, and Should Be*. Princeton, NJ: Princeton UP, 2012. Print.

"Diane Arbus." *Wikipedia*. Wikimedia Foundation, 8 Dec. 2013. Web. 16 Jan. 2014.

Dissanayake, Ellen. "The Arts After Darwin: Does Art Have an Origin and Adaptive Function?" *Ellendissanayake.com*. U of Washington P, n.d. Web. 16 Jan. 2014.

Dreisinger, Baz. "Marching On: James McBride's '*Good Lord Bird.*'" *NYTimes.com*. New York Times, 15 Aug. 2013. Web. 4 Jan. 2014.

Duncker, Karl. "On Problem Solving." *Psychological Monographs* 58:5 (1945) Whole no. 270. Web. 3 June 2015.

Edwards, Betty. *Drawing on the Right Side of the Brain: A Course in Enhancing Creativity and Artistic Confidence*. New York: Tarcher, 1979. Print.

Ericsson, K. Anders, Ralf Th. Krampe, and Clemens Tesch-Römer. "The Role of Deliberate Practice in the Acquisition of Expert Performance." *Psychological Review* 100.3 (1993): 363–406. Web. 3 June 2015.

Fitzgerald, F. Scott. "Appendix A: Fitzgerald's Correspondence about The Great Gatsby (1922–25)." *The Great Gatsby*. Ed. Michael Nowlin. Peterborough, ON, Canada: Broadview, 2007. 185–87. Print.

Framework for Success in Postsecondary Writing. *Wpacouncil.org*. Council of Writing Program Administrators, n.d. Web. 27 Jan. 2014.

Freeza, Bill. "Is Drug War Driven Mass Incarceration the New Jim Crow?" *Forbes.com*. Forbes Media, 28 Feb. 2012. Web. 2 Jan. 2014.

Frost, Robert. "The Road Not Taken." The Poetry Foundation. Web. 4 June 2015.

Gaiman, Neil. "Advice to Authors." *Neilgaiman.com*. Harper Collins, n.d. Web. 6 Nov. 2014.

Galileo. *The Dialogue Concerning the Two Chief World Systems*. Trans. Stillmann Drake. New York: Modern Library, 2001. Print.

Gazzaniga, Michael S. "The Split Brain in Man." *Scientific American* 217.2 (1967): 24–29. Web. 3 June 2015.

"Genesis." *The English Standard Version Bible*. *ESVBible.org*. Crossway, 2015. Web. 16 Jan. 2014.

Gibson, William. *The Miracle Worker*. Playhouse 90, 1957. Teleplay.

---. *The Miracle Worker*. Dir. Arthur Penn. Playfilm Productions, 1962. Film.

---. *The Miracle Worker*. Samuel French, 1961. Play.

---. *Monday After the Miracle*. New York: Dramatists Play Service, 1983. Play.

Gladwell, Malcolm. *Outliers: The Story of Success*. New York: Little, 2008. Print.

---. *What the Dog Saw: And Other Adventures*. New York: Little, 2009. Print.

Gladwell, Malcolm, and Robert Krulwich. "Secrets of Success." *Radiolab*. WNYC. 26 July 2010. Podcast. 21 Dec. 2013.

Gonzales, Laurence. *Deep Survival: Who Lives, Who Dies, and Why*. New York: Norton, 2004. Print.

Gutkind, Lee. "Home." Lee Gutkind. Web. 5 Nov. 2014.

Hochschild, Adam. "'Why's This So Good?' No. 61: John McPhee and the Archdruid." *Nieman Storyboard*. Nieman Foundation for Journalism at Harvard, 2 Oct. 2012. Web. 4 Jan. 2014.

Hohn, Donovan. *Moby-Duck: The True Story of 28,800 Bath Toys Lost at Sea and the Beachcombers, Oceanographers, Environmentalists, and Fools, Including the Author, Who Went in Search of Them*. New York: Viking, 2011. Print.

Johnson, Harriet McBryde. "Unspeakable Conversations." *NYTimes.com*. New York Times Magazine, 16 Feb. 2003. Web. 4 Jan. 2014.

Keller, Helen. *The Story of My Life*. *Gutenberg.org*. Project Gutenberg, 4 Feb. 2013. Web. 17 Jan. 2014.

---. *Teacher: Anne Sullivan Macy*. Garden City, New York: Doubleday, 1955. Print.

---. "Vaudeville Speech." Quoted in Dorothy Hermann, *Helen Keller: A Life*. Chicago: U of Chicago P, 1998. Print.

---. *The World I Live In*. *Gutenberg.org*. Project Gutenberg, 1 Jan. 2009. Web. 17 Jan. 2014.

Kolbert, Elizabeth. *Field Notes from a Catastrophe: Man, Nature, and Climate Change*. New York: Bloomsbury, 2006. Print.

Lamotte, Anne. *Bird by Bird: Some Instructions on Writing and Life*. New York: Anchor, 1995. Print.

Lee, Colonel Robert E. "Colonel Robert E. Lee's Report Concerning the Attack at Harper's Ferry." 1859. *Famous Trials: The Trial of John Brown*. U of Missouri Coll. of Law, n.d. Web. 7 Jan. 2014.

Lepore, Jill. "Battleground America: One Nation, Under the Gun." *Newyorker.com*. New Yorker, 23 Apr. 2012. Web. 21 Jan. 2014.

---. *Book of Ages: The Life and Opinions of Jane Franklin*. New York: Knopf, 2013. Print.

---. Interview by Sasha Weiss and Judith Thurman. "Out Loud: Jane Franklin's Untold American Story." *Newyorker.com*. New Yorker, 30 June 2013. Podcast. 5 June 2015.

---. "Poor Jane's Almanac." *NYTimes.com*. New York Times, 23 Apr. 2011. Web. 23 Dec. 2013.

---. "The Prodigal Daughter: Writing, History, Mourning." *New Yorker*, 8 July 2013: 34–40. Print.

Lethem, Jonathan. "The Ecstasy of Influence: A Plagiarism." *Harpers.org*. Harper's Magazine, Feb. 2007. Web. 21 Jan. 2014.

Lightman, Alan. "The Accidental Universe." *Harpers.org*. Harper's Magazine, Dec. 2011. Web. 31 Dec. 2013.

Lincoln, Abraham. "Gettysburg Address." *Gutenberg.org*. Project Gutenberg, Web. 24 Jan. 2014.

The Matrix. Dir. Andy Wachowski and Lana Wachowski. Warner Bros., 1999. Film.

McBride, James. *The Good Lord Bird*. New York: Riverhead, 2013. Print.

---. Quoted in Julie Bosman. "Traveling with John Brown Along the Road to Literary Celebrity." *NYTimes.com*. New York Times, 24 Nov. 2013. Web. 7 Jan. 2014.

McPhee, John. "John McPhee, The Art of Nonfiction No. 3." Interview by Peter Hessler. *Paris Review* 192 (Spring 2010). Web. 1 Jan. 2014.

---. "Structure." *Newyorker.com*. New Yorker, 14 Jan. 2013. Web. 4 Jan. 2014.

Morrison, Toni. Interview by Elissa Schappell. "Toni Morrison, The Art of Fiction No. 134." *Theparisreview.org.* Paris Review 128 (Fall 1993). Web. 26 Dec. 2013.

Notaro, Tig. *LIVE.* Secretlycanadian.com. 3 Aug. 2012. MP3 file.

Obama, Barack. "Remarks by the President on the Nomination of Dr. Kim Jim for World Bank President." *Whitehouse.gov.* 23 Mar. 2012. Web. 27 Dec. 2013.

---. "Remarks by the President on Trayvon Martin." *Whitehouse.gov.* 19 July 2013. Web. 27 Dec. 2013.

Osifchin, Chris. "Abu Ghraib Ruminations." Message to Richard E. Miller. 29 Jan. 2014. E-mail.

Pink, Daniel. "The Puzzle of Motivation." TED. July 2009. Web. 11 Nov. 2014.

---. *A Whole New Mind: Why Right-Brainers Will Rule the Future.* New York: Riverhead, 2005. Print.

Plato. "The Apology." *Plato: Complete Works.* Eds. John M. Cooper and D. S. Hutchinson. Indianapolis: Hackett, 1997. 17–36. Print.

---. *The Republic.* Trans. G.M.E. Grube. 2nd ed. Indianapolis: Hackett, 1992. Print.

Pollan, Michael. "An Animal's Place." *NYTimes.com.* New York Times, 10 Nov. 2002. Web. 31 Dec. 2013.

---. *The Botany of Desire: A Plant's Eye View of the World.* New York: Random, 2001. Print.

Rose, Erik. Student Writing. n.d. TS. Rutgers UP. Contacted 12 Jan. 2014.

Sacks, Oliver. "The Mind's Eye." *Newyorker.com.* New Yorker, 28 July 2003. Web. 18 Jan. 2014.

Sagan, Carl. *Cosmos.* New York: Ballantine, 2013. Print.

Said, Edward. *Orientalism.* 2nd ed. New York: Vintage, 1994. Print.

Saint Anselm. *Basic Writings: Proslogium, Mologium, Gaunilo's In Behalf of the Fool, Cur Deus Homo.* Trans. S. N. Deane. 2nd ed. Peru, IL: Open Court, 1998. Print.

Schlosser, Eric. "Eric Schlosser." Interview by Robert Boynton. *The New New Journalism.* New York: Random, 2005. Print.

Shakespeare, William. *Romeo and Juliet.* Gutenberg.org. Project Gutenberg, 25 May 2012. Web. 24 Jan. 2014.

Simon, David. "HBO's 'Treme' Creator David Simon Explains It All for You." *Nola.com.* Times-Picayune, 11 Apr. 2010. Web. 15 Nov. 2014.

Singer, Peter. *Animal Liberation: A New Ethic for Our Treatment of Animals.* New York: Random, 1975. Print.

Skloot, Rebecca. "How Rebecca Skloot Built *The Immortal Life of Henrietta Lacks.*" Interview by David Dobbs. *Theopennotebook.com.* The Open Notebook, 22 Nov. 2011. Web. 4 Jan. 2014.

---. *The Immortal Life of Henrietta Lacks.* New York: Crown, 2010. Print.

---. "What's the Most Important Lesson You Learned from a Teacher?" *Rebeccaskloot.com.* Rebecca Skloot, 8 May 2012. Web. 29 Dec. 2013.

Smith, Zadie. "Fail Better." *Theguardian.com.* Guardian, 13 Jan. 2007. Web. 20 Dec. 2013.

---. *NW.* London: Penguin, 2012. Print.

Sontag, Susan. "America Seen through Photographs, Darkly." *On Photography.* New York: Farrar, 1977. 27–50. Print.

---. "Looking at War." *New Yorker,* Dec. 2002: 82–98. Print.

---. "Regarding the Torture of Others." *NYTimes.com.* New York Times Magazine, 23 May 2004. Web. 20 Dec. 2013.

Sotomayor, Sonia. *My Beloved World.* New York: Knopf, 2013. Print.

Spiotta, Dana. *Stone Arabia.* New York: Scribner, 2012. Print.

Stern, Daniel. "Life Becomes a Dream." Rev. of *The Benefactor* by Susan Sontag. *NYTimes.com.* New York Times, 8 Sept. 1963. Web. 3 June 2015.

Stiver, Annie. "The Time Is Ripe." Apr. 2012. TS. Rutgers UP. Contacted 29 Jan. 2014.

Talbot, Margaret. "Stealing Life." *Newyorker.com.* New Yorker, 22 Oct. 2007. Web.

Tharp, Twyla. *The Creative Habit: Learn It and Use It for Life.* New York: Simon, 2003. Print.

Thoreau, Henry David. "Walden." *Walden, and On the Duty of Civil Disobedience.* Project Gutenberg. Jan. 1995. Web. 26 Dec. 2013.

Toy Story. Dir. John Lasseter. Pixar Animation Studios, 1995. Film.

Trainer, Laureen. "The Missing Photographs: An Examination of Diane Arbus's Images of Transvestites and Homosexuals from 1957 to 1965." *Americansuburbx.com*. American Suburb X, 2 Oct. 2009. Web. 16 Jan. 2014.

Tremmel, Michelle. "What to Make of the Five-Paragraph Theme: History of the Genre and Implications." *TETYC* Sept. 2011. 29–41. Print.

Waking Life. Dir. Richard Linklater. Fox Searchlight, 2001. Film.

Walk, Kerry. "Teaching with Writing." Princeton Writing Program. Princeton U, n.d. Web. 27 Dec. 2013.

Wallace, David Foster. *This Is Water: Some Thoughts, Delivered on a Significant Occasion, About Living a Compassionate Life*. Transcription of 2005 Kenyon Commencement Address—May 21, 2005. Purdue U, n.d. Web. 23 Dec. 2013.

Walzer, Michael. "Political Action: The Problem of Dirty Hands." *Philosophy and Public Affairs* 2.2 (1973): 160–80. Print.

Webster, Daniel W., and Jon S. Vernick. "Introduction." *Reducing Gun Violence in America: Informing Policy with Evidence and Analysis*. Eds. Daniel W. Webster and Jon S. Vernick. Baltimore, MD: Johns Hopkins UP, 2013. Print.

Woolf, Virginia. Letter to Vita Sackville-West. 26 Feb. 1939. MS. *Woolf in the World: A Pen and Press of Her Own*. Mortimer Rare Book Room. Smith College. Web. 31 Dec. 2013.

---. *A Room of One's Own*. *Gutenberg.org*. Project Gutenberg Australia. Web. 11 Nov. 2014.

---. "Street Haunting: A London Adventure." *Virginia Woolf: Selected Essays*. Oxford: Oxford UP, 2008. 177–87. Print.

---. *Three Guineas*. 1938. Blackwell Publishing. Web. 20 Dec. 2013.

"WPA Outcomes Statement for First-Year Composition." *Wpacouncil.org*. Council of Writing Program Administrators, n.d. Web. 27 Jan. 2014.

Zakaria, Fareed. "The Case for Gun Control: Why Limiting Access to Guns is Intelligent and American." *Time.com*. Time, 20 Aug. 2012. Web. 27 Jan. 2014.

---. "A Statement from Fareed." Fareed Zakaria GPS. *Globalpublicsquare.blogs.cnn.com*. CNN, 10 Aug. 2012. Web. 3 June 2015.

INDEX